Godliness and Governance
in Tudor Colchester

STUDIES IN MEDIEVAL AND EARLY MODERN CIVILIZATION
Marvin B. Becker, General Editor

Charity and Children in Renaissance Florence:
The Ospedale degli Innocenti, 1410–1536
  Philip Gavitt

Humanism in Crisis: The Decline of the French Renaissance
  Philippe Desan, editor

Upon My Husband's Death: Widows in the Literatures
and Histories of Medieval Europe
  Louise Mirrer, editor

The Crannied Wall: Women, Religion, and the Arts
in Early Modern Europe
  Craig A. Monson, editor

Wife and Widow in Medieval England
  Sue Sheridan Walker, editor

The Rhetorics of Life-Writing in Early Modern Europe: Forms of
Biography from Cassandra Fedele to Louis XIV
  Thomas F. Mayer and D. R. Woolf, editors

Defining Dominion: The Discourses of Magic and Witchcraft in
Early Modern France and Germany
  Gerhild Scholz Williams

Women, Jews, and Muslims in the Texts
of Reconquest Castile
  Louise Mirrer

The Culture of Merit: Nobility, Royal Service, and the Making of
Absolute Monarchy in France, 1600–1789
  Jay M. Smith

Clean Hands and Rough Justice: An Investigating Magistrate
in Renaissance Italy
  David S. Chambers and Trevor Dean

"Songes of Rechelesnesse": Langland and the
Franciscans
  Lawrence M. Clopper

Godliness and Governance in Tudor Colchester
  Laquita M. Higgs

Godliness and Governance in Tudor Colchester

LAQUITA M. HIGGS

Ann Arbor

THE UNIVERSITY OF MICHIGAN PRESS

Copyright © by the University of Michigan 1998
All rights reserved
Published in the United States of America by
The University of Michigan Press
Manufactured in the United States of America
∞ Printed on acid-free paper

2001   2000   1999   1998   4   3   2   1

A CIP catalog record for this book is available from the British Library.

Library of Congress Cataloging-in-Publication Data

Higgs, Laquita M., 1937–
    Godliness and governance in Tudor Colchester / Laquita M.
Higgs.
        p.   cm. — (Studies in medieval and early modern civilization)
    Includes bibliographical references (p.   ) and index.
    ISBN 0-472-10890-5 (acid-free paper)
    1. Colchester (England)—Politics and government. 2. Great
Britain—History—Tudors, 1485–1603. 3. Colchester
(England)—Church history.   I. Title.   II. Series.
    DA690.C7   H54   1998
    941.05—dc21   98-8957
                                                           CIP

Figure 1 was reproduced from the *Victoria History of Essex,*
volume IX, page 43, by permission of the General Editor.
Figure 2 was reproduced by courtesy of Elton Higgs, photog-
rapher. Figure 3 was reproduced from an article by Miller
Christy, W. W. Porteous, and E. Bertram Smith, "The Monumental Brasses of Colchester," in the *Transactions of the
Essex Archaeological Society,* n.s., 13 (1915): 46, by permission of the editor of *Essex Archaeology and History.* Figure 4
was reproduced from Foxe, *Acts and Monuments of John
Foxe,* ed. Stephen Reed Cattley (London: R. B. Seeley and
W. Burnside, 1841), VIII, 154.

To Elton, who never complains
but always encourages;
and to my three daughters,
Liann, Cynthia, and Rachel,
who give me joy and
keep me in touch with reality

Acknowledgments

Large projects are never accomplished alone, so it is most appropriate to acknowledge help given along the way. My first work on Colchester, a doctoral dissertation, was suggested by a professor of mine at the University of Michigan, William Hunt, an expert on Essex Puritanism. When Professor Hunt left the university, Professor Marvin B. Becker kindly took on the role of advisor. Even after graduate school, Dr. Becker continued to prod me on; his encouragement has truly been invaluable.

It has been a pleasure to use the excellent libraries at the University of Michigan, and gaps in the holdings have been patiently acquired by Margaret Kruszewski at the Mardigian Library of the University of Michigan–Dearborn. The Essex Record Offices at Chelmsford and Colchester kindly allowed me to spend many days perusing their records, and my thanks for special assistance go to Mr. Paul Coverley, who located for me the large volumes of Benham's handwritten translation of the cumbersome borough court rolls. Former ERO personnel also helped: the late Dr. and Mrs. Frederick Emmison encouraged me and even permitted me to work in their home to read some unpublished manuscripts; and the late Miss Hilda Grieve saved me a trip to Oxford by loaning her transcripts of some documents housed there. I am also grateful for the use of the Public Record Office, the Guildhall Library, the British Library, and the library at the Institute of Historical Research, all in London.

Most helpful, though, was the staff at the *VCH Essex* office in Chelmsford, who were compiling their volume on Colchester. The editor, Dr. Janet Cooper, saved me from some egregious errors.

My thanks to colleagues at the University of Michigan–Dearborn, especially to Elaine Clark, Peter Amann, and Gerald Moran for their continuing interest as my work progressed; to Rex Clark and Ricardo Singson for their wizardry in digitizing illustrations; and to friends who encouraged me, kept little Rachel, and even promised to read the book. A big thank you goes to my husband, Elton, who helped in so many ways, from proofreading to baby-sitting; and, above all, I must offer my *Gloria Deo.*

Contents

Abbreviations

Record Repositories

BL	British Library
ERO	Essex Record Office
Guildhall	Guildhall Library, London
PRO	Public Record Office

Manuscripts

CR	Court Rolls, Borough of Colchester
D/ABW	Registered and Original Wills, Commissary Court of the Bishop of London
D/ACA	Act Books, Court of the Archdeacon of Colchester
D/ACR	Registered Probate Wills, Court of the Archdeacon of Colchester
D/ACV	Visitation Act Books, Court of the Archdeacon of Colchester
D/ACW	Original Wills, Court of the Archdeacon of Colchester
D/B5 Gb	Assembly Books, Borough of Colchester
D/B5 R5	Book of Examinations and Recognizances, 1562–72, also known as *Liber ordinacionum,* Borough of Colchester
D/B5 R7	Monday Court Book, 1571–76, Borough of Colchester
D/B5 Sb	Book of Examinations and Recognizances, Borough of Colchester
D/P	Parish Registers, Colchester Parish Churches
D/Y2	Morant Manuscripts

T/R   Parish Registers, Colchester Parish Churches,
                        Transcript

Printed Primary Sources

APC   *Acts of the Privy Council of England*
CPR   *Calendar of Patent Rolls*
CSPD   *Calendar of State Papers, Domestic*
CSPSp   *Calendar of State Papers, Spanish*
Essex Fines   *Feet of Fines for Essex*
Foxe   John Foxe, *Acts and Monuments of John Foxe*
LP   *Letters and Papers, Foreign and Domestic, of the
                        Reign of Henry VIII*
OB   *Oath Book or Red Parchment Book of Colchester*
RPB   *Red Paper Book of Colchester*

Secondary Sources: Books

DNB   *Dictionary of National Biography*
Emmison, *Disorder*   F. G. Emmison, *Elizabethan Life: Disorder*
Emmison, *Home*   F. G. Emmison, *Elizabethan Life: Home, Work,
                        and Land*
Emmison, *Morals*   F. G. Emmison, *Elizabethan Life: Morals*
Hasler   P. W. Hasler, ed. *The House of Commons,
                        1558–1603*
Morant   Philip Morant, *The History and Antiquities of the
                        Most Ancient Town and Borough of Colchester*
Newcourt   Richard Newcourt, *Repertorium Ecclesiasticum
                        Parochiale Londinense*
Oxley   J. E. Oxley, *The Reformation in Essex to the
                        Death of Mary*
RCHM, *Essex*   Royal Commission on Historical Monuments, *An
                        Inventory of the Historical Momuments in Essex*
VCH Essex   *Victoria History of the Counties of England:
                        Essex*

Secondary Sources: Journals

EAH   *Essex Archaeology and History*
EHR   *English Historical Review*

ER	*Essex Review*
JBS	*Journal of British Studies*
JEccH	*Journal of Ecclesiastical History*
PP	*Past and Present*
TEAS	*Transactions of the Essex Archaeological Society*

Other

HMSO	Her Majesty's Stationery Office
JP	Justice of the Peace
MP	Member of Parliament
SPCK	Society for the Propagation of Christian Knowledge
£	pound sterling
s.	shilling
d.	pence

Introduction

Situated in a lush valley of the river Colne, the borough of Colchester, which included four neighboring villages, was dominated in the sixteenth century by the walled town set on a hill. With a population of around five thousand in the early Tudor era,[1] Colchester was not a wealthy borough compared to London; yet, among English towns, Colchester was revealed by the lay subsidy of 1523–25 to be twelfth in riches, and it was perhaps higher—some experts say it was ninth in terms of taxable wealth.[2] The wealth of the town had long been based on the manufacture of cloth, but a diversity of occupation added to the town's resilience through the years. Commerce was important, thanks to Colchester's use of the

---

1. For a discussion of Colchester's population, see R. H. Britnell, *Growth and Decline in Colchester, 1300–1525* (Cambridge: Cambridge University Press, 1986), 201. G. H. Martin, *The Story of Colchester from Roman Times to the Present Day* (Colchester: Benham Newspapers, 1959), 36, made the same estimate, basing his figure on J. C. Russell's calculations in his *British Medieval Population* (Albuquerque: University of New Mexico Press, 1948). However, Nigel Goose, "The 'Dutch' In Colchester: The Economic Influence of an Immigrant Community in the Sixteenth and Seventeenth Centuries," *Immigrants and Minorities* 1 (1982): 263–64, concluded that the population in the 1520s was 3,500, though ninth in taxable wealth. The best general history of Colchester is the *Victoria History of the County of Essex*, 9 vols. (Oxford: Oxford University Press, 1903–94), vol. 9, but see also Martin, *Story of Colchester,* and the pioneering eighteenth-century history by Philip Morant, *The History and Antiquities of the Most Ancient Town and Borough of Colchester* (1748; reprint, Wakefield: S. R. Publishers, 1970); Morant had access to some documents that are now lost. Two nineteenth-century histories were Thomas Kitson Cromwell, *History and Description of the Ancient Town and Borough of Colchester,* 2 vols. (London: Robert Jennings, 1825), and Edward L. Cutts, *Colchester* (London: Longmans, Green, and Company, 1888).

2. W. G. Hoskins, *Provincial England: Essays in Social and Economic History* (New York: St. Martin's Press, 1963), 70, compared the riches of English provincial towns, based on the lay subsidy rolls. Actually Colchester was probably thirteenth in wealth, since Newcastle was exempt from the taxation of 1523–25; Hoskins estimates that Newcastle would have been third or fourth in the ranking. Alan R. H. Baker, "Changes in the Later Middle Ages," in *A New Historical Geography of England,* ed. H. C. Darby (Cambridge: Cambridge University Press, 1973), 243, placed Colchester as tenth in wealth in 1524–25, again with Newcastle having been omitted.

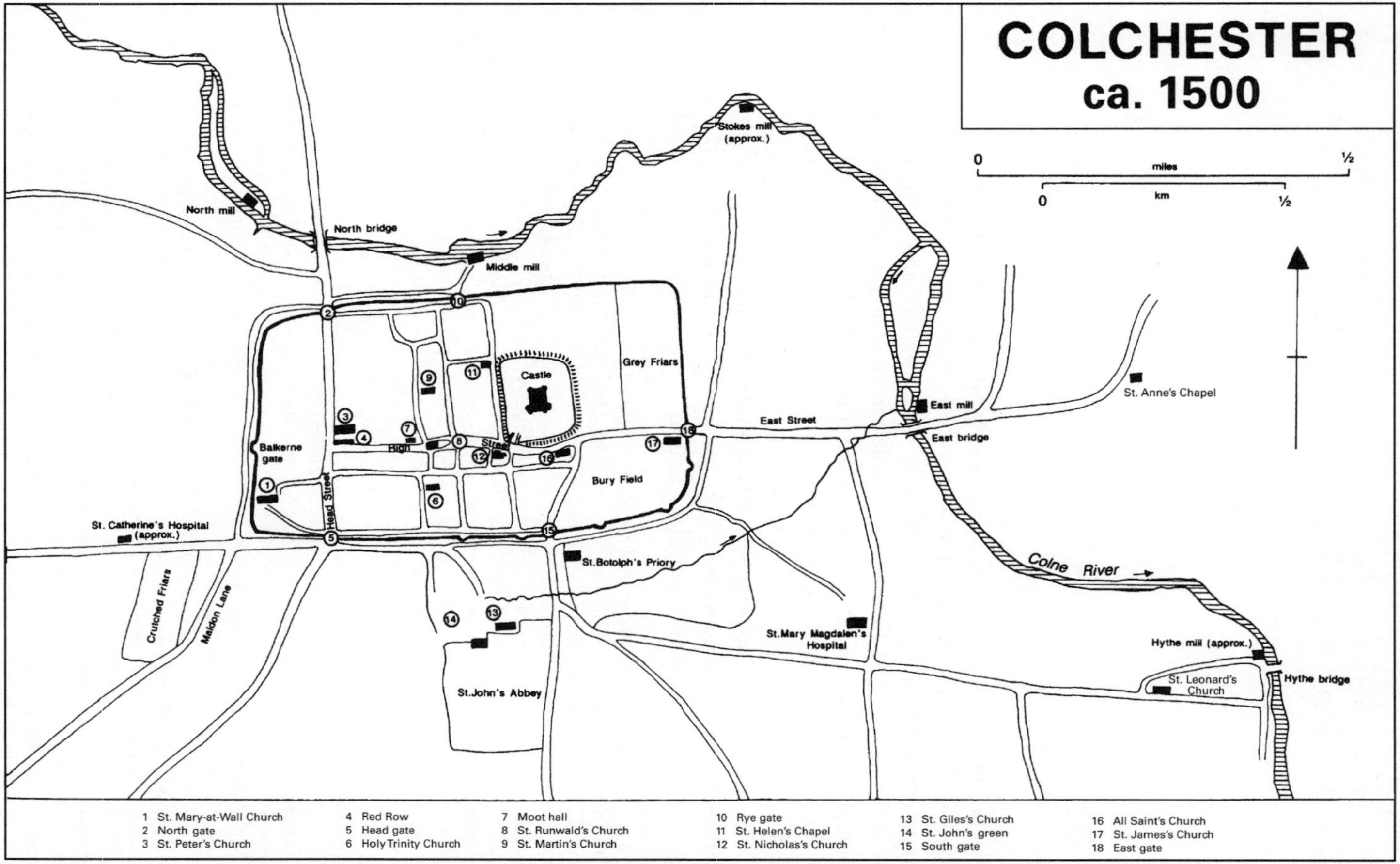

COLCHESTER
ca. 1500

0   miles   ½
0   km   ½

St. Anne's Chapel

Colne River →

East mill

East bridge

East Street

Stokes mill (approx.)

Grey Friars

Bury Field

Hythe mill (approx.)

Hythe bridge

St. Leonard's Church

St. Mary Magdalen's Hospital

St. Botolph's Priory

St. John's Abbey

Castle

Middle mill

North bridge

North mill

St. Catherine's Hospital (approx.)

Crutched Friars

Maldon Lane

Head Street

High Street

Balkerne gate

1   St. Mary-at-Wall Church
2   North gate
3   St. Peter's Church

4   Red Row
5   Head gate
6   Holy Trinity Church

7   Moot hall
8   St. Runwald's Church
9   St. Martin's Church

10 Rye gate
11 St. Helen's Chapel
12 St. Nicholas's Church

13 St. Giles's Church
14 St. John's green
15 South gate

16 All Saint's Church
17 St. James's Church
18 East gate

FIG. 1. Map of Colchester, ca. 1500

Ipswich port and its own small port on the river Colne, which provided access to the North Sea. Another vital connection was its overland proximity to London, fifty-one miles away, and its location on the London-Ipswich road. Though Colchester was the leading market town for northeastern Essex, it was not a cathedral city, nor was it a county town, though a county jail was housed in the Colchester Castle.

Towns and their moneymaking burgesses were viewed with suspicion by a society whose values were those of the landed gentry, but Colchester, as a royal borough with a long tradition of self-governance, had a certain pride that lent confidence to its burgesses. The powerful force of religion also helped the townsman to validate his profit making, provided that he cultivated a life pleasing to God. Religion was an integral part of life, affecting all phases, even secular governance, and Colchester officials saw themselves, in their own words, as governing "to the honour of God and the Borough."[3] This study will show how the sacred was integrated with civic governance in Tudor Colchester, especially during Elizabeth's reign, after the return from exile of reformers who had observed and admired the Genevan model of city and church governance. The evidence of the Colchester experience constitutes a casebook of an early attempt to meld godliness and governance, an experiment that met with both success and failure.

The stimulating urban environment was the natural spawning ground for more intense religious ideas and radical practices. Not only were the inhabitants more frequently exposed to new ideas, but the process was helped by a greater incidence of literacy among merchants, professional men, and independent craftsmen, all of whom needed a certain amount of learning in their occupations.[4] Just as in London, Colchester was experiencing a growth in literacy; according to historian Geoffrey Martin, lit-

---

3. *The Red Paper Book of Colchester,* trans. W. Gurney Benham (Colchester: *Essex County Standard* Office, 1902), 103.

4. In her study of London, Sylvia L. Thrupp calculated that some 50 percent of fifteenth-century lay male Londoners could read English and that among the merchant class, all the men read English and most of them had facility in Latin. Remarkably, most of the women from the merchant class were able to read and write English. See Thrupp, *The Merchant Class of Medieval London* (Ann Arbor: University of Michigan Press, 1962), 156, 158, 161; Jo Ann Hoeppner Moran, *The Growth of English Schooling 1340–1548* (Princeton: Princeton University Press, 1985), 150–84. Studying a slightly later period, David Cressy, *Literacy and the Social Order: Reading and Writing in Tudor and Stuart England* (Cambridge: Cambridge University Press, 1980), 130–31, 176, concluded that literacy from 1580 to 1700 among merchants and the commercial elite of the country towns was in the range of 85–95 percent, with skilled craftsmen and businessmen, such as clothiers, in the 67–86

eracy, even in fifteenth-century Colchester, was a "common accomplishment among most merchants who had more than parochial interests."[5] The relatively high incidence of literacy in the towns not only made an informed laity more possible but contributed to the rise of a more personal holiness, especially with the reading of the greater number of devotional books available in English.

A recent study of the diocese of Salisbury has shown that both orthodox piety and dissent were more intense in the towns than in the countryside.[6] The church was vulnerable to the charges made by reformers that certain practices and beliefs did not follow biblical teaching, and problems in the church only added to the arguments of the reformers. Most obvious was the immoral behavior of some of the clergy, but even more important was the poor financial base of the Colchester churches, which made them subject to pluralism and absenteeism, and which too often resulted in the clergy's engagement in sharp business practices and involvement in petty quarrels over tithes. Even after the Reformation, the financial problems remained, and they increased with the progressive inflation of the Tudor century, which further weakened the Colchester churches and gave Elizabethan town leaders an excuse to hire their own town preacher.

Certainly, religion had a flavor of its own in late medieval Colchester. Contemporaries recognized Colchester as being more radical than most other towns; indeed, for decades Colchester had entertained the underground heretical Lollard teachings, which had sympathizers even at the highest levels of town governance. The emphasis of the Lollards on having the Scripture in English so that one could better know God and his will appealed to the urban laity; furthermore, Lollardy was not necessarily incompatible with Catholic lay piety and lay initiative in religious matters, both of which fostered a desire for a life of service to God and a closer walk with him. The emphases of the Reformation—on the sole authority of Scripture, on the priesthood of all believers, on the faith of the individual in the saving power of Jesus alone, and on the worthiness

---

percent range. Weavers and fullers in the textile industry, brewers, and tailors had a literacy rate of 48–63 percent, while lesser tradesmen, such as blacksmiths, carpenters, butchers, and millers, were 32–44 percent literate. Rosemary O'Day, *Education and Society, 1500–1800* (London: Longman, 1982), 9–24, discusses the role of literacy in that society.

5. Martin, *Story of Colchester,* 39.

6. Andrew Brown, *Popular Piety in Late Medieval England: The Diocese of Salisbury 1250–1550* (Oxford: Clarendon Press, 1995), 222.

of the ordinary Christian's work in the world—were only a natural culmination of the religious forces already at work in Colchester. Undergirding the whole process of change was the force of laicization and its rebellion against a special clerical class that often felt superior to the laity, but perhaps the single most important force behind the continuing religious changes in Colchester was the English Bible itself, which over the years exerted its influence through various forms: the avidly read manuscripts secretly passed around and memorized by Colchester Lollards; the dearly bought, smuggled copies of Tyndale's new English translation; the Great Bibles surprisingly mandated by Henry VIII for all the churches; or the small and readable Geneva Bible so valued by its Elizabethan owners.

Social and religious conditions came together in Colchester to form a favorable environment for a comparatively rapid embrace of Protestant church reforms, but the process was also helped by a salutary political situation, with the borough being comparatively free to govern itself through a royal charter. Geography also played a part. Colchester's location on the eastern seaboard meant that the town had easy access to the most advanced ideas from the Continent, especially through its merchants, who must have encountered Protestant teaching. Contacts in England were also influential. Through frequent trade with Londoners, Colchester inhabitants were exposed to the radical religious teachings so much in evidence in the larger city. Moreover, one of the roads from Colchester led to Cambridge, the center of early Lutheran beliefs, and at least some of the Colchester people were listening to Lutheran preaching.

Colchester became a regional center for Protestant discussion and activity, as well as a haven for some of the radical London preachers during Queen Mary's reign. A number of Colchester people were in the reformers' camp, led in the later 1530s by influential town governors who permitted the acceptance and promulgation of Protestant teaching. Nevertheless, decades passed before the majority of the people in Colchester were fully Protestant in their thinking. Old ways and habits of thinking change slowly for most people. Some of the town leaders were ardent in their Protestant beliefs, but most were probably just being pragmatic, like their own Thomas Audley at the king's court, who instructed them in the value of following the dictates of the king.

The governors of Tudor Colchester have been examined as closely as the records permit, and it is obvious that all, whether their personal piety was shallow or deep, recognized the importance of religion in the town.

Their lives were sometimes paradoxical: though leaders in pious deeds, they were usually more concerned about hierarchy, status, and power; though early Protestants, they welcomed Mary on her way to London to be proclaimed queen and eventually helped her burn Colchester heretics. Though they might be religiously progressive, they were the holders of power, and as such were usually a cautious group, certainly not given to martyrdom, and seldom willing to take strong stands in religion unless they were fairly certain that it was safe to do so. They knew that they owed their liberties to the Crown; they might drag their feet in enforcing the laws of central government, as they did under Queen Mary, but in the end they conformed.

Yet, after Elizabeth's accession to the throne, the borough's rulers were transformed into a more assertive and more intrusive town leadership. Mary's attempt to restore Catholicism was a pivotal time in Colchester, as several Protestant townspeople were burned at the stake for their faith. Those drastic acts polarized the borough, laid the foundation for future divisions, and made Protestants aware that, if given the chance, they needed to take stronger measures to promote their ideas and practices. Elizabeth's accession to the throne provided that opportunity, and reformers gradually took control of town governance.

With the Colchester leadership firmly in the reformist camp by the early 1560s, conditions were right for an experiment in godly governance. The local church was badly weakened, so the town leaders, buttressed by the forceful preaching of zealous Calvinists returning from Geneva, became increasingly concerned with matters that had been the province of the institutional church, especially the provision of preaching in the town. They hired a town preacher; extended more relief to the poor; and, aware of the larger Protestant struggle, invited Protestant Flemish refugees to live in Colchester. A new alliance of power and piety was being forged; Henry's reforms had resulted in a more complete alliance of church and state, with the secular power having ultimate control over religion. A similar alliance, though on a reduced scale and without the attempt to have full control of the church, was cultivated in Elizabethan Colchester. The additional seed of Calvinistic ideas gave body and strength to the attempt by the leaders to fashion godly governance and to shape religious practice in the town.

Other towns also experimented, but if the Calvinist attempt to blend the sacred and the secular was going to succeed anywhere, it should have done so in Colchester. London was much larger and had more Protestants, but London, at the center of political power, too readily came to the attention of those who would thwart such ambitions. Smaller Colchester was much less of a threat and did not so often come to the notice of the authorities. Vibrant London was the center of new ideas, but Colchester was less provincial than its distance from London and its comparative smallness might suggest.

Colchester's early attempt at Puritan governance was unsophisticated and halting, and it was not even articulated, as far as we know. The experiment succeeded for a time—as long as the town had a united leadership and a town preacher who was respected by most people—but those halcyon days could not be sustained, even though godly governance continued in attenuated form. The Colchester experience is a study in the problems inherent in the melding of religion and secular governance. The failure began from within, with quarrels within the leadership and a fading of zeal, particularly when challenged by authorities in London. But the problem was more than the failure of leadership; it was also an institutional failure, for the uneasy marriage of governance and Calvinistic Protestantism was a hybrid form that compromised the purity of Christian teaching and imposed a task that secular governance was ill equipped to handle. The experiment was bound to fail, but, sadly, the Puritans had yet to learn the lesson that the Colchester experience might have taught them.

Historical studies are shaped by the availability of records, and at the heart of this study are the excellent group of court rolls and testamentary wills from Tudor Colchester.[7] The borough court rolls date from the early fourteenth century, but, unfortunately, those from the reign of Henry VII are missing.[8] Likewise, there are fewer wills from the first fifteen years of Henry's reign, thus dictating a less thorough analysis of the governance and piety of those early Tudor years.

---

7. For a discussion of Colchester records, see Martin, *Story of Colchester*, 25, 38; R. H. Britnell, "Colchester Courts and Court Records, 1310–1525," *EAH* 17 (1986): 133–40; Britnell, *Colchester*, 122–23; and Britnell, "The Oath Book of Colchester and the Borough Constitution, 1372–1404," *EAH* 14 (1982): 94–101. On the "Colchester chronicle," see Philip Crummy, *Aspects of Anglo-Saxon and Norman Colchester*, CBA Research Report 39 (London: Council for British Archaeology, 1981), 26–27.

8. Only the fourteenth-century court rolls have been published. Each court roll consists of some twenty to thirty closely written membranes, parchment skins each two or three feet long. A bound, handwritten translation of the court rolls made by W. Gurney Benham, *Translated Abstracts of the Court Rolls, 1310–1602, Borough of Colchester*, 33 vols. (Colchester: handwritten by Benham in the 1930s and 1940s), is helpful, as the original

Each court roll recorded the business of the twice-weekly Colchester court for one borough year, from Michaelmas (September 29) to Michaelmas, as well as the proceedings of the lawhundreds, the courts leet, held three times a year. The rolls do not deal directly with the mechanics of governance, but they do provide useful lists of the borough officers for each year, as well as occasional glimpses into problems that surfaced and some information about the relationships between the governors and between them and the people. A book of examinations and recognizances, useful for tracing some continuing disputes over elections and other problems of governance, was begun in the 1560s.

More directly connected with the governance of the borough are two books of record begun in the fourteenth century, the Red Paper Book and the Oath Book, both of which have been published, which contain lists of officers and new burgesses, judicial precedents, a chronicle of Colchester's history, some deeds and wills, a summary of the court rolls, and, in the Oath Book, the oaths of office to be taken by borough officials.[9] More thorough records of governance are not available until the Elizabethan period, when the minutes of the town assembly began to be recorded, thus permitting a more detailed look at civic rule during those latter years of the Tudor reign. Official records, of course, have limitations, since information is likely to be presented only from the official point of view, so some degree of caution is necessary.

The use of last wills and testaments for investigating the religion of the people has come under criticism, with some justification. Wills were most often made by the more prosperous people, and they indicate little about earlier deeds of piety or the depth of spirituality of the testator; yet wills remain quite helpful as a limited barometer of religious concern. Some information about the institutional church may be found in the registers and visitation act books of the bishop of London, but more useful are the records of the Court of the Archdeacon of Colchester, which dealt more frequently and more closely with the parish churches. Unfortunately, most of the archidiaconal records date only from 1569. The best information about Lollards and the Protestant Reformation in Colchester is

---

rolls are cumbersome and difficult to handle. In the Tudor period, some of the business of the courts began to be recorded in books as well as rolls. The earliest surviving books, in poor condition, are from Henry VII's reign, but the first usable ones are from the 1560s.

9. The Oath Book is also known as the Red Parchment Book. Entries in the Red Paper Book continued through the mid-sixteenth century, and the Oath Book was used up to the eighteenth century.

found in an early printed book, John Foxe's *Acts and Monuments,* first published in 1563.[10] Finally, the dissolution of chantries may be traced through the chantry certificates in the Public Record Office.

Personal information about the town leaders is scanty, but scraps of information have been obtained from the court rolls, wills, deeds, tax assessments, a few extant letters, the incomplete parish records, and even inscriptions on memorial brasses. One would like to put more flesh and blood on the dead bones of the past, but even a "bare-bones" Colchester story is worth the telling.

In the following chapters, Colchester's readiness for the Reformation in the early Tudor years is examined in part 1, with part 2 probing into the years of reform beginning in 1529 and including the traumatic reign of Queen Mary; part 3 gives a detailed account of the governance of the Elizabethan years. Each of the four chapters in part 1 considers one of the larger aspects of Catholic Colchester and its readiness for church reform: (1) Colchester's rich tradition of self-governance, including the tendency of the aldermen toward the exercise of greater power; (2) the town's high connections with central government and the Reformation, provided initially by Thomas Audley, Colchester's town clerk who became lord chancellor of England and modeled for the townsmen the importance of having influence in high places; (3) the condition of the Colchester church and its clergy; and (4) the place of traditional Catholic lay piety in Colchester, which itself might have a radical tinge,[11] as it resided alongside Lollardy and anticlericalism. Modern dating and, for the most part, modern spelling have been used throughout.

---

10. John Foxe, *The Acts and Monuments of John Foxe,* ed. Stephen Reed Cattley, 8 vols. (London: R. B. Seeley and W. Burnside, 1841). See also, John Strype, *Ecclesiastical Memorials,* 3 vols. (Oxford: Clarendon Press, 1822), and *Annals of the Reformation,* 4 vols. (Oxford: Clarendon Press, 1824). Both Foxe and Strype used documents that are now lost.

11. L. R. Poos, *A Rural Society after the Black Death: Essex, 1350–1525* (Cambridge: Cambridge University Press, 1991), 273, warns of the difficulty of trying to demarcate between orthodox and heterodox religion in Essex society.

Part 1
Readiness for Reformation

1

The Governing Structure

Shipowner and Colchester alderman Thomas Cock was cited at a lawhundred in 1533 for the regrating of corn, an action said to be contrary to his oath and against "a common wealth," therefore rendering him unworthy to be an officer in such an honorable town.[1] Truly, the borough of Colchester had a heightened sense of its own worth, independence, and honor as a town—with some justification. Being subject only to the king, Colchester's ancient charters allowed many liberties: self-governance, the right to collect its own taxes (with an annual payment to the king), the right to hold its own courts, and the right to regulate its market, its port, and its long-famous oyster fishery. There were no local gentry families who were overly dominant, and although some Colchester merchants gained riches, none were exceptionally wealthy. There was always the possibility of conflict with the two largest independent jurisdictions within the borough, those of the abbot of Colchester and of the manor of Lexden, but those conflicts often served to unify the burgesses. Thus, usually unhampered by dominant local lords, the borough structure flourished and provided a favorable setting for individualistic ideas of religion to grow among rather ordinary laypeople. This chapter will briefly consider the basis of power in the governance of Colchester by looking especially at the role of the bailiffs and the measures taken to maintain their status; it will then discuss the trend in the early Tudor period toward the holding of more power by the town leaders, a tendency that in Elizabeth's reign would manifest itself in their increased prerogatives in matters of religion and the behavior of townsmen; and finally, to better understand the nature of the men who held the

---

1. Borough of Colchester, Court Roll 103, membrane 2 dorse; the rolls are hereafter cited as, for example, CR103/2d. I have used *Translated Abstracts* by W. Gurney Benham, but the numbering refers to the original rolls. Alderman Cock's name was also given as Cok, Coxe, and Cocks.

reins of power in Colchester, it will examine the ninety-eight Tudor aldermen as a whole and then the aldermen of 1530 in more detail.

Over the centuries, Colchester developed a rather sophisticated form of governance that had, at bottom, a sense of community and of the need to be vigilant for the common good. Though the legal basis of governing authority in Colchester lay in the charter from the king, just as important was the commonalty's tacit consent to be governed, and it is significant that official papers often referred to the bailiffs and "the commonalty."[2] The withdrawal of the assent of the commonalty was an immediate and powerful check on the governors, who were expected to take the lead in promoting the common wealth, or the common good of the town. All inhabitants had a certain responsibility for the common good; for example, householders were expected to handle many of the amenities, such as street cleaning, that are today handled by public services. Not all inhabitants had a part in governance, as a sizable number, including women and the poorer people, were not burgesses and so did not have the right to help govern Colchester.[3] In that hierarchical society, the top positions were always held by the wealthier citizens, but even lesser burgesses had a part in the initial election process, and they might serve on juries or be elected as constables or common councillors.[4]

Colchester governance functioned in four broad areas: (1) keeping law and order; (2) administering justice between individuals; (3) promoting the general welfare of the town and its inhabitants, which might include economic regulations, sanitation, defense, and even right behavior; and (4) acting on behalf of the borough in dealings with the outside world. The first complete borough court roll from Henry VIII's reign, in 1510–11, listed the following officers: two bailiffs; a recorder, or *legis peritus;* four justices of the peace, who had the special responsibility of keeping the king's peace in the borough; ten aldermen; a chamberlain, who was the treasurer and chief financial officer; two coroners; four

---

2. For example, *RPB,* 118, 31; CR86/10.

3. Burgesses also had the freedom to trade as middlemen within the borough, freedom from many custom payments, the right of free transferability of land, the right to use the borough common land, and, along with other citizens, the corporate freedom from external interference. There were normally three ways by which one became a free burgess in Colchester: through patrimony, that is, by being a son or a grandson of a free burgess or, until around 1550, by being born within the borough; by apprenticeship with a free burgess, at the end paying a set fee to the town; or by purchase. See Morant, 1:96–98; Britnell, *Colchester,* 24, 36–37; *VCH Essex,* 9:111.

4. W. J. Petchey, *A Prospect of Maldon, 1500–1689* (Chelmsford: Essex Record Office, 1991), 46, estimates that in Maldon one in eight responsible adult males served in an official capacity.

claviers, who held the keys to the town treasure chest and were also ceremonial mace bearers; a clerk of the town; and four sergeants at mace, who were hired to do the ordinary work of the court, such as summoning jurors. Not so many people were involved as first appears, however, as the bailiffs, the JPs, the coroners, and two of the claviers were all aldermen, giving each of the ten aldermen a second title. In addition, the names of the common council, electors, and twenty-four or more citizen constables were often given in the court rolls.[5]

At the top of the political hierarchy were the ten aldermen, from whom were elected each year two bailiffs, who handled the major judicial and administrative tasks during the year. The town leaders were well aware of their role as instruments of God's order and of the king's peace.[6] The oath taken by the bailiffs promised that they would fulfill such a role: "you shall . . . well and faithfully decide all judgments of pleas which shall happen to be determined before you, . . . sparing no one for love, favor, hatred, gift, or promise, but that reason and right be done to each. . . . And the peace of the lord King . . . you shall guard and cause to be guarded. So help you God and the holy gospels of God." An early Tudor Colchester document stated two of the ideals of God's order and governance: truth finding and the administration of justice. On April 3, 1492, the bailiffs of that year, Thomas Christmas and Nicholas Clere, made inquiry into the making of the will of a certain William Bury. They did so at the instance of a daughter and heir, who said that because of a spurious will, she had suffered "great wrong and extreme hurt and hindrance" from other heirs. The record of the inquiry, which was addressed "to all true Christian people" and sent greeting "in our lord God everlasting," stated its purpose: "forasmuch as it is right well known that it is meritorious and meedful to testify and bear record in every matter of truth, to the intent that all collusion and fraud might be

---

5. See appendix 1. For a helpful discussion of borough offices, see Sidney Webb and Beatrice Webb, *English Local Government*, vol. 2, *The Manor and the Borough* (London: Longmans, Green, and Company, 1908), 2:318–27. Richard Dean Smith, "Social Reform in an Urban Context: Colchester, Essex, 1570–1640" (Ph.D. diss., University of Colorado, 1996), chapter 3, discusses constables and other midrank officials in Colchester.

6. For an excellent discussion of the Tudor belief in order and governance, see Stephen L. Collins, *From Divine Cosmos to Sovereign State: An Intellectual History of Consciousness and the Idea of Order in Renaissance England* (New York: Oxford University Press, 1989), 14–28. For political beliefs in towns, see Susan Reynolds, "Medieval Urban History and the History of Political Thought," *Urban History Yearbook*, 1982, 14–23. Also, see J. A. Sharpe, *Early Modern England: A Social History, 1550–1760* (London: Edward Arnold, 1987), 106–7.

repressed and put out of their wrongful course, and right and equity the rather to be more indifferently ministered."[7] Ideals are never fully realized, but the bailiffs, as the instruments of God's justice and order, were expected to try.

The two bailiffs were to be, according to early records, "sufficient men, of good conversation, the most loyal and the most profitable of the community."[8] One of their major tasks was to preside over the borough court, which met twice a week, on Monday and Thursday, and dealt with actions between burgesses, mostly for the recovery of debts and for trespasses of all sorts, such as assaults, encroachments, and petty misdemeanors. Also handled by the court were some kinds of public business, such as the enrollment of deeds and the enrollment or probate of wills that concerned town property. The court that met on Thursday was a foreign court, in which litigants who were not burgesses could bring actions, and in which any other business could be done.[9] Three times a year, at Michaelmas (on the first Monday after Michaelmas Day, September 29), Hilarytide (on the first Monday after January 13), and Hokeday (on the Monday after Easter), a special session of the Monday court became a court leet, or lawhundred, to handle most of the police work of the borough. All the freeholders of the town, but especially the principal landowners, were supposed to appear at those sessions, during which the magistrates made inquiry as to wrongdoing and a special jury made presentments of all manner of public offenses relating to the king's peace and to morals, as well as agrarian and commercial offenses, such as overstocking the commons or overcharging for ale or bread. All sorts of small problems, such as disposing of rubbish in a proper manner and keeping animals under control, were handled, but greater offenses, such as murders, rapes, or robberies, were handed over to the king's justices.[10] The Oath Book spelled out the kinds of offenses that the jurors were to present, and the oath administered to them warned that, with God as a witness, they were to "conceal no man's fault for consanguinity, love, favor,

7. *The Oath Book or Red Parchment Book of Colchester,* trans. W. Gurney Benham (Colchester: *Essex County Standard* Office, 1907), 36; *RPB,* 112.

8. W. Gurney Benham, introduction to *Court Rolls of the Borough of Colchester,* ed. and trans. Isaac Herbert Jeayes, 4 vols. (Colchester: Colchester Town Council, 1921–41), 1:v.

9. Benham, introduction, 1:vi; Britnell, *Colchester,* 26–27; Britnell, "Colchester Courts."

10. Martin, *Story of Colchester,* 26; Benham, introduction, 1:vi; Britnell, *Colchester,* 27; Sir Thomas Smith, *De Republica Anglorum* (London, 1583), 103. One could be fined for failing to attend the lawhundred: see CR144/22; CR145/31, 31d.

meed, or reward, but present every default of every person according to their deserving." The jurors themselves might be presented for failure to do their duty; in 1511 John Martyn was cited for not searching out "any defaults" in New Hythe.[11]

Besides presiding over the court, the bailiffs supervised trade or at least made sure that someone else was supervising properly. There were markets and fairs to oversee and standards of quality to maintain, and, in times of scarcity, supplies of goods and food had to be assured. The town had to be in readiness for its own defense and that of the kingdom, so the bailiffs had to make sure that the town complied with the ancient obligation of arms in the local militia. At times of alarm, they might be called on to supply ships, men, or horses, as they were in 1554, when Queen Mary asked Colchester to ready eighteen armed men for possible service in Calais.[12]

The two bailiffs also served on the commission of the peace, along with the recorder and the four aldermen chosen each year to be justices. Colchester was granted a permanent commission of the peace to be held by its bailiffs and four other men in 1447, a mark of the borough's distinguished status as an independent subject of the king.[13] The Colchester commission of the peace usually met three times a year, on or near the day of the lawhundred, with extra sessions called as needed to handle unusual problems, such as the enclosure riot in 1538. The session of the peace, in the words of the eager new town clerk in 1514, was "for hearing and determining divers felonies and other misdeeds"; the justices especially had the responsibility for law and order in keeping the king's peace in the borough. Presentments at a session were at the instance of a jury, a constable, or another individual, such as a clergyman.[14]

The legislative business of the borough was handled by the bailiffs and

---

11. *OB*, 2–4; CR84/1d.

12. Benham, introduction, 1:v; F. G. Emmison, *Elizabethan Life: Home, Work, and Land* (Chelmsford: Essex Record Office, with Friends of Historic Essex, 1991), 223; Morant, 1:50.

13. The 1447 charter is summarized in Morant, 1:79–80. The 1462 charter of Edward IV added the recorder to the commission of the peace, which was to enforce the observance of certain of the king's statutes; see Morant, 1:82 n. C. In practice, the recorder was seldom present for the sessions of the peace after 1531, as most of the recorders after that date were nonresident. On the work of the JPs in the liberty of Havering-atte-Bower, see Marjorie Keniston McIntosh, *A Community Transformed: The Manor and Liberty of Havering, 1500–1620* (Cambridge: Cambridge University Press, 1991), 327–29.

14. CR107/3; CR86/5; M. S. Byford, "The Price of Protestantism—Assessing the Impact of Religious Change in Elizabethan Essex: The Cases of Heydon and Colchester, 1558–1594" (Ph.D. diss., Oxford University, 1988), 366.

aldermen in assembly with the common council, which after 1519 was composed of a first council and a second council of sixteen men each.[15] Acting as one, the bailiffs, aldermen, and common council were to make "reasonable ordinances and constitutions for the advantage and government of the borough and put them in execution; and likewise alter and revoke them whenever they should think it for the better." They were permitted to "assess reasonable taxes, or tallages, upon the goods, rents, trades, and merchandises, of all persons" dwelling within the borough, "compelling such as refused to pay (if need be) by arrest and imprisonment without any obstruction from the King or his officers." The council and aldermen were to meet together four times a year, and if any of the burgesses had something to propose, they were to deliver it to the bailiffs in writing, to which they would receive an answer at the next assembly.[16]

The work of the bailiffs, which included administrative, judicial, and legislative functions, was demanding both in time and money for men who also had their own work to do. In compensation, each bailiff was receiving £4 10s. annually in 1524, but later figures reflected the inflation of the century. In 1583 the bailiffs and aldermen agreed that each year the two bailiffs should be allowed £5 each for "their charges for executing the said office," and the allowance was raised to £10 in 1592. On the average, an alderman served as bailiff every fifth year.[17]

Part of the ability to govern came from the accepted system of order or degree, or levels of hierarchy, and the townsmen, having not gentle birth but only wealth to put them at the top of urban society, nurtured a hierarchical system within the town to lend legitimacy to their rule. There was a strong expectation that the wealthier citizens should do their duty

---

15. The second council did not have an independent function, but it rather joined with the first sixteen men to become part of the common council.

16. Morant, 1:82, 94. On town councils, see James H. Thomas, *Town Government in the Sixteenth Century* (London: George Allen and Unwin, 1933), 16–26. Mrs. J. R. Green, *Town Life in the Fifteenth Century*, 2 vols. (London: Macmillan, 1894), 2:269–436, has a lengthy discussion of the makeup of the councils in several towns. The word *assembly* was being used in sixteenth-century Colchester to describe the meeting of the bailiffs, aldermen, and councillors.

17. Cutts, *Colchester*, 144; Morant, 1:82; D/B5 Gb1, f. 27; D/Y2/10, p. 100. Robert Tittler, *Architecture and Power: The Town Hall and the English Urban Community, c. 1500–1640* (Oxford: Clarendon Press, 1991), 106, notes that even small towns were giving a substantial allowance to mayors. To compile the average for service as bailiff, only the records of those who had served fifteen or more years as alderman were used. A letter to the bailiffs in 1591 (D/Y2/8, p. 157) suggests that the usual practice was to be elected "but once every four or five years." The letter writer was interceding for his friend, the elderly Master Lawrence, complaining that Lawrence had been bailiff "but this time two years now past."

and serve as aldermen, an attitude revealed by the reactions to those who refused the office, of which there were only five in the entire Tudor period. The court record indignantly reported that mariner John Joones (or Johns) paid 100s. in 1542 "for his exoneration for not executing the office of alderman as he ought to have done, being elected in accordance with custom by the election of twenty-four good and lawful men." A spate of refusals occurred in the early 1570s, probably because of the general economic depression in the town, and substantial fines, £18 and £20, were levied on the three men. The price was higher for Thomas Buxston (or Buckstone) in 1586. The court record stated that Buxston "did not appear to take his oath, therefore, is deprived of his freedom as a burgess." Another hand inserted that he paid £60 "for his contempt and re-admission to his freedom." Furthermore, none of those five men continued service on the council, although they all continued to live for several years. Civic duties were to be taken seriously; as the court record said of John Joones, he "ought to have done" his duty.[18]

Status was preserved in a number of ways, especially through certain accepted paths to leadership[19] and through civic dress and ceremony. Each man was expected to serve on the common council, normally starting on the second council and then moving up to the first council before being elected alderman;[20] of course, not all councillors but only the wealthier ones were elected aldermen. Certain official modes of dress symbolized distinctions of status, with the aldermen having more elaborate clothing. An ordinance of 1447 stated that no one was to be chosen to "the hole clothyng" of the alderman unless he was "in the hodyng of lyuere of the seid toun," that is, on the common council. The "hole clothyng" referred to the full robes of livery worn by the aldermen,

18. CR112/1; CR136/1; CR137/1; CR148/2d. In 1607 William Turner refused office after having served for twelve years, and he was fined £80; see D/B5 Gb2, f. 63.

19. Wallace T. MacCaffrey, *Exeter, 1540–1640: The Growth of an English County Town* (Cambridge: Harvard University Press, 1958), 36–37, describes the regular pattern of office holding and promotion in Exeter, where there were few deviations from the pattern. The pattern in most towns was customary, rather than being set by formal regulations.

20. It was most unusual for council service to be bypassed, but an exception was made in 1593 (CR155/1), when wealthy John Hunwick, probably the heir of a former alderman by the same name, was elected alderman and even bailiff, though he had never been on the common council. However, the aldermen bowed slightly to traditional procedure by first electing Hunwick to the council, then immediately making him an alderman, so that he could be elected bailiff. In Colchester, the onerous office of chamberlain (treasurer) was also a stepping-stone to greater offices, especially if one were an adult immigrant or had no important family connections. Of the ninety-eight Tudor aldermen, only ten never served as chamberlain.

whereas the councillors simply wore special hoods, that is, "the hodyng."[21] A notation in the town records in 1559 described the customary dress of Colchester aldermen: scarlet gowns and short velvet capes, "as the use of all good towns in England." The gowns were to be worn at Michaelmas, at election time, and on the days of the annual fairs; if they were not worn, the aldermen were fined 3s. 4d.[22] The special clothing of the town rulers lent dignity to their office and was therefore considered to be a vital part of maintaining their authority. Undoubtedly, the trappings helped: official dress was worn with pomp and display in special processions and ceremonies, and special seats were reserved for aldermen in parish churches. The preoccupation of the aldermen with the outward signs of authority was often a source of amusement to outsiders, but it seemed necessary to the aldermen themselves, even though they enjoyed delegated legal powers that were comparable to those of the landowning gentry. As tradesmen, they were keenly aware of a certain insecurity of status in a society that valued birth in a gentle family.[23]

Having built up a system of hierarchy in the town, the rulers expected proper deference from their inferiors. The aldermen were beginning to be given the deferential title *master,* the designation for a gentleman or an esquire, which was never used for mere councillors. Even in the complaint against Alderman Coxe for the regrating of corn, he was called "Master Coxe."[24] Usually the aldermen received respect, but there were times when their underlings were quite willing to pierce their bubble of respectability. Lesser burgesses were free to present the aldermen's names at the borough court leet for offenses, even though they might at the same

21. Britnell, *Colchester,* 224–25.

22. D/Y2/2, p. 65. Janet Cooper, "Civic Ceremonial in Tudor and Stuart Colchester," *Essex Journal,* 23 (1988), 65, notes that at this time, the clothing of most men seemed to be black or tawny colored. On the double symbolism of municipal ceremony, see David Harris Sacks, *The Widening Gate: Bristol and the Atlantic Economy, 1450–1700* (Berkeley: University of California Press, 1991), 140.

23. MacCaffrey, *Exeter,* 276.

24. Such titles of honor were also used in other towns. From the 1490s in the city of York, aldermen expected to be addressed by the term *master,* and citizens were not to refer to them by their Christian names or use the familiar pronoun *thou* when speaking to them; see David M. Palliser, *Tudor York* (Oxford: Oxford University Press, 1979), 100, 290. Tittler, *Architecture,* 104, notes that the need to strengthen the "trappings of hierarchy and office remained intense." On seats of honor, see Robert Tittler, "Seats of Honor, Seats of Power: The Symbolism of Public Seating in the English Urban Community, c. 1560–1620," *Albion* 24 (1992): 205–23.

time defer to them with the title *master*. Even the wealthy Thomas Christmas was subject to numerous complaints; for example, Christmas was said to have "overcharged" the common pasture with six pigs and obstructed the watercourse from its ancient path.[25] More serious charges against aldermen might come before a session of the peace that could impose a heavier penalty. In 1538 Alderman Robert Leche was fined £5 for making a gate in the town wall at the top of Balkerne Hill, and at the same time Aldermen Robert Brown and William Thursteyn paid £10 for their presumption in selling a town gate and chains.[26] Spontaneous complaints against the aldermen occasionally erupted. In 1516 a bailiff and a sergeant who were walking on patrol through the town at night were attacked after arresting two men, an action that prompted five other men to shout, "Down with the bayly, down with him!" while knocking down not the bailiff but the sergeant. The attackers were quickly brought to justice, with the smug comment in the court record that "by ancient custom of the town, . . . burgesses are to follow out and observe . . . the lawful commands by the bailiffs of the town."[27]

The aldermanic office, especially when an alderman was serving his turn as bailiff, conferred a certain status and power on the holder, but there were also needed checks on that power. The same forces that gave authority to the leaders of Colchester—the laws of the king and the borough, the tacit assent of the commonalty, ancient custom, the need for God's order in society—could also restrain the power of the rulers. Even the aldermen sometimes placed a check on themselves: the fine levied against Aldermen Brown and Thursteyn for selling the gate in 1538 was an example of the court fining its own members, for both Brown and Thursteyn were justices of the peace that year. More often, though, power needed to be checked, for power often wants more and has a way of enlarging its boundaries. The early Tudor town rulers were attempting to do just that, and the trend toward more power will be considered in the next section of this chapter. Nevertheless, even in the midst of the ungodly grabbing of power, the ideal of godly governance, though seldom achieved, was taken seriously, with right government being an instrument for forging God's justice and mercy in an imperfect world.

---

25. CR82/10d; CR86/21d.
26. CR108/4.
27. CR88/23.

Governance and Power

Increased aldermanic power had been the trend in Colchester governance for decades. Reforms in 1372, initiated to curb abuses by the two bailiffs, created a board of eight auditors, who became known as aldermen in the early fifteenth century. Reforms in the fifteenth century tightened up the election process, insuring that only the wealthier citizens had ultimate control,[28] and sixteenth-century Colchester experienced three periods of reform: 1517–24, 1549, and the mid-1580s. Only the first two periods concern us at this point. In 1519, the ranks of the common council were doubled with the creation of a second group of councillors. No record remains of any deliberations on the action, but it had the effect of enlarging considerably the ruling group, perhaps to spread the burden and cost of governing,[29] though it is just as likely that it was a response to some of the tensions in the borough, such as the riot that broke out on election day in 1514. Four weeks after the fracas, a session of the peace investigated the affair, with the official report stating that at the meeting of the bailiffs, aldermen, and burgesses to elect new officers, about forty men, "malefactors and disturbers of the peace, . . . tumultuously and riotously, with force and arms, namely clubs and knives, assembled themselves and made assault against the bailiffs and other trustworthy men of the Lord King . . . and gave and offered the bailiffs divers opprobrious and contumacious words and most tumultuously and riotously impeded . . . the election of officers." When the bailiffs tried to arrest one of the rioters, the others "resisted the same with all their might." No explanation about the cause of the riot was given, but a look at the named rioters offers some suggestions. Besides the laborer, ten others were named, with two of them being on the periphery of the ruling group. John Bradman, merchant and newcomer to the town, was a new member of the common council, and William Ryche, husbandman from Lexden, at the western edge of the borough, was one of the electors.[30] Perhaps the rioters felt

---

28. Britnell, *Colchester*, 115–30, 221, in his excellent discussion of the early reforms, offices, and governance in Colchester, has demonstrated that an underlying reason for the reform of 1372 was economic growth.

29. Britnell, *Colchester*, 231–32, believes that the income of the community had decreased in that period while expenses of public office had increased, thereby making the larger council necessary in order "to broaden the basis of consent to the financial management of the community." The charter of 1462 had provided for a second council, though it seems never to have been put into effect until 1519 and then only spasmodically at first.

30. CR86/5. Ten years after the riot, the lay subsidy of 1524, PRO E179/108/169, showed that the three men from Lexden were of some means, being assessed for £12 to £30 worth of land at that time. John Bradman became an alderman in 1520.

that the ruling group was too impenetrable and high-handed; in any case they were undoubtedly angry with those in power on that election day in 1514. The leaders of the town perhaps suffered from some paranoia after the riot, as the same session of the peace inquired whether a certain carpenter hid himself in the moot hall to spy on the deliberations of a session of a peace held on the previous August 16. Perhaps they had reason to be wary, as Bailiff John Mayken could later verify. In 1516, Mayken and a sergeant were attacked after arresting two men for vagrancy. Borough officials were particularly incensed that, of seven attackers, three were burgesses who were supposed "to follow out and observe . . . the lawful commands by the bailiffs of the town." At the following lawhundred, six men, three of them being attackers and one the father of an attacker, were deprived of their freedom.[31] Town governance had its ups and downs.

After those challenges to the authority of the bailiffs, the common council was enlarged in 1519. Elections were times of tension and were often the focus of other constitutional reforms, but in the process, the top borough officers often managed to acquire more power, probably in their view a necessary safeguard for keeping peace in the borough. The Red Paper Book recorded that on September 30, 1523, electors were no longer allowed to put from office any of the aldermen "without the agreement, assent, and consent of the bailiffs and aldermen of the said borough, or the most part of them." Sometime in the next year, that provision was made a part of a new formal constitution of borough governance that largely concerned elections but also took away from ordinary burgesses the power of deposing their leaders.[32]

The constitution of the early 1520s was not entirely successful,[33] and by 1549, disputes over elections prompted the central government to appoint commissioners to initiate reform. The imposed remedy increased the restrictions as to who could participate in the first stages of the elective process,[34] stipulated that no one was to take or give any promise or

---

31. CR86/5; CR88/3, 11d, 17, 23. Also deprived of his freedom was Richard Pakke, an alderman up until the previous September. Pakke never again held office, but others paid fines to be readmitted to their freedom.

32. *RPB*, 29–30; Britnell, *Colchester*, 125–26, 221–22. The earlier practice of having two election days was changed to one.

33. Two sets of electors began to be used again in the 1530s, thus going back, at least partially, to the older system of elections.

34. All householders other than common innholders, bakers, brewers, victuallers, attorneys of courts, and "loose journeymen" were to meet yearly on the Monday after the decollation of St. John the Baptist (August 29), in the moot hall, to name four headmen, one from

reward in connection with the election, and for the first time gave the ten aldermen the power to select the sixteen first councillors. However, the new election powers of the aldermen were short-lived, and by 1551, elections had gone back to the earlier system.[35] Even with such a set back, the trend in the sixteenth century was toward the holding of greater power by the bailiffs and aldermen, though their governing power was far from absolute or autocratic. They held substantial power in the town, enough to make them instrumental in the relatively rapid acceptance of King Henry's church reforms and, later, influential in the shaping of religion in Elizabethan Colchester.

Doing One's Duty: The Ninety-Eight Aldermen of Tudor Colchester

The aldermen were at the apex of Colchester governance, as it was from their ranks that the most important officers of the year were selected, the bailiffs and justices of the peace. Ninety-eight men served in the aldermanic office during the Tudor period, and this section will examine among that group of men the characteristics that help explain their power in governance. Although the aldermen had a foundation of moral authority that came from being generally regarded as God's instruments of good governance, other possible grounds for being respected by their fellow townsmen will be discussed: (1) the wealth that gave them the status to be chosen as leaders; (2) their willingness to serve; and (3) their personal piety, integrity, and concern for the good of the town. In addition, their marriage and family connections with each other, their solidarity as a group, and their pride in their role as aldermen contributed to their effectiveness as leaders. These characteristics reinforced the confluence of situations and events that brought about a distinctive degree of merger between religious convictions and secular governance in Elizabethan Colchester.

Prosperity was a prerequisite, and the tax assessments of 1524 and 1525 show that all of the aldermen at that time had at least £40 in movable goods, and everyone who had £100 or more was an alderman. In contrast, the common councillors had goods of £8 or more.[36] The wealth

---

each ward, by free election; and each headman was to select five others from his ward to make twenty-four electors.

35. D/Y2/2, p. 17; *RPB*, 31; *VCH Essex*, 9:113.

36. PRO E179/108/162, 169. In terms of wealth, the councillors were in the top sixth of the town's population. Britnell, *Colchester*, 232, gives £10 as the lowest assessment for

of town leaders and of Colchester was centered on clothmaking, with at least two-thirds of the ninety-eight Tudor aldermen handling or making cloth or clothing. Rule by wealthier burgesses raises questions about oligarchic rule in the town, a system of rule by the few that has sometimes been regarded as a negative aspect of English town governance. Giving another view is R. H. Britnell, who convincingly demonstrates that late medieval Colchester reaped definite benefits from the oligarchic system, in that the leading townsmen used their resources for the benefit of the borough, an especially useful practice whenever community resources were shrinking. Giving privileges and honors to such a group attached them to the interests of the town.[37] In Worcester, the town leaders contributed substantially to the expenses of town government out of their own pockets. In Colchester, an assessment in 1488 indicates that aldermen paid more in taxes than other burgesses; they were certainly more able to pay, but there was also the expectation that because of their greater financial resources, they would assume financial responsibility in the borough.[38] Being an alderman was no job for the poorer burgesses, especially as expenditures rose in the sixteenth century.

Taking on the job of alderman required a high level of commitment and a willingness to serve, possibly for a long time. Though elected annually, aldermen did their duty for lengthy periods, often until death or infirmity removed them from office. The average length of service for the ninety-eight Tudor aldermen was 12.8 years, and nine of them served a very long time, from 32 to 39 years.[39] Of the sixty-five aldermen whose death dates are known, thirty-eight died in office; thirteen retired only a

---

any of the councillors, but Thomas Northern and Thomas Nothak, Jr., had £8 and £9, respectively. Jennifer C. Ward, "Wealth and Family in Early Sixteenth-Century Colchester," *EAH* 21 (1990): 110–17, has analyzed the 1524 tax assessments.

37. Britnell, *Colchester*, 226–27. Reynolds, "Medieval Urban History," 21, contends that the townsmen saw the rule of the wealthy not as oligarchic but as aristocratic, as the rule of the "better sort" on behalf of, and accountable to, the community. Peter Clark and Paul Slack, *English Towns in Transition, 1500–1700* (London: Oxford University Press, 1976), 129–30, note that wealthy officeholders were a "civic necessity" in the sixteenth century because expenditures rose sharply. Green, *Town Life,* 2:240–68, has a good discussion of town oligarchy; and Tittler, *Architecture,* 99, notes that "both local interests and the Crown found oligarchy entirely appropriate."

38. Alan D. Dyer, *The City of Worcester in the Sixteenth Century* (Leicester: Leicester University Press, 1973), 221; Britnell, *Colchester,* 227–28. By contrast, bailiffs in Maldon were never expected to subsidize expenditures; see Petchey, *Maldon,* 160, 162.

39. The longest-serving aldermen were Martin Basell (36 years), John Christmas (34 years), Thomas Christmas I (33 years), Benjamin Clere (36 years), Thomas Heckforde (39 years), Thomas Jopson (38 years), John Mayken (33 years), Robert Mott (32 years), and George Sayer (33 years). See appendix 2.

year or two before death, suggesting illness or infirmity; and a few others were known to have moved from the town.[40] Obviously, the turnover was not rapid.[41]

Although longevity of service sometimes extended to the second generation of the same family, it was rare to have three successive generations from one family serving in town governance, often because of financial problems, the failure to produce male heirs,[42] or inability to provide if there were too many male heirs. The Cleres were an exception, having at least one member of the Clere family serving as alderman continuously from 1511 to 1579. The first Clere, who came from Bury St. Edmunds in the early 1470s, served as alderman before his death in 1500. The Cleres even had a member of the fourth generation to serve as alderman early in the seventeenth century.[43] However, having a fourth generation alderman was not necessarily desirable for urban families, as they usually aspired not to longevity in town governance but to being prosperous enough to buy land and enter into the landed gentry, a process that usually took about three generations. The Cleres seemed to be well on their way into landed society when John died in 1538, as John had been ranked as the fourth wealthiest alderman in the 1524–25 taxation; but his major heir, Benjamin, experienced a slow decline in his fortunes, including costly court suits. In a 1602 document entered into the court

---

40. Seventeen of the ninety-eight aldermen lived for more than two years beyond their retirement from the office. However, the records are incomplete for five of those seventeen, so it is possible that some or all of those five died in office.

41. However, it was not a closed oligarchy; of the seventy-two aldermen whose backgrounds can be traced definitely, thirty-two were natives of Colchester and forty were born elsewhere; see appendix 2. There was more openness to newcomers in the early Tudor years, as over 62 percent (twenty-five) of those aldermen identified as being born elsewhere came to Colchester before 1530, with seven coming in the 1530s and 1540s, and with eight coming in the last fifty-three years of Tudor rule. There were seventy-one different family names among the aldermen, so family dynasties were not a problem.

42. Only eighteen of the ninety-eight aldermen were sons of aldermen, although ten others were stepsons, grandsons, or heirs. On the whole, Colchester aldermen were quite fortunate in having sons. Of the ninety-eight Tudor aldermen, sixty-two had a son or sons. Of the other thirty-six aldermen, twelve had daughters only, and ten died with no children to succeed them; no information remains about the other fourteen.

43. Palliser, *York,* 289; Maryanne Kowaleski, "The History of Urban Families in Medieval England," *Journal of Medieval History* 14 (1988): 58; *OB,* 128. The first Nicholas Clere was bailiff in 1491–92, but his years of service cannot be determined, since the records are incomplete. John was alderman in 1511–39, his son Benjamin in 1540–76, and his son Nicholas III in 1573–79. John's nephew (Emma Becket's son), Nicholas II, served in 1562–70, and another Nicholas, the fourth alderman to be so named, was alderman from 1604 to 1612.

rolls, Benjamin Clere, probably the son of Alderman Benjamin, begged for forbearance and patience from his creditors in Colchester. He had seven children, and his financial situation was "much decayed."[44] In contrast, the Sayer family illustrated a successful rise into the landed gentry. George Sayer, who had a long career of service to the borough as councillor and alderman (forty years), was the son of a Colchester alderman. The early Sayers were fullers and shearers in the town, and George was a clothmaker who began acquiring lands during the dissolution of the monasteries and chantries. By the time he died in 1574, he owned several manors and was styled a "gentleman." George was the last to be involved in borough affairs; he made a marriage alliance for his son George with the daughter of William Cardinal of Great Bromley, Essex, who had himself risen from clothier to lord of the manor. The Sayers acquired a coat of arms, and by the time the younger George died in 1596, he was titled "esquire." Members of the Sayer family in the next two generations attained knighthood.[45]

To have the trust and respect of the townsmen, aldermen needed more than wealth and a willingness to give of their time and means; they also needed integrity and a respect for pious concerns. Sixty of the ninety-eight aldermen made wills before they died, and those wills provide some clues for determining the aldermen's attitudes, including their esteem for pious ways. The general use of wills in charting levels of religious concern in Colchester is discussed more fully in chapter 4, but the interest in pious bequests is higher in the wills of the aldermen than among the general will-making population, with 53 percent of the sixty aldermen testators manifesting a high or the highest concern for charitable and pious deeds or expressing an unusual degree of piety in their preambles (compared with 21 percent among all testators), and with only 10 percent showing a low regard or none at all for pious acts (compared with 28 percent among all testators).[46] It may be asked whether the town leaders were

44. CR163/12d. John was assessed at £120 in 1524 (PRO E179/108/162). Benjamin's wealth was assessed at £100 in 1556; see S. T. Bindoff, ed., *The House of Commons, 1509–1558*, 3 vols. (London: Secker and Warburg, 1982), 1:650.

45. *OB*, 134–35; *Feet of Fines for Essex*, vol. 4, *1423–1547*, ed. P. H. Reaney and Marc Fitch (Colchester: Essex Archaeological Society, 1964), 297; *Feet of Fines for Essex*, vol. 5, *1547–1580*, ed. Marc Fitch and Frederick Emmison (Oxford: Leopard's Head Press, 1991), 3, 113; PRO 25 Daughtry; Morant, 2:7 (Morant incorrectly inserts a second John Sayer as the father of George; the first John was George's father).

46. See chapter 4, tables 1 and 2, which chart the indicators of piety in wills and the levels of religious concern among Colchester testators.

genuinely pious or merely felt that their position required a show of piety. It has been noted that in Coventry, the higher the aspirations of the townsman were, the more frequently he attended church services. Nothing is known about the church attendance of Colchester aldermen, but even if the piety of the town leader was more symbolic than genuine, his need to exhibit piety tells us much about the expectations of the community in regard to its leaders. The community wanted and expected more in deeds of charity from its leaders than was evident in the society at large, both because the leaders were the more prosperous members of the community and because they were expected to have a sense of social responsibility, a part of which was to provide a model of piety.[47]

The wealthiest family of aldermen in the early Tudor years, the Christmases, were by all indications exemplary patterns of piety. In his 1520 will, the younger Thomas Christmas established a school "to teach grammar and other virtuous conditions and learning," gave money to each of the parish churches, provided for the distribution of money to the poor every Friday for twenty years, left money for the repair of highways and the river Colne, provided bedding to the Hospital of St. Anne, left money for prayers in each of the Colchester religious houses, and provided for the maintenance of sermons by the Grey Friars. His father, the elder Thomas, was the burgess MP who helped write the first account of Parliament written in English in 1485, so he had, at minimum, the ability to read and write English. As businessmen, the Christmases were aware of their responsibility before God and the people; in 1489 the elder Christmas and Alderman Richard Barker, "moved with tenderness by the prayer of the Commonalty, undertook that they themselves would make, and build, at their own proper costs and charges," two mills, one for fulling and the other for grain, "to the honour of God and the Borough." The fulling mill helped revitalize clothmaking in Colchester in the 1480s. There is no doubt that the mills also filled the pocketbooks of the two aldermen, but their gestures affirmed that wealth could work for loftier purposes. Christmas probably provided a substantial amount of money for the rebuilding of St. James's Church, where the initials *T. C.* are on the wall of the east end that was built at that time.[48]

47. Charles Phythian-Adams, *Desolation of a City: Coventry and the Urban Crisis of the Late Middle Ages* (Cambridge: Cambridge University Press, 1979), 138; MacCaffrey, *Exeter*, 276–79.

48. Christmas will (1520), PRO 28 Ayloffe; *RPB*, 103; Royal Commission on Historical Monuments, *An Inventory of the Historical Monuments in Essex*, 4 vols. (London: HMSO, 1916–23), 3:36; *VCH Essex*, 2:502–3; ERO D/B5 Gb1, f. 37. The account of

Piety counterbalanced the moneymaking ventures of the community by showing how to use money rightly, not just for oneself, but for others in a way that was pleasing to God. Certainly not all of the aldermen were models of piety, but their task of keeping order and providing for the welfare of the town was made more tolerable both for the leaders and for the other inhabitants when it was combined with piety. Their pious acts endorsed their role as leaders, and both they and the town were well served by that affirmation.

To do their work, Colchester leaders needed wealth, a willing spirit, and the respect of townsmen, but that work was made even more effective by family and marriage connections. Thirty-seven aldermen—and probably another five—were known to be related by blood to other aldermen, and another twenty-one had connections through either their own marriage or that of a parent or a child.[49] Newcomers who had ambitions in the town found it helpful to make such alliances. For example, Thomas Dybney took as his second wife the stepdaughter of Alderman John Neve, a connection that was probably helpful to Dybney, since he was in the lowly occupation of butcher; in fact, Dybney was the only butcher to become alderman in Tudor Colchester. William Beket, arriving in Colchester at an opportune time, married the recently widowed Emma Clere, thus connecting Beket with the influential Clere family.[50]

Not surprisingly, the wills show the bond of trust to be strong among kinfolk, but service in town governance also provided the chance to form lasting bonds of friendship. In the wills, one indication of such a connecting bond was the naming of a nonrelated fellow alderman to be the executor or supervisor of one's will. Usually, a spouse, a son, or other close relatives were named in those capacities, but seventeen aldermen named other aldermen who were not blood relations,[51] thus indicating

---

Parliament is in Nicholas Pronay and John Taylor, eds., *Parliamentary Texts of the Later Middle Ages* (Oxford: Clarendon Press, 1980), 185–89.

49. See appendix 2. In York, three-fourths of Tudor town leaders were related, according to Palliser, *York*, 96.

50. On Dybney, see *OB*, 151; Margery Neve's will (1560), ERO D/ACR3/167; and Aneret Dybney's will (1586), ERO D/ABW12/202. John Swayn was admitted as a butcher in 1466–67, but he was a merchant when an alderman; see *OB*, 126, and Britnell, *Colchester*, 211. On Beket, see Thomas Clere's will (1520), PRO 4 Maynwaryng; and Emma Beket's will (1560), ERO D/ACR5/59.

51. In chronological order, naming nonrelated aldermen executors were Robert Northern (1525), Thomas Cock I (1544), Robert Browne II (1568), and Thomas Lawrence (1594). Naming nonrelated aldermen supervisors were John Colle (1536), William Buxston (1546), William Mott (1562), John Maynard (1565), John Beriff (1566), John Beste (1573),

that strong, trusting friendships had been forged. References to the alder-men friends became more frequent and more fulsome in the Elizabethan period, especially in the 1560s and 1570s; for example, Alderman John Maynard (1565) named two "trusty and well-beloved friends in Christ," both aldermen, as overseers.[52] Those same seventeen aldermen also had great pride in the town and in their position as one of the governors; it was no coincidence that fourteen of those seventeen aldermen died in office, loyal and faithful to the end,[53] and that thirteen designated them-selves as an alderman or bailiff in the preamble of their wills, thus indi-cating a high degree of pride in that position.[54] Pride in the town and the aldermanic role were more likely to be manifested among those who had close ties to other aldermen, and, not surprisingly, 65 percent of those seventeen aldermen testators also had a high regard for piety or pious deeds, higher than the average of 53 percent among the aldermen as a whole.

Serving as an alderman was time-consuming, it could be onerous, and relationships and attitudes could turn ugly. But it could enforce one's sense of personal worth, provide colleagues with whom one could enjoy fellowship and form deep bonds of friendship, and give one the satisfac-tion of serving the community while also serving God by keeping order and encouraging godliness. It produced stalwarts like George Sayer, who served thirty-three years as alderman, with seven of those years as bailiff. Sayer died in 1577 after outliving two wives, and his monument in St. Peter's Church has an epitaph that describes him as a man who had not only a sense of duty but pride in his native town, which was served before God with justice and mercy in love toward his neighbors.

Richard Northey (1573), William Sympson (1575), Thomas Turner (1575), Richard Thurston (1581), William Earnesbie (1588), Robert Lambert (1590), Thomas Lawrence again (1594), and Henry Osbourne (1614). All seventeen had family members nearby, so it was not a case of having no one else to appoint.

52. PRO 15 Sheffeld.

53. Two of the others, Robert Lambert and William Sympson, retired because of great age and infirmity; the third, John Beriff, left office when Elizabeth became queen, but his connection to fellow alderman Benjamin Clere, whom he named as his supervisor (PRO 17 Crymes), endured, possibly because their fathers had served together as aldermen before them.

54. Of the four who did not, John Beriff and Robert Lambert had already retired, and William Earnesbie, a relative newcomer to the town, was listed in his will as being both from Colchester and London, so he had divided loyalties. John Colle (1536) was the fourth one.

Full thyrte years or more cheefe rule or place he bare
In this his native auncient Towne, whereof he had great care.
With Justice he did rule, and eke with mercy mylde,
With love he lyved many years of man woman and chylde.

. . . .

And we, that yet remayne within this vale of teares,
By thyne example maye be taught for to contemne all feares,
And alwayes for to praye that God our stepps so guyde
That we lykewise may hence depart in endlesse blisse to byde.[55]

A closer look at one group of aldermen will now be presented by focusing on those elected in the autumn of 1530, by which time Henry VIII had been king for over twenty-one years, long enough for him to have made all the changes that a king could be expected to make. Yet, although neither Henry nor the aldermen of Colchester knew it, they were on the verge of one of the greatest changes in the history of England, the transforming of the English church from Catholicism to Protestantism, a change that would affect both the lives and the governance of the people of Colchester. Added to that would be economic upheaval and incredible population growth. The group of 1530, therefore, can be seen as a kind of foil, serving as a contrast to the two later groups of 1560 and 1590, which will be examined in later chapters.

The Aldermen of 1530

The ten aldermen elected in the autumn of 1530 had already served one year together, but their collective experience was much greater. At the time of their election, their years of service ranged from William Beket's one year to John Mayken's twenty-seven years; their average length of service was twelve years.[56] Most of them had already served for several years, with half of them having worked together for the past fourteen years. They knew each other well, having experienced together the ups and downs of borough governance. John Clere was finishing his first stint as junior bailiff back during the election day riot in 1514, when the rioters "offered the bailiffs divers opprobrius and contumacious words"; and Clere was with the other bailiffs when they were assaulted as they later

---

55. Morant, 3:49 (appendix to book 3).
56. Some of the earlier records are incomplete, so the average length of service may have been even longer.

tried to arrest one of the ringleaders of the rioters. The elder of the 1530 aldermanic group was grocer John Mayken, who had been with the sergeant at mace on that night in 1516 when, after trying to arrest two men for disturbing the peace, the sergeant was beaten "so that his life was despaired of," while others shouted, "Down with the bayly, down with him!" Such experiences probably helped motivate the leaders to make constitutional reforms in the next few years.[57]

The 1530 group had an unusually high number (at least half of them) who had been born elsewhere, with four of them coming from Suffolk. John Colle and Christopher Hamond even came from the same village, Nayland, which was just across the Suffolk border. The social status of these fellow Naylanders points up one of the anomalies of the social structure: Colle was a clothmaker but much richer than Hamond, the sole "gentleman" among the group, although Hamond also seems to have been practicing as a merchant.[58]

As far as wealth was concerned, John Christmas was clearly the leader of the aldermen in 1530, having been assessed at £600 in 1524, with Aldermen Colle and Flyngaunt tying for second at £140 each. The five wealthiest were clothiers or, in the case of Christmas, had inherited money from a family of clothiers.[59] Four men (Beket, Hamond, Lowthe, and Neve) were at the low end in wealth, having only £40 each. They were aware of their comparative wealth, for even among the aldermen themselves, wealth spoke loudly and clearly. Only once during John Christmas's first year in office did he serve in the lesser aldermanic roles of coroner or clavier, and from then on during his long tenure, Christmas served only in the more prestigious aldermanic offices of bailiff or justice of the peace. Even in the listing of names, the comparative status of the aldermen was evident, as Christmas was almost always listed first. By 1528 John was known as "esquire," the only one among the aldermen and the first of his family to be so designated. By 1530, Christmas was about to be launched into more influence at the county level through the good fortune and influence of a cousin, Thomas Audley, who was still the

---

57. CR86/5; CR88/23; *RPB*, 28–30.

58. Britnell, *Colchester,* 212. Their 1524–25 assessments were Colle, £140 & £80; Hamond, £40. See PRO E179/108/162, 169, from which the following assessments given in text also come.

59. The five aldermen at the lower end of the scale were a grocer, a merchant, another clothier, a "gentleman," and one man of unknown occupation. John Christmas, about forty years of age in 1530, was the fourth generation of Christmases in Colchester governance, with two Thomases and a Richard before him: see CR111/6, 7; *OB,* 137.

Colchester town clerk although he had recently been elected as Speaker of the House of Commons in what came to be known as the Reformation Parliament.[60]

All of the aldermen were well acquainted with their town clerk; in fact, Audley was at the center of one of their controversies a few years before. In June of 1521, five Colchester burgesses, including then alderman William Debenham and later alderman Christopher Hamond, were at Chelmsford before the county justices of the peace to charge three Colchester men, among them Audley and Alderman Flyngaunt, for having entered the house of a certain John Rede. Everyone involved seemed to be taking the law into their own hands; in July, eight men, including Hamond, unlawfully carried away two wagonloads of hay belonging to Audley. It was probably Audley who engineered the bringing of his opponents before a Colchester session of the peace in September of that year. Audley and Flyngaunt seemed to be good friends; they served together in the 1523 Parliament as burgesses from Colchester, and both Flyngaunt and Christmas would later benefit from Audley's position as lord chancellor of England, when they bought former monastic lands in Colchester from Audley.[61] Though not all connections were so advantageous as that with Audley, networks within the 1530 group of aldermen were important, especially family connections, either by blood or through marriage, and newcomers were not slow to establish connections to older families through marriage. For example, William Beket married John Clere's widowed sister-in-law, Emma.[62] There were other kinds of connections, too. Though five of the aldermen came from five different parishes, the other five aldermen (Christmas, Flyngaunt, Colle, Clere, and Neve) lived in St. James's parish, so they would have regularly worshiped and tended to the business of the parish together. A 1521 parish decision shows how the network of connections intertwined. Flyngaunt and Neve, who was not yet an alderman, were the churchwardens of St. James's Church; they

60. Josiah C. Wedgwood, *History of Parliament: Biographies of the Members of the Commons House, 1439–1509*, 2 vols. (London: HMSO, 1936), 186; *Essex Fines*, 4:129, 170; *Letters and Papers, Foreign and Domestic, of the Reign of Henry VIII*, ed. J. S. Brewer, James Gairdner, and R. H. Brodie, 21 vols. (London: HMSO, 1864–1932), 7: no. 454.

61. CR89/12; CR93/3; CR106/3.

62. CR96/19. John Mayken married the widow of a Colchester gentleman, Robert Rokewood: see CR92/18; PRO 17 Horne. Flyngaunt married into the Northern family from Greenstead, and one member of that family seems to have been the alderman Robert Northern: see ERO D/ACR2/53; ERO D/ACR2/73, 74; ERO D/ACR2/190.

and "other trustworthy parishioners," including Alderman John Clere, helped Alderman John Mayken and his wife, Agnes, sell a house earlier than the terms of her late husband's will had specified. The house was sold to Alderman John Christmas, so the needs of several town leaders were served in that transaction.[63] Another connection was the sharing of duties as wardens of the Guild of St. Helen, a religious guild supported by the leaders of the town.[64]

Such close connections did not necessarily produce harmony. Quick-tempered John Colle was at the center of more than one dispute,[65] but Colle met his match for temper in Alderman William Debenham in 1520, when the two aldermen had a fierce exchange before the whole assembly of aldermen and councillors. After Debenham insulted Colle, who was bailiff that year, by saying that his relatives were heretics, Colle charged that Debenham had ridiculed the aldermen behind their backs, to which Debenham replied, "Thou lyest falsely in thy head." The hot exchange continued until Debenham walked out; three months later Debenham appeared before the assembly and was fined and imprisoned for his "disobedience, cruel and seditious words."[66] Colle ended up on top that time, but his biggest blunder was his dispute with fellow alderman John Clere in 1522, which was recorded at some length in the Red Paper Book. The argument was over a meadow "pertaining to the master of the hospital of Mary Magdalen," which was in the borough but outside the walls of the town. Colle lost his temper and said "certain slanderous and rebukeful words . . . uncharitably against the said John Clere, in the presence of the said bailiffs and divers of their brother aldermen . . . in disobedience . . . and contrary to the good order of the said town." The arbitrators in the dispute, the aldermen and the recorder of the town, made Colle and Clere promise to "behave themselves well and charitably to other" and meted

---

63. CR92/18.

64. Christmas and Colle were wardens in 1524 (CR95/6d). In 1516, Clere and a cleric were wardens (CR88/8), as were Lowthe and a cleric in 1529 (CR99/2). Some aldermen also seemed to be business associates, or at least Aldermen Mayken, Christmas, and Colle, along with William Alfeld, jointly sued two burgesses repeatedly (CR89/23; CR90/5d; CR92/5d).

65. Colle frequently sued others for debts owed him (CR89/10d; CR93/10; CR98/7d, 12), but one of the cases was quite lengthy. After farming out the office of examiner of cloth to a certain Matthew Rede, Colle brought Rede to court in 1517 in a dispute over the amount that Rede owed to Colle. The jury deciding the case took a middle course, though more in Colle's favor than in Rede's, and Rede ended up in the moot hall prison (CR87/23; CR88/5d, 7, 17). Rede's son, John, was a part of the dispute mentioned earlier concerning Audley and Flyngaunt, and he, too, was imprisoned (CR89/12; CR93/3,26).

66. CR92/18d.

out certain punishments.[67] Some of the aldermen were hardly paragons of virtue. Four years later, John Neve was one of four clothiers accused of delivering five pounds of wool to their spinners under the pretense that they were delivering four pounds, an offense that was "to the common and serious damage and pauperization of the king's people spinning this kind of wool and against the laudable customs of the town."[68] John Smalpece and especially Ambrose Lowthe were more than once accused of sharp business practices. Smalpece was said to buy by one measure and sell by another, and Lowthe was considered guilty of regrating salt and of selling candles beyond the price fixed by the bailiffs. His offenses were considered so serious that he was threatened with expulsion from the freedom of the borough in 1518.[69] Although the only merchant among the aldermen in 1530, Lowthe was at the bottom end of aldermanic prosperity, having been assessed at £40 of goods in 1524, so he was always scrambling to maintain his position. Before he became alderman, he was even dealing in polecat skins. Lowthe ended up losing his freedom of the borough in 1539 because his son had prosecuted in an outside court, but Lowthe's ruinous wharf and house in 1534 and 1535 signaled money problems, so he served his last year as alderman in 1536, dying ten years later. Lowthe's early retirement from office was unusual, as most of the 1530 aldermen either died in office or served until close to death.[70]

John Colle was the first of the 1530 aldermen to die, making his will in March, 1536, shortly before his death. Despite Colle's sharp differences with John Clere a few years before, they ended as friends; when Colle died in 1536, he named Clere and Clere's son, Benjamin, as supervisors of his will.[71] As the group began to die off, the sons of deceased aldermen began to appear as witnesses to the wills, indicating a continu-

---

67. *RPB*, 27. The punishments were Solomon-like, with Clere winning in the end: Colle had to pay for glazing the east window in the moot hall, but he got the meadow for four years, provided he did not plough it; after Colle's four years, Clere was to have the meadow for "so many years" as he "claimeth to have in the same." In 1532, Colle was in another affray, that time with Alderman Flyngaunt; both were fined at a session of the peace (CR102/5d).

68. CR104/5.

69. CR98/15; CR83/1d; CR89/4. John Neve also was engaging in some shady practices, in 1534 and 1536 (CR104/5; CR106/2, 2d).

70. PRO E179/108/162; CR83/8; CR109/2; CR103/20; CR105/2d; Lowthe's will, ERO D/ABW23/42. Christmas, Clere, Colle, and Flyngaunt died in office; Beket, Neve, and Smalpece died within one or two years of retirement; and the death dates of Mayken and Hamond are unknown.

71. PRO 34 Hogen.

ing relationship between the families. When John Smalpece wrote his will in 1538, James Colle and Benjamin Clere were at his bedside, and when Thomas Flyngaunt was dying in 1541, Benjamin, by that time a first-year alderman, was there.

The seven extant wills from the 1530 aldermen give some indication of their relationship to God, the church, and the community. It is probably no coincidence that the three aldermen who were most often accused of illegal business practices also had the fewest pious bequests in their wills: John Smalpece gave nothing but an obligatory 12d. to the high altar of his parish church of All Saints; John Neve was a bit more generous with his 40s. to the repair of his parish church of St. James; and Ambrose Lowthe mentioned an almshouse that he bequeathed to the care of his wife.[72] The only two aldermen whose bequests indicated a genuine piety were William Beket and John Clere, who both died in 1538. Beket, who married Clere's widowed sister-in-law, gave money to his parish church of St. Peter, but he was obviously concerned about the poor in the town, carefully listing ten other parishes besides his own and the various amounts to be distributed to the poor within those parishes. John Clere had the distinction of writing the first obviously Protestant will in Colchester, with his preamble calling on the blood of Jesus for the forgiveness of his sins, rather than making the usual Catholic commendation of one's soul to God, Mary, and the saints. Clere provided for the preaching of five sermons in his parish church of St. James, "for the true setting forth of His Word," and he further bequeathed money for the repair of the highway and for five poor maidens' marriages, as well as a weekly allowance for five poor people within his parish for five years.[73]

These were the men who would deal with the complexities that the Reformation brought to Colchester. The aldermen had a strong tradition of self-governance that lent confidence, an exalted status that gave them influence in the borough, and a friend, Thomas Audley, in a high place. The Reformation would bring new opportunities, both for the soul and the pocketbook—opportunities they gladly seized.

---

72. Wills of Smalpece (1538, proved 1543), ERO D/ABW33/105; Neve (1541), PRO 1 Spert; and Lowthe (1545), ERO D/ABW23/42.
73. Beket's will, ERO D/ABW3/59; Clere's will, PRO 25 Dyngeley.

2

Governance Facing Outward: Lords, Lawyers, and Influence

Even though the spirit of service among Colchester's sixteenth-century town leaders contributed significantly to the borough's stability and prosperity, the governors could not afford to rest comfortably with their internal exercise of benevolent power; they also needed to cultivate the power and influence of the town in the county of Essex and with the government in London. As a royal borough chartered by the monarch, Colchester, of necessity, had to consider the broader political spectrum. Especially in connection with the shifts of power in the English Reformation, Colchester leaders increasingly employed men of influence outside the borough to represent them. The expanded power base thus enabled town leaders in the 1570s and 1580s to turn their fervent local Puritanism into a more sophisticated participation in national politics.

The Monarchy and Channels of Influence

In a report of an affray in 1514, election day rioters were accused of offering "resistance against the peace of the said Lord King," and the same report described the keepers of the peace in Colchester, the town leaders, as "trustworthy men of the Lord King."[1] The relationship of Colchester officials to the Crown was complex: the king was the source of their authority, and they were the civil servants of the Crown, but the king also needed the town leaders to keep his peace, house his prisoners in Colchester Castle, help fill his coffers, provide soldiers and ships at times of national crisis, and send members to Parliament whenever an assembly was called. Above all, the mandates of the royal government

---

1. CR86/5. Alan Harding, *The Law Courts of Medieval England* (London: George Allen and Unwin, 1973), 121, says that such phrases "emphasized the identity of interest between subject and sovereign."

were to be obeyed, for the liberties of Colchester were by the grace and favor of the king through the charter that each king issued to the borough. Liberties were no defense against interference from the king, however, and he could even revoke those liberties if he chose to do so.[2]

Not only were they agents of the king, but town leaders were also representatives of the borough and its inhabitants, since they acted on behalf of the borough in dealings with the royal government at both national and county levels. From the town's point of view, loyalty to the Crown was the prudent course, even when such loyalty conflicted with the town leaders' personal desires; for that reason, Catholic Mary, on her way to London to claim the Crown in 1553, was welcomed in Protestant Colchester. Serving the king could be expensive and burdensome. Sometimes the expenses were very direct, as when the borough had to entertain royalty, as Colchester did in 1515 when Catherine of Aragon stopped for a night's stay in Colchester while making a pilgrimage to Walsingham; on her departure, the officers of the borough gave the queen a purse containing £10. The total cost to the borough of Queen Mary's stopover in Colchester in 1553 was over £45, but the relationship with the Crown was usually more mundane, with emphasis being on the need of the town for influence in the right places. A town sometimes needed favors, such as the mitigation of an existing burden or the granting of new liberties; for example, in the 1580s Colchester wanted both a charter from the queen to reestablish the grammar school and help in getting the silenced town preacher reinstated.[3]

Towns in Tudor England had little political influence, so help was needed from the group that had long been influential, the nobility and landed gentry. It was vital for a town to cultivate such friends, and gifts

---

2. On the relationship of the town and the royal government, see Rosemary Horrox, "Urban Patronage and Patrons in the Fifteenth Century," in *Patronage, the Crown, and the Provinces in Later Medieval England,* ed. Ralph A. Griffiths (Atlantic Highlands, N.J.: Humanities Press, 1981), 145–66; Palliser, *York,* 40–59; MacCaffrey, *Exeter,* 203–45; Dyer, *Worcester,* 208–14; Susan Reynolds, *An Introduction to the History of English Medieval Towns* (Oxford: Clarendon Press, 1977), 111, 126, 129; Helen M. Jewell, *English Local Administration in the Middle Ages* (New York: Barnes and Noble, 1972), 9. Robert Tittler, "The Emergence of Urban Policy, 1536–58," in *The Mid-Tudor Polity, c. 1540–1560,* ed. Jennifer Loach and Robert Tittler (London: Macmillan, 1980), 74–93, traces the development by the Crown of an urban policy, particularly by the Marian government, which relied heavily on a strong link with the towns. Sacks, *Bristol,* 186, contends that being agents of royal authority took on new meaning after the Reformation.

3. *OB,* 148; Morant, 1:49–50; Cooper, "Civic Ceremonial," 66–67.

were occasionally given just for that purpose; for example, "a horse-load of our Colchester oysters" was sent to the earl of Leicester in 1579 because he had "been such a continual patron to our Town."[4] However, townsmen were in a vulnerable position if they relied exclusively on gentry or nobility to uphold their interests, so towns were not behindhand in taking advantage of the expertise of the rising group of professionals trained in the common law to press their claims. It might be "safer" to employ a professional lawyer than to rely on fickle friends who had their own interests to promote. The king himself was learning to rely on lawyers; a prominent example was lawyer Thomas Audley, who came to be much more than the Colchester town clerk in the 1530s, when he rose to become lord chancellor of England. Audley's success was also Colchester's success, as the town realized that it was possible to have influence at the highest levels.

The two groups that the town needed in its continuing attempt to gain influence overlapped, since a number of lawyers were from the landed gentry. In fact, the combination was ideal. If a town could hire as recorder or town clerk a man who was from the local gentry, had important connections, and was also trained in the law, they were getting both personal political influence and legal knowledge in one man. In addition to the two offices of recorder and town clerk, another channel of influence was the borough's representation in Parliament, to which Colchester had the privilege of sending two members. In the Tudor period, Colchester began to rely to a greater extent on outsiders—on the more influential lawyers and gentry as representatives—rather than on "homegrown" burgesses. They did what was necessary to gain political influence. One of the most important jobs of Colchester aldermen, therefore, was to choose the right men for the three Colchester positions that were outward-looking: recorder, town clerk, and members of Parliament. In the following section of this chapter, I analyze these three positions and the outside personnel selected for them, especially the aldermen's reasons for choosing the men they selected; in this analysis, a picture of the town's attempts to wield influence emerges, as well as the role of the local gentry and nobility in their endeavor to influence Colchester affairs and to take advantage of the opportunities offered in the town.

---

4. Morant, 3:34.

Colchester's Three Outward-Looking Offices

The Colchester offices of both recorder and town clerk were selected from the ranks of professional lawyers, though some men who served in those offices had the added advantage of being from the landed gentry. The recorder and town clerk provided expertise in the law and, it was hoped, the right kind of influence in Westminster and in Chelmsford, the county town. Both drew a regular fee for their services to the borough, although they would have had other sources of income. Following a trend begun in many fifteenth-century towns, Colchester elected yearly from 1463 onward a recorder, or *legis peritus,* who was the chief legal counsel or officer of the borough, representing it in its business with outside authorities.[5] He was one of the seven JPs of the borough and was, according to Edward IV's charter, always supposed to be present at a session of the peace. A recorder for twenty-one years during the reign of Henry VIII, Thomas Bonham, Esq., owned property in Colchester, apparently living there. After Bonham's death in 1532, the recorders were mostly nonresident, so they would not have normally been a part of the sessions of the peace as the charter stipulated, although at times they might have sent a deputy.[6] Some of the Colchester recorders, such as former attorney general Sir James Hobard and successful London lawyer Anthony Stapleton, were top legal practitioners; others had strong noble or gentry connections; and others, such as Sir Francis Walsingham, Sir Thomas Heneage, and Robert Cecil (later earl of Salisbury), were obviously desirable because of their importance within the central government. Sir Francis Walsingham, who combined his Colchester job with the same work for several other towns, was not alone in the practice of multiple recorderships; the job of recorder was apparently welcomed as a chance to supplement one's income, even by someone in the highest circles, since the office had become more rewarding as the towns began to value the office more highly.[7]

---

5. Britnell, "Colchester Courts," 139; Horrox, "Patronage," 160. On the fees paid to recorders, see E. W. Ives, *The Common Lawyers of Pre-Reformation England* (Cambridge: Cambridge University Press, 1983), 289. My appendix 3 lists the Colchester recorders, town clerks, and MPs in the Tudor period.

6. The exceptions to nonresidency were Jerome Gilbert, who held office only one year, 1553–54, and Sir Thomas Lucas, who seemed to be more interested in county and military affairs and so was recorder only from 1572 to 1576.

7. Tittler, *Architecture,* 122. On Hobard, see Ives, *Common Lawyers,* 76, 242–43, 287, 384.

The clerk of the town also supplied the corporation with legal advice,[8] but he was more often resident in the borough than was the recorder. The town clerk was the counselor and prosecuting attorney in the borough courts, the legal advisor at assembly meetings, and keeper of the official records. It is interesting to note the changes in record keeping in 1514 under the new clerk, Thomas Audley, when the records began to be much more complete. The proceedings of the sessions of the peace began to be recorded, as well as the detailed enrollment of deeds. Such thoroughness was probably typical of Audley, who would later catch the attention of authorities in Westminster. The town clerks were no ordinary lawyers, as all were of the gentry during the Tudor years. Colchester historian R. H. Britnell believes that gentlemen probably took over the Colchester town clerk's office during the reign of Henry VII, and so at that time the office would have become more of an outward-looking office than it had been, with the officeholders increasingly expected to have a certain influence outside the town.[9] As the outside interests of town clerks grew, deputy clerks were used to handle the record-keeping duties in the town, and even some of the resident town clerks had deputies. During Elizabeth's reign, there was one long period of nonresidency, 1576–97, when the Puritan lawyer James Morice was town clerk; a letter from the bailiffs to Morice in 1579 requested him to

---

8. Colchester's charters of incorporation, issued by the Crown, made Colchester a legal corporation, so that the corporation of Colchester had an existence apart from its members, thus giving it certain inherent rights and responsibilities. The elected governors of the time represented the corporation.

9. James R. Davis, "Colchester, 1600–1662: Politics, Religion, and Officeholders in an English Provincial Town" (Ph.D. diss., Brandeis University, 1980), 53; Britnell, *Colchester,* 210. For the first year, Audley held the office jointly with John Barnabe. The town clerk in 1486, John Harvy, was only mentioned in one place, in a will (CR111/6); and nothing more is known of him. *Gentry* is an ambiguous term, but all of the other town clerks in the sixteenth century were described as gentlemen or esquires in the town records, with one exception, Robert Gynes (1564–66), who was designated as "senior." Gynes was educated at the Inner Temple and was bencher there in 1567 and Lent reader in 1568, according to P. W. Hasler, ed., *The House of Commons, 1558–1603,* 3 vols. (London: HMSO, for the History of Parliament Trust, 1981), 2:232; so Gynes's training would have given him the title *gentleman.* C. W. Brooks, *Pettyfoggers and Vipers of the Commonwealth: The "Lower Branch" of the Legal Profession in Early Modern England* (Cambridge: Cambridge University Press, 1986), 210–14, describes the role of the town clerk and the opportunity it provided for the gentry.

come to the town, as they had need of his wisdom concerning several libels "cast about this town."[10]

A third, occasional office that dealt with affairs outside the borough was that of burgess member of Parliament to represent Colchester and to lobby on behalf of the town. The custom had long been established that local communities were to be represented in Parliament to agree to royal policies, especially taxation, and to register grievances. Colchester had the privilege of sending two members, and the burgess members from Colchester took their duties seriously. The Colchester Red Paper Book contains a unique account of the 1485 Parliament, written by the two Colchester burgesses Thomas Christmas and John Vertue. The account is significant in the history of Parliament, as it is the earliest account written by members of the Commons and is also the earliest one written in the English language. A 1980 printing makes it accessible to the modern reader. Addressed to "Maister Baillies, and all my masters," the report began, "According to our deute we went to Westmynestr . . . ," and a day-by-day account followed. The burgesses also mentioned that one of their tasks while at Westminster was to pay to the Exchequer Colchester's fee farm, the set amount of taxes paid annually to the Crown. Their account of the passage of an act on December 6 would have been of great interest to the burgesses in Colchester, as the act restored the earl of Oxford and his brothers to the lands they had lost by attainder during the Yorkist reign.[11]

Sending two men to Westminster for a Parliament could be costly. An account in the Red Paper Book of the methods of payment to the Colchester burgesses in three of Henry VII's early Parliaments reveals the creativity needed to meet those payments. The burgess MPs were paid the standard wage of 2s. a day, which could mount up to a sizable sum. In 1490, the corporation owed £17 16s. to Alderman Thomas Christmas

---

10. D/Y2/2, p. 93; Davis, "Colchester," 53. In the same year, the younger Robert Middleton was granted an annuity of £3 "to be attorney and counsel for the town" (D/B5 Gb1, f. 16), but it seems that Richard Symnell was Morice's deputy by 1579; see Morant, 3:34–35 (appendix to book 1). Seldom were the names of the deputies given, but John Gyne was described as "the town clerk deputy of Colchester" when he was made coexecutor of a 1541 will (ERO D/ABW39/51).

11. Pronay and Taylor, *Parliamentary Texts*, 85–89. Several of the borough instructions to MPs are extant: see MacCaffrey, *Exeter*, 225–28; Palliser, *York*, 58. On the relationship of Parliament and towns, see Robert Tittler, "Elizabethan Towns and the 'Points of Contact': Parliament," *Parliamentary History* 8 (1989): 275–88; D. M. Dean, "Parliament and Locality," in *The Parliaments of Elizabethan England,* ed. D. M. Dean and N. L. Jones (Oxford: Basil Blackwell, 1990), 139–62.

and £13 to Alderman Thomas Jopson for serving in the 1487 and 1489 Parliaments. An agreement for the payments was made, significantly just after Jopson became bailiff, whereby Christmas was released from half of the annual rent owed to the corporation for the corn and fulling mills that Christmas had built on corporation property, with the other half of the rent going to pay fellow MP Jopson, each receiving 26s. 8d. annually so that they would be paid over a period of several years.[12]

The corporation was slower in making payments to Jopson and Richard Heynes for the 1491 Parliament. In fact, Heynes had not been fully paid for the 1487 Parliament, so in 1494 the bailiffs, one of whom was former MP Thomas Christmas, took the unusual step of granting all fees from the borough court to Heynes until his £11 4s. was fully paid. Jopson was granted the rents from six borough properties, most of them held by Jopson himself. With such difficulties in making payment, it is no wonder that Colchester, like many other towns, changed their practice of sending their own aldermen to Parliament and instead began electing their town clerks or local gentry who might waive payment in order to obtain a parliamentary seat. It was a pragmatic change, occasioned both by high cost and by the necessity to have the greater influence that lawyers and gentry were thought to be better able to supply.[13]

The Red Paper Book describes the election for Colchester's members of Parliament in 1523, which also happened to be the first time that a nonalderman was elected as MP from Colchester in the Tudor period. Significantly, that new MP was Thomas Audley, who came to be among the new group of lawyers that played so significant a role during the reign of Henry VIII. In the election on March 31, 1523, the bailiffs called the aldermen, burgesses, and common council to the moot hall to elect two burgesses for the Parliament that would first meet on April 15. By the "advice, consent and agreement" of the assembly, they chose "their Right Well beloved and discreet Counsel and Common Clerk," Thomas Audley, and "their Right trusty and discreet and well beloved Ambrose Lowth, one of the aldermen." Colchester was not straying far from its usual practice in electing Audley, though, since he was resident in Colchester, very active in Colchester affairs, and a cousin of the ruling Christmas family. Before the election, a letter had been received from the

12. *RPB*, 129–30. On payment by towns to MPs, see Horrox, "Patronage," 154–55.
13. *RPB*, 124–26; Horrox, "Patronage," 158. On the difficulties of paying MPs in Rye, see Graham Mayhew, *Tudor Rye* (Brighton: University of Sussex Centre for Continuing Education, 1987), 33.

king, and some have speculated that the king nominated Audley in that letter.[14]

The next parliamentary election, in 1529, more clearly deviated from Colchester's usual practice of electing members of their ruling group to represent them in Parliament. Since the borough had traditionally elected townsmen, they granted admission to the freedom of the borough to two men, Sir John Reynsforth (or Raynsford) and Richard Anthony, so that they might serve as Colchester's members of Parliament but yet be nominal citizens of the town. Reynsforth, from Bradfield, some ten miles from Colchester, held his manor from the earl of Oxford, and Anthony was a servant in Oxford's household, so Oxford was probably behind their election. There was no doubt, though, about the source of the change made at the "special request" of Oxford: Anthony dutifully resigned in favor of Richard Rich, who was noted in the borough court roll as being of the council of the earl of Oxford. Thus began Rich's long and notorious career in Westminster, as well as a new trend in selection of parliamentary members in Colchester.[15]

In the remaining Tudor period, only once were aldermen elected to hold both of the Colchester seats, and that was in the second Parliament of 1554, when Queen Mary directed that constituencies select members from "their inhabitants, as the old laws require."[16] Apart from 1554, only five other aldermen after 1523 were elected as MPs in the remaining Tudor years.[17] Although it might appear that Colchester was becoming less independent in its selection of MPs, all of the men selected had definite connections with Colchester. Of the thirty-two different mem-

---

14. *RPB*, 26. Concerning Audley's relationship to the Christmas family, John Christmas, Sr., in his 1534 will, left money to his "cousin, Thomas Audeley, the elder," and made "Sir Thomas Audeley, knight, Lord Chancellor of England," the only supervisor of his will (CR104/7d). Audley was witness and supervisor of the 1520 will of wealthy alderman Thomas Christmas (PRO 28 Ayloffe), and Audley's own will in 1544 (PRO 1 Alen) mentioned his cousins, John Christmas (a Colchester alderman and son of Alderman Thomas Christmas), and John's son, George. On the letter from the king, see Bindoff, *House*, 1:350.

15. Bindoff, *House*, 1:89 and 3:183, 192–93; CR99/1d.

16. Quoted in J. E. Neale, *The Elizabethan House of Commons* (New Haven: Yale University Press, 1950), 287.

17. Benjamin Clere in 1545, John Beste in 1553, Nicholas Clere to replace a deceased MP in 1576, Martin Basell in 1592, and Richard Symnell in 1601. It is probably significant that the only private bill that Colchester was able to get even so far as into Parliamentary committee, a levy of two pence on all ships unloading goods for repair of Colchester harbor (which did not pass), was proposed in the 1592–93 session. Sitting on the committee was Martin Basell, the first alderman to be chosen to represent Colchester in the initial election in almost forty years: see Dean, "Parliament," 147–48; Hasler, 1:435.

bers of Parliament elected to represent Colchester in the Tudor period, fourteen were aldermen, five were town clerks, two were recorders, and ten were Essex gentry or Oxford retainers. Of the ten Essex gentlemen, four were sons of Colchester aldermen. Only one other Colchester MP, Arthur Throckmorton, did not fall into any of the above categories, but his entrée was through his marriage to the daughter of Sir Thomas Lucas, a resident of Colchester who served at various times as Colchester's town clerk, recorder, and MP.[18] Colchester's town leaders were not routinely electing as MP a lawyer or gentleman who was completely foreign to the town; rather, they were prudently trying to gain influence by choosing those men who not only had the ability and connections to make them effective in Westminster but also had linkages and loyalty to the town. That sometimes meant that town leaders followed the suggestion of a powerful friend or neighbor, which in itself could be a way of gaining influence with that patron.

In looking at all of the nonburgess officials selected by Colchester— MPs, recorders, and town clerks—a picture emerges of various connections and tentacles of power. The tentacles went in both directions: power was exerted to influence Colchester's decisions, and the town did its best to exert power in places that would be most helpful to Colchester. The long-standing influence of local nobility and gentry remained, but three events worked to bring changes to the process in the Tudor period. First, with the new power of common lawyers, exemplified by the rise of Thomas Audley, Colchester tasted and recognized the potential in having one's own man in high places, giving the town leaders more sophistication in the use of power. Second, the new fortunes created by the large transfers of land in the Reformation formed new gentry in Essex and Colchester, all with the potential for influence. Third, in the reign of Elizabeth, a perceived need for more power arose in Puritan Colchester as the town felt besieged by the outside forces of anti-Puritanism in the church and militant Catholic threats from the Continent. The result in Colchester was an even more zealous attempt to maximize what power they could. Some historians believe that the trend of towns away from using their own men as representatives in Parliament was an indication of less

---

18. Also, Sir Francis Walsingham recommended Throckmorton as being of "very good credit and ability"; see Davis, "Colchester," 145. There was some overlapping of categories: Thomas Lucas served as both town clerk and recorder, and Richard Symnell was town clerk for one year before becoming alderman; they were counted in the category in which they served longest.

independence in the Elizabethan period. For Colchester, on the contrary, it was an attempt to become more independent by learning and exercising some of the ways of power. If greater independence required using or occasionally being used by outsiders, the town leaders found that condition acceptable.[19]

Influence of the Earls of Oxford and Local Gentry

A discussion of the outside influences exerted on Colchester must include the traditional influence of the local nobility and gentry. No matter how prosperous a town might be, English society was, after all, still dominated by landed gentry and nobility. The authority of one man, the earl of Oxford, was uppermost in northeastern Essex. The earl of Oxford, from the enduring de Vere family of Norman descent, owned extensive properties in the Lexden and Tendring hundreds that adjoined Colchester. Although Castle Hedingham, almost twenty miles northwest of Colchester, was the main residence of Oxford, the earl also had a seat at Wivenhoe, just four miles down the river Colne from Colchester, and a seat at Earl's Colne, where many of the earls were buried, about ten miles up the river from Colchester. No wonder the river played such a large part in Colchester's disputes with the earl in the fifteenth century.[20]

The de Vere family history paralleled the history of England since the Norman Conquest. From their beginning in England, they had the hereditary office of the king's chamberlain, though they were occasionally deprived of it after choosing the wrong side in the various wars of the barons. The earls of Oxford distinguished themselves in most of the important battles of England; for example, in 1356 at Poitiers, the English archers who saved the day were led by the seventh earl of Oxford. Unfortunately, the twelfth earl took the Lancastrian side and was executed when the Yorkists won; eventually his son, the thirteenth earl, fled to France. The de Veres emerged triumphantly, though, when Henry Tudor landed in 1485 with the thirteenth earl as captain general of the invading army. Not only did Oxford regain his role as lord great cham-

---

19. On borough representation in the Elizabethan period, see Hasler, 1:48–60; S. T. Bindoff, *Tudor England* (Baltimore: Penguin Books, 1950), 216–17. Neale, *House*, 162, believes that the only independent boroughs were those that elected their own burgesses; the rest, in Neale's view, "surrendered to the gentry." But see Tittler, "Parliament," 285, who stresses the idea of reciprocal patronage.

20. Morant, 1:86–87.

berlain, but he was made lord high admiral of England, Ireland, and Aquitaine; high steward of the duchy of Lancaster south of the Trent; constable of the Tower of London and Castle Rising; privy councillor to the king; and knight of the Garter. However, Oxford's entertainment of Henry VII at Castle Hedingham for nearly a week in 1498 ended on a sour note. As the king was leaving, an inappropriately large number of the earl's retainers lined the route, displaying Oxford's private power. The story goes that "the King looked startled and said: 'By my faith, my lord, I thank you for your good cheer; but I may not have my laws broken in my sight. My attorney must speak with you.'"[21] The Tudors knew how to use lawyers and the law, in this case the Statute of Retainers, to gain power over the powerful. The lesson was not lost on towns, such as Colchester, that were weak in comparison to their great, landed neighbors. Colchester had already used the law to good effect to retain its rights to the waters of the river Colne in the mid-fifteenth century, so the de Veres were aware of the limitations of their power over Colchester.[22]

Colchester records are too meager during the reign of Henry VII to know what influence, if any, the formidable thirteenth earl of Oxford played in Colchester affairs, but it is quite possible that he swayed the election of James Hobard as Colchester's recorder in the early sixteenth century, since Hobard was also Oxford's chief steward in Suffolk and an attorney for the king. The influence of such a powerful neighbor waned, of course, when an earl of Oxford died and was replaced by a minor or a weak earl, which occurred in 1513, when the new fourteenth earl was only fourteen years of age. He came into control of his inheritance in 1520, but even then he was so irresponsible that he was ordered to allow Wolsey to manage his estates. Fortunately for his barony, he died in 1526, at which time the direct line ended and the family lost the hereditary office of lord great chamberlain.[23]

A second cousin of the de Vere family became the fifteenth earl of Oxford in 1526, and he began to exert some influence on Colchester, at least on parliamentary elections. The fifteenth earl was a courtier and loyal servant of the king, fully cooperating with Henry VIII's policies. He signed the address to the pope for the king's divorce from Queen Catherine, carried the crown at the coronation of Anne Boleyn, and had a part

---

21. William Addison, *Essex Worthies* (London: Phillimore, 1973), 188–89.

22. Morant, 1:86–87; Cutts, *Colchester*, 132.

23. Ives, *Common Lawyers*, 287; Addison, *Essex Worthies*, 189–90. My appendix 4 lists the earls of Oxford in the Tudor period.

in her later trial. No doubt his faithful adherence to the king was behind his intervention in the election in Colchester to the crucial Parliament of 1529. That was the election, mentioned earlier, in which two of the earl's supporters and retainers were elected, with one of them then being replaced by another retainer, Richard Rich, who was used to help carry out the king's less savory policies.[24]

In terms of continuing influence, Rich was Oxford's most successful protégé. A native of Middlesex, Rich had his start in Essex and a big boost to his career as a lawyer when he became a member of the council of the fifteenth earl, a position he was holding when the earl insisted on Colchester's giving Rich a seat in Parliament. When the office of recorder became vacant in Colchester in 1532, the town leaders chose Rich; perhaps they saw Rich's potential influence or wanted to endear themselves to Oxford. During Rich's twelve-year tenure as recorder of Colchester, he gained recognition as the Speaker of the House of Commons in 1536, dubious notoriety as the solicitor general in the trials of Bishop John Fisher and Sir Thomas More, and enough wealth as the chancellor of the Court of Augmentations during the dissolution of the monasteries to become the second largest landowner in Essex, next to the earl of Oxford. Rich and Audley were colleagues in carrying out the business of the Reformation. Audley passed judgment in the Fisher and More trials in which Rich played so large a part, and Rich supposedly helped Audley draw up the act of 1536 dissolving the lesser monasteries and establishing the Court of Augmentations, with Rich becoming the first chancellor of the court and both men being enriched thereby. Audley, then, rather than Oxford, may have been behind Rich's appointment as recorder of Colchester. If Audley was responsible, that may explain why Rich was replaced as recorder in 1544, the year of Audley's death.[25]

The fifteenth earl of Oxford died in 1540, and his successor to the title, being a Protestant, declared in favor of Lady Jane Grey in 1553, though he quickly recognized his folly and supported Mary, officiating as great chamberlain at her coronation. The Privy Council ordered him in 1555 to attend the burning of heretics in Essex, but his official presence at the

---

24. Addison, *Essex Worthies,* 186, 190; CR99/1d.
25. Addison, *Essex Worthies,* 8, 154–55; W. G. Hoskins, *The Age of Plunder: The England of Henry VIII, 1500–1547* (London: Longman, 1976), 132–33; J. E. Oxley, *The Reformation in Essex to the Death of Mary* (Manchester: Manchester University Press, 1965), 252; Bindoff, *House,* 1:352 and 3:193; G. R. Elton, *Reform and Reformation, England, 1509–1558* (Cambridge: Harvard University Press, 1977), 236–37.

executions was not held against him when Elizabeth came to the throne. Oxford officiated at the new queen's coronation, and he entertained her for five days at Castle Hedingham in 1561. During the twenty-two years in which John, the sixteenth earl, held his title, some of the most prominent Colchester officials had connections with him. Town clerk John Lucas and recorder Anthony Stapleton both had significant contact with Oxford before their appointments. Lucas was known to have given legal advice to the fifteenth earl, and he was made steward of the new earl's manor of Harwich in 1540. By 1545 Lucas was a member of Oxford's council. It appears that Lucas became a personal friend of Oxford; a popular story is that, both being gamesters, Lucas won from Oxford the wardship of a young woman whom Lucas then married to his youngest son. That friendship no doubt helped him gain the position of town clerk in 1543 and three or four terms as MP, but probably as important were Lucas's connections with Audley and the Inner Temple, which are discussed later in this chapter. The new recorder in 1544, Anthony Stapleton, also had dual connections with the de Veres and the Inner Temple. Stapleton's first known linkage with the noble family was with the dowager Elizabeth, countess of the powerful thirteenth earl of Oxford, who lived twenty-four years beyond her husband and made her home at Wivenhoe, near Colchester. In her 1537 will, she left £10 to Stapleton, "towards his learning in the law." After his training at the Inner Temple, he was a successful London lawyer, with one of his clients being the sixteenth earl of Oxford. Colchester retained him as recorder for most of the difficult years between 1544 and 1560.[26]

More obviously a protégé of Oxford than were either Lucas or Stapleton was John Ryther, who served with Lucas in Edward VI's first Parliament in 1547. There is no indication that Oxford dictated the selection of Lucas and Ryther, but it is quite possible that Oxford, as an active supporter of the Protestant Reformation, wanted the right people elected and used his influence to get them elected. Ryther's father had been a servant to the thirteenth earl, and Ryther began his service to the de Veres as comptroller of the household of Elizabeth, dowager countess, and, after her death, comptroller of the sixteenth earl's household. Probably the Oxford connections helped bring Ryther to the office of cofferer of the household of Prince Edward and then of the royal household, but even earlier Ryther would have come to the attention of Colchester when

26. Addison, *Essex Worthies,* 190; Bindoff, *House,* 2:554 and 3:374; George Rickword, "Members of Parliament for Colchester, 1547–1558," *ER* 4 (1895): 114n.

he was appointed by Thomas Cromwell to report on the alleged embezzlement by one of the abbot's servants of the jewelry of Colchester abbey. Ryther served only in the 1547 Parliament for Colchester, as he died before another Parliament was elected.[27]

When John, the sixteenth earl, died in 1562, he left only a twelve-year-old son, but his influence lived on for a time. Among his executors were his "servants" Henry Golding and Robert Christmas, both of whom later served as MPs from Colchester in the early 1570s. By that time, Edward, the seventeenth earl, was of age; Christmas was the young earl's estate agent, and Golding was Edward's uncle, his mother's half brother. Christmas also happened to be the son of a deceased Colchester alderman, John Christmas, which probably made his election as MP more favorable to the town leaders. Oxford, wanting to exert his new power, possibly engineered the election to the 1572 Parliament, but he took no more interest in Colchester affairs after that. Moreover, his secret conversion to Catholicism, if it was known in Colchester, would not have endeared him to the town. Edward lived a long time, dying in the year after Queen Elizabeth did, but his unhappy marriage and interest in poetry and the arts led him to travel and later to be a recluse. A measure of the Oxford influence was taken up by the Darcy family. Sir Thomas Darcy had married the sister of the sixteenth earl of Oxford, and those connections probably led to his rise at the royal court, where he was created the first Lord Darcy in 1551, with his seat at the former priory of St. Osyth, which was about ten miles southeast of Colchester. Local lords served on special commissions whenever trouble erupted, and the second Lord Darcy's role as lord lieutenant of Essex (1569–81) gave the Darcys even more reason to intervene if need be. However, the Darcys played only an occasional official role in Colchester affairs.[28]

The influence of the earl of Oxford, then, was only as important as he wanted it to be but was always somewhat limited by the keen sense of the town's independence. The unwritten rule had long been established that Oxford would have a fight on his hands if he tried to interfere directly and forcibly against Colchester's will. Normally, the earls of Oxford did

---

27. Bindoff, *House,* 3:240–41.
28. Addison, *Essex Worthies,* 54, 190–91; Patrick Collinson, *The Elizabethan Puritan Movement* (Berkeley: University of California Press, 1967), 198; Byford, "Religious Change," 107; W. Gurney Benham, "A Parliamentary Election in Colchester in 1571," *ER* 49 (1940): 185–90. On royal commissions, see Penry Williams, "The Crown and the Counties," in *The Reign of Elizabeth I,* ed. Christopher Haigh (London: Macmillan, 1984), 127–28.

not try to dominate political affairs in Colchester; only in a few parliamentary elections did Oxford's wishes seem to prevail (notably in 1529 and probably in 1547 and 1572), but those occasions were rare. Moreover, when Colchester apparently acquiesced with Oxford's wishes, the candidates usually had other abilities or connections to recommend them. Having influence with the earl of Oxford was an advantage to the town, but being dominated by him was unacceptable, so for a candidate to have a connection with Oxford was more advantageous if it was only one of several reasons for choosing him.

Some local gentry connections were important to Colchester at various times, particularly at the county level. But here again the pervasive Oxford influence was evident, since several gentlemen held their land from the earl of Oxford.[29] The town provided opportunities for such men. For example, William Tey, whose family had Oxford connections, was Colchester town clerk (1510–13) and younger son of Sir Henry Tey, sheriff of Essex. Tey lived on St. John's Green in front of the abbey and, being trained at Gray's Inn, apparently practiced law in Colchester. But probably one of the most profitable things he did was to marry Anastace, the daughter of the merchant alderman Thomas Christmas.[30]

If the right opportunities came, the gentry might rise rapidly. For example, Sir Henry Marney of Layer Marney, about six miles southwest of Colchester, became a royal favorite and a member of the council. After receiving a large share of the lands of the executed duke of Buckingham, Marney was created the first Baron Marney, and, for a few years, it appeared that the Marneys might eventually rival the power of the de Veres in Essex. Those expectations came to an end with the deaths of Sir Henry and his son, in 1523 and 1525, ending the male line. Colchester had enlisted the service and goodwill of Sir Henry Marney in 1521 by granting him an annuity of 20s., but of more lasting consequence to Colchester was the marriage of Marney's daughter, Catherine, to Thomas Bonham, Colchester recorder from 1511 to 1532. Probably because of his new Marney connections, Bonham became JP of Essex in 1510, illustrating one of the advantages for Colchester in choosing local gentry. Often the gentry were already officials at the county court in Chelmsford, thus giving Colchester another entrée into official sources of

---

29. For example, Sir John Raynsford, MP for Colchester in 1529, and William Cardinall I, MP in 1554 and 1559 and recorder from 1560 to 1568.

30. *LP*, 1 (1): no. 1803 (p. 822); Bindoff, *House*, 3:436; PRO 22 Fetiplace. Britnell, *Colchester*, 210–11, writes of the opportunities for the gentry in Colchester.

power. Along with Bonham, this official capacity was true of recorders Richard Rich and William Cardinall and of town clerks John Lucas, William Morice, and Thomas Lucas.[31]

Bonham's marriage to Catherine tied him to Colchester. Through Catherine's first husband, she had life interest in more than a dozen manors in Essex, Kent, and Suffolk; one of the manors was Stanway, just outside of Colchester, and Bonham and Catherine made their home there. Bonham took an active role in the local sessions of the peace (probably the last recorder to do so), and he showed his interest in Colchester by buying Trumpingtons, a capital messuage in the town, perhaps for William, his second son. William married the daughter of Alderman John Clere, illustrating one of the advantages for the gentry in making town connections: a marriage alliance with merchant wealth.[32]

The Audley/Inner Temple Connections

Bonham's wealth through his fortuitous marriage with Catherine Marney also gave him enormous influence in Colchester, and it is he who probably began a chain of appointments of men from the Inner Temple to Colchester offices, the most important being that of Thomas Audley. Thus began a second outside influence on Colchester affairs in the first half of the sixteenth century, the Audley/Inner Temple connection. Bonham was at the Inner Temple before 1505; in 1510 Audley was admitted, so they would have known each other there, as Bonham maintained his connections with the Inner Temple, having chambers there as late as 1522, and being a bencher of the Inner Temple in 1530. However, it should be noted that Audley had another significant connection, that with the de Veres. Audley was born in Earl's Colne, where his grandfather was the earl of Oxford's bailiff until around 1466. Audley's father,

---

31. Bindoff, *House,* 1:462. In contrast, Thomas Audley rose to county prominence in 1520 after becoming town clerk in 1514. On county governance, see Williams, "Crown and the Counties," 125–46; Mark Girouard, *The English Town: A History of Urban Life* (New Haven: Yale University Press, 1990), 47–50. F. G. Emmison, *Elizabethan Life: Disorder* (Chelmsford: Essex County Council, 1970), 322–25, has an appendix contributed by Joel Samaha that lists the gentry who attended the Essex quarter sessions in the Elizabethan period.

32. Addison, *Essex Worthies,* 122; *RPB,* 25; Bindoff, *House,* 1:462; CR99/10; CR103/15; CR101/23; CR109/18d. In Clere's 1538 will (PRO 25 Dyngeley), son-in-law William Bonham was named as coexecutor; Clere's daughter seemed to have been dead by that time. Bindoff, *House,* 1:463, mistakenly mentions only one marriage by William, that to Frances Tey, by 1539.

Geoffrey, was bailiff of Earl's Colne in 1496 and 1497 and owned tenements there; Geoffrey died in 1504, leaving his inheritance to his two sons, both named Thomas.[33] Possibly the thirteenth earl of Oxford helped gain admittance for the younger Thomas to the Inner Temple, but Oxford's death in 1513 and the subsequent minority eliminated the patronage of the de Veres at the beginning of Thomas's career as a lawyer. It seems more likely, then, that Bonham, as Colchester's recorder, was a mentor to the bright, young Audley and helped secure the job of town clerk for Audley in 1514, when Audley was about twenty-six years old. In the first year, the post was held jointly by Audley and John Barnabe, a servant of Bonham's, perhaps to train Audley. By 1517 or 1518, Audley had established moneyed gentry connections when he had married Christina, daughter of Sir Thomas Barnardiston, a squire of Suffolk and Lincolnshire; and by 1520, the year that Bonham became sheriff of Essex, Audley was JP of Essex.[34] The careers of Audley and Bonham paralleled in other ways, although Audley, who was probably more capable or ambitious—maybe both—eventually leaped ahead of Bonham. In 1509, shortly after his marriage, Bonham had been appointed receiver general of the duchy of Lancaster for life,[35] and in 1526 Audley was appointed attorney general of the duchy of Lancaster. Bonham may have had something to do with that appointment, but Audley had already come to the attention of higher authorities, presumably through his service in the 1523 Parliament. Perhaps it was through the influence of Cardinal Thomas Wolsey that Audley was appointed, as one learned in the law, to the newly created council for Princess Mary in 1525; certainly Audley had come to the attention of Wolsey by 1527, by which time Audley was a member of Wolsey's household. In 1529, Bonham and Audley were together again, serving in Parliament as knights of the shire for Essex, even though neither were knights—in itself an unusual situation. Audley

---

33. CR86/2d; Britnell, *Colchester*, 259. The town clerks, recorders, and MPs who were educated at the Inner Temple are noted in appendix 3. On the Inner Temple, see Ives, *Common Lawyers*, 36, 42–43; a bencher was a senior fellow who occupied the bench at moot trials and therefore had a part in the teaching process, and the benchers were the governing body at the Inner Temple.

34. Bindoff, *House*, 1:350. Barnabe later married Bonham's widow, Catherine (CR106/9–10). Britnell, *Colchester*, 511, notes that Audley's mother-in-law was one of the richest taxpayers in Colchester in 1524. Ives, *Common Lawyers*, 227, says that a lawyer became a JP once "status in the profession had become recognised, not when his position in the county justified the appointment."

35. Significantly, Bonham's father-in-law, Sir Henry Marney, had been made chancellor of the duchy that year.

was quickly elected Speaker of the House of Commons in that Parliament, so his election as knight of the shire was probably arranged by the central government. In May, 1532, Audley replaced Sir Thomas More as keeper of the great seal; a month later, Bonham died while in London for the fourth session of Parliament, probably of the pestilence then raging at the Inns of Court.[36] Audley's early friend and guide was gone, but by that time, Audley himself was a mentor to others.

That momentous year for Audley, 1532, was also a time of change in Colchester. Audley, though having risen far above the affairs of a provincial borough, retained his influence in Colchester. He had earlier been busy buying and selling property in Colchester, and he continued that practice after becoming lord chancellor. Audley's relatives continued to live there also. The affluent Christmas cousins have already been mentioned, and Audley's older brother, Thomas, lived at Berechurch, one of the outlying parishes within the borough. Colchester no doubt considered itself fortunate to have one of its own in such a high position. Thomas and Christina had made their home in the parish of St. Mary-at-Wall, and they did not sell their capital tenement there until 1536, when they sold it for £100 to Richard Duke.[37]

Duke represented one of the changes in 1532 in Colchester, as he replaced Audley as town clerk. Though Audley had taken on more important concerns, it seems likely that Audley was responsible for Duke's appointment and possibly also for that of Richard Rich as recorder at the same time. Of course, Rich already had the connection with Colchester as MP in the Reformation Parliament, but Duke was an outsider from Devon, the grandson of an Exeter merchant, and he had no connections to Colchester or Essex except that he was educated at Audley's Inn of Court, the Inner Temple. For Duke, it was a significant linkage; in 1536 he was appointed clerk of the council of the Court of Augmentations when it was established. He obtained land in his native Devon, but he also did a lot of buying and selling in Colchester, often in conjunction with Audley.[38]

---

36. Bindoff, *House,* 1:350–51, 462–63; Stanford E. Lehmberg, "Sir Thomas Audley: A Soul as Black as Marble?" in *Tudor Men and Institutions: Studies in English Law and Government,* ed. A. J. Slavin (Baton Rouge: Louisiana State University Press, 1972), 6–7.

37. *OB,* 149; Bindoff, *House,* 1:350; *Essex Fines,* 4:141; CR96/17; CR105/13; CR106/3; CR107/8d; CR114/6d; CR120/10; CR107/8d. Audley lived in the parish of St. Mary-at-Wall in 1525, when the lay subsidy was collected; his house later became the King's Head inn (*VCH Essex,* 9:108).

38. Bindoff, *House,* 2:68; CR106/5, 5d; CR105/8d, 13d; CR107/8d; CR114/16d; CR115/8.

Duke's successor as town clerk was also from the Inner Temple, as was Rich's successor as recorder. The Oxford connections of the new town clerk, John Lucas, have already been mentioned, but more helpful to Lucas's early career was his entering the Inner Temple in 1526, the year that Audley gave the autumn vacation readings there. It is known that Audley recommended Lucas to Cromwell in 1537; in the following year, Lucas gained a post as joint clerk of the Crown in Chancery, which probably led to Lucas's being appointed to the Essex bench four months later and to his first contact with the earl of Oxford.[39] It is very likely, then, that Audley approved of the selection of Lucas as town clerk for Colchester in 1543.

Audley died the next year, but the Inner Temple connections continued for a time. Anthony Stapleton, another Inner Temple man, became recorder in 1544, perhaps recommended either by Lucas or by Audley before his death. The next three successors to Lucas as town clerk were also from the Inner Temple. The first one, John Carowe, was the son of a yeoman from Romford, but the two succeeding town clerks were natives of Colchester, both of them being admitted to the Inner Temple in 1550. Robert Gynes was apparently the son of John Gyne, who had been deputy town clerk to Richard Duke; Thomas Lucas, son of former town clerk John Lucas, eventually became MP (1558), town clerk (1566–72), and recorder (1572–76), but his being the son of John was probably more significant than his Inner Temple connections, as he had a hot temper, at one time being expelled from the inn and imprisoned in the Fleet prison.[40]

The Inner Temple connections were giving way to other influences, such as the new gentry created by the Reformation, but especially the force of aggressive Protestantism. The heady days when Colchester's Thomas Audley was lord chancellor and other Colchester officers were at the forefront of reform were soon gone. By 1562, the sixteenth earl of Oxford was dead, and except for one brief period in the early 1570s, the Oxford influence was essentially eliminated. A vacuum of outside power thus coincided with the ardent Puritanism of the town leaders in Elizabeth's reign, so allegiance to Puritanism became the deciding factor in the

---

39. Bindoff, *House*, 2:553; Ives, *Common Lawyers*, 83. Ives, 44–53, discusses the readings in the Inns of Court; a reading was a seminar on an agreed text, given in a period of three to four weeks.

40. Bindoff, *House*, 2:555; Hasler, 2:232; ERO D/ABW39/51; on John Carowe, see McIntosh, *Havering*, 262, 357.

choice of officers to promote Colchester's interests outside the town. At first Colchester elected as town clerk and recorder committed Protestants who were local gentry or lawyers with some connections to the town, but a shift occurred in 1578 with the selection of an ardent Puritan, Sir Francis Walsingham. Walsingham had no previous connections with Colchester but was already very influential in the royal government. His selection set a pattern for the rest of the Tudor era, so that men perceived to be able to do the most for the town were chosen, with no regard as to whether they were outsiders or native sons. That utilitarian practice continued even when Puritanism lost its political viability, as it did for a time at the end of Elizabeth's reign. The choosing of officers from outside the borough thus changed from local pragmatism to a more sophisticated attempt to wield influence in the affairs of the central government; town leaders were playing the game of politics whether through a lawyer or a lord or with "a horse-load of . . . Colchester oysters." Thomas Audley had taught them well.

3

The Institutional Church and Its
Clergy on the Eve of the Reformation

The borough of Colchester took pride in its supposed connection with one of the saints of Christendom, St. Helen. Though history and legend were freely mixed, Colchester's records proudly related how old King Coel (that "merry old soul" with "his fiddlers three," of nursery-rhyme fame), rebellious governor of the district, gave his daughter, Helen, as concubine to the Roman general who was besieging Colchester. Coel's generous gift brought the end of the siege and relief to the town. Helen's son, born of that union, was later adopted by his Roman father after marriage to Helen, and the son, according to the Colchester legend, became the great Constantine, the first emperor of Rome to become a Christian. Through Helen, then, Colchester believed it had a palpable tie to early Christendom, and in late medieval Colchester, the town guild was named after St. Helen. Even today, overlooking Colchester's High Street is a statue of Helen, facing Jerusalem and with scepter and cross in hand, standing impressively atop the bell tower of the Victorian town hall; furthermore, the modern borough arms show the True Cross, which was revealed to Helen in a vision. Having its own saint to intercede for it in heaven gave Colchester a sense of solidarity and typified the blending of the sacred and secular that was a part of life and of governance in the English town.[1]

The governance of Colchester has been shown to have been tending toward the use of more power in the sixteenth century, which in the Elizabethan period would be increased, whether intentionally or not, by the

---

1. *OB*, 27; *VCH Essex*, 9:19–21; G. H. Martin, *Colchester: Official Guide*, 4th ed. (Colchester: Benham and Company, 1973), 81–82; Sacks, *Bristol*, 142. Tittler, *Architecture*, 151–52, notes that the perpetuation of myths to legitimize power was often associated with town halls, and that Bath's new town hall of 1625 had statues of King Edgar and King Coel. An interesting reference in the borough court records of 1534–35 mentions the town wall near "King Coel's Castle"; see CR104/3.

exercise of certain religious prerogatives, such as the hiring of the town preacher. It will be useful, then, to look at the institutional church and its clergy before the Reformation—first, to know what the normal situation was, so that the effects of the Reformation on the parish church and its people can be appreciated; and second, to understand the weak points of the late medieval church, as those weaknesses, carried over into the early Protestant Church of England, permitted the governors of the town to take such a strong role in the Elizabethan period. Although early Tudor Colchester was known as a religiously radical town, the institutional church was thoroughly integrated into its life, and the radical elements, for the most part, remained within the framework of the medieval church. This chapter discusses the religious foundations and the clergy in Colchester, the role of the parish church in the lives of the people, and the relationship of the Colchester churches to the wider church.

Religious Foundations in Colchester

The Normans were builders. When the Norman lord Eudo built the massive Colchester Castle, he also restored the nearby little chapel of St. Helen, the origin of which is something of a mystery, though tradition says that it was erected by Helen herself.[2] More costly for Eudo was the erection of a Benedictine monastery, St. John's Abbey, on a hill across from the town walls, a location that attracted Eudo because it was also the site of a small wooden church consecrated to St. John the Evangelist, which had a reputation for miracles. After the first abbey church burned in 1133, the church was rebuilt on a cruciform plan, with a great central tower and a decorated west front topped by two towers. This huge abbey church cast its shadow over Tudor Colchester. One of the Colchester parish churches, St. Giles's, originally a chapel in the monastic cemetery, was in the cure of St. John's Abbey, so one of the monks usually acted as parish priest. The abbey was patron of four of the other parish churches outside the walls of the town, as well as two within the walls, giving the abbot the right to appoint the parish priests. Since the greater number of the churches in the patronage of St. John's were outside the walls of the town, the primary influence of the abbey lay there also, which was not

---

2. Crummy, *Aspects,* 47. It has been asserted that St. Helen's was a Roman chapel, but M. R. Hull, *Roman Colchester,* Reports of the Research Committee of the Society of Antiquaries of London, no. 20. (Oxford: Oxford University Press, for the Society of Antiquaries and the Corporation of the Borough of Colchester, 1958), 106, believes that the walls were once part of a Roman theater.

surprising, since landed wealth had founded the abbey. The abbot of St. John's was mitered, which gave him the privilege of sitting in the House of Lords whenever Parliament met. A 1535 ecclesiastical survey showed that St. John's Abbey had twenty-four monks and a yearly value of £523 16s. ¼d. In 1465 the abbey had twenty-six monks, so the number had remained fairly constant.[3]

The abbot's legal jurisdiction over the tenants of the sizable abbey lands within the borough and the abbey's right of chartered sanctuary were time and again sources of hostility between the abbey and the borough. Occasionally in the early Tudor years, fences were broken down and cattle were put on abbey lands, acts justified by the claim that those lands were actually held in common by all the people. Few Tudor townspeople had any sympathy with the lordly detachment of St. John's Abbey, except for wealthy merchant Thomas Christmas and a few of the gentry, who were conscious of the wealth and privilege of the abbey and wanted to be buried in its church. Testators' bequests illustrate the lack of identification of townspeople with St. John's: fewer will makers paid for prayers at St. John's Abbey than at the other religious houses in Colchester, and half of those who did were from St. Giles's parish, which was served by the Benedictines, with the other testators being mostly aldermen or gentry. The appeal of the Benedictines, therefore, was primarily to the upper levels of Colchester society.[4]

In contrast was the house of Augustinian canons at St. Botolph's Priory. Both houses were founded in Colchester around the same time, but St. Botolph's had an early advantage among the townspeople in that it grew out of an already existing company of priests in Colchester, probably an Anglo-Saxon monastic foundation, who had been serving a church dedicated to St. Botolph, a Saxon saint. Sometime before 1100, the priests were brought under the Augustinian rule. Unlike the Benedictines, the Augustinians were not cloistered but were expected to minister among the townspeople,[5] although that involvement in the life of the

3. Crummy, *Aspects*, 41; *VCH Essex*, 2:93–102 and 9:303; Martin, *Story of Colchester*, 30; Oxley, 47, 59.

4. David Stevenson, *The Book of Colchester* (Chesham, Buckinghamshire: Barracuda Books, 1978), 55; Cutts, *Colchester*, 148–50; *RPB*, 51–52, 54–56, 117–21; J. L. Fisher, "The Leger Book of St. John's Abbey, Colchester," *TEAS*, n.s., 24 (1944–49): 114–15; Christmas will, PRO 28 Ayloffe. Out of fifty-seven testators requesting prayers in a religious house, only ten wanted prayers at St. John's Abbey.

5. C. R. Peers, *St. Botolph's Priory, Colchester* (London: HMSO, 1917), 10–12; *VCH Essex*, 2:148–50; Crummy, *Aspects*, 74. Crummy speculates that the Saxon church of St. Botolph's grew out of an earlier church in the Roman cemetery.

town had probably slackened by the Tudor period. They were truly respected by the parishioners of the parish church of St. Botolph, which was housed in the nave of the priory church, and for which the Augustinians had the cure. Some parishioners referred in their wills to their canon/curate as "my ghostly father,"[6] and of the ten testators from St. Botolph's who left money to a religious house, nine of them left it to St. Botolph's Priory, indicating a high regard for the pastoral work of the Augustinian canons among their own populous but poorer parish, composed largely of small craftsmen and laborers. St. Botolph's Priory remained relatively small, possibly never exceeding its original number of thirteen inmates, a number set to typify Christ and his apostles; in 1534 there was only a prior and seven canons. St. Botolph's did not acquire great wealth, having only a yearly value of £134 3s. 4d. at its dissolution in 1536.[7]

Occasionally, the borough had a disagreement with St. Botolph's. For example, a presentment in 1534 charged that the prior had built on some town land near the river. But the priory's fewer properties meant that it was less subject to conflict with the town than was St. John's Abbey. In contrast to the Benedictines, St. Botolph's physical presence near the town, just a few yards outside the town wall, was symbolic of its greater role in the parish churches within the town, with St. Botolph's having the patronage of four churches within the walls and two without (the latter including the one within the priory church). Furthermore, two of those churches in the town were, in terms of their wealth, size, and influence, the most important churches in Colchester, St. James's and St. Peter's.[8] Most of the parish churches, then, were controlled, at least as far as the right to present the clergy was concerned, by the two earliest religious houses. But on the whole, neither had the overwhelming affection of Colchester inhabitants, though St. Botolph's was effective in its own parish.

Held in greater esteem was a newer order, the Franciscans, who in Colchester wills were usually called "the Grey Friars" or "the Friars Minor."[9] The Franciscans were in Colchester by 1237, when they

---

6. Wills of M. Thorne (1503), ERO D/ACR1/112; A. Lanham (1506), ERO D/ACR1/123; E. Ive (1510), ERO D/ACR1/170.

7. *VCH Essex,* 2:150.

8. CR104/2; appendix 5.

9. For example, wills of G. Aleyn (1510), PRO 1 Fetiplace; J. Forster (1516), ERO D/ACR2/44.

received a plot of land from the king. Other gifts enabled the friars to build a church and to enlarge their holdings, so that by the dissolution of the monasteries, they possessed a block of land of at least four acres in the northeast corner of the town walls, the only one of the four religious houses to be within the walls of the town. The mission of the Franciscans was especially to townsmen, and although they were lampooned in four-teenth- and fifteenth-century literature for being too greedy and cunning, their popularity in the towns continued right up to their suppression. More testators (thirty-nine) made requests to the Grey Friars for prayers for the soul than to any other religious house in Colchester. Another attraction for the people were the two guilds for the laity in the Grey Fri-ars, Our Lady Guild and the Guild (or Fraternity) of Sts. Crispin and Crispinian. These saints were the patron saints of cobblers, shoemakers, and leather makers, which would indicate that the Friars were working among the ordinary people.[10] The emphasis of the Franciscans on the loving-kindness of God in sending his son to share humanity's lot was appealing to rich and poor alike. The Franciscans were known for their preaching, and the only two wills in pre-Reformation Colchester that mentioned sermons were referring to sermons at the Grey Friars. In 1520 Thomas Christmas left 20s. yearly for "the maintenance of sermons" at the Grey Friars on every Sunday in Lent. The Franciscans encouraged their preachers to be educated, and there was at least one learned friar in the Colchester house in 1507, when Friar John Spryngwell, B.D., was a witness to a will.[11]

At the opposite corner of the town, just outside the southwest corner of the town walls, lay the fourth religious house in Colchester, the Crossed or Crutched Friars. The English Crutched Friars derived from a Belgium group founded in the early thirteenth century, whose work was chiefly in hospitals, and the hospital in Colchester was apparently founded later in that century by the lord of the manor of Stanway. By the early fifteenth century, the hospital and its chapel were in financial difficulty and badly in need of repair, and in 1407 the king granted a license to burgesses and leading landowners for the foundation of a Guild

---

10. *VCH Essex*, 2:180–81 and 9:306; R. C. Fowler, "The Friars Minor of Colchester," *TEAS*, n.s., 11 (1911): 367; Palliser, *York*, 227; John C. Dickinson, *The Later Middle Ages* (New York: Barnes and Noble, 1979), 200–216. The guilds were named in the wills of W. Smyth (1491; PRO 40 Milles) and J. Hillys (1517; ERO D/ACR2/58); see also CR95/10d.

11. The wills of R. Hervy (PRO 17 Milles) and T. Christmas (PRO 28 Ayloffe) men-tioned sermons; Spryngwell was witness to the will of R. Burgon (D/ACR1/127).

of St. Helen in the chapel of the Holy Cross, to maintain thirteen poor men and to found a chantry of five chaplains. Toward the end of the fifteenth century, the Crossed Friars reasserted their claim to the site by producing papal bulls and were readmitted in 1496; they were subsequently entrusted with the task of daily prayers to fulfill the requirements of some of the chantry foundations that had been housed in their chapel when it was under the Guild of St. Helen, with the provision that they keep four friars in residence, all of whom were to be native Englishmen. Always in need of money for their hospital, the Crossed Friars were granted permission in 1523 to sell indulgences, two copies of which were discovered early in this century in the covers of an old book in Chichester Cathedral Library, preserved because a sixteenth-century bookbinder found the paper useful as backing. The printed indulgence, with a blank for filling in the buyer's name, provided that any visitor to the chapel of the Crossed Friars on certain festival days or on any Friday who "stretched out helping hands towards it" by giving alms could obtain for themselves or others the same remission of sin that they would have received had they visited a church in or near Rome on that same day. If one could not visit the chapel of the Crossed Friars, one could conveniently send in alms and receive the same benefits. Buying one of the indulgences also made one a member of the confraternity, a brotherhood of laypeople attached to the Crossed Friars, whose members could choose their own confessors and receive special benefits of prayer during Lent. Furthermore, if one bought a rosary that had been blessed by the Friars, an indulgence of fifty days could be obtained by using the rosary to recite the Lord's Prayer and Angelic Salutation. Just such indulgences stirred up Luther and helped provoke the Reformation. In fact, the printed indulgence used by the Crossed Friars resembled the one sold by Tetzel that became the object of Luther's ire. Such attempts by religious houses to raise money were forever ended by their dissolution, which came to the Crossed Friars by 1537, when the records show that they had four friars and a yearly value of only £7 7s. 8d.[12]

A few other religious foundations were to be found in Colchester,

---

12. *VCH Essex,* 2:181–82 and 9:307–8; David Knowles, *The Religious Orders in England,* 3 vols. (Cambridge: Cambridge University Press, 1956), 1:203; Morant, 2:41–43 and 3:8–9; Oxley, 61–62; W. Gurney Benham, "The Chapel of the Holy Cross in Crouch Street, Colchester," *ER* 45 (1936), 33–35. Copies of the 1523 indulgence were discovered around 1900; see S. Fraser, "A Pynson Indulgence of 1523," *Sussex Archaeological Collections* 50 (1907): 109–16.

among them two hospitals, that is, residences for the infirm and the poor. The lesser one, St. Catherine's, on the north side of Crouch Street near the Crossed Friars, had been founded for the infirm at least by 1352. It is seldom mentioned in the records, but a 1502 will refers to "the lazer house of St. Catherine," and in 1510 "the Proctor of the Hospice of St. Catherine" was presented in the borough court for harboring thieves and beggars.[13] The older Hospital of St. Mary Magdalen, founded by Eudo as a leper hospital in the early twelfth century, was reconstituted in 1423 under the direction of Humphrey, duke of Gloucester, and was then declared to be for a master and five poor men since leprosy was no longer a problem in England. Since it was under the patronage of the abbot of St. John's and had a small independent endowment, St. Mary Magdalen was seldom the object of the charity of the townspeople.[14] Dearer to their hearts was St. Anne's Chapel, standing on the south side of the Harwich road, where there had been a holy well and hermitage and to which there was a guild attached as early as 1491. A little earlier, John Vertue, who died in 1486, had established there an almshouse and a hostel for poor travelers, and throughout the early Tudor period, sheets and other bedding were bequeathed to St. Anne's. Widow Elizabeth Harmanson left money for masses at both the Grey Friars and the Crossed Friars, but she invested far more, £20, for a priest to pray for her soul for three years at St. Anne's Chapel.[15] Another religious foundation was the ancient St. Helen's Chapel, which continued with a chaplain saying daily prayers. Two chantries had been founded in the chapel in the fourteenth century, at which time the advowson had been put into the hands of the bailiffs and commonalty, but the chapel seems not to have captured the allegiance of the people, as it was seldom mentioned in wills.[16] In addition to the sixteen parish churches within the borough, the religious foundations supplied at least five other churches or chapels: the Benedictine and Fran-

13. Morant, 3:8–9; VCH Essex 9:308; ERO D/ACR1/106; CR82/10d.

14. VCH Essex, 2:184–86; Morant, 2:21–22; Fisher, "Leger Book," 118–23, has information about the 1423 reconstitution. On hospitals, see Christopher Dyer, Standards of Living in the Later Middle Ages: Social Change in England, c. 1200–1520 (Cambridge: Cambridge University Press, 1989), 242–44.

15. Morant, 2:44–45; D/Y2/2, p. 65; CR111/6; PRO 1 Adeane. The guild is mentioned in the 1491 will of William Smith (PRO 40 Milles).

16. The court rolls mention a chaplain at St. Helen's in 1510 (CR82/10d) and 1513 (CR85/5); however, a 1535 document indicates that there were two chantry priests residing on the premises of St. Helen's at that time. See Morant, 2:45–46; J. H. Round, St. Helen's Chapel, Colchester (London: Elliot Stock, n.d.).

ciscan churches, the chapel at the Crossed Friars, and the chapels of St. Anne and St. Helen. Though the people of Colchester called on the services offered by the religious foundations—the praying, preaching, charitable work, and even the occasional indulgence—their first loyalties were usually given to their parish church.

The Role of the Parish Church in the Lives of the People

Tudor Colchester was crowded with churches. The eight parish churches within the walls were all around the market place or within easy walking distance. The huge St. Botolph's Priory church was just outside the wall, and St. Giles's was only a short distance beyond. The church of St. Mary Magdalen was out on the road leading to the Hythe, and farther down the road, St. Leonard's occupied the little hill overlooking the port. Rounding out the sixteen parish churches in the borough were the four village churches, each in a different direction from the town, at Lexden, Berechurch, Greenstead, and Mile End. Colchester's sixteen parish churches were all in existence by the thirteenth century, and at least six, probably more, predated the Norman conquest.[17] Three of them had been listed in the Domesday Book of the late eleventh century because they had sizable lands attached—St. Peter's had the largest amount of glebe land in all of Essex, the equivalent of a rural manor—but after the Normans' greedy seizure of much of the church lands, the Colchester churches would never again be quite so prosperous.[18]

The parish was an ecclesiastical unit with a parish priest, with the inhabitants having an obligatory payment of tithes to the priest. Regular attendance at divine services on Sundays and feast days was expected, and only in the parish church did large numbers of people meet regularly, so it was an important provider of social space. The parish was also a unit of civil governance, with the corporation and national government increasingly finding the parish useful, especially in the collection of taxes. The lay subsidy of 1524–25 was collected by parishes, with subcollectors for each parish appointed by borough leaders. The growing trend during the sixteenth century was to use the parish officers, especially church-

---

17. See appendix 5 for a listing of the parish churches.
18. *VCH Essex*, 1:423–24; J. H. Round, "St. Peter's Church, Colchester," *TEAS*, n.s., 15 (1921): 94; Cutts, *Colchester*, 97–99.

wardens and constables, in secular administrative roles, overseeing road repair, policing, and poor relief in each parish.[19]

The parish church both reflected and reinforced the hierarchical social order, even in its seating, which was installed in many parish churches in the fifteenth century. The wealthiest men were put in front and the women to one side, although there might be some mixed pews for married couples; the servants were in the rear. The dignity of civic leaders was upheld in the church, where Colchester aldermen wore their robes of office, scarlet gowns and velvet tippets, on certain occasions. Even the "holy cake" (as opposed to the consecrated bread) was distributed by the deacons according to each person's degree and status.[20]

The parish church was crucial to the lives of the people: there the great events of life were ritualized and made holy by the church. Within days after birth—sometimes on the same day if the child appeared to be sickly—the father and three godparents, with the mother still lying in, accompanied the infant to church for the rite of baptism, when the child was officially named, brought into Christian society, and, most importantly, freed from original sin. A month after giving birth, the new mother, with head properly covered, came to church for purification, a practice that was changed after the Reformation to a time of thanksgiving.[21] Marriage, which was both a legal contract and a religious sacrament, had increasingly come under the aegis of the church. The marriage ceremony took place in two parts: first the actual marriage was performed at the church door, with the couple holding hands and exchang-

---

19. David M. Palliser, "Introduction: The Parish in Perspective," in *Parish, Church, and People: Local Studies in Lay Religion, 1350–1750,* ed. Susan J. Wright (London: Hutchinson, 1988), 5–7. In the same book edited by Wright, Nick Alldridge, "Loyalty and Identity in Chester Parishes, 1540–1640," 104, found a tenfold increase in parochial personnel in the hundred years from 1540 to 1640.

20. M. D. Anderson, *History and Imagery in British Churches* (London: John Murray, 1971), 142–43; Peter Clark, *English Provincial Society from the Reformation to the Revolution: Religion, Politics, and Society in Kent, 1500–1640* (Hassocks, Sussex: Harvester Press, 1977), 24; D/Y2/2, p. 65; Alldridge, "Loyalty," 94–97. Phythian-Adams, *Coventry,* 137–38, found that in Coventry the mayor wore his ceremonial robes to both matins and evensong on workdays, Sundays, and holidays.

21. John Myrc, *Instructions to Parish Priests,* ed. Edward Peacock (London: Kegan Paul, Trench, Trübner, and Company, 1898), 5; Edward L. Cutts, *Parish Priests and Their People in the Middle Ages in England* (London: SPCK, 1914), 234; J. H. Bettey, *Church and Community: The Parish Church in English Life* (Bradford-on-Avon, Wiltshire: Moonraker Press, 1979), 25–26; John Bossy, *Christianity in the West, 1400–1700* (Oxford: Oxford University Press, 1985), 14–19.

ing words of consent; then the couple went into the church for a nuptial mass, after which a mazer (drinking bowl) containing wine was passed among the couple and their guests.[22] At death, prayers for the deceased commenced at the parish church. First came the vespers service, said the evening before the day of the funeral; next was the matins, or *dirige*, said in the presence of the corpse on the morning of the funeral. The Mass for the Dead was a solemn and dignified service, lent significance by the fact that a funeral was one of the rare occasions on which a priest was permitted to celebrate twice in one day. Most Colchester parishioners (89 percent of testators through 1558) asked to be buried in their own parish churchyard or, if they were more prosperous, in the church itself. The wealthier parishioners, who sometimes had elaborate funerals, might also request that food or money be distributed at burial.[23]

The parish church was more than a place for marking the milestones of life, however; it was primarily a place of worship, providing assurance of salvation and solace from the fears and cares of the world. Central to the worship was the mass, which reenacted Christ's sacrifice, with the grand climax coming when the bread and wine were consecrated so that they miraculously became the very body and blood of Christ. At that point the elements were worshipfully elevated by the celebrant, while a bell rang out, a censer sent clouds of smoke upward, and candles were elevated in homage. Most people actually took Communion only once a year, at Easter, but the priest communed at each mass, standing at the altar with his back to the people so that it was often difficult to see or hear through the screen that separated the nave from the chancel. For the people, the blessing lay in being present at the working of a miracle and in viewing the actual body and blood of Christ that resulted. Almost all of the mass was in Latin, for most people an unknown tongue, but the

---

22. The matrimonial bond was not merely between individuals; it also established a strong tie between families, with new bonds of kinship and aid. See McIntosh, *Havering,* 74; Bettey, *Church,* 26–27; John R. H. Moorman, *Church Life in England in the Thirteenth Century* (Cambridge: Cambridge University Press, 1955), 85–86; P. J. P. Goldberg, "Women in Fifteenth-Century Town Life," in *Towns and Townspeople in the Fifteenth Century,* ed. J. A. F. Thomson (Gloucester: Alan Sutton Publishing, 1988), 114.

23. F. A. Gasquet, *Parish Life in Mediaeval England,* 6th ed. (London: Methuen, 1929), 201–7; Eamon Duffy, *The Stripping of the Altars: Traditional Religion in England, c. 1400–c. 1580* (New Haven: Yale University Press, 1992), 313, 369; H. S. Bennett, *The Pastons and Their England* (Cambridge: Cambridge University Press, 1968), 196–99; Moorman, *Church Life,* 88–89; David L. Edwards, *Christian England,* vol. 2 (London: Collins, 1983), 87; Robert Whiting, *The Blind Devotion of the People: Popular Religion and the English Reformation* (Cambridge: Cambridge University Press, 1989), 17.

people participated in other ways. The people marked parts of the mass by kneeling or standing, and they confessed together with the priest and crossed themselves while the priest read from the Gospel of John. For the literate, there were devotional books that might be used during mass.[24]

Regular attendance was required at mass on Sunday mornings and on holy days; matins and evensong were also said on Sundays, but with fewer in attendance, it seems.[25] Many church services were available on other days of the week. Mass was to be said daily by the parish priest, so one might start the day with a mass at 6 A.M. With its many priests, churches, chantries, guilds, and special masses for the dead, the town afforded many opportunities for church services during the week, and many laity attended weekday masses, which were shorter, low masses, absent of the time-consuming ceremony of the Sunday ritual. In 1497, the Venetian Trevisan described the devotion of the English when he wrote the following, probably about townspeople:

Although they all attend Mass every day, and say many Paternosters in public, (the women carrying long rosaries in their hands, and any who can read taking the office of Our Lady with them, and with some companion reciting it in the church verse by verse, in a low voice, after the manner of churchmen,) they always hear mass on Sunday in their parish church, and give liberal alms.[26]

The church was charged with instructing the people in their duty to God. The priest was to assist even the illiterate to learn about the basis of

---

24. Colin Platt, *The Parish Churches of Medieval England* (London: Secker and Warburg, 1981), 120–21; Dickinson, *Later Middle Ages*, 455; Bettey, *Church*, 21–22; H. Maynard Smith, *Pre-Reformation England* (1938; reprint, New York: Russell and Russell, 1963), 96; John Bossy, "The Mass as a Social Institution, 1200–1700," *PP* 100 (1983): 54–56; Duffy, *Traditional Religion*, 34–35, 123–26; Susan Brigden, *London and the Reformation* (Oxford: Clarendon Press, 1989), 12–18. An excellent example of a medieval wall painting of Christ sitting in judgment can be seen in the village church at Copford, only a few miles from Colchester.

25. Cutts, *Priests*, 200–204. Scholars disagree about the level of church attendance: Phythian-Adams, *Coventry*, 168–69, concluded that the parish churches in Coventry were quite crowded for the Sunday mass, whereas Keith Thomas, *Religion and the Decline of Magic* (New York: Charles Scribner's Sons, 1971), 159–60, wrote that churchgoing was quite lax, noting that some parish churches were too small for all parishioners to attend and that few of the poorer people attended.

26. *A Relation, or Rather a True Account, of the Island of England*, trans. Charlotte Augusta Sneyd (London: Camden Society, 1897), 23; Bettey, *Church*, 20; Gasquet, *Parish Life*, 140–46; Duffy, *Traditional Religion*, 98–99, 112.

belief and the rules of Christian conduct, but there was little organized personal instruction by priests. Even when priests conducted schools, direct religious instruction was sparse, though much was probably imparted in a practical way, such as using the Paternoster in the teaching of reading. For the most part, religious instruction was supposed to be given to the young by parents and godparents. The deficiency in personal instruction made the rite of confession all the more important for its instructional value, since the priest could deal intimately with the individual, probing for undeclared sins. John Myrc's *Instructions for Parish Priests* enjoined priests to ascertain whether the penitent could say his/her Paternoster, Apostles' Creed, and Ave Maria and, if he could not, to give him such a penance that he would know them before he came again. Confession, which was mandatory before one took Communion at least once a year, also seems to have occurred at other times, for example, in connection with the feasts of All Saints' Day, Christmas, and Whitsun (Pentecost) or at certain crises in one's life, making confession more frequent than the taking of Communion for the average parishioner.[27]

Sermons might have great instructional value, of course, but it is uncertain how often the Sunday churchgoer would have heard sermons. Archbishop Peckham decreed in the thirteenth century that there must be a sermon in the vernacular in the parish church at least four times a year. The popular preaching of the friars helped develop a taste for sermons, and the installing of new pulpits and pews indicates that sermons became more common in parish churches in the late Middle Ages. The earliest parish church pulpits for preaching date from the mid–fourteenth century, and seats for the comfort of listeners were added in many churches in the fifteenth and early sixteenth centuries.[28]

---

27. Hubert Jedin and John Dolan, eds., *Handbook of Church History,* vol. 4, *From the High Middle Ages to the Eve of the Reformation,* trans. Anselm Biggs (Montreal: Palm Publications, n.d.), 578; Cutts, *Priests,* 216–23 (Cutts details Archbishop Peckham's 1281 manual for teaching major beliefs, which was influential up to the Reformation); Myrc, *Instructions,* 21–53; Dickinson, *Later Middle Ages,* 201–3, 274–75; Gasquet, *Parish Life,* 197–200; Thomas N. Tentler, *Sin and Confession on the Eve of the Reformation* (Princeton: Princeton University Press, 1977), 80.

28. G. R. Owst, *Preaching in Medieval England* (New York: Russell and Russell, 1965), 145, 165–67; Bettey, *Church,* 24–25; Anderson, *Imagery,* 142–43. R. N. Swanson, "The Problems of the Priesthood in Pre-Reformation England," *EHR* 105 (1990): 853–54, believes that most clerics did not preach.

Since sermons and personal instruction were often spasmodic and poor in quality, the visual and dramatic elements of the liturgy were all the more important in teaching the illiterate about their faith. Popular devotion concentrated on gazing at the Host at the elevation, and other elements of the liturgy were marked by ceremony. The reading of the gospel that culminated the first part of the Sunday mass had its importance emphasized by the Gospel Book being carried in procession. Drama was built into the ceremonies, especially during Holy Week, which included the distribution of palms on Palm Sunday, the creeping to the cross on Good Friday, and the restoration of the cross from the Easter sepulchre to its place on the high altar on Easter Day. Chanting or singing added to the sense of drama of the worship services. By the early sixteenth century, some parish churches had choirs in which even the laity sang, and Roger Burgon's will suggests that there was just such a choir in All Saints' Church and possibly that Burgon was a choir member, as his precise directions indicate that he was knowledgeable about music: "I bequeath to the quire of the said church a dirige book with the mass of requiem noted and the commendation and the burial. Also I bequeath a quayre of the New Fest of the Transfiguration of Christ and the Fest of Jhus and the Fest of the Visitation of Our Lady and all noted with the legends and the octaves of the said festes."[29]

The decoration of the church itself was instructive, being "the poor man's service book," as one historian has put it. The preoccupation with death and judgment in the fifteenth century was revealed in the "dooms," or Last Judgment scenes, on church walls, and the graphic art vividly portrayed the message of the soul's need of the protection from judgment afforded by the sacrifice of Christ on the cross. Popular subjects for painting on the walls of churches were the dance of death, the seven deadly sins, and the weighing of souls, all conveying a strong message to their viewers, but above all was the great rood representing Christ on the cross. The rood loft, a kind of gallery over the screen at the dividing line of the nave and the chancel, contained the rood, or crucifix, for the people to gaze on. Several Colchester testators left money for the enhance-

---

29. ERO D/ACR1/127; Jedin and Dolan, *Handbook,* 571; Duffy, *Traditional Religion,* 22–37; Dickinson, *Later Middle Ages,* 455; Henry Barclay Swete, *Church Services and Service-Books before the Reformation,* rev. ed. (New York: Macmillan, 1930), 35–38; Moran, *Schooling,* 199–200.

ment of the rood loft in their parish churches, with Nicholas Clere's bequest being the most elaborate: £20 was "to be spent on making or mending a crucifix, called 'le Roode,' with Mary and John, to stand over the rood-loft." Images of Mary or the saints in the church also stirred the hearts of worshipers. Each parish church was supposed to have in its chancel the image of the saint to whom the church was dedicated, but churches had other statues that were loved by parishioners. John Leveson bequeathed five marks for the "new dyghting" of St. Paul in St. Leonard's Church (see fig. 2), and Margaret Thorne left her "best beads of jet" for the adornment of the image of Our Lady in St. Botolph's.[30]

The parish church not only provided worship, instruction, and rituals for the passages of life but also helped create a oneness and a sense of community that were especially important in the fluid society of the town. The eating of the holy cake—or holy loaf, as it was more commonly called—was a symbol of that unity. Provided by some of the laity every Sunday, the bread was at the end of the mass censed and blessed before being cut into small pieces and distributed. Some people even took it home to sick friends. Although not sacramental as was the Holy Eucharist, the people valued the custom of the eating of the holy loaf, and even amidst the radical changes of the Reformation, the custom was commended in 1540 as worthy of continuation, "as a godly ceremony . . . to put us in mind that all Christian men be one mystical body of Christ."[31] Also within the worship services was the peace ritual, which promoted the ideal of peace with one's neighbor. The ritual, which dated from around 1000, had evolved into the passing around of a pax, on which was carved or painted a sacred symbol, such as the crucifix, the Agnus Dei, or the sacred monogram *IHS*. The pax was first kissed by the priest and then passed around so that the parishioners could kiss it in turn, all the while observing proper seniority.[32]

---

30. Bernard Lord Manning, *The People's Faith in the Time of Wyclif*, 2d ed. (Hassocks, Sussex: Harvester Press, 1975), 12–13; Platt, *Churches*, 120–35; PRO 17 Moone; PRO 13 Dogett; ERO D/ACR1/112. See Anderson, *Imagery*, for an excellent discussion of the art and imagery in parish churches. Robert Whiting, "Abominable Idols: Images and Image-Breaking under Henry VIII," *JEccH* 33 (1982): 31–39, concluded that the image remained a crucial element in popular religion on the eve of the Reformation. Goldberg, "Women," 110, notes the role of women in beautifying the parish church.

31. Quoted in Smith, *Pre-Reformation England*, 97–98. See also Cutts, *Priests*, 202, 235–36; Gasquet, *Parish Life*, 157–58.

32. Smith, *Pre-Reformation England*, 96–97; Joseph A. Jungmann, *The Mass of the Roman Rite: Its Origins and Development*, trans. Francis A. Brunner, 2 vols. (New York: Benziger, 1951), 2:321–32; Bossy, "Mass," 125.

FIG. 2. The interior of St. Leonard's Church, in the parish where wealthy mariners lived. *Top:* View from the nave, looking toward the rood screen separating the nave from the chancel beyond. *Bottom:* View from the chancel, showing the back of the rood-screen figures and the nave's lovely hammer-beam roof, built in the early sixteenth century.

Processions outside the church building were also a mark of parish solidarity. Parading around the churchyard on Palm Sunday, Ascension Day, and Corpus Christi, the procession moved into the streets and open countryside on the Rogation Days and St. Mark's Day. Heading the procession of parishioners were the processional cross and the priest in his colorful cope, with perhaps a shrine, and following were the people, some with banners and even handbells, all marching together in a symbol of oneness as the body of Christ in that parish. The procession during Rogation Days, which took place on the days just preceding Ascension Day, "beat the bounds," that is, walked around the parish boundaries to mark and recall them, with boys being taken along to ensure that witnesses to the boundaries should survive as long as possible. The occasion was usually enlivened by a church feast following the beating of the bounds.[33]

Oneness within the parish was also created through feasting and fun, with the parish church frequently the center for hearty fellowship. As both principal fund-raisers and social activities, the church ales included sports, dancing, and other festivities. In the period before gravestones, the churchyard was often the site of the fun. Also, religious plays, performed either in the church or in the churchyard, were popular for amusement, for teaching, and for profit. Plays were produced in towns and villages all over Essex in the first half of the sixteenth century, with the plays at Braintree and Dunmow being well documented in the churchwardens' accounts. Unfortunately, those records are not extant in Colchester, but one tantalizing allusion in the borough court roll records the payment of a fine from two men "for gathering of corn for St. Martin's play."[34]

Within the framework of the church, the sense of oneness and community might also extend in time and give a sense of continuity. Every

---

33. Swete, *Church Services*, 132–33; Bettey, *Church*, 23, 56; Charles Phythian-Adams, "Ceremony and the Citizen: The Communal Year at Coventry, 1450–1550," in *Crisis and Order in English Towns, 1500–1700: Essays in Urban History*, ed. Peter Clark and Paul Slack (Toronto: University of Toronto Press, 1972), 57–85; Mervyn James, "Ritual, Drama, and Social Body in the Late Medieval English Town," *PP* 98 (1983): 3–29; F. G. Emmison, "Tithes, Perambulations, and Sabbath-Breach in Elizabethan Essex," in *Tribute to an Antiquary: Essays Presented to Marc Fitch*, ed. F. G. Emmison and W. B. Stephens (London: Leopard's Head Press, 1976), 183–93; Duffy, *Traditional Religion*, 136, 279–80.

34. CR97, detached roll; Bettey, *Church*, 50–53; John Christopher Coldewey, "Early Essex Drama" (Ph.D. diss., University of Colorado, 1972), 25–28.

Sunday morning, the names of the recent dead were solemnly pronounced in the beadroll, an observance that must have given the living some sense of oneness with those of the past. In 1504 Colchester testator Edith Algood left money for the priest of her parish "to rehearse every name" of her two dead husbands and herself for ten years, "when he biddeth the bodies in the beadroll."[35] Parishioners would also be aware of the daily intercession for the dead conducted by the chantry priests, but more affordable, and more popular, were the obits observing the anniversaries of the deaths of former parishioners. John Bardefield, Colchester alderman, bequeathed the profits from a certain field for a yearly obit to be kept for himself, his parents, his two wives, and all Christians for one hundred years.[36] Bardefield obviously did not want his name to be forgotten. Such intercessions created connections not only with the past but also with the future, since the living knew that following generations would in turn be praying for their souls.

The parish church also provided a less esoteric reminder of time that united the parish in a very practical way: the church bells, which awakened people from their night's slumber and sent them to bed at curfew time. The Angelus bell, also known as the Ave bell or the Gabriel bell, sounded the first thing in the morning and the last at night, with church bells also calling the faithful to attendance at the services of the church or to other events, both joyous and sad. St. Leonard's Church went a step further and installed a large clock on its tower around 1500.[37]

The parish church gave much to the people, providing a contact with God, assistance during times of trial, fellowship and a sense of community with others, reinforcement of the social order, certitude in an uncertain world, and the promise of salvation in the afterlife. In turn, many parishioners were both willing and expected to give of themselves to their church, in time, effort, and loyalties. Each parish church normally had a parish council of laity, later called the vestry, which met at least once a year around Easter. Theoretically, that meeting was for the whole parish to elect churchwardens and constables, but parish councils, usually from

---

35. ERO D/ACR1/99; Smith, *Pre-Reformation England*, 127–28; Duffy, *Traditional Religion*, 124–25, 334–37.

36. PRO 18 Adeane; Palliser, *York*, 228. Forty-nine testators, or 24 percent of the 203 wills from 1485 to 1529, requested obits.

37. Gasquet, *Parish Life*, 162; Dickinson, *Later Middle Ages*, 443–44, 466–67; RCHM, *Essex*, 3:45.

twelve to twenty-four in number, had developed to handle many church matters, including supervision of funds and fund-raising activities, assessments for maintenance and church repair, and overseeing the work of the churchwardens. The unpaid wardens, usually two in number, handled the details of the responsibilities belonging to the laity in the parish, which included the maintaining—both cleaning and repair—of the nave of the church (whereas the priest maintained the chancel), supervising any rebuilding, managing church property or stock that had been bequeathed to the church, distributing bequests to the poor, organizing church festivities, and providing the books and utensils needed for services. The parish council could be summoned anytime during the year by the parish priest or the churchwardens to help make decisions, but all parishioners might be consulted for the more important activities, as was done by the churchwardens of St. Botolph's in 1515 when they sold a house "by the unanimous assent, consent and permission of the whole body of the parishioners of the parish." St. James's Church likewise sold a house that had been bequeathed to the church "at the special request" of the two churchwardens and eleven other named men, probably the church council, "and of all other trustworthy parishioners dwelling within the parish of St. James." The council at St. Peter's Church built for themselves in the early sixteenth century a meeting room opening off of one of the side aisles and large enough for at least twenty people to sit comfortably, indicating the value placed on the council and its work.[38] At the end of each church year, the accounts of the churchwardens were examined by the parish council at the same Easter meeting where the new wardens were elected. The wardens were sworn in at the next archidiaconal court, so they had dual allegiance, being subject to the ecclesiastical court and a key link in its disciplinary function, and being required by oath to provide "presentments" to the court four times annually on the physical condition of church buildings and on the behavior of the incum-

---

38. A. Tindal Hart, *The Man in the Pew, 1558–1660* (New York: Humanities Press, 1966), 23–24, 58–88; CR93/26; CR92/18; RCHM, *Essex*, 3:41; Palliser, "Parish," 11; William J. Pressey, "The Essex Churchwarden," *ER* 51 (1942): 145–50; McIntosh, *Havering*, 220. The vestry developed out of the parish council, according to Smith, *Pre-Reformation England*, 122–23: see also W. E. Tate, *The Parish Chest*, 2d ed. (Cambridge: Cambridge University Press, 1951), 12–14; Emma Mason, "The Role of the English Parishioner, 1100–1500," *JEccH* 27 (1976): 23–27. Gervase Rosser, *Medieval Westminster, 1200–1540* (Oxford: Clarendon Press, 1989), 264–71, describes the lay-supervised rebuilding of the parish church of St. Margaret and the fund-raising projects for it in the early Tudor period.

bent and parishioners. The latter duty was often an onerous and thankless task.[39]

With so much of the lives of the people connected to the parish church, it is not surprising that, after family, the church often had the first loyalty of the ordinary people, as was evident by the bequests in wills. Forty percent, or eighty-one of all the Tudor wills through 1529, gave something to the parish church beyond the usual offering to the high altar for any unpaid tithes, with almost half (thirty-eight wills) contributing toward the fabric (the structure) of the church—often toward repair, but sometimes toward new building. In 1503 the church of St. Mary-at-Wall was building a new steeple, according to the will of parishioner William Ball, who bequeathed 6s. 8d. toward its construction; ten years later, it was finished when another parishioner, Robert Cowbridge, left 20s. for the "hanging of the bells in the new steeple of St. Mary." It was a time of pride in church buildings, with most of the parish churches in Colchester engaged in some rebuilding of their fabric in the late fifteenth and early sixteenth centuries; the additions to the two richer parish churches of St. James and St. Leonard were quite extensive.[40] Colchester testators were also creative in the furnishings they supplied for their parish churches. Margaret Bayly directed her executors to have made for her parish church, All Saints', a cloth of silk with a picture of All Saints' Church on it. There was no mistaking where her loyalty lay.[41]

Colchester Clergy

With the abundance of churches and religious foundations in Colchester, there was no shortage of clerics to serve and pray, and Colchester had the gamut—both the learned and the unlearned, the virtuous and the immoral, the competent and the incompetent. The impression that the people had of the institutional church was obtained largely through the clergy, both those who served within the parish and the regular clergy in the religious orders.

---

39. Jay Pascal Anglin, "The Court of the Archdeacon of Essex, 1571–1609" (Ph.D. diss., University of California, 1965), 58; F. G. Emmison, *Elizabethan Life: Morals and the Church Courts* (Chelmsford: Essex County Council, 1973), 231. For an excellent assessment of the relationship of wardens and council, see Alldridge, "Loyalty," 112.

40. Palliser, "Parish," 11; *VCH Essex*, 9:105; PRO 30 Blamyr; PRO 22 Fetiplace. John Glede (ERO D/ACR1/138) mentioned the building of the new steeple in 1508. Hoskins, *Plunder*, 33, wrote that church rebuilding in the early Tudor period "rivalled the great wave of ecclesiastical building of the twelfth to fourteenth centuries."

41. ERO D/ACR1/106.

Historian Edward Cutts, relying on the list of those swearing allegiance to Henry VIII in 1535, counted eighty priests and monks in Colchester at that time, but those figures do not include the Grey Friars, who for some reason were not listed. Even without the Grey Friars, there was a cleric for every sixty-two people or so, assuming that Colchester had a population of around five thousand.[42]

If the Colchester clerics were typical, their social and economic origins were generally similar to those whom they served. Evidence for the origin of Colchester clerics is scanty, but at least a few came from local families. For example, two priests, Richard Caumond, vicar of St. Peter's, and James Forster of St. Leonard's, had brothers living in Colchester,[43] and a few testators mentioned clerical relatives in their wills.[44] But local family connections did not seem to be a significant factor in the influence held by the clerics.

More important was that the priest be a godly man of upright life, compassionate toward his people, and eager to teach and serve them. John Adam, "parson of St. James," as he described himself in his will of 1491, seemed to be such a man. In his will, Adam left money so that each poor person of the town could be given 1d. and a loaf of bread at Adam's burial and at the one-week and one-month anniversaries of his death. Bedding was to be given to St. Anne's for poor folks, a gown to his parish clerk, and two tenements to his servant for his lifetime. Adam also wanted to promote the learning of fellow parish clergy, asking that all his unbound books be distributed among them, but even more remarkable was his desire to share the Word of God with the people. He directed that his "portuse," a portable breviary, and all his books that were bound be chained in one of the chapels in St. James's, by the Bible. Having a Bible in the parish church might simply mean that the Bible itself was being read in the church services, or, even more unusual, it might mean that the Bible was available for perusal by people who could read Latin. Some

---

42. Cutts, *Colchester,* 102.

43. Wills of Caumond (1535), PRO 27 Hogan; and John Forster (1504), ERO D/ACR1/90. Forster's will shows him to be a brother to James Forster, who, in the will of J. Bardfield (1506; PRO 18 Adeane), was said to be the parish priest of St. Leonard's. A few clerics had names that were common family names in Colchester, such as Fennyng, Forde, and Lowth.

44. Wills of R. Burgon (1507), ERO D/ACR1/127; M. Burgon (1512), ERO D/ACR2/17; T. Garrard (1512), ERO D/ACR1/194; A. Garrard (1514), ERO D/ACR2/10; John Brich (1501), ERO D/ACR1/17; Joan Brich (1512), ERO D/ACR1/191.

parish churches in England had Bibles, but there is no indication that any other church in Colchester had one, particularly in a place where it might be accessible to the laity. But, lest one think that Adam was a proto-Protestant, he also asked for prayers for his soul at several religious houses. Adam's love for his parish church was evident in his bequest of a blue coverlet to lie before the high altar on holy days, £10 toward work on the windows, and cushions and bunkers (seats) to be laid in the seats in the chancel on holy days; moreover, Adam gave money toward the repair of every church in the town. A last warm touch, almost an afterthought, was the gift of his mantle "to some poor woman for to lay on her bed."[45] An unusual request nine years later testified to the respect accorded to Parson Adam: Alderman Nicholas Clere asked to be buried next to Adam's grave.[46]

The parish priest had many duties. He was expected to administer the sacraments and provide regular church services, including matins and vespers; teach his flock to love and serve God and to maintain at least rudimentary catechetical instruction; visit the sick; provide hospitality; use any excess revenues to support the poor; and keep the chancel, churchyard, rectory, and barns in good repair.[47] The church expected its priests to be well informed and literate, but success in that area was elusive, and one of the continuing criticisms of the church concerned the poor learning of many of the clergy. The elite clergy were those with university degrees, such as John Wayne, rector of St. James's Church, who was said to be a "doctor of laws of either kind," that is, of both canon and civil law, and who sometimes served as an official in the archdeaconry court. In comparison to some other regions, the borough of Colchester had a respectable percentage of parish priests with university degrees. There were at least sixty-six beneficed parish priests in the borough between 1485 and 1536, and at least eighteen, or 27 percent, were known to have university degrees, which compares well with the 20 per-

---

45. PRO 7 Vox; Moran, *Schooling*, 186–91; Brigden, *London*, 59–60. Norman P. Tanner, *The Church in Late Medieval Norwich, 1370–1532* (Toronto: Pontifical Institute of Mediaeval Studies, 1984), 128, noted the Norwich priests who left devotional books to be chained in the parish church.

46. PRO 17 Moone. Other examples of beloved, compassionate priests can be given, such as two Augustinian canons, John Grewe (or Grene) and Richard White, both of whom served the cure of souls in the parish of St. Botolph around 1500 and were often mentioned by name in wills.

47. Platt, *Churches*, 48–49; Swanson, "Problems," 846–47; Harding, *Law Courts*, 117.

cent of university graduates in the diocese of Canterbury (1454–86) or the 17.6 percent in the diocese of Norwich (1503–28). However, the Colchester figure does not compare well with larger towns; in 1522, 75 percent of London beneficed priests were graduates, and in the city of Norwich from 1500 to 1532, 42 percent were.[48] In Colchester the better endowed parishes were more likely to have educated men serving the cure. In the early Tudor years, five Colchester churches had from 40 to 50 percent of their clergy with university degrees. Of those, all but St. Runwald's had a benefice valued at the highest Colchester level of £10 or above, and the learned priests at St. Runwald's were probably subsidized by the patron, the Tey family.[49] Of the known university-educated clergy in Colchester, only Richard Caumond, M.A., left a will, revealing a continuing Cambridge connection; though vicar at St. Peter's from 1494 to his death in 1535, Caumond still retained a chamber at Clare Hall when he died.[50]

The income of parish priests varied according to the worth of the benefice attached to the church. Of the twelve Colchester parish churches listed in the 1535 *Valor Ecclesiasticus,* seven had a yearly living of £10 or above, with three having less than £7 a year and the other two between £7 and £10. Of the eight churches within the walls of the town, John Adam's church, St. James's, was a little ahead of the others, with a benefice valued at £11 8s. 4d. It has been calculated that around 1500 a parish incumbent needed an income of £15 a year if he employed a chaplain to help him in his work, £10 a year if he worked alone in his parish. By that standard, some Colchester incumbents had an adequate income, though they hardly lived in the lap of luxury, whereas others had such little income that they were hard pressed to keep up the duties of hospitality and repair. Even so, the beneficed position was sought after. Once appointed by the patron of the church and instituted by the bishop, the parson had job security, since he could not be dismissed except through

48. CR98/6; Platt, *Churches,* 53–55; appendix 6; Richard L. Greaves, *Society and Religion in Elizabethan England* (Minneapolis: University of Minnesota Press, 1981), 77; Claire Cross, *Church and People, 1450–1660: The Triumph of the Laity in the English Church* (London: Fontana, 1976), 46; Margaret Bowker, *The Secular Clergy in the Diocese of Lincoln, 1495–1520* (Cambridge: Cambridge University Press, 1968), 179; Tanner, *Norwich,* 29.
49. The other four churches were St. James's, St. Mary-at-Wall, St. Nicholas's, and St. Leonard's.
50. PRO 27 Hogen.

condemnation by an ecclesiastical court for failure to live a holy life or tend adequately to his duties.[51]

One of the traditional solutions to offset the poorer benefices was for a cleric to obtain a license to hold more than one benefice, a continuing problem known as "pluralism," though in some poorer parishes it was a necessary expedient. For example, St. Michael's Church in the parish of Mile End, north of the walled town, had one of the poorer benefices, being worth only £7, so several of their rectors also held other livings. Robert Alwether, while still rector at Mile End, was appointed to the parsonage at St. Nicholas's within the town, although after doing double duty for three years, he resigned at Mile End to serve only the more prosperous town parish. Likewise, Mile End's next parson, John Lowth, after serving at Mile End for five years, took on another parish, that of St. James's, thus replacing Parson John Adam. After a year of serving both parishes, Lowth resigned at Mile End. Other examples of pluralism can be found among the parishes of the borough, most often a combination of an outlying parish and a town parish, but usually no cleric tried to serve more than one town parish at a time, although that would later occur in the Elizabethan period when inflation rendered the benefices inadequate.[52]

Along with pluralism, the connected practice of absenteeism was also subject to sustained criticism. If a clergyman held two or more benefices, it was obviously impossible to live and work in each parish. Of the forty-eight parish priests in the twelve beneficed Colchester parishes from 1500 to 1536, there is no evidence that nineteen of them ever lived in the parishes. Some of the absentees were pluralists, especially those at the churches of Holy Trinity and St. Mary-at-Wall. Others, such as Richard Langryge, absent rector of St. Nicholas's Church from 1531 to 1537, who held the degree of doctor of divinity from Oxford, moved in high

---

51. *Valor Ecclesiasticus*, 6 vols. (1810), 1:443; Cross, *Church and People*, 43; H. G. Alexander, *Religion in England, 1558–1662* (London: University of London Press, 1968), 14. According to Brigden, *London*, 49, London clergy were much better paid, with almost half of the benefices being worth more than £20. The income from a benefice derived mainly from three sources: tithes and offerings, income from the parson's glebe, and fees for certain services offered by the priest, such as christenings, weddings, and burials.

52. See appendixes 5 and 6. Thomas Wilkynson was an exception to the holding of two Colchester town parishes; as rector of St. Nicholas's Church, Wilkynson obtained a bull from Pope Leo X in 1514 to unite his parish with that of St. Mary-at-Wall, but by 1531 the parishes were again separate. See Morant, 2:14.

circles and apparently received the appointment to St. Nicholas's as a sinecure for additional income while he was chaplain to the archbishop of York.[53] The Colchester churches that were under the patronage of St. John's Abbey, such as St. Nicholas's, Holy Trinity, and Greenstead, were more likely to have absentee clerics, probably a result of the higher standing and connections of the Benedictine monastery, which made it more subject to the "friendly persuasions" of high churchmen. More surprising was the number of absentee priests at St. Mary-at-Wall, which was in the patronage of the bishop of London.

In any town, there were a number of other clergy besides the parson and the monastics and friars in religious houses. For a minimum fee, clergy were hired as curates to replace absentee priests, with the latter then pocketing the profits from the benefice without doing any work; for example, in 1534 Robert Borowe served as curate for the parish of St. Nicholas in place of the absent Dr. Langryge.[54] In addition to the parish priest or his curate, almost every parish church had one or more extra priests serving the chantries by saying prayers for the dead. Chantry chapels were built within churches, sometimes in aisles or adjoining the choir area, or chantry altars were set up to accommodate the priest hired to say the prayers. Chantries fell into two categories, perpetual and stipendiary, with the perpetual chantry having a permanent endowment and the temporary or stipendiary chantry set up for a limited period of time, which might be anywhere from one-fourth of a year to five years, although most were usually for one year. The chantry priest was independent of the parochial incumbent, yet many were required to assist the parish priest in addition to saying prayers for the soul of the chantry founder. Such duties were imposed on the chantrists at St. Leonard's Church, as revealed by the 1548 chantry certificates; both chantrists were "to sing mass . . . and to help to serve the cure there."[55] The livings of the

53. Brigden, *London*, 57, says that about a quarter of the London clergy were habitually absent. Langryge served Wolsey as chaplain and then became chaplain to Edward Lee, archdeacon of Colchester, when Lee succeeded Wolsey as archbishop of York in 1531; see Richard Newcourt, *Repertorium Ecclesiasticum Parochiale Londinense*, 2 vols. (London, 1710), 2:177. This is probably the Dr. Richard Langrysh who committed suicide by leaping from the steeple of St. Magnus's in London into the waters of the Thames in 1547, seemingly in reaction to the coming ecclesiastical reforms; see Brigden, *London*, 427.

54. The parishioners had probably never seen Langryge, so the town records (*RPB*, 88) and the will of W. Roberts (1534; ERO D/ACR3/1) incorrectly referred to Borowe as "parish priest" and "rector."

55. PRO E301/19; Kathleen L. Wood-Legh, *Perpetual Chantries in Britain* (Cambridge: Cambridge University Press, 1965), 278–90; Alexander Hamilton Thompson, *The English*

perpetual chantry priests varied in Colchester, from as low as £6 (the Harmanson Chantry in St. Leonard's Church) to £9 a year (the Heynes Chantry in St. Peter's Church). When those figures were compiled in the ecclesiastical survey in 1535, five perpetual chantries in parish churches were listed: two at St. Leonard's and one each at St. Mary-at-Wall, St. Peter's, and St. Nicholas's. Some earlier chantry foundations, the oldest being from the fourteenth century, had been partly consolidated and were being celebrated outside of parish churches. Two were housed in the ancient St. Helen's Chapel in Maidenborough Street, for which a priest was still regularly appointed, and four chantries, which earlier had been consolidated under the Guild of St. Helen, had prayers celebrated by the Crossed Friars in their chapel.[56] Though not on the same level as the beneficed parish priests, the perpetual chantry priests had a reasonably secure place and income, whereas the "floating" priests who served the stipendiary chantries were in a more precarious position.

Each parish church, then, even the smaller ones, usually had several clergy as well as a parish clerk, whose duties included reading part of the liturgy during the services, saying mass in the priest's absence, teaching children at the parish school (if there was one), and distributing holy water to households to rid them of evil and invoke good.[57] By the sixteenth century, the parish clerks were usually laymen, as was the clerk of St. James's, his lay status being apparent because he was married, a fact known to us because his wife proved to be too tempting to Parson John Wayne. Wayne, though he must have been at least sixty years old, was charged in 1536 of consorting with the clerk's wife "at unlawful hours in several nights," for which the borough court levied a 20s. fine on Wayne, who died in the same year.[58]

Parson John Wayne's fornication with the wife of his parish clerk may not have been typical, though there were certainly other examples of sex-

---

Clergy and Their Organization in the Later Middle Ages (Oxford: Clarendon Press, 1947), 133–35, 143–45. On duties of stipendiary priests, see Clive Burgess, " 'By Quick and by Dead': Wills and Pious Provision in Late Medieval Bristol," *EHR* 102 (1987): 849–50.

56. *Valor Ecclesiasticus*, 1:443; Morant, 2:45–51; Martin, *Story of Colchester*, 33–34; appendix 7.

57. The last task gave him the name of "holy water clerk." The clerk might also perform such mundane tasks as cleaning the church and preparing it for services, putting out the priest's vestments, ringing the bells, and accompanying the priest when he visited the sick. The parish clerks were originally in minor orders: see Platt, *Churches*, 61–63; Bettey, *Church*, 33–34; Duffy, *Traditional Religion*, 124, 281–82; Cross, *Church and People*, 43.

58. CR105/5. By the following year, the parish clerk's wife had found another lover, and court records (CR107/2) proclaimed her to be a "common strumpet."

ual sins among the Colchester clergy, but the behavior of priests was enough of a concern that testators who were asking their executors to hire a priest for prayers for their soul often stipulated, as Robert Hervy did in 1488, that "a priest of good and honest conversation" be found. There were few occasions when common people had any authority over the hiring of priests, so the expressions in the wills about what was wanted in a stipendiary priest aptly articulated the general desire for upright priests. Harry Bear requested "an honest and well bespoke priest," and George Aleyn demanded that the chaplain who was to sing for his soul be "an honest and an able priest." Of the 203 testators from 1485 to 1529, 38 left money for a stipendiary priest, and all but 8 added instructions about the priests' manner of life.[59]

Such concerns about clerical behavior indicate that some priests led a less than virtuous life. The stipendiary priests, who might be idle much of the time, since their work was spasmodic, were often the focus of complaints, but stipendiaries did not have a corner on clerical misbehavior, as can be seen from the borough court records. The behavior and morals of the clergy were normally in the province of the ecclesiastical courts, but, unfortunately, those records from pre-Reformation Colchester are lost. Such offenses were occasionally brought before the borough court, though usually only at the lawhundred held three times a year, when burgesses reported on the behavior of people within their wards.[60] Jurors were not shy about presenting clerical misbehavior, even that of the parish priests; lesser examples range from unclean ditches to being too much the sportsman, but more serious were charges of thievery, such as that leveled against the rector of Holy Trinity for stealing cartloads of wheat and barley from the rector of St. Nicholas's Church, possibly reflecting a tithe dispute. The ethics of some of the priests were questioned: Richard Caumond, the vicar of St. Peter's, was accused of receiving stolen goods, and William Grant, rector at Lexden, was said to be a "common regrator of divers grains with intention to sell them at exces-

---

    59. PRO 17 Milles; ERO D/ACR1/200; PRO 1 Fetiplace.

    60. Robert E. Rodes, *Ecclesiastical Administration in Medieval England* (Notre Dame: University of Notre Dame Press, 1977), 120, 138–39; Smith, *Pre-Reformation England*, 65. Only an ecclesiastical court could actually punish a priest, and only a church court could deprive the wayward priest of his living, but secular courts could and did charge clerics with wrongdoing and even gave their own verdicts, over theoretical canonical objections, as to whether the cleric was guilty or not. Another complication was that to impose the death penalty on a cleric, the bishop had to hand the cleric back to the civil authorities.

sive price, to the great detriment of the King's liege people."[61] Some parishioners were on the side of the parsons; certainly Mother Wolman showed her loyalty when she carried an ax to her imprisoned rector so that he could break out of his prison in the moot hall. His incarceration probably resulted from the accusation that he had stolen a wallet containing two hundred marks from a deceased widow.[62] The clergy could be violent, too. Thomas Chanon, rector of St. Leonard's, was charged with striking an alderman with a vessel called a "berecruise," and at the same lawhundred, the rector of St. Runwald's was presented for assaulting another clerk, "against the king's peace and to the evil example of other unruly people."[63] It should be emphasized that none of these charges indicated opposition to the clerical system, but they were objecting to unruly and immoral behavior of certain priests; after all, priests were the "mediators and means unto God for men," the holders of knowledge that set them apart from the laity. John Colet preached to the clergy at St. Paul's in 1511 that "the dignity of the priesthood is equal with the dignity of the angels." As a channel of divine grace, the priesthood was to eschew the world and fleshly behavior; it is no wonder that priests were subject to ridicule when less than angelic behavior was exhibited.[64]

It is easy to point out the problems of the poor behavior of priests, but of course many were of exemplary behavior, though the good behavior seldom made it into the official records. Hugh Fetherston's role as peacemaker was recognized in Colchester; Fetherston, the rector of All Saints' Church, was assigned the role of arbitrator by the borough court in at least four local disputes.[65] Though the clergy quarreled and even fought with each other, they also relied on each other in times of need, as can be observed in the five clerical wills written between 1485 and 1537. Three of the testators named other clerics as executors, and the other two had

---

61. CR82/6; CR83/8; CR96/13.

62. CR91/2, 13. Though not named in the record, the imprisoned rector of St. Runwald's would have been John Farforth; see Newcourt, 2:180. Not surprisingly, Farforth resigned a few months later.

63. CR84/16. Chanon's attack on the alderman was considered far more serious, meriting a £5 fine, whereas the rector of St. Runwald's was fined only 40s.

64. Swanson, "Problems," 846, 868–69; Brigden, London, 43.

65. CR89/20d; CR90/21d, 24; CR97/10. In each case, four arbitrators were appointed; and in the first three cases, Fetherston was the only clergyman chosen to serve as an arbitrator.

clerics present to witness the writing of their wills.[66] Four of the wills were full of concern about prayers for the soul and the giving away of worldly goods; the exception was the will of Richard Caumond, who seemed most interested in providing for his brother's family and in setting up a marble monument for himself in St. Peter's Church. In his early years in Colchester, Caumond obviously had the trust of his parishioners, serving as executor and supervisor of several of their wills,[67] but in later years, few asked Caumond for that service, and Caumond's own will, written at the end of forty-two years as vicar of St. Peter's, gave the impression that he was little concerned about spiritual matters. Confirming the perception that he had departed from his original commitment were the graphic charges brought against him in the borough court in his later years, for sexual misconduct and other unlawful acts.[68] The evidence of only five clerical wills is meager, but those contrasting wills point up a basic problem faced by the clergy and the institutional church in early Tudor England: one wayward priest out of five overshadowed the goodness of the other four and made the institutional church vulnerable to the charges of reformers.

Colchester and the Larger Church

As part of the larger Western Christian church headed by the pope in Rome, the Colchester churches were at the bottom of the hierarchical structure within the English church. Under the oversight of the archbishop at Canterbury, the bishop of London headed the diocese of London, in which Colchester was situated. Many pre-Reformation Colchester testators left small amounts to St. Paul's, their cathedral church in London, so they were certainly aware of the connection. In his first year of office and in every third subsequent year, a bishop was directed to carry out an official visitation of his diocese, but the people probably saw

---

66. Wills of J. Adam (1491), PRO 7 Vox; J. Longe (1504), PRO 8 Holgrave; J. Dey (1520), ERO D/ACR2/102; R. Caumond (1535), PRO 27 Hogen; J. Raynolde (1537), ERO D/ABW31/24.

67. Supervisor: wills of J. Tyall (1500), printed in G. Montagu Benton, ed., "Essex Wills at Canterbury," *TEAS,* n.s., 21 (1937): 260–61; A. Bownde (1508), PRO 8 Bennett; R. Cowbridge (1513), PRO 22 Fetiplace; R. Northern (1525), ERO D/ACR2/190. Executor: wills of J. Stanford (1501), ERO D/ACR1/28; R. Heynes (by 1508), ERO D/ACR1/133 (see CR84/10); A. Piggisley (1506), ERO D/ACR1/113; R. Salman (1533), ERO D/ACR2/262.

68. For receiving stolen goods, CR96/13; rape, CR100/9d; continuing fornication, CR104/2d, 5; illegally holding land and houses, CR104/5d.

little of their bishop, for he could appoint a suffragan bishop if he needed to be absent or was hampered by age or ill health.[69]

More in contact with the parish churches was the archdeacon. For administrative purposes, every diocese was divided into large districts, each one under an archdeacon, with the diocese of London having five archdeaconries: London, Essex, Middlesex, Colchester, and St. Alban's. The archdeacon of Colchester had direct control over the ecclesiastical structure in Colchester and the surrounding northeastern area of the county of Essex, though judicial decisions were always subject to appeal to the bishop. The archdeacon of Colchester, whose work was both administrative and judicial, conducted two yearly visits to Colchester, which were primarily inquisitory and administrative, to ensure that the church fabric and church property were kept in good repair and that the church had the proper utensils, books, and records; that the licenses of clergy, schoolmasters, and physicians were valid; that the incumbent carried out his duties; and that both the clergy and the laity conformed to good moral standards. The judicial function of the archdeacon was performed through regular sessions of the archidiaconal court, often with the archdeacon's appointed assistant, the Official, presiding. Such sessions might be held as often as every three weeks, usually at St. Peter's Church in the Elizabethan period (most of the Colchester archdeaconry court records date from 1569), handling testamentary business, disciplinary prosecutions, causes of litigation, and even the granting of marriage licenses. The archdeaconry court also held ad hoc sessions as needed, in which case the archdeacon himself might preside. Both clergy and laity used the ecclesiastical court to bring disputes for redress; for example, clergy could sue laymen for failure to pay tithes, and laymen could bring cases involving marriage and family disputes, probate problems, and slander and defamation.[70]

---

69. Alexander, *Religion*, 17–18; Dickinson, *Later Middle Ages*, 166–68.

70. Anglin, "Court," 11, 16, 31, 59, 65–67; Hart, *Pew*, 63; Dickinson, *Later Middle Ages*, 179–82; Rodes, *Administration*, 103. For a description of the ecclesiastical court system, see Martin Ingram, *Church Courts, Sex, and Marriage in England, 1570–1640* (Cambridge: Cambridge University Press, 1987); Ralph A. Houlbrooke, *Church Courts and the People during the English Reformation, 1520–1570* (Oxford: Oxford University Press, 1979); and Christopher Hill, *Society and Puritanism*, 2d ed. (New York: Schocken Books, 1967), 298–381. For a good description of the visitation process, see John Addy, "The Archdeacon and Ecclesiastical Discipline in Yorkshire, 1598–1714: Clergy and Churchwardens," *Borthwick Papers* 24 (1963): 9–12. See Oxley, 38–43, for biographical details of the bishops of London and the archdeacons of Colchester in the early Tudor period; see also Newcourt, 1:83–84.

Though the archdeaconry court served a useful function, it was also seen as intrusive, as implied by the popular name sometimes given it because of its concern with adultery and fornication, that is, "the bawdy court." The archdeaconry court was only doing its duty in Colchester in 1545 when it was revealed that John Case stayed away from church and kept a wench "beside his wife." Whether the court was respected or not depended much on the character and competence of the archdeacon and his assistants.[71] The court was periodically subject to criticism, and Elizabethan Puritans tried to do away with it altogether.

The church was at the center of Colchester life, and it seemed as if it would last forever. But the church was vulnerable to the charges made by reformers that certain practices and beliefs did not follow biblical teaching, and problems in the church only added to the arguments of the reformers. Most obvious was the immoral behavior of some of the clergy, but even more crucial was the poor financial base of the Colchester churches, which made them subject to pluralism and absenteeism, and which too often resulted in the clergy's engagement in sharp business practices and involvement in petty quarrels over tithes. Also preparing the way for King Henry's reforms was an underground movement, Lollardy, as well as traditional lay piety. Eventually, the religious way of life in Colchester would be drastically altered.

---

71. Dickinson, *Later Middle Ages,* 180; Oxley, 146.

4

Traditional Lay Piety and Lollardy—
A Potent Mixture

Around 1500, a Venetian observer wrote about the English—though he might easily have been describing Colchester—"nor do they omit any form incumbent upon good Christians; there are, however, many who have various opinions concerning religion."[1] The Christian faith in Colchester was strong and healthy. Many testators were zealous in their provision for prayers and pious deeds; yet problems in the institutional church and among the clergy would be grist in the mill of reform. This chapter explores three conditions that made Reformation ideas and practices attractive to Colchester laity. First was traditional piety, especially its expression in the involvement of the laity in setting up chantries, in service as churchwardens and executors, and in lay associations of piety, especially guilds, which helped to ready the laity for the Protestant emphasis on the priesthood of all believers. Second was the role of the town leaders in the religious life of Catholic Colchester, which set a pattern that made it easier for the Elizabethan governors to intensify their involvement in the religion of the town. Last was Lollardy, which, with its emphasis on the English Bible and its negation of many Catholic practices, prepared the ground for the Protestant emphasis on the authority of the Word and for the rejection of anything considered unbiblical.

Lollardy was admittedly radical, but traditional piety, though seemingly quite conservative, had the potential of planting the seed of change, especially in the town, where urban lay piety was slowly transforming the ideal of monastic separation from the world into an affirmation of the spirituality of the layperson who lived and worked in the world. It was a theme that the Protestant Reformation would openly develop. Though orthodox religion maintained much of its strength in Colchester, the radical sympathy of the borough, even among the town leaders, was shown

---

1. *A Relation, or Rather a True Account, of the Island of England,* 23.

by its reaction to the investigation of Colchester Lollardy in the 1520s, when the town court began going beyond its usual bounds by calling the local clergy to task for its sexual immorality. Colchester was fertile ground for reform, with traditional lay piety and especially Lollardy contributing to the zeal for renewal and change.

Involvement of the Laity in Traditional Religion

The history of the English church has showed time and again that the church was not the hierarchy, the priests, or the building; it was the people. It was the parishioners who had endowed the parish churches so that they could afford to pay a priest; it was the parishioners who had built the church buildings; and it was the parishioners who maintained most of the property. This section looks at the continuing lay piety in early Tudor Colchester as it was manifested in the bequests in wills, in the control exercised by the laity over the hiring of chantry priests and in guilds, and in the roles of two groups of laity: churchwardens and executors of wills, whose combined efforts in the administration of good works and prayers were substantial.

Lay Piety in Wills

In an age that stressed certain works for the release of the soul from purgatory and for the attainment of salvation, the last wills and testaments of Catholic Colchester give some indication of the commitment, energies, and resources devoted to God. Undoubtedly, some of the marks of piety manifested in the wills reflected only conventional ideals of devotion rather than personal holiness, yet pious deeds were a reflection of accepted standards of piety and indicated the value placed on piety. The works of charity, provisions for prayers, and other indicators of piety have been charted in the 203 lay wills of early Tudor Colchester, from 1485 to 1529 (see table 1).[2] The rapidity of probate after the writing of

---

2. There are seven earlier Colchester wills, but this study uses the wills dating only from 1485. Three clerics also made wills in this period. Most of the Colchester wills were proved in the court of the archdeacon of Colchester, but those records only began in 1500, so many more wills are extant from 1500 on, making them more of a reflection of the attitudes of the total population than are the fewer number of wills dating from 1485 to 1499. Most of the early wills were enrolled in the Prerogative Court of Canterbury, so those sixteen testators were from a higher social and economic stratum than the general will-making population.

TABLE 1. Indicators of Piety in Lay Wills, 1485–1529

| Years | No. of Wills | Bequest for Prayers (includes guilds and chantries) | Charitable Benefactions | | | Mention of a Specific Clergyman | Owned Religious Artifact or Book (not a Bible) | Godchildren (only the unrelated) |
			Poor, hospitals almshouses, prisoners	To the community	Parish church or religious house* (fabric or furnishing)			
1485–99	16	15 94%	10 63%	6 38%	15 94%	13 81%	0	1
1500–1509	81	51 63%	21 26%	6 7%	38 47%	49 61%	2 3%	1
1510–19	64	47 73%	18 28%	4 6%	25 39%	43 67%	2 3%	5 8%
1520–29	42	22 52%	16 38%	1 2%	11 26%	22 52%	0	5 8%
Total	203	135 67%	65 32%	17 8%	89 44%	127 63%	4 2%	12 6%

*Excludes bequests to the high altar for tithes or offerings. Many testators gave in more than one category.

a will shows that wills were almost always drawn up on the deathbed, so they are as honest a group of documents as one can expect to find, for they are concerned with what the testator found to be of ultimate importance in life. Wills cannot give a complete picture,[3] yet they provide a glimpse into the psyche and values of the will-making population. Skepticism about the use of wills has been most often leveled against the attempt to measure religious thinking;[4] nevertheless, wills remain a valu-

---

The wills from the archdeaconry court are housed in the Essex Record Office in Chelmsford, and the wills from the Prerogative Court of Canterbury are at the Public Record Office in London. Six of the early wills were published in Benton, "Essex Wills."

3. Not everyone made a will, and married women, children, prisoners, traitors, heretics, and those of unsound mind generally were not permitted to do so, although a few married women in Colchester made wills with the consent of their husbands. The majority of testators, 81 percent of the 203 testators in Colchester between 1485 and 1529, were males; see Laquita M. Higgs, "Wills and Religious Mentality in Tudor Colchester," *EAH* 22 (1991): 88. Thrupp, *Merchant Class,* 109, found that London testators were above the average in wealth, but Margaret Spufford, "Peasant Inheritance Customs and Land Distribution in Cambridgeshire from the Sixteenth to the Eighteenth Centuries," in *Family and Inheritance,* ed. Jack Goody, Joan Thirsk, and E. P. Thompson (Cambridge: Cambridge University Press, 1976), 169–71, found that the poorer groups produced the most wills in Cambridgeshire. Robert S. Gottfried, "Bury St. Edmunds and the Populations of Late Medieval English Towns, 1270–1530," *JBS* 20 (1980): 8, determined that the testamentary population in Bury St. Edmunds was also very broadly based. Using the categories set forth in Gottfried's *Bury St. Edmunds and the Urban Crisis, 1290–1539* (Princeton: Princeton University Press, 1982), 127, my charting of the bequests to the high altar show that 53 percent of the testators gave only 20d. or less, verifying that the lower economic groups in Colchester indeed made wills, though with the realization that bequests to the high altar were not always an accurate measure of wealth.

4. The pioneering studies of Wilbur K. Jordan, *Philanthropy in England, 1480–1660* (New York: Russell Sage, 1959), and A. G. Dickens, *Lollards and Protestants in the Diocese of York, 1509–1558* (London: Oxford University Press, 1959), have been subject to much criticism, but they were valuable beginning points. It has been argued that wills only reflect the thinking of the writer of the will, often a cleric who might have a vested interest in promoting pious bequests; but in Colchester the dying testator had other choices, such as an attorney or notary, and a few testators wrote their own wills. I found that 55 percent of the lay wills from 1500 to 1529 listed a cleric witness who was possibly the writer, though the cleric may have been there simply to administer the last rites while someone else wrote the will. Another cited problem is that the wills may possibly draw a picture of a greater percentage of pious people than was actually the case, since the desire to provide for prayers or for the giving of alms was one of the motives for making a will. On problems in the use of wills, see Peter Heath, "Urban Piety in the Later Middle Ages: The Evidence of Hull Wills," in *The Church, Politics, and Patronage in the Fifteenth Century,* ed. R. Barrie Dobson (New York: St. Martin's Press, 1984), 212–13; Clive Burgess, "Late Medieval Wills and Pious Convention: Testamentary Evidence Reconsidered," in *Profit, Piety, and the Professions in Later Medieval England,* ed. Michael Hicks (Gloucester: Allen Sutton, 1990), 14–33. In defense of the use of wills, see Duffy, *Traditional Religion,* 355; and J. J. Scarisbrick, *The Reformation and the English People* (Oxford: Basil Blackwell, 1984), 11–12.

able clue to the importance placed on certain beliefs, actions, and institutions.

The most ubiquitous and the most Catholic of indicators of piety was the request for prayers for the soul after death, whether said in a parish church, in a religious house, or by the laity. As table 1 shows, 67 percent of pre-Reformation Colchester testators wanted such prayers. The belief behind the zeal to provide for prayers had to do with the doctrine of purgatory; according to that belief, even the person who died in a state of grace was not yet pure enough to enjoy the glories of heaven and so must be purged from the stains of sin by the sufferings in the intermediate state called purgatory. Happily, the suffering in purgatory could be lessened and shortened by good works and by the prayers of others, as John Tey explained when he asked that prayers for his soul be said quickly after his death, with the purpose "that my soul through prayer may be the sooner succoured and relieved."[5] The problem with the doctrine of purgatory was that it was vulnerable to the charge of the Reformers that it was not a biblical doctrine and that salvation depended on the mercy and grace of God rather than on the "works salvation" that the many provisions for prayer and good deeds implied. Prayers in the parish church were especially valued by testators, with 118 (58 percent) wanting additional prayers in the parish church, even though every Christian had prayers said at burial. The single most popular type of prayer was the obit, or anniversary mass, requested by forty-nine testators. The obit had the advantage of being affordable to many people, since it could be elaborate or spartan, as resources required. To supplement entreaties for the soul in the parish church, the testator might also commission prayers in religious houses, as fifty-seven testators did; however, most did not rely exclusively on the prayers of friars and monks. Twelve testators also turned to the poor laity for prayers, leaving money to the poor with the proviso that they were to pray for the soul of the donor. Prayers of the poor were thought to have exceptional influence with God, whose son was once a poor man. With so much attention given to the provision of prayers to aid in the release from the sufferings of purgatory, there was a heavy investment in the dead. Unhappily, the doctrine of purgatory, with its

---

5. PRO 17 Hogen. For history of the doctrine of purgatory, see the early work by Thomas Wright, *St. Patrick's Purgatory* (1844); Jacques LeGoff, *The Birth of Purgatory* (Chicago: University of Chicago Press, 1984); Lionel Rothkrug, "Popular Religion and Holy Shrines," in *Religion and the People, 800–1700*, ed. James Obelkevich (Chapel Hill: University of North Carolina Press, 1979), 32–40; Duffy, *Traditional Religion*, 338–47.

TABLE 2. Levels of Religious Concern, 1485–1603

Years	No. of Wills	Ratings						
		0 No Religious Concern	1 Nominally Religious	2 Moderately Pious	3 Above Average in Piety	4 Highly Pious	5 Extremely Pious
Catholic Years								
1485–99	16				1 6%	3 19%	12 75%	
1500–1509	81		11 14%	14 17%	26 32%	16 20%	14 17%	
1510–19	64		4 6%	16 25%	19 30%	9 14%	16 25%	
1520–29	42		4 10%	11 26%	17 40%	6 14%	4 10%	
Total: 1485–1529	203		19 9%	41 20%	63 31%	34 17%	46 23%	
Transition Years								
1530–39	58		15 26%	19 33%	10 17%	9 15.5%	5 9%	
1540–49	68		15 22%	27 40%	20 29%	2 3%	4 6%	
1550–59	92	1 1%	49 53%	25 27%	13 14%	4 4%	0 0%	
Total: 1530–59	218	1 0.5%	79 36%	71 33%	43 20%	15 7%	9 4%	
Protestant Years								
1560–69	75	3 4%	22 29%	33 44%	9 12%	4 5%	4 5%	
1570–79	107	2 2%	39 36%	32 30%	18 17%	8 7.5%	8 7.5%	
1580–89	126	4 3%	30 24%	41 33%	25 20%	18 14%	8 6%	
1590–99	134	8 6%	36 27%	31 23%	22 16%	18 13%	19 14%	
1600–1603	65	2 3%	20 31%	16 25%	18 28%	8 12%	1 2%	
Total: 1560–1603	507	19 4%	147 29%	153 30%	92 18%	56 11%	40 8%	
Total Tudor Period: 1485–1603	928	20 2%	245 26%	265 29%	198 21%	105 11%	95 10%	

Note: A "0" rating was given to any testator who gave no indication of religion whatsoever, and a "1" was given to those exhibiting only the marks of a conventional religion found in most wills of the period, such as the religious preamble and the bequest to the high altar. Points were garnered from the indicators, with each indicator conferring a point on the chart for the testator, but allowance was made if an indicator went far beyond the expectations of ordinary piety, in which case two points (but no more) were given. Points from the indicators were then added to the basic "1" of nominal religiosity, up to the score of "5." Thus, a "2" marks an average, or moderately pious, testator; a "3" an above average testator; a "4" a highly pious testator; and a "5" a testator with the highest concern for piety.

dependence on a kind of salvation by works, left the devoted often wondering if they had done enough, particularly when they had the resources for doing more. Many of their bequests went into charitable benefactions.

Charitable bequests were made by 113 testators, somewhat less than the 135 testators wanting prayers. Almsgiving to the poor, who could not repay the favor, was the highest form of charity and was favored by sixty-five testators, but more popular was giving to the parish church, with eighty-one testators leaving money for repair, rebuilding, or new furnishings. Also included were benefactions to the community, with the most popular being for the repair of highways (sixteen testators)—in Richard Ball's descriptive phrase, for the "reparation of fowle waies."[6] For the townspeople, it was all right to make money as long as it was used in the right way, in which case money could help achieve salvation and win a home in heaven.

By charting the bequests for prayers and charity, as well as other indicators of piety (such as the ownership of a religious artifact or book, the mentioning of specific clergymen, or having godchildren who were not related), I have outlined in table 2 the level of religious concern shown in the wills. The table shows that all testators in Catholic Colchester were at least nominally religious, whereas the later Protestant years spawned a few testators who seemingly had no concern for religion. At the other end of the scale, the first forty-four years of the Tudor period had a high number of its testators, 23 percent, who were extremely pious, but a more accurate figure is obtained from the wills from 1500 onward, when the wills were more broadly based,[7] with an average percentage of the extremely pious at 17 percent. Most testators, over 50 percent, were in the broad middle range of the moderately pious and the above average in piety.

Traditional religion was obviously an important force in Colchester, yet there is some evidence that Colchester was less traditional and less reliant on the clergy than some other towns were. Norman Tanner's study of Norwich wills is especially helpful in making a comparison. For example, 13 percent of Colchester testators named a cleric as an executor or supervisor of their wills, whereas between 25 and 33 percent of Norwich testators did so, and most of the Colchester clerics named were for

---

6. PRO 15 Horne.
7. Because the wills dated before 1500 were lost from the court of the archdeacon of Colchester.

the post of supervisor, an advisory position only, rather than executor.[8] In Norwich, between 10 and 11 percent of sons mentioned in wills were secular or regular priests, but only 4 percent of those mentioned in Colchester wills were, another sign that Colchester people were not so close to the institutional church and its clergy as were the people of Norwich.[9] Compared to Norwich, Colchester wills showed less devotion to votive lights and to prayers for the dead, and there was less support of the friars in Colchester than in Norwich, York, or London.[10] On the whole, Colchester was apparently less traditional; nevertheless, it is safe to assume that faith remained a significant part of the mental world of Catholic Colchester. It was too integral to the ordinary life of the people to be left only in the hands of the clergy.

Control over the Chantries and Guilds

The laity exercised a large measure of control over chantries, with the donor giving detailed instructions about the kind of person to be hired and the kind of prayers wanted. Only the wealthy could afford to set up a perpetual chantry, but the moderately prosperous could arrange for the employment of a stipendiary priest for a set period of time, as forty testators did in early Tudor Colchester, making that method of praying for the dead in the parish church second only to obits in popularity. The enthusiasm for chantry priests must have been, at least partially, the product of the donor's being able to have some power over the process.

Even more elaborate in organization were the cooperative chantries, the religious guilds or fraternities that encompassed a broad range of people and were especially popular in towns. The laity exercised extensive authority over the guilds, hiring their own priests and determining the kind, place, and frequency of services. Several towns have been described as having guilds in every parish church in town,[11] and references in the wills and other records indicate that most of the sixteen

---

8. Tanner, *Norwich*, 126. Nine Colchester clerics were named as executor, and only two of those were sole executors.

9. Tanner, *Norwich*, 25; in Colchester there were only 6 clerical sons among the 135 sons definitely named in the wills from 1485 to 1529.

10. Tanner, *Norwich*, 104–5, 118–19; John A. F. Thomson, "Piety and Charity in Late Medieval London," *JEccH* 16 (1965): 189–90, 192; Palliser, *York*, 227.

11. Alan Rogers, "Late Medieval Stamford," in *Perspectives in English Urban History*, ed. Alan Everitt (New York: Harper and Row, 1973), 33; Palliser, *York*, 231; Colin Platt, *The English Medieval Town* (London: Book Club Associates, 1976), 164; Scarisbrick, *Reformation*, 24; Duffy, *Traditional Religion*, 114.

parish churches in Colchester had a guild at one time.[12] The parish guilds in Colchester were apparently very much in the business of praying for the deceased, both at burial and at obit time.[13] Half of the references to guilds named the Guild of Jesus Mass in St. Peter's Church, which seemed to be fully organized into a cooperative chantry, with the guild having its own chapel in the church, including an altar, images of Jesus and Mary, and large torches and smaller lights that were burned at burials, on Sundays, on holy days, and on Fridays at the elevation of the eucharistic bread. Probably all members of the guild were expected to attend the Friday mass in honor of the name of Jesus, at which time the guild chaplain would also celebrate obits for deceased guild members.[14] The guild seemed to be self-governed and independent of clerical control, as the two listings of the masters or governors of the guild in the borough court records show them to be laymen who were busy taking care of the affairs of the guild, selling inherited property, and even leasing water rights. The voluntary lay association of the guild was a means of expressing the laity's devotion to God, in a setting largely controlled by themselves, though in the context of the church.[15]

---

12. Mentioned only once were the Guild of St. James "in the old hithe" (ERO D/ACR1/101); St. Leonard's Guild (PRO 40 Milles); the Guild of St. Mary's Chapel in St. Botolph's (PRO 20 Milles); Trinity Guild, probably in Holy Trinity (ERO D/ACR1/200); the Guild of St. Katherine in the parish of St. Mary Magdalen (CR93/6); and the Guild of St. John the Baptist in St. Runwald's Church. Mentioned twice were the Guild of the Mass of Jesus in St. Nicholas (PRO 12 Godyn and ERO D/ACR1/205; ERO D/ACR1/200 mentions St. Nicholas Guild) and the Guild of St. Barbara in All Saints' Church (ERO D/ACR1/127, in the wills of John Barker and Roger Burgon). Mentioned in the 1525 subsidy assessment (PRO E179/108/169) were the Guilds of St. Anne and of St. James in St. James's Church, the Guild of St. Barbara in St. Peter's Church, and the Guild of St. John the Baptist in St. Runwald's Church.

13. Out of the twenty-five wills that mentioned guilds, only two, those of M. Barty (1513; ERO D/ACR2/9) and P. Borow (1512; ERO D/ACR1/205), left money both to a guild and for an obit in their parish churches, indicating that the testators were relying on the prayers of the guilds. Three other wills left money for both an obit and a guild, but in each case the guild was in a parish church other than their own. There is no indication that the guilds were mutual benefit or "friendly" societies.

14. Herbert Francis Westlake, The Parish Gilds of Mediaeval England (New York: Macmillan, 1919), 44. Especially helpful were the wills of R. Hervy (PRO 17 Milles), W. Bownde (1508; PRO 8 Bennett), and R. Norman (1518; ERO D/ACR2/91). See also Duffy, Traditional Religion, 115–16; Wood-Legh, Chantries, 288; Scarisbrick, Reformation, chapter 4. The Guild of Jesus Mass was also called the Guild of St. John's in earlier records; see Morant, 2:51, and the will of N. Cooke (1502; ERO D/ACR1/51).

15. CR91/11d; CR116/13; Gervase Rosser, "Communities of Parish and Guild in the Late Middle Ages," in Parish, Church, and People: Local Studies in Lay Religion, 1350–1750, ed. Susan J. Wright (London: Hutchinson, 1988), 32–38.

Churchwardens

The laity were entrusted with much of the administration of pious deeds, and one of the groups relied on were the annually elected lay churchwardens, usually two in every parish church. Two testators with no family named their churchwardens as executors of their wills,[16] but more often wardens were named as recipients of money, property, or animals bequeathed to the church, since the wardens were the legal guardians of all parochial church property. Some of the bequests handled by churchwardens were relatively simple: Margaret Barty wanted "two kine bought and delivered to the churchwardens of St. Giles to maintain the light of St. Anthony perpetual." Other legacies required more work: two women left houses to the churchwardens of St. Leonard's parish to be used as almshouses, which meant that the wardens would have to select poor people to live in the houses and would have to keep the houses in repair.[17] An even greater trust was placed in the wardens by ten testators who depended on the wardens to supervise the continuation of prayers in obits, or anniversary masses for the repose of the souls of the deceased. Even John Dey, a chantry priest at St. Leonard's Church, entrusted the wardens to keep his annual commemoration with the yearly rent from a house, and the more prosperous William Breton wanted obits kept for himself and six relatives with the yearly profits from lands in Wivenhoe, but he was thoughtful enough to pay the wardens 8d. annually for their trouble.[18]

Executors

Testators placed the greatest confidence in the executors of wills for the implementation of pious deeds and prayers. Naming an executor was legally mandated, for if no executor was named, the testator was considered to have died intestate. Most testators named their closest family members as executors, so a preponderate number of executors were laypeople. In the 198 wills whose executors are known, 295 executors were named, with only 9 of them being clerics. Of the 295 executors, 178 were first-order kin (wives, sons, brothers, daughters, mothers, and hus-

16. ERO D/ACR2/1; ERO D/ACR2/91.
17. ERO D/ACR2/9; ERO D/ABW21/1; PRO 3 Fetiplace.
18. ERO D/ACR2/102; PRO 39 Horne.

bands), and 28 were affines (related by marriage) or other relatives, with a total of 206 executors, or 70 percent, who were relatives. A high degree of confidence was placed in wives, as 122 were named executors and 78 of those were sole executors.[19]

Not only did executors handle secular legacies, but they were repeatedly mentioned as being responsible for administering varied spiritual business for the testator. Margaret Bayly bequeathed to her parish church "a cloth of silk with the picture of All Hallows therein and to be bought by my executors." Elizabeth Harmanson left £26 "to one priest or to students in the university [Cambridge] after the discretion of mine executors," and the will of her husband, beer brewer Edmund Harmanson, designated "to the Cross Friars £10 to be paid by my executors as they see their reparations done or else none." Testators were especially careful to put laypeople in charge of prayers that were to take place over a period of time; for example, George Aleyn wrote "that my executors shall cause to be sung for my soul every year during the term of five years, every quarter of a year a trental, paying for every trental 10s. and then to distribute to poor and needy people every quarter . . . with every trental 3s. 4d."[20] The giving of alms was almost completely handled by laypeople, especially if the alms were to be given weekly. Thomas Christmas kept his executors very busy, directing "that my executors and their executors for twenty years after my decease do every Friday distribute to twelve lame, poor, and needy persons in Colchester and the twelve poor persons shall every Friday come to St. John's monastery to devoutly hear mass and prayer for my soul about my tomb, 12d.," and also directing his executors "to distribute every Friday for twenty years to the prisoners of the castle in meat and drink, 12d."[21] Whether relatives, churchwardens, or trusted friends, the lay executors epitomized the reliance of the laity on one another rather than on the clergy. They were accustomed to handling a substantial part of the spiritual business of Catholic Colchester; it was a trend that blended well with Luther's doctrine of the priest-

---

19. Actually the number of relatives was probably higher, since the relationships were not always designated. See Anthony J. Camp, *Wills and Their Whereabouts*, 4th ed. (London, 1974), xv. On women as executors, see Rowena E. Archer and B. E. Ferme, "Testamentary Procedure with Special Reference to the Executrix," *Reading Medieval Studies* 15 (1989): 3–34.

20. ERO D/ACR1/106; PRO 1 Adeane; PRO 8 Blamyr; PRO 1 Fetiplace.

21. PRO 28 Ayloffe. Four other Colchester testators left money for weekly almsgiving: J. Salough (1511; PRO 3 Fetiplace), W. Wheler (1493; PRO 24 Doggett), M. Aleyn (1511; PRO 3 Fetiplace), and A. Norman (1523; ERO D/ACR2/153).

hood of all believers and Calvin's emphasis on the governance of the church by both laity and ministers.

Involvement of Town Leaders in Religious Matters

With religion being so much a part of everyday life in Colchester, there was no anomaly in secular governors taking a role in religious matters in the town, and as their own wills show, many of them valued pious works. Of the fourteen aldermanic wills from 1500 to 1529, eight wills, or 57 percent, showed a high degree of interest in piety or pious deeds, with five aldermen having only a moderate interest, and with only one being merely perfunctory in his mention of religion. Town leaders and their families were not shy about being seen to be religious; for example, a memorial brass in St. Peter's Church depicts Alderman John Sayer, whose will is not extant, at prayer with his family (see fig. 3). By using red enamel, the craftsman showed Sayer, who died in 1509, proudly wearing his robe of office—a long, fur-trimmed scarlet aldermanic gown, complete with a tippet draped around his neck.

Fig. 3. A memorial brass in St. Peter's Church depicting Alderman John Sayer and his family at prayer; made after Sayer's wife died in 1530.

The leaders of Colchester had, at least by the fourteenth century, developed a tradition of religious responsibility in the town, a tradition that would reach a climax in the hiring of the town preacher during Elizabeth's reign. The founders of the three earliest chantries in Colchester, all in the fourteenth century, designated the two annually elected bailiffs, the highest officers in the town, as the holders of the advowson of each of the chantries, thus giving the bailiffs the continuing right to present the chantry chaplains. One chantry, the well-endowed Elianore Chantry, was housed in the church of St. Mary-at-Wall, and the other two chantries were in the ancient St. Helen's Chapel in Maidenborough Street, as the first chantry had been partially endowed with the chapel itself and the land on which it stood. The second chantry in St. Helen's Chapel, established in the will of Richolda, widow of Richard de Cosford, was challenged by Chancery Court officials, but the case was successfully pleaded on the grounds that the custom of Colchester allowed lands and tenements to be devised by will. Thus, the ancient liberties enjoyed by Colchester permitted a greater involvement of its leaders in religious matters. Richolda had astutely given the bailiffs and commonalty a vested interest in the chantry by inserting the clause that the chantry priest was to pray not only for her and her husband but for the bailiffs and the commonalty as well.[22]

Three other leading citizens of the town established perpetual chantries in the first half of the fifteenth century, but they gave the right to present chaplains to the Fraternity and Guild of St. Helen, which was incorporated by a charter issued by Henry IV in 1407. Named after the patron saint of the borough, the guild was composed of leading townsmen and local gentry. The guild established its own chantry, called the Holy Cross, and having obtained possession of the chapel of the decayed hospital of the Crutched Friars, the guild founded there a chantry of five chaplains, including its own chantry of the Holy Cross, and incorporating the three chantry foundations established in the early fifteenth century. The guild also provided for the maintenance of thirteen poor men to pray for the king and for the brothers and sisters of the guild. The town leaders, then, were directly or indirectly in control of all seven perpetual chantries established in fourteenth- and early fifteenth-century Colchester. Right up to the dissolution of the chantries, the bailiffs continued to present chaplains to the Elianore Chantry in the church of St.

---

22. See appendix 7; Morant, 2:45–48.

Mary-at-Wall and to those in St. Helen's Chapel, and they shared control over the other chantries with members of the Guild of St. Helen. Their continuing presentations of chantry chaplains represented a kind of extraecclesiastical jurisdiction within the town.[23]

In 1496, the Crutched Friars were reinstated to their house, and a portion of the chantry lands and duties was delegated by the guild to the friars. By that time the Guild of St. Helen seemed not to have had as its primary role the provision of prayers for the dead, or if that provision was primary, it was not appealing to testators, as only two mentioned the guild.[24] The guild seemed to have become a fraternal society, a change that had occurred in several towns. In 1491 the guild had eighty-seven members, among them the abbot of St. John's Abbey and local gentry, and if they were like similar guilds in other towns, they would have participated in borough ceremonial and had elaborate annual feasts. Membership in the town guild gave outsiders a role in the town and established good contacts for the burgesses. A like guild in Stratford had four general meetings a year as well as an annual guild mass and dinner after Easter, on which occasion all guild members wore a common livery and processed through the town to the feast. In some towns the town guild was a kind of surrogate town council, but Colchester's well-established borough governance had precluded the dependence on guilds that some towns experienced; nevertheless, Colchester's town guild would have served the purpose of affirming the status and enhancing the reputation of the town and its leaders, as well as helping to maintain harmonious relationships among the rulers of the town.[25]

Not only were the town leaders supervising the perpetual chantries, but in various other ways they were encouraging religion in the town. From 1349 to 1508 the bailiffs and commonalty granted to Holy Trinity Church a dwelling house for the rector, thus assisting one of the older

---

23. Morant, 2:41–42, 48–50; *VCH Essex*, 2:181; R. N. Swanson, *Church and Society in Late Medieval England* (Oxford: Basil Blackwell, 1989), 257. The 1407 license says that St. Helen's Guild was founded anew; see Morant, 3:11. The continuing presentations of chantry chaplains by the bailiffs may be found in the registers of the bishop of London (Guildhall MSS 9531). Brown, *Popular Piety*, 175, 181, 189, 200–201, found that in the diocese of Salisbury, corporate bodies were also overseeing obits, almshouses, and hospitals.

24. *VCH Essex*, 2:181 and 9:64; PRO 40 Milles; ERO D/ACR2/44.

25. Morant, 2:42; Cutts, *Colchester*, 102–3; Rosser, "Parish and Guild," 32–34; Ben R. McRee, "Religious Gilds and Civic Order: The Case of Norwich in the Late Middle Ages," *Speculum* 67 (1992): 95–97; Scarisbrick, *Reformation*, 21–24.

parishes in the heart of town, and the help of the bailiffs was essential for the reestablishment of the Crossed Friars at the end of the fifteenth century. In 1516 the town leaders used their connection with the Crossed Friars to establish a special annual mass to be celebrated for the prosperity of the town; a piece of land adjacent to the priory was granted to the Crossed Friars on the condition that the Prior and his successors celebrate yearly in their church, "at an altar, *de skala celi* there, a solemn mass" on Monday after Hokeday, *"pro salutari prosperitate ville."* The bailiffs also administered at least one anniversary mass for the repose of the soul; in 1523 Robert Everard entrusted the bailiffs to oversee his obit in perpetuity.[26] The town governors thus had a tradition of assuming some responsibility for spiritual matters in the town; Elizabethan town leaders would assume a much greater role, but their involvement did not arise out of a vacuum.

Evidence of a Radical Religious Culture: Lollards and Anticlericalism

Lay involvement in religion, including that of the town leaders, was one of the preconditions that made the coming religious changes more acceptable in Colchester than in many other places, but evidence of a more radical religious culture was to be found in the presence of Colchester Lollards, who even had sympathizers among the town leaders. Also, when the Lollards were under attack in the 1520s, there was a surge of anticlericalism, often mentioned as a possible sign of the readiness for reform.

Lollards must have been at least partially responsible for the less traditional religious culture evident in Colchester, for Lollards had been in the borough long enough for their teachings to have taken deep root. In 1429, exactly a hundred years before the Reformation Parliament began its work, a Colchester Lollard, tailor William Chiveling, was condemned by church officials in a heresy trial at St. Nicholas's Church. Since the church could not enforce capital punishment, Chiveling was committed to the custody of the Colchester bailiffs, who quickly obtained a writ from the king to burn the tailor in front of Colchester Castle. Heresy was whatever the church defined it to be, so anyone who willfully defied church teachings could be condemned as a heretic, though it was the duty

---

26. Morant, 2:12, 42, 53–54; *VCH Essex,* 2:181; *OB,* 144; CR87/11.

of the church to try to dissuade the person from heretical thinking before condemnation. Ecclesiastical officials were obviously feeling that the social order was threatened by the Lollard heresy; only the year before the unfortunate tailor's burning in Colchester, John Wycliffe's body had been disinterred from its grave in Lutterworth churchyard and burned, so the authorities were determined to do all that they could to stamp out Lollardy.[27]

Chiveling was not the first Lollard to be linked with the borough of Colchester, as is shown by the early history of Lollardy. Followers of the teachings of the Oxford don John Wycliffe were derisively called Lollards, a term coming from the Dutch word meaning "mumbler" or "mutterer" of prayers. Despite the contemptuous label, the teachings had at first appealed to some of the leading gentry, but all of that changed when the tide of nonconformist thinking was forcibly checked by the events provoked by Sir John Oldcastle, the earlier boon companion of King Henry V. After being tried and convicted of heresy because of his Lollard beliefs, Oldcastle was imprisoned in the Tower of London in the autumn of 1413, but he escaped and was joined by insurgent groups of Lollards who, according to official reports, were prepared to overthrow the nobility and church hierarchy. In early 1414, the king easily scattered the gathering Lollards, and Oldcastle remained in hiding until his capture and execution by burning three years later. Official investigations uncovered several Lollard groups, among them one at Colchester, where the Lollards were said to have many English books that were read day and night, "secretly and openly, sometimes in company, and sometimes individually." The effects of the Oldcastle rebellion were threefold: officials thereafter viewed Lollardy as a threat to the social order of the kingdom, although Lollardy was without political leadership and so was no longer a political threat; Lollardy was subsequently without theological guidance that could ensure a measure of theological orthodoxy; and Lollardy moved even deeper underground, where it remained mostly among small farmers and lesser craftsmen, though it had occasional clerical, professional, and more prosperous adherents. Church officials became alarmed about heresy in the late 1420s, and they not only tightened up the legal process for fighting heresy but uncovered various Lollard groups. In the

---

27. *RPB,* 52–53. Information about Lollards in this and the following paragraphs is from A. G. Dickens, *The English Reformation,* rev. ed. (London: Fontana/Collins, 1967), 41–46; and John A. F. Thomson, *The Later Lollards, 1414–1520* (London: Oxford University Press, 1965), 121–26, 130, 134.

process, more was discovered in Colchester than a tailor whom officials wished to burn. For one thing, Lollard beliefs were being taught in the town by John Abraham. A tailor from Norfolk confessed that he had been "conversant, familiar, and homely with heretics . . . in the house of John Abraham, cordwainer of Colchester, [who was] keeping and holding schools of heresy." Abraham was executed in Colchester either in 1428 or 1429. Another investigation in 1430 revealed that John Fynch of Colchester had lied when being examined by a commissary of the bishop of London in Colchester two years before; Fynch had sworn falsely on a mass book that he did not believe the heresies and errors of which he was accused. Fynch's belated honesty must have saved him, but a less fortunate priest who was connected with the Colchester Lollards, William Caleys, was burned at the stake in that same year.[28]

Lollardy was not stamped out by persecution, though it remained only a shadowy presence, but Cade's rebellion in 1450 was followed by indictments that revealed Lollardy among some of the rebels who came from villages just a few miles west of Colchester. Once more Lollardy was connected with rebellion, and extreme social beliefs were indeed held by a few Lollards, such as Robert Helder from Bocking in Essex, who was reported to believe in 1450 that "all goods and chattels of every person should be common to all, and should be divided equally among all people, so that no person should have property separately."[29] For the most part, Lollards were concerned not with social reform but with perceived abuses in the church, but because of the way Lollardy evolved in the fifteenth century, Lollard beliefs were not uniform. The early theological leadership of Wycliffe and other university scholars had long disappeared; instead, beliefs developed among the people in the many informal discussions in homes and other meeting places.

Calling themselves "known men," Lollards followed Wycliffe in a desire for the Bible in English, but the fear of Lollardy prompted church authorities in 1409 to prohibit English translations unless sanctioned by a bishop. Although anyone who possessed a Bible in English was suspect, the Word was basic to Lollard beliefs. When Lollards met, it was not to pray but to read and discuss the forbidden English Scripture, although if a text was available, it was usually only a portion, such as one of the

---

28. Poos, *Essex*, 254–55, 265–67; Margaret Aston, *Lollards and Reformers* (London: Hambledon Press, 1984), 77, 81, 96–97; David Loades, *Politics, Censorship, and the English Reformation* (London: Pinter, 1991), 127; Brigden, *London*, 87.

29. Poos, *Essex*, 255–59, 267–69.

Gospels, the Ten Commandments, the Apocalypse, or one of the Epistles of Paul or James, with the latter being especially preferred by Colchester Lollards. Other writings, such as *The Prick of Conscience* or *Wycliffe's Wicket,* were also used. Portions were read aloud for those who could not read, and storytelling from the Bible was also a favorite activity. During ecclesiastical examinations, a youth told of hearing James Brewster, a Colchester carpenter, tell the story of Moses and the golden calf, as well as hearing William Sweeting tell about the conversion of Paul. Knowledge of the Scriptures was at the heart of Lollardy, and many Lollards memorized large portions.

From the Word, Lollards sought to recover a sense of the person and spirit of Jesus, but Lollard beliefs were more easily described in the negative. Lollards were opposed to the papacy, pilgrimages, the veneration of images (which they considered superstitious and idolatrous), the doctrine of transubstantiation (the belief that the Communion elements became the actual body and blood of Christ), the validity of indulgences, the necessity of a special order of priests, and auricular confession (because confessions were to be made only to God, not to priests). Some Lollards went further than others in wanting to alter the sacraments. Some opposed the baptism of infants and contended that a child should not be baptized until fourteen years of age, while others said that marriage could be solemnized without the holy church. The Norfolk man who reported in 1428 that he had been taught in Colchester believed that "only consent of love between man and woman is sufficient for the sacrament of perfect matrimony without any contract of word and without any solemnization in church," whereas other Lollards believed that a written contract, but no church ceremony, was necessary. The Lollards' antisacramentarian beliefs were logically connected with their anticlericalism. If a Christian could make contact with God without the sacramental process, the special role of the priest was unnecessary. Most threatening to the organized church was the Lollard denial of transubstantiation, the centerpiece of the mass, since that denial took away the necessity for the special role of the priest in the mysterious transformation of the eucharistic bread and wine. Lollards were convinced that the Catholic priesthood had perverted the true teachings of the Bible.[30]

Lollardy seemed to be having a revival toward the end of the fifteenth century, or perhaps the ecclesiastical authorities were again becoming

---

30. Poos, *Essex,* 268–69; Brigden, *London,* 87–88, 90–93.

zealous to stamp out the heresy. In 1505 heresy was again investigated, at which time two Lollards with connections to Colchester were before the bishop's interrogators. William Sweeting had lived and worked in the Colchester region most of his adult life. He opposed pilgrimages and the veneration of images, often chastising his wife for wasting her money and time on those useless exercises, and Sweeting also believed "that the sacrament of the priests' altar was not the present very body, but bread in substance, received in memorial of Christ." Sweeting taught his beliefs to the unlearned Colchester carpenter James Brewster, with some of the instruction occurring when Sweeting was in the fields looking after farm animals, where the literate Sweeting regularly read to others "many good things out of a certain book." Brewster was an especially apt pupil. When Sweeting and Brewster were called to London in 1505, they were imprisoned in the Tower, and perhaps it was their experience in the Lollards' Tower that persuaded them to abjure. Sweeting and Brewster were ordered to do penance in London and Colchester, with a part of the penance being the wearing of the faggot—that "infamous badge," as Protestant martyrologist John Foxe later called it—on their outer clothing for the rest of their lives. For a time they obeyed. Sweeting wore his faggot on his left sleeve for two years, but the parson of St. Mary Magdalen's Church in Colchester recruited Sweeting as his parish clerk and "plucked the badge from his sleeve." Brewster wore his faggot on his left shoulder for two years, but likewise his employer, the comptroller of the earl of Oxford, "plucked it away." Obviously the people around Sweeting and Brewster thought the punishment harsh or unfair, but the church hierarchy was not so lenient, and the bishop sentenced the two men to death. Sweeting and Brewster burned in the same fire in Smithfield in London on October 18, 1511. One of Brewster's crimes was that he carried on his person a "certain little book of Scripture in English, of an old writing almost worn for age, whose name is not there expressed," thus emphasizing the importance of Scripture to the Lollards, even if, like Brewster, they could not read.[31]

The bishop also examined a certain Thomas Man in 1511, and it was revealed that Man had preached Lollard doctrines in several counties in England, with Colchester being one of the towns in which he taught. Despite the best efforts of the bishops, heretical opinions were growing,

---

31. Foxe, 4:180–81, 214–16; Thomson, *Lollards,* 137, 162. J. W. Martin, *Religious Radicals in Tudor England* (London: Hambledon Press, 1989), 15–16.

not declining; Man and his wife were said to have converted six to seven hundred people to Lollard opinions. Man, who went to the stake in 1518, was particularly anticlerical; he was charged with calling certain priests "pilled knaves," saying "that pulpits were priests' lying stools," and believing that "the popish church was not the church of God." Striking at the heart of the sacerdotal system was Man's belief that "all holy men of his sect were only priests" and were "the true church of God," thus presaging Martin Luther's "priesthood of all believers."[32]

Undaunted by the burnings of such men, Lollards continued on. Taking Man's place as a traveling Lollard teacher was John "Father" Hacker, who was the leader of a secret London conventicle (religious meeting) of Lollards that met on Coleman Street, not far from Guildhall. Hacker's group in London had formed a kind of Lollard scriptorium, a heretical activity, and it was to Coleman Street that Lollards traveled when they wanted to buy a manuscript copy of the Scripture in English. By the late 1520s, printed texts had come on the scene, and the Lollards provided a network to promote the heretical printed book trade. William Tyndale's translation of the New Testament published at Worms began appearing in early 1526, and both Lutheran texts and Tyndale's translation found an eager market in England, including Colchester, though they had to be sold surreptitiously. Colchester Lollards later revealed that they bought in Colchester one of Tyndale's New Testaments for 4s. from a Lombard of London, and at least one man was exporting Lutheran books through the Colchester port for the London market, with smuggled New Testaments being concealed in bolts of cloth in Colchester warehouses.[33]

Though Lollards were still involved, the spread of heretical books and ideas had grown beyond the Lollard movement. Secret groups of men in London were eager to promote Scripture in the vernacular; among them were sophisticated merchants, such as Humphrey Monmouth, a wealthy draper and patron of William Tyndale. Secret cells of brethren were formed in the city's top trade guilds, and in the drapers' guild, Colchester had a significant connection through a former Colchester citizen, Henry Patmore (or Patmere, alias Brykys or Briggis in the Colchester records), who had moved to London by 1509, though he and his son were still buying property in Colchester in 1517. In London, Patmore became a

---

32. Foxe, 4:208–11, 214.
33. Strype, *Memorials*, 1 (1): 121; Davis, "Colchester," 84.

member of the Drapers' Company, and later his son, Thomas, a priest in Hertfordshire who sometimes lived incognito in London by posing as a member of the Draper's Company, helped form a secret cell that called itself the Christian Brethren. The younger Patmore had been to Wittenberg to study at the feet of Martin Luther, and he became an ardent leader of reform, never backing down, and finally being condemned in 1531 to perpetual imprisonment by his former associate at Magdalen College in Oxford, John Stokesley, the new bishop of London by that time. Thomas Patmore was released only after the queen, Anne Boleyn, took up his cause, and his story was told in the House of Commons, where the Speaker of the House was the Colchester town clerk, Thomas Audley.[34]

Hacker's Lollard group in London had connections with Colchester Lollards, and his testimony in 1527 opened a Pandora's box in Colchester. By then, Cuthbert Tunstall, bishop of London, was determined to stamp out the old heresy that was being infused with new life from the Lutheran Reformation and the vernacular Scripture movement. After Tyndale's translation began appearing in England, Bishop Tunstall moved quickly, sending notice to the archdeacons of his diocese on October 23, 1526, prohibiting the reading or possession of the English New Testament and certain other books. The examination of John Hacker, the traveling Lollard teacher, by Tunstall's vicar-general Geoffrey Wharton implicated the two leading Lollard teachers resident in Colchester, John Pykas, a thirty-three-year-old baker, and tailor William Reylond, as well as an influential Colchester supporter, fishmonger Thomas Matthew. By the testimony of Pykas and Reylond, others were named and called to London to appear before the bishop himself in March and April, 1527. A year later the testimony of Lollards from Steeple Bumpstead in Essex revealed more Colchester Lollards, and as a result Thomas Bowgas of St. Leonard's parish in Colchester was called before the bishop on May 14, 1528, when he publicly abjured and was then absolved from his sentence of excommunication and ordered to do penance at his parish church. In July of that year, Wharton came to Colchester, holding court in St. John's Abbey and examining others suspected of heresy, many of them women. A few more Lollards were

---

34. Brigden, *London*, 103–6, 121–22, 124–25, 197, 205–7, 222; Foxe, 4:683 and 5:34–35; *LP*, 1 (1): no. 438 (p. 268); CR89/8; CR93/22. A close relative, John Patmore, probably a brother or uncle, remained in Colchester until at least 1534; see CR103/14.

detected in 1530 and 1531, so around forty persons were named as Lollards in the years from 1527 to 1531.[35]

All of the Colchester people investigated during those five years renounced their heretical opinions except for one Edward Freese. Freese (or Freez) was a former monk at Jervaulx Abbey in Yorkshire. He had come to Colchester in 1526, where he lived quietly for over five years. During that time, he married and had children. Having once been an apprentice to a painter in York, Freese was hired to paint some cloths for a new inn in the marketplace, and he injudiciously painted some Scripture texts in the upper border of the cloths, which immediately labeled him as a heretic. It was later revealed that he had kept a heretical night school in his house. Taken to London, Freese and others from Essex were "straitly kept" in the bishop's house at Fulham, with sawdust mixed into their food and no family allowed to visit. Freese's wife tried to see him, but the porter cruelly kicked her "on the body," although she was "great with child." The baby died immediately, but she died "at length . . . of the same." Freese and the other prisoners were finally sent to the Lollards' Tower, where they were kept for a long time in the stocks, and when they were set loose in the prison, their legs were manacled with irons. Freese often wrote on the walls with chalk or a coal, but again his writings got him in trouble, and his wrists were then manacled so that he could not even comb his hair. After his brother appealed to the king, Freese's case was finally heard in an ecclesiastical court, but the authorities gave him nothing to eat for three days before his court appearance. By the time Freese got to court, he had gone mad, so he was released; but he never regained his wits. Others died during incarceration, including a boy from Colchester, whose crime was helping Richard Bayfield, a priest turned book agent, to distribute forbidden books. Only the most resolute refused to renounce their heretical opinions; in fact, some of the leading London reformers felt that the cause was better served if they feigned submission and lived on to continue evangelizing.[36] Such pragmatism was also characteristic of most of the Colchester Lollard reformers.

The depositions from those investigations beginning in 1527, most of

---

35. Foxe, 4:666–67, 694–95; Strype, *Memorials,* 1 (1): 113–21, 124–33; Brigden, *London,* 159; Dickens, *English Reformation,* 50. John Davis, "Joan of Kent, Lollardy, and the English Reformation," *JEccH* 33 (1982): 225–33, believes that Joan of Kent, who was burned for heresy in 1550, lived in Steeple Bumpstead in 1528 and had connections with Colchester Lollards.

36. Foxe, 4:694–95 and 5:38; Brigden, *London,* 190, 193–94, 196.

them published by John Strype in 1823, provide revealing details about the practice and spread of Lollardy in Colchester, as well as the extent to which the newer influences were beginning to be felt. John Pykas, a leader of the Colchester Lollards, had the readiest tongue, disclosing that, about five years before, his mother, who then lived in Bury St. Edmunds, persuaded him that he should not believe in the sacraments of the church. She gave Pykas a book of Paul's Epistles in English and bade him "live after the manner and way of the said Epistles and Gospels, and not after the way that the Church doth teach." Though only a baker by trade, the literate Pykas owned other books of "heresy and reprobate reading," some of them standbys of Lollardy, such as *The Prick of Conscience*. A friar of Colchester, whose name is unknown, gave Pykas *The Seven Wise Masters of Rome,* but Pykas was most eager to procure Tyndale's translation of the New Testament, which he obtained from the Lombard of London for 4s. Ever the enthusiast, Pykas traveled to Ipswich to hear the early Cambridge reformer Thomas Bilney dispute with a friar about the veneration of images. Confident in his beliefs, Pykas taught in a number of homes in Colchester and surrounding villages. Some Lollards named by Pykas, such as Dorothy Long and Thomas Parker, had long been active in Lollard circles, whereas others, such as Robert Best, had been brought into the "same sect and learning" more recently. Pykas had known Best for about six years, but only in the last year had Best been taken as a *"known man,* and a *broder in Christ,* amongst them be called *brothren in Christ,* and *known men."* It is speculation, but that description may refer not only to Best's Lollardy but also to his being a part of the Christian Brethren, the promoters of vernacular Scripture in London, since Best and Thomas Patmore had probably grown up together. Best had borrowed from Pykas the New Testament in English, probably Tyndale's translation, keeping it for about a month, during which time he learned the Epistle of James by heart. Reformist thinking was converging in Colchester, with the old Lollard beliefs being transformed by Tyndale's translation and other reformist teaching—and not just by that of Thomas Bilney. Some of the guests from Steeple Bumpstead who "souped at John Pycas's house" were reading and discussing Erasmus's iconoclastic *Colloquies* and listening to the preaching of another Bible translator and reformer, Miles Coverdale.[37]

37. Strype, *Memorials*, 1 (1): 119–23, 126–27, (2): 53; Claire Cross, " 'Great Reasoners in Scripture': The Activities of Women Lollards, 1380–1530," in *Medieval Women,* ed. Derek Baker (Oxford: Basil Blackwell, 1978), 373–75; BL, Harley MS 421; Dickens,

The beliefs of the Colchester Lollards were detailed by Pykas, who gave the names of nineteen people who, according to Pykas, "steadfastly believed them [the beliefs], and did affirm them to be of truth." Pykas maintained that the "Sacrament of the Altar" was not "the *very body* of Christ, but only *bread* and *wine*." After discarding that crucial doctrine of transubstantiation, Pykas denied the validity of another sacrament, baptism, believing only in the baptism of the Holy Spirit, and he also rejected the sacrament of confession. However, Pykas admitted that he was yearly "confessed and housled, but for no other cause, but that people should not wonder upon him." There was no desire for martyrdom there. Pykas spoke against fasting, holy days, pardons, pilgrimages, and images, with the addendum that one should "pray only to God, and to no saints." Pykas and those of his "conversation and learning" were fiercely conscious of their right to pray to God without the need for clerics or saints to intercede for them. Other Colchester people who described their beliefs most often expressed their opposition to pilgrimages and praying before images; William Reylond reported hearing Pykas and Henry, Reylond's son, remark that "it is missavory to go on pilgrimage to Walsingham, Ipswich, and any other place. For they be but idols; and it is idolatry for to go to them in pilgrimage; and that they cannot help themselves therefore they cannot help another man." Maryon Matthew added her disdain for the practice of setting up lights before images, boasting that "she had set up as few candles to images as any woman had, for it was not lawful." Pykas affirmed that "none of the *known men* did ever set up light before any images, as far as he knoweth."[38]

Lollardy in Colchester was found throughout all social and economic groups.[39] In the 1524–25 lay subsidy rolls, the baker and Lollard teacher John Pykas was listed as receiving 20s. in wages, as was young fletcher and Lollard John Thompson. Most of the other Lollards, however,

---

English Reformation, 100–101, 112, 117–18. See John F. Davis, "The Trials of Thomas Bylney and the English Reformation," *Historical Journal* 24 (1981): 775–90, who finds a movement called "evangelism" in this period, especially in Thomas Bylney, whom Pykas mentions having heard preach in Ipswich. Sensitive to Lollardism, evangelism espoused the doctrine of faith—especially faith in the all-sufficiency of Christ's passion and atonement—while remaining in communion with Rome.

38. Strype, *Memorials,* 1 (1): 121–23, 128–30.

39. Derek Plumb, "The Social and Economic Spread of Rural Lollardy: A Reappraisal," *Studies in Church History* 23 (1986): 115–16, 119, 121–22, 129, found this to be true of the flourishing Lollard groups in southern Buckinghamshire.

owned from two to four pounds in goods. "Weaver, or a maker of cloth," Robert Best, had £3 6s. 8d., placing him above the ordinary weaver, such as Thomas Parker, who had goods worth 40s. Fletcher Robert Hedil had £3 in goods, and tanner John Hammond had £4 in goods.[40] Not all of that "sect and learning" were of lower status. One Thomas Matthew was something of a patron of the Lollards, since he was more prosperous than the others, being assessed in 1523 as having goods worth £30. A fishmonger born in London, Matthew was admitted to the freedom of the borough on June 30, 1516, and sometime before that he married Maryon Wesden, widow of Thomas Wesden, a respected parishioner of St. James's parish. Maryon was reported by Pykas to have been a *"known woman,* and of the brotherhood, that is to say, as a woman suspect of heresy, by the space of twelve years, as he hath heard say." Pykas had heard Maryon Matthew speak of the Epistles and Gospels in her own house many times, and "she had them well by heart." The house of the Matthews was the overnight stop for the "known men" of Steeple Bumpstead, where they were treated to a recitation from memory by William Pykas, brother to John, of the *Dispute between the Friar and the Clerk.* The Matthews housed Robert Necton several times as he traveled throughout East Anglia selling English translations of the New Testament. Necton read aloud "divers times" from the Tyndale New Testament before Thomas and Maryon Matthew and their servants, and it was also at their home that Necton heard "old Father Hacker speak of prophecies," again showing the convergence of various reforming influences in Colchester. Matthew was one of the first to be called to London by Dr. Wharton in March, 1527, and Matthew, with no desire to be a martyr, pragmatically abjured "and submitted himself to correction" on March 5. Wharton enjoined penance on Matthew, directing him to distribute in alms 6s. 8d. weekly during the five weeks of Lent. Matthew's example seemed to set the standard for submissive truth telling, and the fact that his punishment had not been too harsh must have helped the lesser men make their decision to submit. Wharton made sure that Pykas was present when Matthew was examined, and at the next sitting of the court, two days later, the floodgate of Pykas's confession was opened and all was revealed about Colchester Lollards. Matthew's greater prosperity gave him a natural leadership of the Lol-

---

40. PRO E179/108/154; PRO E179/108/169; Dickens, *English Reformation,* 51.

lards in the borough, although it was probably Maryon Matthew who was the more ardent.[41]

Although not quite wealthy enough to be an alderman, Thomas Matthew still had a certain standing in the borough, a status that was seemingly undamaged by his connections with Lollardy. All of the aldermen in 1524–25 were recorded in the lay subsidy assessments as having at least £40 in goods, whereas Matthew had only £30, but Matthew was elected to the second council in 1519, only three years after being admitted to the freedom of the borough, and he continued to serve in that body until September, 1533, when he was elected to the first council, where he served until his death in late 1534. Matthew's advancement came after his examination and imposed penance by the bishop in 1527, after which he was also elected as one of the seven constables of the East Ward, was appointed an arbitrator in a dispute, was a pledge in a court suit for Alderman John Colle, and above all was chamberlain of the town in 1532–33, which was an important step for advancement in borough affairs. Matthew had other well-placed friends among the aldermen; Thomas Flyngaunt was a business associate, and another close associate, Austin Beriff, became an alderman in 1537. The two executors of Matthew's will, stepsons-in-law George Sayer and William Mott, later became aldermen, with the Sayers eventually becoming the leading aldermanic family and staunch supporters of Protestantism. Clearly, as far as the borough was concerned, neither Matthew nor his sons-in-law were adversely affected by Matthew's "heretical" past. Colchester was a town in which nonconforming ways were acceptable up to a point, especially if one had the prudence to submit to authority when necessary.[42]

The acceptance of Matthew was consistent with the fact that there were a number of Lollard sympathizers in aldermanic families, with two of the "known women" being widows of aldermen. John Pykas mentioned that Katherine Swayne, widow of Alderman John Swayne, had heard his teaching, but when asked about her, Pykas cautiously pleaded ignorance, though he also noted that Swayne was reputed to be "a

41. Strype, *Memorials,* 1 (1): 120, 128–29, (2): 53, 63–65. On public penance, see Houlbrooke, *Church Courts,* 46–47. W. T. Whitley, "Thomas Matthew of Colchester and Matthew's Bible of 1537," *ER* 43 (1934): 1–6, 82–87, 155–62, 227–34; 44 (1935), 40–44, speculated that Thomas Matthew was the translator of Matthew's Bible, which was published in 1537. Whitley was mistaken, as he misread some of the court rolls and thought that Matthew was alive until 1543.

42. CR98/7d, 8; CR99/17; CR100/8d; Matthew's will, ERO D/ABW25/35.

known woman." All indications point to "known man" Robert Best being the oldest son of Alderman Robert Best, who had died in 1508 and whose will showed only the bare minimum of orthodox piety. Also named as a listener to John Pykas was Margaret Cowbridge, whose family was a good example of the perilous ambiguities of the situation. Margaret, the widow of Alderman Robert Cowbridge, was, according to Lollard William Reylond, a "known woman." Cowbridge was not content with that label, and at the July, 1528, visitation by Wharton, she brought eight compurgators who swore that she was not a heretic, and she was therefore "lawfully purged" and restored "to her former fame." She then had to swear to "keep the Catholic faith, that she should not knowingly favour heretics, nor conceal them, nor contract familiarity with them: and that if she knew any heretics, she should denounce them with their heresies, as soon as she could." Ten years later (in 1538), her only son, William Cowbridge, was burned as a heretic at Oxford, and John Foxe described William as "of good stock and family, whose ancestors, even from Wickliff's time hitherto, had been always favourers of the gospel, and addicted to the setting forth thereof in the English tongue." The 1513 will of William's father, Alderman Robert Cowbridge, manifested minimal orthodox piety in the request for an obit and in the gift of 10s. to the Crossed Friars, but one of his witnesses was a Lollard, Thomas Foxe.[43]

Other wills subtly revealed the close connections between Lollards and leading families; an example was the 1503 will of John Vertue, whose father of the same name was an earlier alderman, MP, and coauthor with Thomas Christmas of the first account of Parliament written in English. The younger Vertue was the first husband of Alice Gardiner, who was briefly imprisoned as a heretic in 1527, and his will, showing only a bare minimum of orthodox piety in the preamble, had as one of his executors Thomas Wesden, who was the first husband of Lollard Maryon Matthew. John Colle, a future alderman who was accused in an angry outburst by another alderman in 1520 of having heretical relatives, was also an executor. One of Vertue's daughters later married a Christmas, and another daughter and her husband, Thomas and Margaret Bogas,

---

43. Strype, *Memorials,* 1 (1): 121, 129, 131–33; CR93/6d; BL, Harley MS 421, f. 266; will of R. Best, PRO 5 Bennett; will of R. Cowbridge, PRO 22 Fetiplace; Foxe, 5:251–53 (where William Cowbridge was mistakenly listed as Mark Cowbridge). Plumb, "Rural Lollardy," 120, 129, found that Lollards sometimes held local office, and that Lollard testators sometimes included traditional Catholic bequests.

were among the Lollards charged in 1528.[44] With so much intermarriage between leading families, one family's unorthodox beliefs affected another, so that by 1527–28, when ecclesiastics investigated Colchester so closely, at least four of the ten aldermen had close relatives who were either "known" people or attending their conventicles or who were reading Tyndale's new English translation; so radicalism was an undercurrent in several aldermanic families.[45] The aldermen, then, were aware of and at least somewhat sympathetic with reformist teachings, since they made no move against the accused persons. Even though they were not willing to jeopardize their positions and be openly radical themselves, their sympathy would later be a crucial element in the acceptance of the Reformation in Colchester.

The town was less sympathetic to some of its clergy, especially when the church hierarchy was exerting its power against Colchester heretics. In 1511, the year in which Sweeting and Brewster were executed by burning at Smithfield, the jurors at the lawhundred courts presented several unruly priests in Colchester who were brawling, "against the King's peace and to the evil example of other unruly priests." The parish priest of St. Leonard's assaulted Alderman John Reynold with a "berecruse," and the rector of St. Runwald's assaulted another clerk.[46] Such presentments were uncommon, particularly since clerical behavior was in the province of ecclesiastical, not civil, courts; so to have several in one year was extraordinary. It would be going too far to conclude that those presentments represented true anticlericalism, that is, against the sacerdotal system, but they were certainly expressing disapproval of the unseemly behavior of clerics, from whom the people expected higher standards than those of ordinary folk.

---

44. CR107/18; will of J. Vertue, CR105/14; will of A. Gardiner, ERO D/ACR4/70; Foxe, 5:39, 42; Strype, *Memorials,* 1 (1): 121–22, 124–25, 131–32; CR87/22d; CR92/18d.

45. The four aldermen with Lollard connections were (1) John Smalpece, who was a close relative of the Bests, probably a brother-in-law of Alderman Robert Best, whose son was a Lollard; (2) John Christmas, whose brother, Thomas, married the daughter of Lollard Alice Gardiner; (3) John Clere, whose sister married Alderman Robert Best and was the mother of heretic Robert Best; and (4) John Colle, whose wife was sister-in-law to Alice Gardiner. Jennifer C. Ward, "The Reformation in Colchester, 1528–1558," *EAH* 15 (1983): 85, also notes the Lollard connections with aldermanic families. Brown, *Popular Piety,* 217–18, found that some Lollards in the diocese of Salisbury were influential people who were active in communal affairs.

46. CR84/8d, 16. The dating of the court rolls is confused at this point, but I follow the dating of Benham, *Translated Abstracts,* so all of the assaults were either in 1511 or early 1512.

Not until 1527 did the court rolls evince a like outburst against clerical misbehavior, but then the offenses were of a sexual nature. Such charges were serious, since, theoretically, no cleric could remain a priest once he was found guilty of fornication, although in practice the rule was usually not followed. There was probably a reason for bringing the sins of the priests into the borough court. In March and April of that year, ecclesiastical authorities called many Colchester citizens to London; some were imprisoned, many secrets were revealed, and all who were called were forced to abjure. In May, in the first lawhundred after those two traumatic months, the presentments in the less conservative South Ward, home of the port area and several of the alleged heretics, suddenly read like a gossip column: "Sir Roger, soul priest at the Hythe, ill rule with Hurry's wife. . . . John Blaksall, for maintaining his wife in ill rule with priests and other knaves. . . . Dominus John Thixstyll, Sacrist of St. Botolph's, ill rule with the wife of the late Richard Rychold." After that, one or two such presentments against clerics were made at each lawhundred, but on January 16, 1531, a new tone of conflict emerged, this time between town leaders and clerics. The jurors at the lawhundred on that day reported that the parson of St. James's and one of the sergeants at mace had fought. On the same day, a session of the peace convened. This session was the king's court in the town, with six of the ten aldermen serving as JPs, so bringing clerical wrongdoing before the session of the peace signified a new aggressiveness on the part of the town leaders. John Wayne, rector of St. James's since 1510 who sometimes acted as the bishop of London's Official, was found to have disobeyed the sergeants of the town who came to announce a mandate of the bailiffs. Unfortunately, the content of the official announcement is unknown, but Wayne and another man and his wife were fined 6s. 8d. The same jurors chose that day to report belatedly that several months before, on May 20, 1530, the vicar at St. Peter's for thirty-six years, Richard Caumond, had forcibly entered the home of Richard Feks and assaulted and raped Feks's wife, having "his pleasure and lust with her." Another priest, Roger Pereson, was said to have stolen a ewe sheep six months before, and thereafter other priests, including both Caumond and Wayne, were occasionally mentioned in the court rolls for sexual misconduct.[47]

There were probably at least three root causes for the outcropping of charges against the long-established Colchester priests on January 16,

---

47. CR98/19; CR100/9, 9d; CR104/2; CR105/5; Oxley, 84; Brigden, *London*, 64.

1531. One was the long-existing annoyance in England about both the special privileges of clergy and the flagrant misconduct of some of the priests. When those privileges permitted clerics to escape punishment for obvious wrongdoing, laypeople were particularly incensed. Colchester had begun making inroads into the jurisdiction of the church courts. Sixteen months earlier, the burgesses had tested the waters by trying the curate of Lexden in a session of the peace on a charge of regrating grain; earlier charges against clerics had been made only in the milder court leet, the lawhundred, so the 1531 session of the peace was a victory of sorts for the lay court. A second cause was possibly pent-up frustration against the ecclesiastical hierarchy, which had been so persistently investigating Colchester residents in what must have felt like harassment. Just two months before, former Colchester resident Thomas Patmore had done public penance in London under the new and harsher bishop of London, John Stokesley, and Patmore was headed toward far more severe punishment. Third, the actions of the Colchester court mirrored the attacks on the privileges of the clergy at the national level, which must have given courage to the Colchester leaders to proceed. The first session of the Reformation Parliament called in 1529 had passed three acts against the privileges of clergy that infringed on the exclusive jurisdiction of the Courts Christian within the realm. On January 12, 1531, four days before the Colchester session of the peace, the convocation of the clergy began meeting, and by the end of January the clergy formally submitted to the charges against them, after which they received royal pardon and a fine of over £100,000. The laity were winning a major battle over the clergy.[48]

The complaints against the clergy in the 1529 Parliament provoked Bishop Fisher to remonstrate before the House of Lords, "My lords, you see daily what bills come hither from the Commons House, and all to the destruction of the Church. For God's sake, see what a realm the kingdom of Bohemia was, and when the Church went down, then fell the glory of the kingdom; now with the Commons is nothing but down with the Church; and all this, me seemeth, is for lack of faith only." Enraged at what they considered a slanderous charge of heresy, Thomas Audley, the Speaker of the House, led thirty members to the king to complain: "Are we infidels, are we Saracens, are we pagans and heathens, that the laws

---

48. J. J. Scarisbrick, *Henry VIII* (Berkeley: University of California Press, 1968), 250–52, 273–75; on Scarisbrick's p. 243 is an excellent discussion of anticlericalism.

which we establish should be thought not worthy to be kept by Christian men? I beseech your Highness, to call that bishop before you, and bid him speak more discreetly of such a number as be in the Commons House."[49] Such talk by mere laymen was audacious and a portent of more radical measures to come.

Both Catholic lay piety and heretical Lollardy were powerful religious forces. Orthodox piety could be a mighty catalyst for change when it produced a yearning for a more personal, direct relationship with God, not one mediated through the clergy or the tradition of the church. If allegiance was to God himself, rather than to a tradition, then Catholic piety did not preclude reform. Wycliffe and the Lollards, though radical and sometimes misguided, planted seeds of discontent with certain practices of the institutional church that were viewed as superstitious substitutes for the real presence of God in the heart, and perhaps even more powerful were the seeds of desire in the people to have the Word of God in their own language. As resentment against the clergy grew, the king's need for a divorce provided an opportunity for change, but laymen were needed to lead the way. The king found them in the lawyers sitting in Westminster in 1529 and, by 1531, in the moot hall in Colchester.

---

49. Quoted in Dickens, *English Reformation*, 139.

Part 2
Reforms: There and Back Again

5

The Henrician Reformation, 1529–47

The forces impelling the calling of what came to be known as the Reformation Parliament were a complex mixture, driven, first, by the king's
need for a divorce and a male heir and, second, by pressures to reform
abuses in the church. Also affecting proceedings were reforming impulses
coming out of the Lutheran Reformation and the increasing desire for the
Scripture in English, as well as Henry's new appreciation for Erastian
thought. In 1529 life in Colchester seemed much the same as ever, with
the court rolls reporting the usual uncleaned ditches and persons guilty of
"ill rule." The powerful abbot of St. John's Abbey sued John and Joan
Thomson for not maintaining a fence, a carelessness that had permitted
animals to enter and damage the abbey's herb garden.[1] Ten years later,
conditions had changed so drastically that another abbot of St. John's
had rather more to worry about, for on December 1, 1539, the abbot was
hanged outside the city gate of Colchester for not handing over the
monastery to the king. The new Parliament, which first assembled on
November 3, 1529, gradually unleashed forces of momentous change
that reformed church and society in Tudor England. This chapter looks
at some of the effects of the reforms as they unfolded in Colchester in the
final years of Henry VIII's reign, from the meeting of the Reformation
Parliament in 1529 to Henry's death in 1547—almost two decades. The
period of the Henrician Reformation has been divided into three sections:
(1) 1529–35, during which time Henry and his Parliament tamed the
English clergy, officially severed connections with Rome, and declared
Henry to be the supreme head of the English church; (2) 1536–39, the
years of the suppression of the monasteries, transactions that drastically
altered the patronage of Colchester churches, made unstable the parish
churches serviced by the monasteries, and transferred monastic lands,
thus raising protests against the fences built by the new owners and cre-

---

1. CR99/6d.

ating new wealth and three new gentry families in Colchester; and (3) 1536–47, which saw in the churches doctrinal and practical changes that began to affect the people more directly, especially the teaching in English rather than Latin and the availability of the English Bible.

For Colchester governance, the Reformation was a time of full cooperation with the king's policy of taking the middle road between the extreme reformist outlook and Catholic orthodoxy, though Colchester governors were also tolerant of radical sympathies as long as those views were kept quiet. They were especially eager to join with the king against the exalted powers of the clergy and the church courts. It was a formative period for Colchester leaders. Being allowed to follow their moderately radical religious tendencies while at the same time being obedient servants to the king afforded them a new freedom to explore different directions. There were no immediate effects on governance—none would occur until Elizabeth's reign—but town leaders were being schooled in the combination of power and lay piety that the king so aptly modeled for them after his severance from Rome. In addition, their connection with Thomas Audley gave them a taste of influence at the national level, which they would later cultivate more fully.

Reform of the Clergy and the Road to Royal Supremacy, 1529–35

All seemed normal in Colchester in 1529, but some entries in the court roll were a portent of change. On September 30, a first order of business was to admit new burgesses, but some of the admissions in that year were unlike any other, one being an Essex knight and the other being recommended by the earl of Oxford, with both excused from any fines, since they were to serve as "burgesses of Parliament" representing Colchester. Apart from town clerk Thomas Audley, who served as Colchester's burgess in the last Parliament of 1523, Tudor Colchester had been represented only by its own aldermen, so the intrusion by the earl of Oxford was striking. The current earl was the king's man, perhaps more eager to please Henry because he was only a cousin of the de Veres and the first to serve as earl of Oxford after the direct hereditary line ended in 1526. The interests of the king were obviously behind the election of Oxford's men, and Audley, now knight of the shire for Essex and designated to be Speaker of the House of Commons in the new Parliament, probably encouraged the Colchester burgesses to acquiesce willingly, as there is no indication of rancor in the process. Audley's service in the 1523 Parliament had brought his skills as an attorney to the attention of authorities in Westminster, and Colchester's longtime recorder Thomas Bonham was also MP for Essex, so the 1529 Parliament was unexpectedly bringing Colchester's town lawyers into high places.[2]

Soon afterward, another change gave Colchester an additional influential connection: one of the first MPs stepped down to make way for Richard Rich, who would later serve for twelve years as the recorder of Colchester while going on to greater fame in the central government, eventually becoming lord chancellor of England. Even earlier, Thomas Audley was the first of Colchester's lawyers to become lord chancellor, and both Rich and Audley were later lieutenants to the king and to Thomas Cromwell in their revolutionary reform of the English church. The rebels in Lincolnshire and Yorkshire in the 1536 Pilgrimage of Grace were referring to just such men when they demanded that baseborn councillors be supplanted by men of decent birth. Most of the burgesses of Colchester would have disagreed with the rebels, for Audley and Rich began as ordinary laymen like themselves and were representative of the changes that could be wrought by lay initiative, especially with the backing of the king. As a royal borough, Colchester was usually ready to do the monarch's bidding, but having Thomas Audley, whom they considered one of their own,[3] at the highest levels of government was also a marvelous incentive toward cooperation, as Audley's friendship put Colchester leaders in line for possible benefits.

The focus of the new Parliament was on the clergy, with acts against the privileges of the clergy resulting in the latter's submission to the king in 1531. Colchester leaders obviously agreed with the policy of curtailing the clergy, as it was in the same year (as noted in chapter 4) that borough records were swollen with charges of clerical wrongdoing made in the wake of Bishop Stokesley's unrelenting investigations of heretical practices. The judicial privileges of the church courts were especially vulnerable, as the laity were beginning to perceive actions against heretics in the ecclesiastical courts as being arbitrary and sometimes cruel, since the laity were not allowed to challenge accusers and had little recourse against the learned arguments of the clergy. In small ways the Colchester borough court began intruding on ecclesiastical jurisdiction. Two accu-

---

2. CR99/1d; Bindoff, *House*, 1:350, 462; see appendixes 3 and 4 and chapter 2.

3. The Audleys retained a home in the parish of St. Mary-at-Wall until 1536; see chapter 2 and *VCH Essex*, 9:108.

sations of witchcraft were made in 1532, the first recorded in the Tudor court rolls. The wife of Henry Page was supposed to be making three women believe that they should have a "sely" plough when they broke the ground, for which the borough authorities imprisoned Page's wife and then pardoned her. Mother Colet, also charged with witchcraft, was fined 12d.[4] Here was the borough court accusing and punishing for an offense normally left to the ecclesiastical courts. It was possibly a reflection of the same spirit that was challenging the church courts at the national level. The *Supplication against the Ordinaries* was a long litany of complaints against the workings of the church courts, clerical fees, frivolous excommunication, and tithes, a list apparently drawn up in 1529 by the House but presented to the king by Speaker Audley on March 18, 1532. Shortly after, the House heard the story of Thomas Patmore, former Colchester resident who was suffering a harsh imprisonment under Bishop Stokesley; it was a sad story calculated to keep the MPs intent on checking the powers of the clergy. The clergy resisted, of course, but the royal will prevailed, and on May 15 the convocation of the clergy yielded to the king, though the intransigent Bishop Stokesley did not sign his name to the Submission of the Clergy. Sir Thomas More immediately resigned as chancellor, opening the way for the appointment of Thomas Audley.[5]

A small incident in early 1534 illustrates the prudent middle course taken by Colchester town leaders who, though supportive of the king, realized that they had to be careful in the presence of influential church officials. Thomas Cromwell, the designer and administrator of many of the policies of the king and the mentor of Thomas Audley, had his agents in Colchester, one of whom, Henry Fasted (or Fayrsted), reported an affair that centered around some pamphlets issued by the Crown in an attempt to explain the king's position to the people. Fasted, according to his report, had "certain books of the King's print" in his possession, which "the holy fathers of the Spirituality cannot abide to read, hear, nor see, nor yet suffer the King's subjects to read them." Fasted provocatively tried to show the books to John Wayne, who, said Fasted, "openly

---

4. CR101/9. Two earlier accusations of witchcraft were made in 1420 and 1456 (*VCH Essex*, 9:66).

5. Elton, *Reform*, 150–52; Scarisbrick, *Henry VIII*, 297; Brigden, *London*, 204–7. The ordinaries were the highest church court officials. Audley was knighted and appointed lord keeper of the great seal on May 20; in January, 1533, he became lord chancellor, and he held that office until his death in 1544 (Bindoff, *House*, 1:350–51).

preaches against these new books, and says he will prove them to be naught, charging his parishioners not to meddle with them." Wayne would not look at the books brought by Fasted, but he asked "certain worshipful men of Colchester" who were present, that is, bailiffs or aldermen, to confiscate the books. Wayne, as official of the bishop of London and rector of St. James's Church, where half of the aldermen were parishioners, was the most influential and learned parish clergyman in Colchester, but the town officials declined to act, although they did go so far as to write down the titles of Fasted's books. They were becoming practiced in the ability to tread the middle way without giving too much offense to either side, an art that would be quite useful in the coming years.[6]

Around the time that Parson Wayne was preaching against the king's books, new policies that would bring Wayne to compliance were being enacted by the fifth session of the Reformation Parliament. The Act of Succession, which bastardized Catherine's daughter, Mary, and declared that the heirs of Henry and Anne would succeed to the throne, was not simply a political document but a necessary part of the policy of royal supremacy in religion, which was Henry's answer to his dynastic dilemma, permitting him to obtain the divorce from Catherine that the pope had refused to grant. Since the Act of Succession stated that anyone disputing the newly declared succession was treasonous, subjects were to swear an oath admitting its validity and thereby agreeing with royal supremacy. Sir Thomas More was asked to sign first. He refused, but 1,136 inhabitants of Colchester signed, including parson John Wayne and all the other clergy in Colchester.[7]

As the town leaders saw the local clergy having to comply, they gradually became bolder in the stand taken in support of the king's policies, especially after the sixth session of the Reformation Parliament, which began meeting in late 1534, brought England to a complete break with Rome. The Act of Supremacy openly stated the king's headship over the

---

6. Fasted was probably the same man who had earlier abjured his heretical ways before an ecclesiastical court: see Foxe, 4:585; Scarisbrick, *Henry VIII*, 265, 270; *LP*, 7: no. 406; Oxley, 84; CR97/19. On the first Sunday in Lent during that same year of 1534, a sermon was preached against the king's books at Grey Friars by Dr. Thystell, who bade men "beware of these books, for they were naught," being like "the fig tree which Christ cursed."

7. Brigden, *London*, 222–23; Philip Hughes, *The Reformation in England*, rev. ed., 3 vols. (London: Burns and Oates, 1963), 1:258; *RPB*, 87–92; Henry Harrod, *Report of the Records of the Borough of Colchester, 1865* (Colchester, 1865), 35.

English church and declared that the spiritual allegiance of English subjects was henceforth to be accorded to the monarch, rather than to the
pope. The clergy, who had already sworn to the pope as head of the
church, had to transfer their allegiance to the king, but several resisted to
the death, including the London Carthusian monks, Cardinal John
Fisher, and Sir Thomas More, who were executed in the summer of
1535. Only weeks before, William Havens openly expressed his disagreement in Colchester. A session of the peace that met on April 19
erupted with charges against those who had been religiously indiscreet,
and the jurors said that Havens, rector of All Saints' and curate at St.
Nicholas's Church in the place of the absentee parson, had boldly read at
St. Nicholas's "a certain book called 'le sentence'" and that he had "then
and there prayed for the very Holy Father in Christ, the Bishop of Rome,
with the College of Cardinals and then and there said, in accordance with
certain articles contained in the said book of sentences, we cannot have
absolution unless we are willing to be subject to the holy court of Rome."
The jurors charged that Havens "said and propounded very many other
words against the laudable statutes of the Lord King in this case lately
issued and provided."[8]

The same session of the peace that charged Parson Havens for being
too conservative also accused five laypersons, including a parish clerk, of
having radical opinions that were considered heretical, thus reflecting the
support of the town officials for the middle way adopted by the king.
Although Henry had moved to curtail the power of the church, he was
not yet ready to countenance all of the reforms advocated by the more
radical elements. The session of the peace was eagerly doing its duty in
taking up the matter of heresy for the first time, as a popular parliamentary statute passed the year before demanded initial indictment in common law courts, thus taking away some of the powers of the church
courts and the bishops. Four Colchester laypersons were charged with
having blasphemous opinions "against the sacrament of the altar," and
their colorful statements were recorded just as they were said in English.
Robert Danyell did not believe that "the priest can make God's own
body," and Thomas Heyward rather crudely noted: "the sacrament of
the altar is not very God flesh and blood. And if it so be he would not be

---

8. CR104/3. The *Book of Sentences* was the encyclopedic compilation of the writings of
the church fathers by Peter Lombard that became the authoritative handbook of theology
for medieval churchmen.

champed and chawed and so depart through a man's body into a vile place." William Wodcok included other heretical beliefs in his statement:

> the sacrament of the altar is made of dough, and they would make us believe that it is God in form of bread, and so they make us believe that the moon is made of a green cheese, and that a "torde of his arse" is as good as any picture in the church, and that the water running in the gutter is as good as the holy water and that he had as leave to be buried in the high way as in the church yard for any hallowing that is there.

The parish clerk of St. Peter's, John Faley (or Valey), was also charged for his opposition to auricular confession to a priest for particular sins, although he acknowledged the necessity to make a general confession of sinfulness. The statements made by the radicals were generally a rehearsal of the older Lollard beliefs, though with some new variations that were echoes of reformist preachers.[9]

The indictments made in the April 19, 1535, session of the peace did not end there; the accused laypersons were sent to London, and a Colchester bailiff became implicated. A bailiff, probably William Beket (Beket and John Colle were the bailiffs for the year), sent the five persons to London to Thomas Audley, who by then was lord chancellor of England, and Audley transferred them to Bishop Stokesley. Four were quickly "dispatched . . . according to their deserts," but the case of Faley, the parish clerk, required special attention. Faley, who had been before the bishop once before, held beliefs that undermined the priestly office itself, and he refused to answer before Bishop Stokesley, demanding that Audley hear his case. The bishop consulted Audley, who replied that he and Cromwell would examine Faley and "John Coole." The records made no earlier mention of a John Coole charged with heresy, so his inclusion is surprising and quite interesting, as Coole was more than likely the bailiff of Colchester whose name was usually given as "Colle" or "Cole" in the Colchester records. According to depositions taken

---

9. CR104/3; Elton, *Reform*, 231. See Brigden, *London*, 231, 260, 263, 266–68, for similar statements by reformist preachers. Sister Mary Justine Peter, "A Study of the Administration of the Henrician Act of Supremacy in Canterbury Diocese" (Ph.D. diss., Loyola University, 1959), 117–19, found an active and influential Protestant radical group in Canterbury by the mid-1530s.

before the earl of Oxford, which would have been a venue suitable for a bailiff, Coole had been indicted for errors concerning the sacrament of the altar. It may be that the pugnacious Faley accused Colle, the bailiff, after the April session of the peace, for which Colle would have been one of the JPs. As noted earlier, Colle was related to Lollard Alice Gardiner and had been accused in 1520 of having heretical relatives, though no official action had ever been taken against him.[10] If "Coole" was the Colchester bailiff, as seems likely, his examination in high places was an object lesson in the prudence of keeping to the king's middle way and keeping quiet about any reformers among them.

Even so, the reformist sympathies of the town leaders were showing on January 10, 1536, when the rector of the Lexden parish church was presented at the lawhundred for saying in English "That the blodde of hayles is the blood of Jesus Christ and that Sir Thomas of Strotford is an heretic." The rector was defending the relic at Hailes Abbey in Gloucestershire, which had long been a destination for pilgrims, and he was incensed by a priest who apparently had pro-Reformation tendencies at nearby Stratford St. Mary in Suffolk. The bailiffs of 1536, John Christmas and John Neve, did not care for the rector's speech, and they punished him with an unusually large fine in a court leet, 10s.[11] Thus, on the eve of the dissolution of the monasteries, town leaders were indulging in their own brand of cooperation with authorities, being sympathetic to reform but pragmatic enough to remain with the king's moderate position between extreme reformist views and Catholic orthodoxy. Furthermore, Thomas Audley's presence in Westminster put Colchester even more firmly in the king's corner, and the coming dissolution of the monasteries would give at least some of them an economic vested interest in the Reformation.

---

10. CR92/18d; see also chapter 4. The account of events published in *LP*, 14 (1): no. 1001, although mistakenly labeled by the editor as being written in 1539, was in a letter written to Thomas Cromwell on May 21 from Bishop Stokesley, who was at his house in Fulham. The report of a previous conversation between Faley and Parson Havens showed them both to be argumentative, and their contentiousness was possibly the reason why both were charged in the April session of the peace. It may be that the examination of Faley and Coole played a small part in convincing Cromwell that caution was needed at this point, as it was after this event that he later began to check zealous reformist preachers.

11. CR105/5; information about Stratford St. Mary from a note in Benham, *Translated Abstracts*.

Dissolution of the Monasteries, 1536–39

The king's policies were gaining momentum in the eventful year of 1536, when King Henry executed one wife and married another, and when church doctrine and practices were altered; but rebellion sprang up, partly caused by the concluding work of the Reformation Parliament, which met for the last time in early 1536 and forced the closure of all the smaller monastic houses in the kingdom. It was another move to curb the power of the clergy. To prepare the way, Thomas Cromwell instituted in 1535 a comprehensive survey of English monastic wealth, the *Valor Ecclesiasticus,* and Parliament, using the evidence in the report, concluded, as they were supposed to do, that corruption was rife in the monasteries. The legislative body passed an act, said to have been written by Audley and Richard Rich, dissolving all houses worth less than £200 a year and placing the properties in the hands of the Crown,[12] and eventually the greater houses fell also. In Colchester the dominant effects were economic. With the transference of monastic properties, new wealth was created, especially for those lawyers who were in a position to help the king execute his policies, such as Thomas Audley and town clerk John Lucas. Eventually three new gentry families were established in Colchester. Aldermen of the town were drawn into the prosecution of the reluctant abbot of St. John's, but some of the aldermen also benefited economically, gradually acquiring some of the former monastic lands, though not without enduring the resentment expressed against those who put up fences around their newly attained property. Closure of the religious houses also had personal and ecclesiastical consequences, especially on the monks, friars, and canons themselves, but also on the churches of Colchester, almost all of which acquired new patrons. In general, lay power increased at the expense of the church, and thus the foundation was laid in Colchester for greater lay involvement in religious affairs.

Of the four religious houses in Colchester, all but the Benedictine St. John's Abbey eventually fell under the Act for the Dissolution of the Lesser Monasteries in 1536. The first to be dissolved was the Augustinian St. Botolph's Priory, which seems to have surrendered on May 4, 1536, and it was granted to Sir Thomas Audley on May 26. The first

---

12. For the act of 1536, see Joyce Youings, *The Dissolution of the Monasteries* (New York: Barnes and Noble, 1971), 155–59. For history of the *Valor Ecclesiasticus* and the first stage of the dissolution, see Elton, *Reform,* 232–37.

mention of the dissolution in the borough court rolls was a triumphantly worded deed, dated September 10, 1536:

> I, Thomas Audley, Knight, Lord Chancellor of England, have granted to Thomas Flyngaunt, Alderman, a certain meadow in St. Botolph's parish and a certain moor which were late part of the lands of the late Priory of St. Botolph's, recently suppressed and dissolved by authority of Parliament, and which I, the aforesaid Thomas Audley, lately had to myself and my heirs in perpetuity, by the gift and grant of the most dread and unconquered Prince and Lord, Henry VIII, King of England and France, now Defender of the Faith, Lord of Ireland and on earth Supreme Head of the English Church.

The priory itself had at first been granted to Audley for an annual rent of just over £13, but in September, 1540, Audley received permission to alienate the site to John Golder (or Golding), whose wife was Anastasia, the daughter of deceased Alderman Thomas Christmas and, therefore, a cousin of Audley's. Alderman John Christmas, Anastasia's brother, was a major purchaser of former priory lands from Audley, but even the last prior of St. Botolph's, Thomas Turnour, and his sister purchased some of the property in 1542.[13]

Friaries were handled separately from other religious houses, and both the Crossed Friars and the Grey Friars had surrendered their houses by 1538. The struggling house of the Crossed Friars was first. The prior of the Crossed Friars early saw the handwriting on the wall, and on November 20, 1535, he sold land to three men, among them Colchester town clerk Richard Duke and Colchester native Francis Jobson, both of whom were serving as officials on the Court of Augmentations, which supervised the closure of monasteries and incidentally enriched its officials. At least by January, 1537, the priory of the Holy Cross was surrendered to the king, and on April 24, 1542, it was granted to Thomas Audley. With such lessons before them, the Grey Friars, anticipating their doom, sold most of their valuables and such items as water pipes and lead from the

---

13. CR106/3; Oxley, 105–6. The wills of Joan Breton, CR111/6d, and of Thomas Christmas, PRO 28 Ayloffe, show relationships of the Christmases. Anastasia's second husband was William Tey, who preceded Audley as Colchester town clerk; see Tey's will (PRO 22 Fetiplace), which also notes that Anastasia had a son by a first marriage, Arthur Clark (or Clerke), to whom she granted the priory in 1548. For Christmas's purchases, see CR120/10; CR111/14; Morant, 2:40–41. For Turnour's purchase, see CR112/6d; Turnour was by that time rector at Wigborough Magna (CR111/22).

roofs, and they sold eight and one-half acres of land to Alderman John Christmas in 1537, for "a certain sum of money" and "for many gifts and benefactions by the same John and by his parents to us." The king kept the friary for a time, leasing it to Francis Jobson in 1539 for an annual rent of £2 10s., but in 1544 it was fully granted to Jobson.[14]

By 1538 the dissolution of the richer monasteries was also being considered. Ironically, the abbots with seats in the House of Lords, such as the abbot of the Colchester monastery, had voted for the suppression of the lesser houses, and now, one by one, they surrendered their own monasteries. At first Audley pleaded for the continuance of St. John's Abbey, not as a monastery, but as a collegiate church, with Audley arguing that numerous poor people in Colchester were relieved by St. John's charity. Nothing was to save St. John's, however, not even a reluctant abbot, Thomas Beche (alias Marshall), who was arrested in October, 1539, on a charge of treason. His actual offense was his unwillingness to hand over his monastery to the king. Beche blamed his problems on the men around the king, especially the upstart lawyers, such as Thomas Audley. Beche asserted that "two or three of the King's council had brought his grace to such a covetous mind that if all the water in Thames did flow gold and silver it were not able to quench his grace's thirst." Speaking of the rebellion in 1536 known as the Pilgrimage of Grace, Beche described the Northern rebels as "good men, muckle in the mouth, great crackers, and nothing worth in their deeds," adding "I would to God, the rebels in the North Country had the Archbishop of Canterbury [Cranmer], the Lord Chancellor [Audley] and the Lord Privy Seal [Cromwell] amongst them, and then, I trust we should have a merry world again." The abbot was sent back to Colchester to be tried by an appointed commission of Essex gentry and a grand jury of Essex men, including the ten aldermen of Colchester. Not surprisingly, the abbot was found guilty and was drawn on a sledge through the streets of Colchester to his execution by hanging on December 1, 1539.[15] It must have been a sobering sight for the people of Colchester to see the great abbot brought so low, though they had never had any particular love for him. A town

14. Morant, 2:43–44; CR106/5, 5d, 10; Oxley, 121; VCH Essex, 9:306; Christopher Kitching, "The Disposal of Monastic and Chantry Lands," in Church and Society in England: Henry VIII to James I, eds. Felicity Heal and Rosemary O'Day (London: Macmillan, 1977), 119–36.

15. Hughes, Reformation, 1:321; G. H. Cook, ed., Letters to Cromwell and Others on the Suppression of the Monasteries (London: John Baker, 1965), 194–96; VCH Essex, 2:99–100; Oxley, 126, 129–30; Morant, 2:20, 36; LP, 14 (2): no. 43.

tradition suggests that the burgesses helped bring about Beche's downfall; according to the tradition, Beche was invited by the burgesses to a feast and was there presented with his death warrant from the king. It did not happen that way, since the abbot was tried judicially, but it is speculated that the abbot may have been lured out of his abbey by an invitation to the municipal feast held at the annual fair of St. Denis in October, as his arrest would have been much easier outside of his abbey.[16] In any case, the Colchester aldermen did their part in bringing down their powerful neighbor, St. John's Abbey, but again the king's officials profited most.

The new wealth created by the transferral of monastic lands altered the social structure in the borough, as three new gentry families gradually emerged. Sir Thomas Audley was eager to have the lands from the dissolution of St. John's Abbey, but they were not to be his, except for the manor of Berechurch, which was granted to Audley by the abbot of St. John's in a vain attempt to stave off dissolution. However, Audley was rewarded for his work in the Reformation with the great abbey at Walden in northeastern Essex, and from there Audley went on to greater things, taking as his second wife the daughter of the marquess of Dorset, a cousin of the king, and being raised to the peerage, becoming Baron Audley. Since Walden was some distance from Colchester, Audley's direct contact with the borough lessened somewhat after he took the Walden property as his family seat, but he maintained contact with Colchester by installing his brother, also named Thomas, as lord of the manor of Berechurch. In his will written just before his death in 1544, Lord Audley also bequeathed to his brother the property formerly belonging to the Colchester Crutched Friars and remembered his Christmas cousins, so his ties to Colchester continued throughout his life.[17] Ironically, the Audley manor at Berechurch later became a center of Elizabethan Catholicism and a thorn in the side of Protestant Colchester.

The lands from the dissolution of St. John's Abbey stayed in the hands of the king until the wars with France and Scotland forced the massive selling of monastery lands in the early 1540s. Francis Jobson bought St. John's Abbey from his wife's half brother, John Dudley, the earl of Warwick, in 1547, but Jobson kept it for less than a year, selling it in 1548 to John Lucas, who built near the abbey church a mansion that became the family seat. Lucas had begun serving as deputy steward of the Court of

16. Stevenson, *Colchester,* 56.
17. Bindoff, *House,* 1:350–53; Morant, 2:30, 43.

Augmentations in 1542, the year before he became Colchester's town clerk. As the third son of a Bury St. Edmunds gentry family, Lucas's acquisition of the monastic lands was another example of the gentry benefiting from the dissolution of the monasteries, and this gentry family did well indeed, with Lucas's son, Thomas, gaining knighthood in 1571.[18] Francis Jobson was also drawn back to his native Colchester. The son and grandson of Tudor aldermen, Jobson became secretary to John Dudley and tutor to his children, and at Dudley's persuasion Jobson married Dudley's half sister, who was the daughter of Arthur Plantagenet, the natural son of King Edward IV. Through Jobson's work on the Court of Augmentations, he gradually took possession of seventeen Crown manors, and his increasing wealth brought knighthood around 1549. He eventually settled in the borough of Colchester, taking for his family seat the manor of Monkwick, a former abbey property in the parish of Berechurch, though he was in London frequently, fulfilling his duties as Elizabeth's lieutenant of the Tower (1564–70). Thus, three new gentry families were established on properties formerly belonging to St. John's: the Jobsons, the Lucases, and the Audleys of Berechurch Hall.[19]

As benefits from the new wealth of the king's officials trickled downward, a few of the town leaders also gained economically. From Audley, the ambitious John Christmas acquired Dilbridge, a manor in St. Botolph's parish, but the townsman who eventually gained most from the opening up of monastic lands and later the chantry properties was clothmaker George Sayer. The son of an alderman, Sayer began his acquisition of significant property with his first purchase of priory lands in January, 1537, two years before he became an alderman. By the time he died in 1574, his family had attained gentle status.[20]

There are indications that lesser folk disliked some of the changes that came after the dissolution of the monasteries, though broader economic resentments were also at work in the enclosure riots occurring in Col-

18. Bindoff, *House*, 2:553. Before Dudley was granted the abbey, it had been leased to Roger Williams in 1544 and then to Sir Thomas Darcy in 1545 (*VCH Essex*, 9:303). Lucas was the third son of Thomas Lucas, the secretary to the duke of Bedford. Lucas's second wife was the daughter of George Christmas, son of the wealthy alderman John Christmas; Bindoff mistakenly says that Lucas was married to the daughter of John Christmas.

19. Bindoff, *House*, 2:444–46; Morant, 2:29–30. The grandfather of Francis Jobson (or Jopson), was the alderman and MP Thomas Jopson, and his father was Alderman William Jopson, who died in 1524, having been assessed as having £100 of movable goods.

20. For Christmas's purchase, see Morant, 2:17; CR120/10. Christmas sold Dilbridge to John Lucas in 1552, in whose family it remained until 1917 (*VCH Essex*, 9:386). For Sayer's purchases, see CR106/5d; CR110/19; Morant 2:28; *Essex Fines*, 4:297.

chester on two succeeding days in August, 1538, followed on the third day by a riotous assembly opposite the moot hall. The rioters tore down fences and hedges, but the lengthy account in the borough records gives nothing of the rioters' side of the story. Enclosure of land had long been an emotional issue. Putting fences or hedges around a property, considered an advanced practice in husbandry, was usually for the purpose of converting the land from arable to pasture for sheep or cattle, but inhabitants were used to having land free and open, much of it for common usage, so enclosure represented an action imposed on the community by the elite. The first day's rioters were objecting to the enclosure of some large areas of rich meadowland, with three properties being the object of the rioters' wrath: a two-acre meadow belonging to the dean and chapter of St. Paul's Cathedral; forty acres of meadow and pastureland at the manor of Dilbridge, former St. Botolph's property that had been recently acquired by Alderman John Christmas; and four acres of meadow that had belonged to the abbot of St. John's Abbey and was in the tenure of Alderman Thomas Flyngaunt. The nine men named as rioters were not the poorest of the town; four were clothmakers, and the others were artisans and tradesmen. One of them, John Baker, was on the common council, though it would be the last year he was elected to that body, perhaps because of his participation in the riot. In the late 1540s, three of the rioters even became aldermen.[21] Their action was directed at the privileged, including the elite of the church and the richest alderman in the town, John Christmas, whose "hedges, ditches, and enclosure fences" around the manor of Dilbridge must have been only recently completed. The elite had gained yet another advantage, at the expense of lesser men, such as the rioters. There was possibly also a tinge of resentment against the wealth of the church, as two of the men, Thomas Dybney and John Best, both of whom eventually became aldermen, later proved to be ardent reformers. In any case, the rioters were taking action against what must have seemed to be a rapacious and selfish use of the land by those who were already rich, whether it was the elite of the church or the new owner of former church lands.

---

21. Hoskins, *Plunder*, 68–72; CR107/3. Ralph Fynche and John Beste became aldermen in 1547, and Thomas Dybney did in 1549. In September, 1539, there was a problem in the borough: the son of former alderman Ambrose Lowthe was accused of prosecuting a suit against Bartholomew Cowey, one of the 1538 rioters, outside the court of the town, and he was accused of stirring up trouble by putting up slanderous writings on posts (CR109/2, 2d). It is unclear whether that conflict had anything to do with the riot or the religious problems of the time.

The second day of enclosure riots involved a completely different group of men, suggesting that the first group had carefully planned and executed their work and had stopped when it was completed. Apparently spurred on by the example of the first group, the fifteen men named in the second group were of a slightly lower status, with only two of them being clothmakers and one a draper. The rest were clothworkers, artisans, an innholder, a barber, a tanner, and three husbandmen, none of whom were in town governance. Their object on that August day was to tear down fences around small fields in Mile End parish that were probably being converted to pasture. One of the fields belonged to the earl of Oxford; one belonged to parish clergyman Richard Sharples of Mile End, who earlier had a sharp encounter with Lollard Margaret Bowgas, sister-in-law of one of the rioters, draper Thomas Christmas; and one belonged to parish clergyman Henry Beck, parson at St. Peter's, who would later be cited repeatedly for sexual offenses and for opposing reforming mandates. Here again the resistance was against the privileged, even those of the church, and again at least three of the rioters were reformers or of reforming families. In fact, glazier William Bongeour was executed for his faith nineteen years later, almost on the same day in August on which he had rioted. Their being reformers probably had nothing directly to do with the action taken in 1538, but both a reforming spirit and the tearing down of fences indicated a willingness to defy the established authorities. The bailiffs had apparently taken no action about the first group of rioters—it was probably handled privately—but the second group was ordered to appear before the bailiffs. Instead, the second day's rioters assembled before the moot hall with other persons, up to the number of thirty, and openly declared their intention to "stand alike against the said bailiffs." Five days later, a session of the peace was called to investigate both the riots and the defiance of the bailiffs, but unfortunately the outcome is not recorded.[22] Though the primary motives for the riots may have been economic, the religious upheavals had certainly set the stage for the civic disorder, and at least in the case of Christmas's fences around Dilbridge, the rioters were taking a hostile action in regard to former religious lands. The ordinary man was not interested in reforms that only created a new privileged group at the expense of others.

---

22. CR107/3, 3d; Foxe, 5:39; CR112/3d, 4d, 5; CR113/3. Two of the rioters were eventually elected to the common council. The other two reformers were John Damsell (CR122/3) and Robert George, from whose family two women were burned in the 1550s: see Foxe, 8:151–56, 467–68; will of John George, ERO D/ACR3/2.

Though the economic consequences of the closing of the monasteries were far-reaching, other effects touched lives in a dramatic way, with the greatest personal impact being felt by the monks, canons, and friars themselves. Whereas Abbot Beche lost his life, Thomas Turnour, the last prior of St. Botolph's, became rector at Wigborough Magna. Few of the lesser men can be traced, but a few of the names from the list of those monastics swearing allegiance to the king in 1534 reappeared as curates in Colchester parish churches. A John Pepper was at St. John's in 1534, and a man by the same name was the beneficed incumbent at All Saints' from 1546 to 1553. The William Patch who served as canon at St. Botolph's was probably the same William Patch who was the rector at Greenstead in the early 1540s. Also from St. Botolph's was John Gyppys, who was presented to the church in Mile End in 1542. Less in tune with his calling was former Grey Friar William Parker, who found his refuge in the house of Margaret Fysshe, with whom he had previously been illicitly consorting. Colchester churches also received former inhabitants of religious houses outside of Colchester; for example, William Wright, incumbent at St. Leonard's from 1539 until his deprivation in 1550, was probably a monk at Hatfield Regis.[23]

There is no indication that the people of Colchester were particularly sorry about the closing of the religious houses, but certainly affected were those who lived in the parishes of St. Botolph and St. Giles, whose parish churches had been serviced by the religious houses. Both parish churches had difficulties maintaining curates after the dissolution, which probably explains why an archidiaconal visitation in the early 1540s reported that less than half of the houseling people (those eligible to take Communion) in St. Giles's parish went to church on Sundays and holy days. Apparently thinking that St. Botolph's should be consolidated with the parish of All Saints, Audley awarded the tithes of St. Botolph's to the rector of All Saints', making it all the more difficult for St. Botolph's. In the Elizabethan period, St. Botolph's became the site for some of the sermons by the Protestant town preachers, and St. Giles's, under the patronage of the Lucas family, finally had a stable curacy by the 1580s.[24]

23. CR111/22; *RPB*, 92; Newcourt, 2:164, 173, 287, 420; CR107/13; CR109/10d; Oxley, 114. Also, John Francis, monk at St. John's, may have been the man who became rector of St. Mary's in 1556.

24. Oxley, 145; ERO D/Y2/2, p. 113; Newcourt, 2:163. William Cock was the curate of St. Giles's in 1585 and the incumbent from 1586 until his death in 1619; see Thomas William Davids, *Annals of Evangelical Nonconformity in the County of Essex* (London: Jackson, Walford, and Hodder, 1863), 114.

The closing of the monasteries had long-reaching effects on the parish churches, since many of them had been in the patronage of the religious houses. Most of the churches formerly in the patronage of St. John's came under the aegis of the Crown, whereas the churches formerly under St. Botolph's fell to the patronage of Thomas Audley. One of Audley's appointments seemed to be designed to promote reform; Sir John Cornisshe (or Coringshe), whom Audley appointed to the rectory of St. James's, not only was made the supervisor of Alice Gardiner's will but was given a small legacy as well. Since Gardiner was a Lollard, it is unlikely that she would have mentioned any priest unless he was a reformer. Although Cornisshe was the only incumbent appointed by the lord chancellor for whom there is any evidence of reformist thinking, it should be noted that little is known about the others. One presentation by Audley turned out to be a poor choice: Henry Beck, presented to the vicarage of St. Peter's in 1537, was far too eager to entertain women in his chamber, nor did he adhere to reforming practices mandated by the king.[25] Audley does not seem to have grasped the opportunity given him by the right of patronage to influence parishioners toward reformist thinking,[26] but the change in patronage affected the parish churches for

---

25. See appendix 5; Newcourt, 2:169; ERO D/ACR4/70. For charges against Beck, see CR112/3d, 4d, 5; CR113/3.

26. There are several possible explanations for Audley's failure to present reformers: lack of foresightedness, preoccupation with his new home in Saffron Walden, a shortage of reforming priests, reluctance to pay the extra money required to hire one of the leading graduate reformers; or even a lack of commitment to Protestant evangelizing. Audley's role in the Reformation is not entirely clear. His objection to Cromwell in 1535 about an iconoclastic tract (see Duffy, *Traditional Religion*, 386) seemed to indicate caution about going too far too quickly with reformist thinking. However, one account said that Audley and Richard Rich originated the idea to dissolve the monasteries by statute, rather than by a slower method suggested by Cromwell; see David Loades, *Revolution in Religion: The English Reformation, 1530–1570* (Cardiff: University of Wales Press, 1992), 24. In any case, Audley was, to use Scarisbrick's phrase (*Reformation,* 162), the "cold-statute" Protestant, rather than the "hot gospeller." His was a lawyer's and administrator's mind whose concern was to keep order as the loyal servant of the king and as Cromwell's lieutenant, but his pragmatic nature also meant that he was not behindhand in using the church to his own advantage. When a parliamentary act was passed in 1534 establishing a number of suffragan bishoprics, including one at Colchester, Audley asked Cromwell to help Audley's steward, William More, obtain the nomination: see Oxley, 101, 133; Morant, 1:77. More, a pluralist with several profitable benefices, served as suffragan bishop of Colchester from 1536 until his death in 1540 (the next suffragan bishop of Colchester was not appointed until 1592), but More had no known effect on Colchester. No doubt Audley profited enormously from the dissolution of the monasteries, as did many others, but there was also a certain commitment to Protestantism itself, even if it was not of the evangelizing variety. By the end of his life, the leading reformers counted Audley to be among the "chief supporters

years to come and generally made them weaker. Thus, the dissolution of Colchester's monasteries both gave the gentry a greater position in the borough and lessened the strength of the ecclesiastical structure, but that was not the end of the changes wrought by the Henrician Reformation, for other forces were at work to change church doctrine and practices.

Reformation Doctrine and Practices, 1536–47

During the last years of Henry's reign, statements of doctrine were issued, supposedly to insure "unity and concord in opinion," with the declarations becoming increasingly Protestant until they were checked by a conservative reaction in 1539. Throughout, the town leaders seemingly continued their support of the new tenets, which were increasingly affecting the ordinary parishioner, taking away many longtime practices and beliefs, but making church teaching more understandable by teaching in English and by the availability of the English Bible. In August of 1536, just after the first monasteries were closed, the Ten Articles were issued by convocation at the wish of the king. The statement of doctrine cast grave doubt on the existence of purgatory, but prayers for the dead were allowed to continue, though not the "abuses" of the "Bishop of Rome's pardons." The Ten Articles mentioned only three sacraments (penance, baptism, and the mass) and allowed images to remain in churches, although they were not to be worshiped. The royal injunctions promulgated in the same month by Thomas Cromwell, the king's vicegerent in spiritual matters, ordered clerics to teach children the Pater Noster, the Apostles' Creed, and the Ten Commandments, not in the usual Latin, but in English.[27] Two years later, images had become a principal focus of attack by reformers who preached of the "spiritual whoredom" of idola-

---

of the Gospel," and his 1544 will revealed Protestant thinking. For example, he provided for that most Protestant of practices, the sermon, in each of the Colchester churches of which he was a patron. But the sermons were only for the limited period of Lent each year. (See Ward, "Reformation," 87; Brigden, *London,* 363.) Even so, Audley's effect on Colchester and its official acceptance of the Reformation was profound, not theologically, but in the adoption of the practical stance of support for the king and the suppression of anything too radical that might cause trouble.

    27. The documents mentioned in this section may be found in A. G. Dickens and Dorothy Carr, eds., *The Reformation in England to the Accession of Elizabeth I* (New York: St. Martin's Press, 1968), 74–79. For a summary of the documents, see Ken Powell and Chris Cook, *English Historical Facts, 1485–1603* (Totowa, N.J.: Rowman and Littlefield, 1977), 110–11; Brigden, *London,* 244.

try, so a second set of royal injunctions appeared on September 5, 1538, denouncing "superstitions," including pilgrimages, and stating that abused images were to be destroyed. The injunctions declared that parishes were to keep registers to record all births, marriages, and deaths, and, most amazing of all, they enjoined the parish clergy to provide a copy of the English Bible and make it readily available to parishioners. Clergy were to "provoke, stir and exhort" their people to read the "very lively Word of God," and they were to persuade their flock to "works of charity, mercy and faith . . . and not to repose their trust . . . in any other works devised by men's phantasies beside Scripture." The effects of the mandates began to be noted in the Colchester court records. In April, 1539, a session of the peace charged the curate of Lexden with teaching "his scholars the *pater noster* [in Latin], against the mandate of the Lord King," for which he was fined 6s. 8d. Both the new teaching in English and the availability of the English Bible were profoundly significant and would gradually bring the desire for reform to a far larger number of ordinary people. A man in Chelmsford told of the eagerness of many people to read "that glad and sweet tidings of the Gospel" in the Chelmsford parish church.[28]

The king was disturbed by the fast-paced reformist thinking that, in the king's view, brought disorder. Though he was generally in favor of reforming the cult of the saints and images, he remained a fierce defender of the traditional mass, so in the summer of 1539 the Act of Six Articles was issued. Transubstantiation was reaffirmed, thus spurning Lutheran and the more radical Zwinglian interpretations of Communion, and auricular confession, which had so disturbed some Colchester radicals, was firmly upheld. Anyone who denied transubstantiation was to be declared a heretic and burned. In London, people rejoiced, joining the king in his orthodox views on the sacrament of the mass. It was a dark time for reformers; Hugh Latimer resigned as bishop of Worcester and was in custody for a year. The summer of 1540 was particularly difficult; in one two-week period, five hundred Londoners were arrested. Even the powerful Thomas Cromwell was felled by the conservative backlash and

---

28. Powell and Cook, *Historical Facts*, 111; Brigden, *London*, 286–91; CR108/8d; Oxley, 141–42; Duffy, *Traditional Religion*, 406–10. One of the immediate effects was the destruction of the shrine of St. Thomas Becket at Canterbury. On image breaking in Devon and Cornwall, see Whiting, "Idols," 30–47. On the English Bible, see Dickens, *English Reformation*, 183–96.

was executed by hanging, and the popular reformist preacher Robert Barnes was burned.[29]

Despite the turn toward conservatism, burgesses in Colchester continued supporting the king's policies, which was undoubtedly the prudent course to follow, as mercer Richard Rouse had decided. Rouse had been a friend of the abbot of Colchester, but after hearing the abbot insist that the pope was still head of the Church of England and that the king's covetousness was behind the dissolution of the monasteries, Rouse dropped his friendship with the abbot. The testimony about the abbot's defiance of the king's policies came out in early November, 1539, when three Colchester men were examined in London and Brentwood. Edmund Trowman confessed to being terrified when he faced Thomas Cromwell; if loyalty was not there before, fear was enough to make men quickly find their allegiance to the king's policies. The ten aldermen of Colchester cooperated by sitting with Essex gentry in judgment on Beche, the Colchester abbot, who was condemned to being hanged and disemboweled in late 1539.[30]

It seems that the corporation was rewarded for its loyalty to the king's policies. In between the examination of witnesses against Abbot Beche and his trial for treason, the bailiffs and commonalty of Colchester were presented on November 12, 1539, with a gift from King Henry. If the gift was not a reward for the loyalty of the borough leaders, the timing of the gift was amazingly coincidental. The chantries in St. Helen's Chapel and in St. Mary's Church, along with their attached lands, were given to the corporation, though the properties attached to the Guild of St. Helen's went to Thomas Audley. Termination of those particular chantries would not have been too disturbing to the townspeople, as the chantry priests were not serving a sizable number of people. A condition was attached to the gift: the bailiffs were to maintain a free school, which was to be set up according to statutes and ordinances drawn up by Lord Audley. So the creation of a school by Audley, as well as the guild properties, may have been a sop to him for not receiving St. John's Abbey. The

---

29. The persecutions were brought to a halt on August 1; accounts differ, but either Henry himself or Lord Chancellor Audley—or perhaps both—interceded for the prisoners. See Duffy, *Traditional Religion*, 421–23; J. D. Mackie, *The Earlier Tudors, 1485–1558* (Oxford: Clarendon Press, 1952), 427; Brigden, *London*, 305–7, 320, 322.

30. Oxley, 126–30. *LP*, 14 (2): no. 43, seems to be a list of jurors for the trial of the abbot; Alderman John Smalpece is missing from the list, but John Johns, who was elected alderman in 1541 but refused the office, was apparently taking his place. Smalpece was probably ill, as he wrote a will in 1538, although he did not die until 1543.

chantry in St. Mary's Church was under the patronage of the bishop of London, so taking it over was probably part of the king's attack on episcopal estates; the chantry in St. Helen's Chapel was already under the supervision of the town, but the new grant gave them the freedom to alienate the property, as long as they maintained the school. Audley, dying in 1544, never got around to drawing up official statutes for the school, but the town leaders continued to hire the services of a schoolmaster with funds from the former chantry properties.[31] The chantry properties were useful to the corporation and would certainly have gone a long way toward discouraging disagreement with the king's conservative stance in 1539.

In any case, a number of Colchester burgesses were genuinely supportive of the king; in his will of 1540, Richard Colbrand left 6s. 8d. to his parish church "to make a sermon in setting out of the glory of God and the honor of our most noble prince."[32] The borough court continued its policy of supporting the king's middle way, as is shown by the 1541 case against the radical carpenter Matthew Estwood, described as "an enemy of God." Estwood was brought before a session of the peace for publicly uttering words against Jesus and for a radical statement opposing kneeling before a crucifix: "I will do no more reverence to the cross made in the similitude of the cross of Christ than I would do to the bathhouse; and he said that he loved the cross the worse because that Christ died upon it." The same view against the veneration of the cross was expressed by a young man in Chelmsford, who had been so taken with the reading of the Bible that he learned to read and saved his money to buy a New Testament in English, thus gaining him the wrath of his father.[33] The outcome of Estwood's case is unknown, but certainly the Colchester leaders were attempting to quench the most radical fires.

Just such incidents must have moved the king to push through Parliament in 1543 the Act for the Advancement of True Religion, which limited Bible reading. Conservatives had become alarmed at the "insolent and indiscreet" behavior of the gospelers, and the convocation of the

31. VCH Essex, 2:502; Morant, 3:9; Martin, Story of Colchester, 51; Ward, "Reformation," 86; CR117/13d; appendix 7. At least some of the former land of the "confraternity or guild of St. Helen" remained in the hands of the Audley family in 1550. The schoolmaster taught in the school (Westons) set up in 1520 by Thomas Christmas; in 1584 Queen Elizabeth issued a new charter for the Colchester school.
32. ERO D/ACR4/82.
33. CR111/3; Dickens, English Reformation, 263–64.

clergy had debated whether the Great Bible might be retained "without scandal, error, and a manifold offence to Christ's faithful people." Henry had ambivalent feelings, wanting the English Bible in each parish church, but being fearful that it would provoke disputes. The resulting 1543 act stipulated that certain persons—women of less than gentle status, apprentices, serving men, and persons of low degree—were not to read the Bible at all, but it conceded that "the highest and most honest sort of men" gained from studying Scripture.[34] A speech made by the king before Parliament in 1545 indicates the impact made by the English Bible. Always eager to avoid extremes so as to keep peace and quiet, Henry cautioned the laity in the Parliament:

> And although you be permitted to read Holy Scripture and to have the Word of God in your mother-tongue, you must understand that it is licensed you so to do only to inform your own conscience and to instruct your children and family, and not to dispute and make Scripture a railing and a taunting stock against priests and preachers, as many light persons do. I am very sorry to know and hear how unreverently that most precious jewel, the Word of God, is disputed, rhymed, sung and jangled in every ale-house and tavern, contrary to the true meaning and doctrine of the same.[35]

The Word of God had indeed penetrated into the alehouse, and the delight taken in the reading and discussing of the Word was not to be stopped. Significantly, officials continued to encourage the use of English in churches. In 1544 Archbishop Cranmer introduced a litany in English into the churches, and during the following year a primer in English, authorized by the king, was issued. Its preface, supposedly by Henry, emphasized the need for the people to understand the prayers they used. The *King's Primer,* as it was called, reflected the reforms approved by the king: only four saints' days were commemorated; the usual prayers for the dead were omitted or shortened; prayers to Mary, the saints, and even to the Blessed Sacrament were omitted or replaced with Scripture texts.[36] Thus, the use of the native tongue was being used to instill reformist ideas.

---

34. Dickens, *English Reformation,* 264–65; Brigden, *London,* 332, 339, 346–47; Duffy, *Traditional Religion,* 430–33.
35. Quoted in G. R. Elton, ed., *Renaissance and Reformation, 1300–1648* (New York: Macmillan, 1963), 199
36. Duffy, *Traditional Religion,* 444–47.

In small ways, the borough court was affected by the new teachings. For example, the new attitude toward saints had an impact on the dating of court records. The Ten Articles had declared that saints were to be reverenced "for their excellent virtues," but not with that honor that is due only to God; and the first set of injunctions had reduced the number of saints' days. Beginning with the 1539–40 court roll, the usual dating from saints' days was replaced by modern dating by month and day. No longer was a court said to be held, for example, on the Thursday after St. David's Day, or on the Monday after St. Gregory's Day. The approved accessibility of the Bible also brought a new procedure into the Colchester court. When Alderman Thomas Flyngaunt sued town clerk Richard Duke for payment of a debt in October, 1540, Duke acknowledged the debt and offered to swear, "if the complainant so wished, . . . on the book of the evangels of God." Flyngaunt agreed and accepted "the oath on the book" as promise of payment. In 1542 another defendant was said to swear "on the Gospels of God" that he did not owe a certain debt.[37]

The borough court was used to keep reluctant clergy on the path of reform. Along with the usual charges against priests for moral wrongs,[38] the rector of St. Mary's Church, Thomas Kyrkham, was charged in early 1543 with not having "left in the church the Injunctions of the Lord King, as he ought to have done." He was the same rector of whom it was said later that he "maintaineth bawdry," "keeps a whore," and, again, "has not published the Injunctions or Statutes of the Lord King in the aforesaid church four times annually, according to the effect of the same statutes as he ought to have done." The second set of royal injunctions had stipulated that all clergy were to read the injunctions once every quarter "openly and deliberately" before all parishioners, to remind both the priest and the people of their duty. For not doing so, Kyrkham paid 12d., but his fine for keeping the whore was 10s. Perhaps the Colchester magistrates calculated that Bishop Bonner, who had presented Kyrkham, was more likely to approve of their punishment of Kyrkham's sexual wrongdoing than of punishment for his failure to promote the religious reforms. At the same time, Henry Beck, vicar of St. Peter's Church, was charged with much the same offenses, but his punishment was somewhat more severe. Beck had "a woman in his house illicitly, in evil example," but he was also charged in 1543 with preaching neither "the Gospel of

---

37. CR110/6; CR111/24; Duffy, *Traditional Religion*, 394–96.
38. The master of the Hospital of St. Mary Magdalen, Ralph Lee, did the most to feed anticlerical sentiments with his repeated lechery, rape, eavesdropping, and ill rule: see CR107/2d, 18d; CR108/8; CR109/10d; CR111/13; CR112/2d, 3d, 5.

God nor the Statute of the Lord King." Beck was fined 10s. for each offense.[39]

As is shown by the charges against hesitant clergymen in the borough court, Colchester officials continued their judicious allegiance to the king and his policies. An unusual memorandum in the Oath Book, written after Henry's forces had taken Boulogne in September, 1544, thankfully prayed for the king, "In his designs, may God give good fortune." Nevertheless, Colchester continued to be viewed by higher authorities as a center of radical opinions. Under the government's continuing repression of radical views under the Act of Six Articles, four men and a woman were examined and proven to be guilty of heretical views on the Eucharist in May, 1546. The Commission for the Six Articles, which included Colchester's former recorder, Sir Richard Rich, and Colchester's town clerk, John Lucas, ruled that the woman and two of the men were to be executed at Colchester and at "two other places within that county most meet for the example and terror of others." In July, three other men of Colchester—John Damsell, innholder and common councillor who participated in the enclosure riot of 1538; Robert Smythe, clothier and former churchwarden at St. Peter's; and a William Harvy—were examined by the Privy Council, seemingly for their reformist opposition to the Six Articles. The three were released after being given a lesson "by the Council for their better behavior in their words hereafter." In the same month, William Wright, the rector of St. Leonard's, was also examined, but he showed himself "to be of honest opinion" and so was dismissed on bond to reappear again if summoned. Anne Askew, a Lincolnshire gentlewoman who had commemorative views of the sacrament of the altar, was apparently considered to be of less than honest opinion, as she was burned at the stake that same summer, so broken by her torture on the rack that she could not stand. With Askew at her London arraignment in June, 1546, was a Colchester tailor, John Hadlam, who was burned with Askew. Hadlam, who had been sent to the Privy Council by John Lucas, had been "detected of evil opinions

---

39. On Kyrkham, see CR112/3; CR113/10; CR114/2, 2d. On Beck, see CR112/3d, 4d, 5; CR113/2, 3. See also Guildhall MS 9531/11, f. 33; Guildhall MS 9531/12, f. 130; Dickens and Carr, *Reformation*, 84–85. A Thomas Kyrkham, perhaps the Colchester priest, was earlier deprived of his benefice in London by Bishop Stokesley, and all the parish in London was said to know that Kyrkham spent his nights with a woman; see Brigden, *London*, 65–66.

against the Blessed Sacrament of the altar."[40] It was not an easy time to harbor radical views, and if the town leaders were favorable to them—some of them probably were—they managed to contain their sympathies. After all, the old king was nearing the end of his life, and the tide would soon turn in favor of the reformers.

Undoubtedly, the Henrician reforms had changed the religious scene, and for those people supportive of Protestantism, as the town leaders generally were, the changes were all for the better. The religious houses were gone, and the parish churches would never be quite the same again. Still, there were people who thought that reform had not gone far enough, but the cautious town leaders circumspectly realized the value of adopting the king's middle way. Lending their support to the king had been financially profitable for the corporation; a few of the aldermen were themselves enjoying a new sense of wealth; and they undoubtedly enjoyed having a friend, Thomas Audley, at the center of power. Under the tutelage of the king, they were learning a lesson for future years: that political power can advance ecclesiastical reform, a worthy cause in the eyes of reformers. Only the most astute would have also cautioned that when piety begins to be used to enhance earthly power, the piety becomes so tainted that it is no longer true piety but only a weak imitation. Only later would that lesson be forced on the people of Colchester; at the moment, the future looked bright, for when Henry was dead, his son and successor, young Edward, would favor complete reform.

---

40. *OB*, 164, 166; *Acts of the Privy Council of England*, ed. J. R. Dasent, 32 vols. (London: HMSO, 1890–1907), 1:418, 464, 475, 485; *LP*, 21 (1): nos. 836, 1119, 1180 and note, 1204, 1302; CR107/3; CR115/17; Brigden, *London*, 374–75. The Hadlam who burned with Askew was described as an Essex tailor, but they must be the same man.

6

The Reigns of Edward and Mary and the Evidence of Wills

With young Edward coming to the throne at Henry's death in January of 1547, it soon became clear that Protestants were in the ascendancy. A number of conservatives went into exile, but former Colchester clergyman Dr. Richard Langrysh rejected that solution and committed suicide by jumping from a church steeple into the Thames.[1] Under the regency of the boy king's uncle, Edward Seymour, who was created the duke of Somerset, and then under the regency of the duke of Northumberland (the former earl of Warwick), the halfway measures of Henry were left behind, and England became increasingly Protestant. The Catholic altar became a Protestant Communion table, the Latin services gave way to English, and the ideal of the celibate priesthood yielded to the marriage bed. This chapter looks at the effects in Colchester of the Protestantization under Edward and then of the attempt by Queen Mary to restore Catholicism, with the information pieced together from official borough records, wills, and the accounts given in Foxe's *Book of Martyrs*. Some of the leading townsmen were early Protestants, since they already had a certain sympathy with reformist ways; others apparently came into the Protestant camp when they were able to buy former chantry and guild lands, thus acquiring a vested interest in the Reformation. Among the townsmen, Catholic practices continued well into the mid-1540s, as is shown by the wills; nevertheless, compared with that of other towns, Colchester's acceptance of Protestant ways was fairly rapid.

The Edwardian Reformation, 1547–53

The first official reforms came in the summer of 1547, with the publication of royal injunctions that did away with the conservative measures of

---

1. Brigden, *London*, 427.

Henry's last years and went back to the 1538 injunctions, though more definite stands were taken in opposition to superstitious images and ceremonies. Incumbents were enjoined to declare the Word of God and to warn parishioners that "works devised by men's fantasies," such as the lighting of candles before images and the recitation of the rosary, were "great threats to God, for they be things tending to idolatry and superstition."[2] It was the beginning of a period of enormous change in the parish churches of England: chantries, guilds, and obits disappeared; the physical appearance of the buildings was transformed; and even the ceremonies and liturgy were altered.

Also in 1547, Parliament passed the Act Dissolving the Chantries, a natural product of the earlier downplaying of purgatory, and a measure useful for filling the coffers of the Crown. Colchester's largest two chantries, a consolidation of several of the earliest chantries, had already been dissolved in 1539 when Henry gave them to the borough, but St. Peter's and St. Leonard's still had one chantry each to be disbanded.[3] Guilds were also terminated with the chantries. The largest religious guild in Colchester, the Guild of the Jesus Mass, was housed in St. Peter's, and Nicholas Bushe, the chaplain for the Heynes Chantry, had been responsible for saying the Jesus Mass, so both the chantry and guild came to an end at once. The interest in guilds, however, already seemed to be disappearing; the last two bequests to Colchester guilds came in 1533 and 1534, although the first openly Protestant will, by Alderman John Clere in 1538, left 40s. to "the new making up of the Guild in St. James's Church." Clere wanted the parish guild to continue, but apparently on more Protestant lines; if Clere's other bequests are any indication, he would have had a guild sponsor sermons rather than prayers for the dead.[4] Obits were also abolished along with chantries and guilds; no doubt some parishioners missed the obits, but the creation of obits was already in decline in Colchester. Nine testators had established obits in

---

2. Brigden, *London,* 427–28; Duffy, *Traditional Religion,* 450–53.

3. See appendix 7; PRO E301/19, no. 29; PRO E301/20, no. 56, m. 5 and 6; Duffy, *Traditional Religion,* 454–56; Alan Kreider, *English Chantries: The Road to Dissolution* (Cambridge: Harvard University Press, 1979), 116, 186. The properties attached to a second chantry at St. Leonard's, the Harmanson Chantry, had already disappeared, having been given to Lord Audley sometime before his death in 1544; see Ward, "Reformation," 88.

4. PRO E301/20, no. 56, m. 5 and 6. The last wills mentioning guilds were by R. Salman (1533; ERO D/ACR2/262), who gave to the Mass of Jhus in St. Peter's, and by W. Robertes (1534; ERO D/ACR3/1), who gave to the Guild of St. Nicholas; see also Clere's will, PRO 25 Dyngeley.

the 1520s, but only six had done so in the 1530s, with the last obit instituted in 1535, twelve years before obits were officially eliminated. The chantry certificate in 1548 listed eleven obits that were being continued in seven parish churches just prior to the dissolution of obits. A good portion of the proceeds from those dissolved obits went to the poor, and the rest went to the Crown.[5] On the whole, the effects of the Chantries Act seems not to have been so disastrous for Colchester as it is reported to have been for some parts of the country.[6]

The Crown's takeover of the chantry and guild lands and their eventual sale certainly benefited the central government, but it also benefited ambitious townsmen. At first the corporation, for a payment of almost £300 in November, 1550, was granted the properties attached to the Barwick and Heynes Chantries for the express purpose of enhancing and maintaining port facilities, but the borough was unable to pay the fee, so the benefits went to individuals with the resources to buy and resell the properties. Five months later, "Spycers" in East Thorpe was sold to Alderman Robert Leche, mercer John Byrd, and draper Robert Middleton, who in turn sold the land two months later to a husbandman at East Thorpe. The same three townsmen were also buying other chantry lands. Lexden lands were sold to Thomas Rich, and in 1552 three more local men, Richard Godfrey, William Peverell, and Robert Lambert, were buying former chantry lands, this time through the Mildmays of Moulsham. Several of the men involved in the transactions sooner or later became councillors or aldermen, positions that their increased wealth would have helped them obtain. Some guild lands also came on the market; a Lexden meadow formerly belonging to the Jesus Mass came into the hands of clothier Robert Maynard in 1550, and the following year, although other factors were surely at work, Maynard was elected alderman. Thus the dissolution of the chantries and guilds meant that more of the leading men of the corporation acquired a vested interest in the Reformation.[7]

---

5. Except for 2s. 8d. to the lord of the manor of Greenstead: see PRO E301/19, no. 29; Morant, 2:51–52. The will of Joane Roberts (ERO D/ACR3/9) established the last obit for a layperson in Colchester; Patrick Collyns, parson of Greenstead (Guildhall MS 9531/12, 1, f. 182), established an obit in 1540.

6. Duffy, *Traditional Religion,* 454–55.

7. *Calendar of Patent Rolls: Edward VI,* 6 vols. (London: HMSO, 1924–29), 3:420–21; CR118/5, 20d; Morant, 2:28; CR119/17–19; CR121/10d; Ward, "Reformation," 88. Scarisbrick, *Reformation,* 128–31, shows how towns were profiting from the Reformation. Byrd died soon thereafter, but Godfrey, Peverell, and Ryche became common councillors, and Middleton and Lambert eventually became aldermen.

The dissolution of the chantries disrupted the lives of yet more priests and took away opportunities for employment. Nicholas Davye was luckier than most, though his career certainly had its ups and downs after his chantry was disbanded. Chaplain of the Barwick Chantry in St. Leonard's Church and described in the 1548 report as being about fifty years of age and of small learning, Davye was also said to be of good conversation, so he was respected as living a life worthy of a priest. Fortunately, after dissolution of the Barwick Chantry, Davye found another position quickly, being presented to the small church in Greenstead in 1548 by the king. When the rector of St. Leonard's was deprived of his position in 1550, possibly because of his unwillingness to conform to Protestant practices, Davye was appointed rector at the church where he had served as chantry priest. In turn, during Mary's attempt to restore Catholicism, Davye was ousted in favor of the former rector. Possibly Davye's deprivation was a result of his marriage, as his will of 1560 shows him to have married and fathered a son. The 1549 act of Parliament permitting priests to marry was repealed by Mary, and priests were deprived of their positions if they would not renounce their marriages. At the time of Davye's death, he was called the "parson" of St. Leonard's; he was serving as curate in place of the absent rector, Peter Walker, so Davye's service to St. Leonard's had gone full circle.[8]

Not only did the Edwardian Reformation take away chantries and guilds, but even the appearance of the church was altered. A general visitation of the church in England was proclaimed after Edward became king, and the 1548 reports of the visitors in Essex revealed that the churchwardens in at least twelve of the sixteen parish churches in Colchester were selling some of their ornaments and presumably obeying the order in the 1547 injunctions to take away "all shrines . . . pictures, paintings, and all other monuments of feigned miracles, pilgrimages, idolatry, and superstition." Fourteen years earlier, St. Mary's Church had prudently begun the process of vending excess church goods by selling some of its silver plate, using the money to put up a steeple and bell and to help the poor, and at some point they whitewashed the church and inscribed the walls with scriptural texts to replace the medieval wall paintings. True reformers, they had defaced and glazed the church windows; that is, the medieval stained glass was replaced with plain glass. They had also bought a chest bound with iron, presumably for keeping

---

8. See appendix 6; Newcourt, 2:173, 287; ERO D/ACR5/100; PRO E301/19, no. 29; Eric Josef Carlson, "Clerical Marriage and the English Reformation," *JBS* 31 (1992): 1–31.

the parish register mandated by King Henry. Since St. Mary's was Thomas Audley's parish church when he lived in Colchester,[9] it is probable that the churchwardens had Audley's informed advice to sell church goods early so that the parish could benefit rather than the central government. St. Martin's Church had begun selling its goods around 1543, but the date of the selling of the goods of the other churches was not given, though most churches probably acted at a later date. In addition to St. Mary's, only two other churches mentioned the reformist practices of whitewashing the walls or glazing the windows. The money from the sale of goods was put to various uses in other churches, with several using the money for repairs, but St. Runwald's also bought a "pair of organs," and St. Botolph's paid for a law suit against the parson of All Saints', who was claiming tithes from St. Botolph's. Though with varying degrees of ardency, several Colchester churches were quick to leave saints behind, another evidence of the relatively rapid acceptance of Protestantism in Colchester. In contrast, conservative areas, such as Oxford and York, had made only token compliance by 1548, and wall paintings in some York churches were not whitewashed until a long time after. Those churches that kept all their extra church plate had cause to regret it when in 1551 the Privy Council declared that, since "the Kinge's Majestie hath neede presently of a masse of money," a commission would "take into the Kinge's hands suche church plate as remayneth, to be emploied unto his highnesse use." Only the essentials for worship were left in the churches: a surplice, two tablecloths, a Communion cup, and a bell.[10]

Again, some of the elite profited from the religious changes. For example, one of the commissioners who was to receive plate from Colchester churches was the town clerk, Sir John Lucas, who by that time had married the granddaughter of Alderman John Christmas and was residing in

---

9. Edward P. Dickin, "Embezzled Church Goods of Essex," *TEAS*, n.s., 13 (1915): 165; *VCH Essex*, 2:26–31; J. R. Tanner, ed., *Tudor Constitutional Documents*, A.D. *1485–1603, with an Historical Commentary* (Cambridge: Cambridge University Press, 1948), 101. Audley's parish is mentioned in PRO E179/108/147 and BL, Stowe MS 831, f. 27d.

10. The Privy Council's declaration is quoted in Bettey, *Church*, 66. See also Dickin, "Church Goods," 165–68; Platt, *Churches*, 150–55; Oxley, 169–72; David M. Palliser, "Popular Reactions to Reformation, 1530–70," in *Church and Society in England: Henry VIII to James I*, ed. Felicity Heal and Rosemary O'Day (London: Macmillan, 1977), 40; idem, "The Reformation in York, 1534–1553," *Borthwick Papers* 40 (1971): 27; Scarisbrick, *Reformation*, 94–95. Duffy, *Traditional Religion*, 462, 476–77, 482–92, warns that the cooperation of churchwardens and the selling of church goods should not be read as approval but were pragmatic actions. See McIntosh, *Havering*, 222–23, for the effects in another part of Essex.

a mansion on the former grounds of St. John's Abbey. Lucas was a stalwart of the Reformation, having been on the Court of Augmentations to oversee the dissolution of the monasteries under Henry VIII, and he was appointed by Edward VI in 1551 to serve with one other layman and six clergymen to revise the ecclesiastical laws of the kingdom. Only the year before, Lucas had been charged by the Privy Council to search out the origin of seditious libels published in Colchester, which apparently came from the hand of Jerome Gilbert. Gilbert was possibly opposing the religious reforms, as his 1583 will showed him to be a close friend of the leading Catholic gentry family in the area, the Audleys of Berechurch. Apart from Gilbert's possible opposition, no other hostility to religious reforms made itself known in the Colchester records.[11]

Church ceremony and liturgy also changed during Edward's reign. Ceremonies, such as the use of holy water and holy bread, were revoked, and the destruction of remaining images was encouraged. A new Prayer Book came into use on June 9, 1549, abolishing all Latin services, although in other ways the Prayer Book was conservative in tone. A revolt in late spring and early summer was engendered both by social grievances and by objections to the new Prayer Book, though troubles in London in the summer were led by religious radicals. In December, 1549, the government issued pardons to two Colchester men who had probably been caught up in the uprising. Both shoemaker Peter Jenkyn (alias Cleyshe) and cooper Robert Baryngton were charged with treason and insurrection, but it is unclear whether their actions sprang from religious convictions or social unrest. Somerset's vacillation in dealing with the rebellion was the beginning of his downfall, and with Warwick's ascendancy, the Protestant doctrinal position gained supremacy. The English Ordinal, introduced in the spring of 1550, transformed the Catholic priest into a Protestant minister and the altar into a Communion table, and by the end of 1550 every London church had a Communion table, though one church determinedly kept its altar. The revised Book of Common Prayer, used from November, 1552, went further and abolished the mass, prayers for the dead, private confession, and many ceremonies. The medieval church was no more.[12]

In Edward's reign, not only were the parish churches transformed,

---

11. Oxley, 169–70; Bindoff, *House*, 2:553–54; *APC*, 3:138; PRO 38 Rowe.

12. *CPR: Edward VI*, 3:2; Brigden, *London*, 468; Duffy, *Traditional Religion*, 464–65, 472–75; Powell and Cook, *Historical Facts*, 114–16. For a good discussion of the changes in doctrine and worship in this period, see C. W. Dugmore, *The Mass and the English Reformers* (London: Macmillan, 1958), 111–75.

with their brightly painted walls whitewashed and their window glass made plain rather than colored, but the services were altered, being wholly in the language of the people for the first time. Many traditional ceremonies were no more, and the number of priests and services were fewer with the dissolution of the chantries, religious guilds, and obituary masses. Most Colchester clerics were now presented to their livings by a layperson, either by the king or by a member of the Audley family, but that did not seem to have much effect on the quality of the priests. The English Bible continued to be welcomed; by 1557, thirty editions of the whole Bible and fifty editions of the New Testament had been published.[13] Like Humpty Dumpty, the traditional church had taken a great fall, and though Queen Mary would try valiantly, she could not put it all back together again.

Was Colchester Protestant? The Evidence of Wills

One way of assessing the progress of Protestant thinking in Colchester is to analyze the wills surviving in sixteenth-century records. The following analysis is based on careful examination of the 218 lay wills written in the three decades of transition from Catholic Colchester to the advent of Elizabethan Protestantism (1530–59), a period of flux and uncertainty, as noted by testator Robert Saunderson, whose 1540 will said that it was an "unstable and mutable world."[14] The wills, which indicate that the years of 1545 and 1546 were a pivotal period in the acceptance of Protestantism in Colchester, were examined for signs of the relinquishing of Catholic practices and indications of active Protestantism, such as the commendation of the soul in the preamble;[15] emphasis on the "once-for-all" redemptive sacrifice of Jesus; and the neutral instruction for "Chris-

---

13. H. S. Bennett, *English Books and Readers,* 2d ed., 3 vols. (Cambridge: Cambridge University Press, 1965–70), 1:26. Some of the best descriptions of the changes in the parish churches are in Scarisbrick, *Reformation,* 163–64, and Patrick Collinson, *The Birthpangs of Protestant England: Religious and Cultural Change in the Sixteenth and Seventeenth Centuries* (New York: St. Martin's Press, 1988), 50–55.

14. ERO D/ACR4/80.

15. The use of the preamble is still debated among historians of the Reformation. Though testamentary preambles may be only a crude index to the changing nature of religious belief and, therefore, caution should be exercised in the analysis of preambles, they are certainly of value. Even in the 1530s, preambles were cited as evidence of religious opinion; in 1532 a convocation of the clergy ruled that the corpse of a Gloucestershire man should be exhumed and burned as a heretic because his will omitted the mediation of the saints, according to Clark, *Provincial Society,* 420 n. 72.

tian burial," rather than for burial in hallowed ground. More difficult to chart but often valid indicators were the use of fellow reformers to act as executors, supervisors, or witnesses to the will or the use of a scribe known to have reformist sympathies. Found less frequently were requests for sermons; giving biblical names to children; and, in the Elizabethan period, the ownership of a Bible.

The first openly Protestant will in Colchester was written at the end of 1538, by which time the official reform of the church was well under way and the three lesser religious houses in Colchester had been disbanded. Such wills were relatively new in England; the first London testator to put her faith only in the saving power of Christ did so in 1530, and a Bristol widow made a Protestant will only the year before. By contrast, one was not made by a citizen in conservative York until 1547.[16] The first Protestant testator in Colchester was not an obscure townsman but Alderman John Clere, who, in Colchester affairs, was second in power only to Alderman John Christmas. Only four months before, an enclosure riot against Christmas property had occurred, and it is notable that the first three witnesses to Clere's will, Bartholomew Cowie, John Best, and Nicholas Maynard, were leading instigators of the riot, suggesting that

---

The most thorough attack against the use of preambles to measure Protestant belief has been made by historian Eamon Duffy (*Traditional Religion,* 504–23), who gives two main objections. Duffy notes that leaving out the commendation to Mary and the saints could have been merely an expedient measure prompted by the external pressures of official policies and that it was not inconsistent for Catholic wills to use Christocentric phrasing, usually considered a sign of Protestantism in that period, because, says Duffy, such phraseology was actually a return to basic Catholic doctrine. Yet, a point that Duffy overlooks is that the Protestant emphasis on Jesus was subtly but crucially different from the Catholic practices of the time. In looking at atonement for sin, Protestant teaching emphasized the all-sufficient, onetime sacrifice of Jesus, which was made efficacious by the faith of the believer. Moreover, the theology of English Protestants did not stress the faith of the testator as much as Lutheran theology did; rather, the emphasis was on the object of the faith, that is, Christ's Passion and Atonement, according to Davis, "Bylney," 788. Reformist theology had the effect of making unnecessary several key Catholic traditions: the need for the intercession of the prayers of the saints and Mary in heaven, since, in the reformist view, the mediation of Jesus alone was sufficient; the ongoing sacrifice of Jesus on the parish church altar as observed in the Catholic mass; and a "works" salvation involving, for example, pilgrimages or the buying of prayers and indulgences, rather than reliance simply on the grace of God for salvation.

See chapter 4 n. 4 for other objections that have been raised against the use of religious preambles. The objectors raise valid considerations, but Colchester wills give enough additional evidence of Protestant thinking to confirm the use of commendations in the preambles as a sign of Protestantism. Ward, in her study of Colchester wills ("Reformation," 87), assumed that preambles can "be taken as an indication of religious opinion."

16. Brigden, *London,* 382; Palliser, "Reactions," 40.

the riot may have been a power play between Christmas and Clere. John Best was Clere's nephew, and he and his children were among Clere's legatees. Another nephew, Robert Best, was the Lollard discovered by the authorities in the 1527 investigations, but even without the Best connections, Clere's will could never be mistaken for anything other than Protestant. He requested "that five sermons be made in the parish church of St. James by the most discretist, wisest, and best learned men that can be gotten within the space of one whole year after my decease, and they to have for every sermon so to be made 10s., to the laud, honor, and praise of almighty God and to the true setting forth of his word." In Catholic Colchester, 10s. bought a trental, a set of thirty requiem masses for the soul in purgatory, but now it was buying a learned sermon. Clere had no need for prayers for his soul after death or for the intercession of Mary or the saints, but, in his words, Clere put his soul into "the hands of almighty God, trusting that by his mercy and by the merits, passion and bloodshedding of his dear and only son, Jesus Christ, to have forgiveness of my sins."[17]

Colchester wills show that medieval orthodoxy continued well into the early 1540s. An excellent example of Catholic piety was expressed in the will of brasier Thomas Preston, written in May, 1536, at the time when the Ten Articles that would undermine belief in the existence of purgatory were being contemplated. Preston had an unusual sense of the drama of the burial service, requesting that six of his godchildren bear tapers of wax at his *dirige* and mass of requiem and that every child in the parish who could sing be there for a payment of 1d. each. Prisoners and the poor were to be given bread on Preston's burial day, and even the priests hired to say six masses were to have a dinner.[18] The wills of Clere and Preston illustrate the diversity in the religious thinking in Colchester of the 1530s, though orthodox ways certainly continued to prevail.

The wills of the transition years show a relinquishing of Catholic practices in two areas: prayers for the soul of the deceased, and the commendation of the testator's soul to Mary and the saints in heaven. After the 1536 demotion of purgatory in the Ten Articles, there was a sharp and sudden decline in bequests for prayers for the soul. In the whole decade of the 1530s, 40 percent of the wills requested such prayers, well below

---

17. Clere's will, PRO 25 Dyngeley; CR107/3; Strype, *Memorials* 1 (1): 117. Robert Best was not mentioned in Clere's will, but that could have been a result of Robert's lack of children, rather than his Lollardy.
18. ERO D/ABW28/36.

the 52 percent of the wills of the 1520s (see table 3). However, in the wills from 1530 through 1536, the first seven years of the decade, 33 percent of the testators requested prayers, whereas only 9 percent did in the last three years of the decade, verifying the dramatic drop in reliance on such prayers. The percentage went down to 4 percent in the 1540s and to 2 percent in the 1550s. The widow of Alderman Ambrose Lowthe, Katherine, was the last of the laity to bequeath money especially for a priest to pray for her soul. In 1545 she left £6 13s. 4d., desiring that "an honest priest sing for me and my friends' souls one whole year." In the 1550s the two testators requesting prayers asked only that the poor, rather than priests, pray for their souls; for example, during Mary's reign William Wyseman set up two almshouses in 1557, requesting that the two inhabitants "pray for my soul."[19]

Significantly, Wyseman's will was one of the few in the 1550s to include in the preamble a commendation of the soul to the Virgin Mary "and to all the holy company of heaven" (see table 4). The Catholic preamble had been a fairly set formula, similar to that written early in the Tudor reign by John Vertue, who commended his soul "to almighty God and to our blessed and glorious Virgin Mary and to all the saints of heaven."[20] The vast majority of the wills through the pre-Reformation years included such phrasing, with only slight variations, but beginning in the 1530s uncertainty was revealed in the language of the preambles. In that decade, only 57 percent of the testators included Mary or the saints in their commendation; in London the figure was much higher—85 percent. A few Colchester testators omitted the commendation altogether, and two confused men bequeathed their souls and bodies but failed to say to whom they were bequeathing them. The inclusion of the Virgin Mary in the preamble was rare after 1546; only four lay testators did so, all of them during Queen Mary's reign, indicating a definite lessening in commitment to traditional Catholicism by that time, at least in contrast to the city of York, where almost 89 percent of the wills retained traditional preambles.[21]

---

19. ERO D/ACR3/100; ERO B/W39/198. See Ward's useful analysis of Colchester wills, "Reformation," 87–91, which comes to many of the same conclusions but divides the years differently.

20. CR111/6.

21. Brigden, London, 383; Palliser, York, 251–53. A few other Colchester testators included saints but omitted Mary. The four lay testators were J. Herde (1555; ERO D/ABW18/161), W. Buk (1556; ERO D/ABW4/70), R. Stampe (1557; ERO D/ABW33/313), and W. Wiseman (1557; ERO D/ABW39/198).

TABLE 3. Indicators of Piety in Lay Wills, 1485–1603

Years	No. of Wills	Bequest for Prayers (includes guilds and chantries)	Charitable Benefactions			Mention of a Specific Clergyman	Owned Religious Artifact or Book (not a Bible)	Godchildren (only the unrelated)	Unusually Pious Preamble or Statement	Owned a Bible	Bequest for Sermons	Use of Unusual Biblical Names
			Poor, Hospitals, Almshouses, Prisoners	To the Community	Parish Church or Religious House* (fabric or furnishing)							
Catholic Years												
1485–99	16	15 94%	10 63%	6 38%	15 94%	13 81%		1				
1500–1509	81	51 63%	21 26%	6 7%	38 47%	49 61%	2 3%	1				
1510–19	64	47 73%	18 28%	4 6%	25 39%	43 67%	2 3%	5 8%				
1520–29	42	22 52%	16 38%	1 2%	11 26%	22 52%		5 8%				
Total: 1485–1529	203	135 67%	65 32%	17 8%	89 44%	127 63%	4 2%	12 6%				
Transition Years												
1530–39	58	23 40%	12 21%	4 7%	11 19%	28 48%	2 3%	1 2%	4 7%		1 2%	
1540–49	68	3 4%	19 28%	7 10%	7 10%	33 49%	0 0%	6 9%	12 18%		2 3%	
1550–59	92	2 2%	27 29%	2 2%	0 0%	10 11%	0 0%	3 3%	11 12%			2 2%
Total: 1530–59	218	28 13%	58 27%	13 6%	18 8%	71 33%	2 1%	10 5%	27 12%		3 1%	2 1%
Protestant Years												
1560–69	75		27 36%	2 3%	4 5%	22 29%		2 3%	12 16%		5 7%	1 1%
1570–79	107		36 34%	4 4%	3 3%	18 17%		3 3%	40 37%	3 3%	8 7%	1 1%
1580–89	126		45 36%	2 2%	2 2%	28 22%	1 1%	4 3%	68 54%	3 2%	3 2%	
1590–99	134		51 38%	1 1%	3 2%	41 31%	1 1%	1 1%	68 51%	3 2%	5 4%	5 4%
1600–1603	65		14 22%		1 2%	17 26%	1 2%	1 2%	37 57%	1 2%		1 2%
Total: 1560–1603	507		173 34%	9 2%	13 3%	126 25%	3 1%	11 2%	225 44%	10 2%	21 4%	8 2%

TABLE 4. Commendations of Testators' Souls, 1485–1603

Years	No. of Wills	Traditional					GA	Almighty God	God, Maker & Redeemer*	GH	Protestant					No Inc
		GMS	GS	TMS	GJMS	JMS					T	GJ	J	Om	Pre	
Catholic and Transition Years																
1485–99	16	14				1										1
1500–1509	81	77						2	1							1
1510–19	64	58	1	2				3					3			
1520–29	42	32				2		4			2					1
1530–39	58	31		1		1		12	2		4	1		8		
1540–49	68	32		1		2		13	8			4	3	1		
1550–59	92	3	2	1	1		1	35	32			11	5		1	1
Total: 1485–1559	421	247	3	5	1	6	1	68	43	0	6	16	11	9	1	4
Protestant Years																
1560–69	75							43	14	1	4	7	2	2	2	
1570–79	107							26	31		27	18	2	1	2	
1580–89	126							31	15		35	32	4	5	4	
1590–99	134							23	10		40	48	1	1	11	
1600–1603	65							14	7		20	19	2		3	
Total: 1560–1603	507							137	77	1	126	124	11	9	22	

* Or a variant, such as "creator and redeemer." The use of *redeemer* is interesting; it may or may not be referring to God the Son, as the Old Testament sometimes used *redeemer* when speaking of Jehovah God.

A = angels
G = God
H = Holy Spirit
Inc = Incomplete; only an incomplete transcript has survived.
J = Jesus
M = Mary
No Pre = No preamble included.
Om = Omitted commendation in preamble; many were noncupative, that is, given orally and later reported by witnesses.
S = saints
T = Trinity

In Colchester, a small but increasing number of testators commended their souls either to Jesus alone or to both God and Jesus; the single will so doing in 1538, by John Clere, was followed by seven (10 percent) in the 1540s and sixteen (17 percent) in the 1550s (see tables 4 and 5).[22] Typical of the commendation of the soul to Jesus or, in this case, to both God the Father and Jesus the Son, was the 1546 will of Alderman William Buxton: "I commend my soul unto Almighty God, Jesus Christ, my maker and redeemer in whom and by the merit of whose blessed passion is all my whole trust of clean remission of my sins." After 1546 the number of commendations to Jesus outnumbered those to Mary and the saints; however, most testators by that time were taking the safe route and commending their souls to God alone. None of those testators with commendations to Jesus asked for prayers for the soul, but very few in Colchester, only five in the two decades, were doing so by that time. However, two paid money to the high altar of their parish church, though that practice was also in drastic decline. Significantly, the two wills including payments to the high altar were written by John Thorpe, who was a priest at St. Peter's Church and was therefore due to benefit from the bequest to the high altar.[23] As an active writer of wills, Thorpe's role brings up the problem of whether the wording of the preamble was simply the choice of the scribe and was therefore possibly not a reflection of the wishes of the testator. Colchester testators had a number of choices of scribes, so it seems unlikely that they would choose a scribe whose opinions were radically different from their own.[24] Three scribes wrote

---

22. Three testators who commended their souls to Jesus in the 1520s probably had reformist sympathies, though their wills also reflected Catholic practices (ERO D/ACR2/178; ERO D/ACR2/200; ERO D/ACR2/208). The three wills were all apparently written by Sir John Thixstill, curate at St. Botolph's, who in 1534 preached a Lenten sermon at the Grey Friars against the king's new religious policies; see Oxley, 84.

23. Buxton's will, ERO D/ACR3/120. Henry Harrison, ERO D/ACR3/107, and Richard Hampken; ERO D/ACR3/80, gave to the high altar.

24. Colchester testators were increasingly using laymen rather than clerics to write their wills, and some of the notaries, such as John Andrewes and William Mauncell in the 1540s and 1550s, began to identify themselves as the writers of the wills; see ERO D/ABW39/48; ERO D/ABW23/42; ERO D/ACR3/100; ERO D/ABW4/57; ERO D/ABW28/229. See also Margaret Spufford, *Contrasting Communities: English Villagers in the Sixteenth and Seventeenth Centuries* (Cambridge: Cambridge University Press, 1974), 320–25; Brigden, *London,* 384; Palliser, "Reactions," 39–40; Palliser, "Reformation in York," 19–20, 28, 32; Michael L. Zell, "The Use of Religious Preambles as a Measure of Religious Belief in the Sixteenth Century," *Bulletin of the Institute of Historical Research* 50 (1977): 246–49; Matlock Population Studies Group, "Wills and Their Scribes," *Local Population Studies* 8 (1972): 55–57; N. R. Evans, "Testators, Literacy, Education, and Religious Belief," *Local Population Studies* 25 (1980): 42–50.

the seven Colchester wills commending the soul to Jesus in the 1540s: Bevys Wright, priest at St. Botolph's, wrote three wills; John Thorpe, priest at St. Peter's, wrote two; and committed lay reformer Nicholas Wilbore wrote two in St. Runwald's parish.[25] Protestants were therefore active in at least those three parishes. Thorpe,[26] one of the first to identify himself as a writer of Colchester wills, first appeared in the Colchester records as the "Jhus priest," so he was initially the priest for the Guild of the Jesus Mass in St. Peter's, which meant that he was first hired by the lay members of the guild and then appointed by the Protestant Audley family as the vicar of St. Peter's when that position became available.[27] By the 1550s, the sixteen testators commending their souls to Jesus were from several different parishes, and their wills were written by various scribes, so Protestant sympathies—if we assume that a "Jesus will" indicates such—were more widespread by that time.

TABLE 5.   Reformist Practices in Lay Wills

	Commendation of the Soul to Jesus or to God and Jesus	Asked for Christian Burial*	Provided for Sermons	Use of Unusual Biblical Names	Number of Testators Using These Reformist Practices
1530–39	1	1	1	0	2
1540–49	7	5	2	0	13
1550–59	16	19	0	2	27
Total	24	25	3	2	42

*Includes such phrases as "where it please God" or "to the earth."

25. Wright wrote the following wills: ERO D/ABW3/104; ERO D/ABW3/104; ERO D/ABW39/94. Thorpe wrote ERO D/ACR3/107 and ERO D/ACR3/80. Wilbore wrote ERO D/ACR3/120 and ERO D/ACR3/107. Wilbore's daughter later married the Calvinist preacher John Pullen.

26. Thorpe seems to have been from the same family that produced two early "Jesus" wills in the 1520s, but at that time Thorpe, apparently a priest at St. Osyth's Priory, was asked to pray for the soul of his brother; see the wills of brothers H. Thorpe (1527; ERO D/ACR2/200) and R. Thorpe (1528; ERO D/ACR2/208), both of whom lived in St. Botolph's parish, though their father, Robert Thorpe, Sr., lived in St. Peter's parish (ERO D/ACR2/227). St. Osyth's was early infiltrated by Lollard teaching; see Foxe, 4:214–15.

27. Will of H. Harrison (1545), ERO D/ACR3/107; Newcourt, 4:179. Thorpe wrote or witnessed at least four other Colchester wills, only one of which included any Catholic traditional practices: Agnes Preston (ERO D/ACR3/112) bequeathed her soul to Jesus, Mary, and the saints.

The twenty-three Colchester "Jesus wills" from the 1540s and 1550s reveal other evidences of Protestantism. A close look at the friends, relatives, and associates of reformers shows that there were networks among them, so one of the possible marks of a Protestant will was the use of other Protestants as executors, supervisors, or witnesses. Such evidence is difficult to ascertain, since the historian must have an intimate acquaintance with the records and be able to determine from other sources the religious views of some of the people mentioned in the wills. At least nine of the twenty-three "Jesus wills" mentioned other Protestants; for example, Robert Middleton, who was a witness, a coexecutor, and a supervisor in three of the wills,[28] was one of the three men elected as aldermen in the Protestant coup at the first election after Elizabeth's ascension to the throne. Two wills mentioned John Valey, the radical reformer and parish clerk at St. Peter's who was called before the bishop for his unorthodox views.[29] Another sign of possible reformist views, the committal of the body to the earth, to "Christian burial," or "where it please God," was in nine of the "Jesus wills," all from the 1550s.[30] Beyond the commendations to Jesus, then, there is additional internal evidence in the wills indicating that at least sixteen of the twenty-three testators were reformers, and a good case could be made for several others. In Colchester, then, a commendation of the soul to Jesus was a highly probable indicator that the testator was a reformer.

The committal of the body simply "to Christian burial" first appeared in Colchester wills in 1534, in the will of Lollard Thomas Matthew, in contrast to the usual practice of designating a burial place, usually the testator's parish church or churchyard. It was important to medieval men and women to be buried in hallowed ground, and burial in one's own parish was practical and economical, since the parish church could demand a share of burial fees if the parishioner was buried elsewhere. Some reformers, however, rejected the necessity for burial in hallowed ground, and such thinking was a part of William Wodcok's crude statement when he was before the borough court in 1535 for having opinions "against the sacrament of the altar." Wodcok stated that "he had as

---

28. Wills of Alderman William Buxston (1546), ERO D/ACR3/120; John Byrde (1555), ERO D/ABW4/48; Nicholas Wilbore (1557), ERO D/ABW39/196.

29. ERO D/ACR3/80; ERO D/ABW33/275; Oxley, 144.

30. Wills of G. Fawkes (1551), ERO D/ABW14/33; J. Byrde (1555), ERO D/ABW4/48; R. Thurston (1556), ERO D/ABW37/91; J. Roper (1557), ERO D/ABW31/123; J. Bat (1558), ERO D/ABW4/167; W. Panton (1558), ERO D/ABW28/217; R. Glanville (1559), PRO 23 Mellershe; J. Hall (1559), ERO D/ACR5/36; J. Payne (1559), ERO D/ABW28/229.

leave to be buried in the high way as in the church yard for any hallow-
ing that is there."[31] In the 1540s, other testators began to follow
Matthew's and Wodcok's thinking, often asking for "Christian burial
where it shall please God," with five testators in the 1540s and nineteen
in the 1550s making such requests (see table 5). Only one of those wills,
that of former alderman Ambrose Lowthe, had any vestige of Catholic
tradition; Lowthe curiously commended his soul to God, Mary, and the
saints, but he requested that his body be buried "where it shall please
God."[32] Eighteen of the wills show additional signs of reformist thinking.
Nine of those testators also commended their souls to Jesus, and there
was no mistaking the evangelical intent of John Smyth, who left 5s. in
1545 to the parson of his parish church of St. Leonard "for preaching the
holy gospel of our Savior Jesus Christ." Reformer John Beste, brother of
Lollard Robert Beste, was Smyth's supervisor, and the writer of the will
seems to have been Robert Lambe; described as a scrivener in a 1549
deed, Lambe wrote six more of the wills requesting Christian burial.[33]

As indicated by the wills, Robert Lambe was an excellent example of
a scribe with reformist views. Not until 1547 did Lambe describe himself
as the writer of a will,[34] but he probably wrote most of the nineteen wills
that he witnessed from 1534 to 1556. The first will Lambe wrote was
that of Lollard Thomas Matthew, so Lambe was a scribe used by some of
the most radical reformers, and the neutral committal of the body seemed
to be a mark of the most radical elements of their wills, even more so
than the commendation of the soul to Jesus. One of the testators who
used Lambe's services in 1554 and who asked for Christian burial was
Robert Fawkon, the son-in-law of reformer Nicholas Wilbore. Two
items in Fawkon's will pointed to his radical beliefs: a witness was clan-
destine preacher Thomas Putto, and Fawkon had given two of his daughters the names of Christian virtues, Faith and Grace, a mark of the true

31. ERO D/ABW25/35; CR104/3; Philippe Aries, *The Hour of Our Death*, trans. Helen
Weaver (New York: Alfred A. Knopf, 1981), 71–74.
32. ERO D/ABW23/42. Lowthe's wife was certainly Catholic, as she was the last lay testator to ask a priest to pray for her soul; see her will, ERO D/ACR3/100, also written in
1545, a few months after her husband's. Another testator, Alice Maynard (ERO
D/ABW25/64), had a curious mixture, requesting that her body be buried in Christian
burial, but within the parish church of St. Botolph; her will was not counted in table 5.
33. ERO D/ABW33/126; CR118/5d. The rector of St. Leonard's was William Wright
(alias Smith).
34. ERO D/ABW1/46. A Robert Lambe, probably another man, also witnessed a 1520
will, that of M. Godfrey, ERO D/ACR2/235. The writer of a will usually put his name first
or last in the group of witnesses; Lambe put his name last.

reformer. None of the wills written by Lambe mentioned saints, with one exception. In 1556, shortly after Queen Mary's fires had burned four respected Colchester men for heresy, the testator William Buk commended his soul "to God Almighty, my only savior and redeemer," the usual commendation used by scrivener Lambe, but above it was inserted in different ink, "and to our blessed lady and to all the holy company of heaven." Again, reflecting the pressure of that time, Buk's body was committed to Christian burial, but those words were marked through and were replaced by the direction for burial in the parish churchyard of St. Leonard's.[35]

Not one of Lambe's nineteen wills commended the soul to Jesus; in his early wills, three were commended to the Trinity, but all the rest were commended to God alone, a commendation that would appear to be neutral and an easy way out of the religious confusion. It was a practice increasingly used by Colchester testators (see table 4), but it was probably not so neutral as it would appear and as many historians have assumed it to be. In fact, the simple commendation to God was used by many reformers, including some of the most radical; for example, two known Lollards, Thomas Matthew and Alice Gardyner, bequeathed their souls to "Almighty God" in the 1530s.[36] Of the twenty-one testators in the 1540s commending their souls to God alone, only one had a request for prayers for the soul, and fifteen had evidence of reformist views in their wills. Two left money for sermons; six hired reformist scrivener Robert Lambe; five asked for simple burial; and eight mentioned friends or relatives who were reformers. For example, Peter Hawke's daughter-in-law was a Marian fugitive; and the wife of John Leveron's son-in-law burned as a heretic under Mary.[37] Of the twenty-four wills in the 1540s and 1550s requesting simple Christian burial or having some other neu-

35. Wills of Matthew, ERO D/ABW25/35; Fawkon, ERO D/ABW14/77; Buk, ERO D/ABW4/70.

36. Foxe, 4:585 and 5:42; will of Matthew, ERO D/ABW25/35; will of Gardyner, ERO D/ACR4/70. In the troubled 1530s, eight testators omitted altogether the usual bequest of the soul (see table 4). Palliser, *York,* 250–51, says the phrase was neutral, as does Ward, "Reformation," 87. However, McIntosh, *Havering,* 189, counts the wills as Protestant if they commend their testators' souls to God only and do not contain any Catholic elements. Of the fourteen Colchester testators in the 1530s who commended their souls to God alone, only two requested prayers for the soul; in the 1520s, out of the four testators with that commendation, only one asked for such prayers.

37. Will of Hawke (1547), ERO D/ABW18/69; will of Leveron (1548), ERO D/ABW23/50; CR122/4. Joan Hawke had fled by August 27, 1556; Helen (or Ellen) Ewring, wife of miller John Ewring, Leveron's son-in-law, was burned on August 2, 1557; see Foxe, 8:387, 389–90, 392.

tral request for burial, thirteen bequeathed their souls to God alone, confirming the impression that a commendation to God was often used by reformers. Usually the phrasing in the commendation was "to Almighty God," but by the 1550s the commendation of the soul to "God, my maker and redeemer" (or "my creator and savior") was frequent. Though *redeemer* could refer to God the Father, it was more commonly used in reference to Jesus, so it was possibly a disguise of Protestant sympathies during Mary's Catholic reign. One example was the use of the phrase "almighty God my maker and redeemer" by former Lollard Margaret Bowgas (or Bogus) in 1558.[38]

Tracing reformers through the wills is tenuous, but the evidence from Colchester indicates that a high proportion of the testators who commended their souls to Jesus or to God and who omitted the usual burial in hallowed ground were either committed reformers, sympathetic to reform, or had close friends and relatives who were. Table 5 charts the obvious signs of a reformist testator, but those indicators only scratch the surface; just as significant were the more subtle signs in the networks of friends and relatives or the scribes with reformist views. After 1546, and certainly by the 1550s, reform had made significant inroads into the thinking of many Colchester testators.

The dramatic decrease in the traditional prayers for the soul and reliance on saints, as well as the increasing evidence of Protestantism, were not the only effects of reform shown by the Colchester wills. Bequests to the parish church were in a striking decline, and testators showed a marked decrease of dependence on the clergy. However, charitable gifts remained fairly constant,[39] and there was a slightly greater emphasis on family and education, though the latter was probably not directly linked to the religious changes of the time.[40] There were bequests to the churches (aside from offerings to the high altar) in 44 percent of

---

38. ERO D/ABW4/140; Spufford, *Communities*, 335. New phraseology in reference to God was also emerging. In 1540 John Prestney (ERO D/ABW28/51) commended his soul to "the hands and mercy" of God, and in 1541 gentleman Richard Weston (ERO D/ABW39/51) left his soul "to the infinite and inestimable mercy and goodness of almighty God, the very creator and redeemer of the same," indicating what would seem to be a belief in a more personal and caring God. See Higgs, "Wills," 93.

39. According to Ward, "Reformation," 89, there was an increase in giving to the poor, but that increase is explained by Ward's different division of the years.

40. Concern about minor children was more evident in the wills of the transition years. In the 203 pre-Reformation wills, only nine testators said something about the upbringing of minor children, but in the 218 wills from 1530 through 1559, twenty-two testators gave such directions, often wanting the children to be brought up in virtuous learning. Surprisingly few testators (only three in each period) referred to children's learning to read and write.

the pre-Reformation wills, but that figure went down to 19 percent in the 1530s, to 10 percent in the 1540s, and to an astonishing zero in the 1550s (see table 3). Even more striking was the decrease in bequests to the high altar for tithes withheld or forgotten. Ninety percent or more of the pre-Reformation testators made a bequest to the high altar, but that offering was made in only 69 percent of the wills of the 1530s, in 53 percent in the 1540s, and in only 2 percent in the 1550s. One would think that there would have been more of a resurgence of traditionalism in Mary's reign, but that was not the case.[41] As the mediation of the church and of its priests became less important, so the need to support the church was taken away, but another factor may be that the early selling of church goods had paid for the repairs to the parish churches that had so often been the reason for bequests to the churches. Also, the Reformation made unnecessary many of the special items that had previously been bequeathed to churches. Colchester wills likewise showed a diminishing dependence on the clergy. That clergy were no longer asked to pray for the souls of the deceased partly accounts for the fewer clergy mentioned in wills, but testators were also less reliant on clergy when it came to making and executing their wills, with the figure declining dramatically in the 1550s. In the 1540s, a cleric was named in some capacity in 49 percent of the wills, but that figure declined to 11 percent in the wills of the next decade. On the whole, the Reformation lessened the necessity for the priest, though he was still needed at the Communion table.[42]

Though the religious reforms were imposed by the king, acceptance came relatively quickly in Colchester, with borough leaders eagerly supporting their "most noble prince."[43] The southeast of England was gen-

41. Wilbur K. Jordan, *Philanthropy*, 301, 316, also found that there was an abrupt decline in giving to the parish church beginning in the 1530s, and Dyer, *Worcester*, 243, likewise found a striking collapse in the bequests to the church in Worcester. Duffy, *Traditional Religion*, 551–55, notes that the laity in some counties immediately began to endow parish churches but that most places did not, a fact he attributes to the greater problem of the poor, the heavy demands already placed on all parishioners to restore the parish church furnishings, and the lack of confidence, engendered by the history of religious upheaval, that legacies would be enduring.

42. There was probably a gap between the beliefs of some of the people and their priests. Only six clerical wills survived from the 1530s through the 1550s: they are those of R. Caumond (1535; PRO 27 Hogen), J. Reynolde (1537; ERO D/ABW31/24), P. Collyns (1540; Guildhall MS 9531/12, pt. 1, f. 182), R. Scharples (1542; ERO D/ABW33/96), P. Bolden (1543; ERO D/ABW3/88), and T. Gale (1557; ERO D/ABW16/128). All of those wills avowed traditional beliefs and practices.

43. Phrase from the will of R. Colbrande (1540), ERO D/ACR4/82. Colchester's openness to reform was not typical of all English towns. Many areas in England were much

erally more receptive to the new ideas and practices of the Reformation, partly because of its proximity to the Continent, and such receptivity was especially evident in Colchester, where Protestantism made itself known early. Through long exposure to the Lollards, many burgesses of Colchester seemed to have a preexisting sympathy for nonconformity, so King Henry's reforms generally accorded with their views, and their personal tie to Thomas Audley, one of the power brokers of the Reformation, was an added incentive. Even so, changes come slowly, and Colchester wills show that traditional Catholic practices were not generally discarded until the mid-1540s.

Tested in the Fire: The Reign of Mary, 1553–58

Since Colchester had moved comparatively easily into the Protestant camp, it would seem that Mary's accession on the death of Edward on July 6, 1553, would occasion immediate resistance from the Colchester burgesses. But town officials welcomed Mary in Colchester with a silver cup and £20 in gold as she made her way to London,[44] triumphant in her victory over Northumberland's attempt to place Lady Jane Grey on the throne. Mary was known to be an ardent Romanist, but the burgesses, even those with equally earnest reformist beliefs, had no reasonable choice but to welcome the rightful heir to the throne and to be obedient to her lawful authority. Their strength and freedom lay in the Crown. Without the authority of the Crown behind them, they had no power, and if they failed to support Mary, they could completely lose their rights

---

slower to accept the ways of the Reformation; see Christopher Haigh, "The Recent Historiography of the English Reformation," *Historical Journal* 25 (1982): 995–1007. For some categorizations of approaches, see ibid.; Christine Carpenter, "The Religion of the Gentry of Fifteenth-Century England," in *England in the Fifteenth Century: Proceedings of the 1986 Harlaxton Symposium,* ed. Daniel Williams (Woodbridge, Suffolk: Boydell and Brewer, 1987), 53–55; Norman P. Tanner, "The Reformation and Regionalism: Further Reflections on the Church in Late Medieval Norwich," in *Towns and Townspeople in the Fifteenth Century,* ed. J. A. F. Thomson (Gloucester: Alan Sutton, 1988), 130–32; Loades, *Revolution*), 1–5. A. G. Dickens, *English Reformation,* and others contend the Reformation was rapid in Colchester because of its ready acceptance by the people inspired by Lollardy and tired of a corrupt church; on the opposing side, Haigh, "Historiography," Scarisbrick, *Reformation,* and Duffy, *Traditional Religion,* stress that it was imposed from above on a reluctant people who wanted to retain their flourishing traditional religion.

44. Martin, *Story of Colchester,* 47. Palliser, "Reactions," 42, says that it is now accepted that the ease with which Mary ascended to the throne was due to her legitimate hereditary claim, not to her religion.

as a corporation. It was no empty fear, as the common council of London learned when they were threatened with having their liberties taken away if they did not keep under control the people rioting against the restoration of the Catholic mass.[45]

The burgesses were not the only ones to make peace with Mary; the gentry of Colchester who had grown rich off of the demise of Catholic institutions were scrambling to save their privileges and even their lives. On the very day that Mary was proclaimed queen in London, July 19, the Privy Council permitted three men of Colchester, servants of Sir Francis Jobson, to return to their homes. Five days before, the Privy Council had issued a warrant for the arrest of Jobson, who, in the vanguard of the forces under the duke of Northumberland, was in East Anglia attempting to depose Mary while she was in the castle at Framlingham. Jobson, the son and grandson of deceased Colchester aldermen, owed his great advancement in life to Northumberland, but now that connection was hardly an advantage. Mary triumphantly entered London on August 3, and Jobson was arrested and committed to the Tower five days later, although he was pardoned in December.[46] In trouble along with Jobson was his servant, clothier William Beriff, probably an estate manager for Jobson's Colchester properties. Beriff, also the son of a deceased alderman, was reported to be a "great doer for Francis Jobson, and a great traveler for the Duke of Northumberland." Beriff was put into the custody of Colchester bailiffs until he was called for examination by the Privy Council, when he was released under bond.[47] Colchester town clerk John Lucas had been one of the twenty-four signers supporting the alteration of the succession in favor of Lady Jane Grey, so he was placed in the Fleet prison. He was released five days later and put under house arrest, though that lasted only two weeks because of his ill health.[48]

Though the town leaders pragmatically received Mary as queen and aided her in the apprehension of her enemies, the lesser folk of Colchester provided plenty of resistance during her reign, causing one of her chief courtiers, Sir Anthony Browne, to comment that Colchester "is a har-

---

45. Brigden, *London,* 529.

46. *APC,* 4:304, 313, 344; Bindoff, *House,* 2:445; CR124/13. Jobson's pragmatism allowed him to serve whatever master he was under, and he served Mary loyally by representing Colchester in two of her Parliaments, the first one being Mary's first Parliament of 1554, which prepared the way for the Spanish marriage.

47. *APC,* 4:311, 313, 317, 323, 418.

48. *APC,* 4:322; Bindoff, *House,* 2:555.

bourer of heretics and ever was." Wanting to make her position clear, Mary quickly issued a proclamation stating her attachment to the Catholic faith, and the first indication of resistance came on October 3, when, in the first lawhundred in Colchester after Mary's accession, seven people were named for failure to attend divine services. The accusations were noteworthy since such charges had previously come only infrequently before the borough court. One of the men was said to be an idle person, but the other six were said to be working on Sundays and feast days and were consequently absent from church services. At least some of the accused were probably expressing displeasure at being expected to attend Catholic services again,[49] but just as significant was the fact that other churchgoers, no doubt the traditionalists, were so quick to charge them. Mary definitely had Catholic sympathizers in Colchester.

The events of 1554 were disquieting. In early January, the Privy Council ordered bailiffs Benjamin Clere and John Maynard and two aldermen to appear before the council, but the reason for the summons is unknown. For the town governors, such uncomfortably close scrutiny from the council possibly confirmed for them the wisdom of conforming to Mary's policies, especially after they saw the results of the armed rebellion in Kent that broke out later in the same month, in opposition to Mary's proposed marriage with the Spanish Prince Philip. Mary punished those rebels harshly, with some one hundred of them dying for treason, and in February of that year Mary's council ordered that punishment be given to lewd (unlearned) persons around Colchester "that have gone about to dissuade the Queen's people there from frequenting such Divine Service as is presently appointed by the laws to be observed in the realm."[50] One such person was Thomas Putto, resident at Mile End, who had been chastised for "lewd" preaching during the time of King Edward. Sent to Archbishop Cranmer for correction in 1549, he finally recanted his Anabaptist opinions, and in 1552 the reformist bishop of London, Nicholas Ridley, ordained Putto. In 1554 Putto was quietly

---

49. Browne quotation in Oxley, 197; CR120/2, 2d. One of the persons charged was the wife of John Matthews; a John Matthews was sergeant at mace, but there is no indication that he was related to Lollard Thomas Matthews. More certainly one of the reformers was Hawkes the shoemaker, who was probably Thomas Hawkes, the husband of Agnes Hawkes. Agnes was among the congregation of reformist preacher Thomas Putto (CR122/4) and was the daughter of Robert Smith (CR124/9), who had been called to London for examination in 1546 (APC, 1:485).

50. APC, 4:383, 395; Oxley, 180; VCH Essex, 2:32.

preaching his heretical doctrines and opinions; it was later charged that on a certain day in November he preached to about twenty persons.[51]

As the Marian persecution of heretics heated up, testimony revealed the extent to which Colchester was a center of Protestant teaching. An informer priest, Stephen Morris, told of the close connections between the London and Colchester Protestants. Morris named three preachers from "King Edward's days," Master John Pullen, also called Smith, Simon Harlestone, and William, a Scot. Morris added that "their most abiding is at Colchester," although in London they had "much resort" to a center of Protestant teaching, an "ale-house in Cornhill." Pullen, an Oxford graduate who had forfeited the rectory of St. Peter's Cornhill, London, preached privately to the godly in Colchester and was probably active in the distribution of seditious literature for which Colchester was a center. Pullen finally had to flee to Geneva in 1557, but he eventually returned to Colchester to preach again another day. Some London Protestants—among them Thomas Mowntayne, rector of St. Michael's, Tower Hill—fled to Colchester to get a boat for passage to the safety of the Continent.[52]

The inns of Colchester became centers of Protestantism. Pullen and the other preachers from London most commonly resorted to the King's Head, whose mistress eventually got in trouble with the bishop for harboring Protestants. William Wilkinson, writing more than two decades later, spoke of that time in Colchester.

The ancient and famous city of Colchester was, in the troublesome times of Queen Mary's persecution, a sweet and comfortable mother of the bodies, and a tender nurse of the souls of God's children, and was at that time the more frequented, because it afforded many zealous and godly martyrs: who continually with their blood watered those seeds, which by the preachers of the word had been sown most plentifully in the hearts of Christians in the days of good king Edward. This town, for the earnest profession of the gospel, became like unto the city upon a hill; and as a candle upon a candlestick, gave light to all those, who, for the comfort of their consciences, came to confer

51. Oxley, 166–67; CR122/4.

52. Foxe, 8:384; Dickens, *English Reformation*, 375–76; Christina Hallowell Garrett, *The Marian Exiles: A Study in the Origins of Elizabethan Puritanism* (1938; reprint, Cambridge: Cambridge University Press, 1966), 262–63; Oxley, 197. Pullen returned in 1559 to become archdeacon of Colchester; see Newcourt, 1:92.

there, from divers places of the realm. And repairing to common inns, had by night their Christian exercises: which in other places could not be gotten.[53]

The testimony of one Henry Orinel painted a vivid picture of activity in the inns. Orinel, a husbandman from the Cambridgeshire village of Willingham, over fifty miles away, traveled to Colchester so that, in his words, "my conscience should not be entangled with the popish pitch." At Colchester he found many old acquaintances and met strangers who had come there "to confer concerning the safety of their consciences." One of the strangers had come not to confer, however, but to persuade others of his extreme doctrines. Christopher Vitells, a joiner from Delft and follower of the Family of Love, a Dutch sect, was viewed by Orinel as holding "many strange opinions," denying even the divinity of Christ. A local man who came to argue with Vitells was stymied by the wily Dutchman, who "put Barry to silence, and blanked him. So that he had not a word to say; to the great offense of divers; and especially of two women gospellers."[54]

Such activity was sure to gain the notice of authorities, particularly that of the restored conservative bishop of London, Edmund Bonner. As authorities began to ferret out heretics in 1555, they found them with the cooperation of such men as Lord Richard Rich, former Colchester recorder, and the earl of Oxford. While awaiting examination, some of the heretics were imprisoned in Colchester Castle, where the prisoners of better estate were personally visited by Bishop Bonner in his attempt to dissuade them from their heretical opinions. A nineteen-year-old man, William Hunter from Brentwood, and five other Essex men were burned in March, but not without protest by the common people. The Venetian ambassador reported that large crowds gathered in Essex and heard the heretics exhort the people to persevere in their faith; Rich even became fearful of attack on his person. In what was probably an attempt to put fear in the heart of the inhabitants, the men were burned in different towns, Colchester being one of them. Obvious sympathy was displayed

53. The 1579 Wilkinson quotation is from Strype, *Annals,* 2 (2): 282. See also Foxe, 8:384.
54. Oxley, 193; Strype, *Annals,* 2 (2): 284–86; Martin, *Radicals,* 203–9. Orinel's name was given as Crinel by Strype, who copied it from William Wilkinson. Spufford, *Communities,* 246–48, found that Orinel in 1575 was a husbandman, farming a half-yardland at that time. According to the *Oxford English Dictionary,* a yardland was 30 acres in 1684.

at the execution in Colchester of John Lawrence, an ex-friar, whose legs were so damaged by the heavy prison irons that he had to be burned while sitting in a chair. While at the stake, Lawrence was surrounded by young children who were reported to cry, "Lord, strengthen thy servant, and keep thy promise."[55] The open sympathy was a strong hint that many people in Colchester were not so easily intimidated.

In June, Thomas Hawkes, a gentleman from Coggeshall and a member of the earl of Oxford's household, was burned because he refused to have his newborn child christened as a Catholic. Rich and one of the local gentry, Sir John Raynsford, were especially asked to be present at the burning of Hawkes, making their compliance an example to the townsmen. The executions of Hawkes and of two of the earlier martyrs were notable because they were among the few people of a higher social status to burn in the Marian persecutions; others of the highborn recanted or simply fled to the Continent, leaving martyrdom to the lesser people. The government policy of selecting a favored few as examples, rather than attempting to search out every Protestant, applied to the clergy as well. The bishops who were unwilling to revert to Catholicism were burned at the stake, including the bishop of London during King Edward's time, Nicholas Ridley, and the great Protestant preacher and bishop Hugh Latimer. During the year 1555, uncooperative clergymen were being deprived of their benefices, including the rectors of St. Mary-at-Wall, Mile End, and St. Leonard's.[56]

During the spring of the burnings in Essex, the burgesses of Colchester were taught a lesson. In May, bailiff Thomas Dybney was called before the Privy Council, as a complaint had been received about "his evil behavior in matters of religion." Only months before, the two burgess MPs for Colchester in Mary's third Parliament, Aldermen Robert Browne and George Sayer, had faced the legislation restoring Catholicism and measures against heretics. Thirty-seven MPs walked out in protest, and by one report, Robert Browne was among them. Both Sayer and Browne had strong Protestant connections, as did most of the Colchester aldermanic group. The wife of George Sayer was Lollard Thomas Matthew's stepdaughter, and Browne's father was a close friend of town clerk and Protestant John Lucas. It is quite remarkable that Colchester men had been immune from investigation for so long; it is possible that

55. Oxley, 210–14; *VCH Essex*, 2:34; Davids, *Annals*, 34.
56. Oxley, 214–16; *APC*, 5:141, 153; *VCH Essex*, 2:33.

they had been protected by friends in high places, but in the climate of repression of heresy under the restored laws, such protection could go only so far. Thus, Colchester bailiff Thomas Dybney was called before the Privy Council at Hampton Court, where Dybney, unwilling to burn with the other Essex men, promised to "confess his offense on Monday or Tuesday next in two parish churches of Colchester at service time." The government made sure that town leaders took notice, as Dybney's penance had to be documented by "some of the chiefest and most honest of that town."[57] The question is why Dybney in particular was singled out. His social status may have had a lot to do with it, as Dybney was the only butcher ever to be elected alderman in Tudor Colchester. He must have been prosperous, or he would not have been elected, but a butcher was definitely of a lower status. Also, Dybney's Protestant beliefs were probably more radical than those of his fellow aldermen, who were more pragmatic about the folly of holding stubbornly to extremist views. Dybney's relatives were less circumspect. Dybney's brother-in-law, apothecary John Mace, burned a year later for his faith, and the Joan Dybney who went into exile in Aarau was probably Dybney's daughter-in-law.[58] With the Colchester aldermen experiencing so much pressure from the central government, it is no surprise that they increasingly began to cooperate with the authorities.

The persecution of ordinary laymen started in earnest in 1556; it was the beginning of a two-year period that would be among the most difficult in Colchester's history. Town records revealed unusual tension between the Crown and the town over secular matters in late 1555 and early 1556,[59] and a charge in the first lawhundred of 1556 signaled that the supporters of the queen's policies were coming into the ascendancy in Colchester. On January 20, innkeeper and Protestant John Damsell was

<hr />

57. APC, 5:134, 137; Oxley, 217; Davids, Annals, 29; Mackie, Earlier Tudors, 548–49; will of T. Matthew (1534), ERO D/ABW25/35; will of R. Browne (1548), ERO D/ABW3/146. Browne's action in leaving the House did not necessarily imply Protestantism, as some Catholics were unhappy with giving the papacy such free reign over the English church; see Bindoff, House, 1:525. On town leaders and the Reformation, see Bob Scribner, "Religion, Society, and Culture: Reorientating the Reformation," History Workshop Journal 14 (1982): 6–7.

58. CR94/22; CR122/4; ERO T/R108/2; Foxe, 8:138–39. Mace was Dybney's brother-in-law through Dybney's first wife, Amice, the daughter of butcher John Mace, who had a son named John; see wills of J. Mace (1533), ERO D/ACR2/158; E. Mace (1540), ERO D/ACR4/97; J. Dybney (1571), ERO DACR6/219. Garrett mistakenly gave Joan's first name as Margaret.

59. CR122/10d, 15, 19.

fined 10s. for not receiving travelers who had come "to render service to the Lord King and the Lady Queen, to the great dishonor of the whole town."[60] On March 28, just a week after Archbishop Cranmer suffered in the flames at Oxford, several Essex men were sent to Bishop Bonner. Among them were four Colchester men: tanner John Hammond, apothecary John Mace, weaver Richard Nichols, and weaver John Spencer. The men asserted their belief that there were only two sacraments in the church; Spencer added that the church of Rome was malignant and therefore not a part of Christ's catholic church; and Nichols related that "he had more plainly learned the truth of his profession by the doctrine set forth in king Edward the sixth's days." For Hammond, it was déjà vu, as he had been forced to abjure in 1530 for his Lollard views. But this time his resolve was stronger. Hammond was burned at Colchester on April 28 with the others who did not recant their heretical opinions (see table 6). Elizabethan martyrologist John Foxe reported that they "most cheerfully . . . ended their lives, to the glory of God's holy name, and the great encouragement of others."[61]

It was probably no coincidence that on the day before the execution, some of the Colchester burgesses belatedly began to enforce Mary's policies through the borough court. At the lawhundred on April 27, 1556, the jurors from the head ward, but not from any of the other wards, reported that five women and one man had failed to receive the Eucharist at Easter, three weeks earlier, and had absented themselves from divine services. Four of them were now fled "in contempt of the laws of the church and kingdom." The parishes of Holy Trinity and St. Runwald noted smugly that all of their inhabitants attended divine services and were fully obedient to "the laws of the Catholic Church and of the King and Queen."[62]

On the same day, a session of the peace, which handled the more serious cases, was held before bailiffs Sayer and Strachie and JPs Beriff, Dybney, Clere, and Beste. Two other aldermen, Browne and Robert Maynard, were also present, which was highly unusual, and Jerome Gilbert, probably acting as deputy recorder, was in attendance. The recorder was supposed to sit with the bailiffs and JPs at each session of the peace, but

---

60. CR122/3. In 1546 Damsell had appeared before the Privy Council, seemingly because of his Protestant beliefs on the Eucharist (*APC*, 1:485). Damsell died in 1558.
    61. Oxley, 222; Davids, *Annals*, 43–44; Foxe, 4:385–86; Foxe, 8:138–40.
    62. CR122/4.

TABLE 6. Colchester Residents Executed during Mary's Reign

Name	Status or Occupation	Parish	Age at Death	Heresy	Place and Date of Execution
John Hammond	Tanner			Opposed Roman church; belief in only two sacraments	Colchester April 28, 1556
Richard Nichols	Weaver			Same	Same
John Mace	Apothecary			Same	Same
John Spencer	Weaver			Same	Same
Agnes George†	Wife of husbandman Richard George	Berechurch	26	Same	Stratford-le-Bow June 27, 1556
Edmund Hurst	Laborer	St. James's	50	Same	Same
Elizabeth Pepper	Wife of weaver Thomas Pepper	St. James's	30 Pregnant	Same	Same
Thomas Benold	Tallow chandler			Opposed the mass	Colchester August 2, 1557
William Bongeor	Glazier	St. Nicholas's	60	Same	Same
Ellen Ewring	Spinster; wife of miller John Ewring		45	Same	Same
Elizabeth Folkes	Servant to clothier Nicholas Clere		20	Opposed the mass; opposed confession to priest	Same
Agnes May Smith Downes Silverside	Widow of priest		60	Same	Same
Agnes Bongeor	Wife of carrier Richard Bongeor		Had an infant	Opposed the mass	Colchester Sept. 17, 1557
Christian George†	Wife of husbandman Richard George				Colchester May 27, 1558
William Harris†					Same

†There is some doubt as to whether these were residents of Colchester, but circumstantial evidence indicates that they were; see text.

in practice, the recorder, often a nonresident, usually did not. Gilbert, a Colchester burgess, had been elected as recorder for the first year of Mary's reign, but after that, Anthony Stapleton, a successful London lawyer, was the recorder. As a committed Catholic, Gilbert may have been behind the events of that April day. Gilbert's parish, Holy Trinity, was said to be complying fully with the queen's policies, and Gilbert had encouraged house by house searches for heretical strangers, as well as the reporting of anyone suspected of heresy. An indictment for unlawful assembly was brought by the jurors against seventeen persons, but, curiously, the charge against them, including Thomas Putto, an Anabaptist tanner from Berechurch, was for an event that had happened eighteen months earlier. All of the people indicted, including Putto, who alone was indicted for unlawful preaching, were said to have already fled the town. That the charges did little to hurt anyone was possibly the intent of most of the jurors and aldermen. It seems the officials were scared into making a show of loyalty to the queen's policies but were not really wanting to bring harm. Gilbert and Robert Maynard, as later events would show, may have been more serious about detecting heresy, but they were in the minority. The indictment said that Thomas Putto was "a heretic and most hateful enemy of Christ" and that he had schemed "damnably to engage, induce and ensnare numerous men by his heresies, errors of unbelief, and accursed opinions." He had taught a number of persons either to flee or "to resist the royal power and the doctrine of Christ and Holy Mother Church . . . to the manifest weakening of all Christian faith." The sixteen other persons who were said to be "obstinate and fugitive heretics" were four couples; three men, among them a haberdasher, a barber, and a carrier; and five women, two of them wives, one a widow, and the marital status of the other two not given. Nothing more was heard of several of the people, but the widow, Joan Dybney, ended up in exile on the Continent, probably helped by her father-in-law, Alderman Thomas Dybney. Ellen Ewring, wife of a miller, was burned at the stake the following year.[63]

The burnings resumed in late June of 1556, this time at Stratford-le-Bow, just east of London. Among the martyrs were three Colchester people: fifty-year-old laborer Edmund Hurst and Elizabeth Pepper, wife of a

---

63. CR122/4, from Benham, *Translated Abstracts;* Ward, "Reformation," 91; *VCH Essex* 9:123. Gilbert was the father of the scientist William Gilbert. On the exiles from Essex, see Oxley, 195–97, 201–4.

weaver, both from St. James's parish; and twenty-six-year-old Agnes George of Berechurch, wife of a husbandman. The accused had been gathered up by the usual Essex authorities, such as the earl of Oxford, Lord Rich, and Master Mildmay of Chelmsford, but the women reported that, because they would not attend church, they had been committed to prison by Colchester authorities and then sent on to Bishop Bonner. Agnes George mentioned in particular "one master Maynard, an alderman of the town," probably Robert Maynard. George also added that it was in the time of Edward VI that she "went from her old faith and religion," again confirming the importance of the Edwardian period in the conversion to Protestantism. After condemnation, the thirteen wrote a letter in reply to the scathing charge by the dean of St. Paul's Cathedral that they "had as many sundry opinions as they were sundry persons." The letter proclaimed their unity, their "one voice," in their belief that there were only two sacraments; that their baptism was valid because it was "in the faith of Christ's church" and not "in the faith of the church of Rome"; that Rome was "the see of Antichrist, the congregation of the wicked, whereof the pope [was] head, under the devil"; and that the mass was "a blasphemous idol." Those were strong opinions, and Bonner told them that people who held such beliefs had to be "cut off like wicked branches." The sheriff tried to get the heretics to recant by separating them into two groups and telling each group in turn that the others had renounced their Protestant beliefs. It did not work, and the thirteen died together, with the eleven men tied to three stakes and the two women loose in the middle. A dramatic picture was included in Foxe's recounting of their suffering (see fig. 4). Pepper, who was about thirty, had been pregnant for eleven weeks; when asked why she did not tell the authorities that she was with child, she replied that "they knew it well enough."[64]

In August a new commission was issued to the earl of Oxford, Lord Darcy, and other Essex gentry to deal with heresy, giving them permission to seize the goods of those who had fled overseas and to proclaim the

---

64. Foxe, 8:151–56, 726; Oxley, 224. Sixteen were condemned, but only thirteen burned. Brigden, *London,* 616, says that such statements of unity by the reformers were also made to counter the views of the extremist groups, such as the "free willers" or the Anabaptists. Some historians have said that the Georges were from West Bergholt, but I believe they were from Berechurch, also known as West Donyland. Otherwise, Robert Maynard would not have had the authority to apprehend George. There were a number of Georges living in Lexden.

Fig. 4. A woodcut, first published in the sixteenth century in John Foxe's *Book of Martyrs*, showing the burning of thirteen martyrs at Stratford-le-Bow. Three of them were from Colchester, including the two women left loose in the middle, one of whom was pregnant.

queen's warrant for the restitution of church goods. A letter to Bishop Bonner from his commissary described the proceedings of the commissioners in Colchester, which had created tumult among the people. The commissary complained that, while delivering some heretics to the commissioners, "I was going betwixt the castle and St. Catherine's chapel, two hours and a half, and in great press and danger," and he asked the bishop to require the town bailiffs to aid him with men and weapons. After jockeying between church and secular officials, the commissioners decided to send the accused heretics to the bishop for examination; one Colchester woman, Alice, the wife of William Walley, quickly "abjured her erroneous opinions" and promised to do penance at St. Peter's on the next Sunday. She was "big with child" and so was probably eager to stay home. That left fourteen men and eight women to be bound with rope and taken to London; eight were Colchester inhabitants, with two of them, Ellen Ewring and Alan Simpson, having been among the seventeen indicted as heretics by the April session of the peace in Colchester. In London the prisoners created quite a stir, according to a letter Bonner wrote to Cardinal Pole. The Essex men and women insisted on going through Cheapside; Bonner said that the "naughty heretics . . . both exhorted the people to their part and had much comfort" from them. Followed to the bishop's palace by about a thousand people, the twenty-two were examined by Bonner, who described them as being "desperate and very obstinate." Their view on Communion presented the greatest difficulty, but they were finally released to return home after signing an ambiguous document that allowed both Roman and Protestant interpretations.[65]

On their return home from London, one of the prisoners made clear her distaste for bailiff Robert Maynard, whom Foxe called "a special enemy to God's gospel." Maynard welcomed Ellen Ewring with a kiss, but she openly called it a Judas kiss, remarking that Maynard would betray her in the end. Foxe noted that soon after her prediction, she was indeed apprehended again by Maynard and imprisoned until her death by burning in August of 1557. The martyrs would brook no compromise and had no patience with the politically expedient course the aldermen had chosen. In comparison, churchmen thought the Colchester authori-

---

65. Foxe, 8:303–10; Oxley, 226–28. Foxe mistakenly labeled this event as happening in 1557. Martin, *Radicals*, 132, offers the interesting speculation that the twenty-two prisoners sent to London formed a conventicle, since Foxe says that they were "apprehended at one clap."

ties were far too sympathetic to the Protestants. In December of 1556, priest Thomas Tye reported to Bishop Bonner on conditions in Colchester since the twenty-two "rank heretics" had come back from London.

> the detestable sort of schismatics were never so bold . . . as they are now at this present. . . . The rebels are stout in the town of Colchester. The ministers of the church are hemmed at in the open streets, and called knaves. The blessed sacrament of the altar is blasphemed and railed upon in every house and tavern. Prayer and fasting are not regarded. Seditious talks and news are rife, both in town and country, in as ample a manner, as though there had no honourable lords and commissioners been sent for reformation thereof.

Tye further complained that mariner John Love had come home again and had "nothing said or done to him." According to Tye, Love had twice been indicted of heresy, he had fled with his family, and his goods had been seized, yet when he returned to Colchester the authorities had done nothing.[66] It appears that the town leaders were cooperating with the Crown when it was necessary but, for the most part, remaining sympathetic to Protestantism, though not willing to die for it.

In February, 1557, Queen Mary issued additional commissions against heresy, and by March more heretics were imprisoned in Colchester Castle, including five from Colchester: glazier William Bongeor, tallow chandler Thomas Benold, aged widow Agnes Silverside, young Elizabeth Folkes, and Ellen Ewring, who had rejected Maynard's welcoming kiss. At the same time, the jailer of Colchester Castle was to be examined, possibly for being too lenient with heretics. A letter written in June by Bishop Bonner to his subordinates complained of heretics in Essex and said that they must be either converted or excommunicated and handed over to the secular authorities for punishment. On June 23 the prisoners in Colchester were tried before Dr. Chedsey (the archdeacon of Middlesex), Commissary Kingston, and the two Colchester bailiffs for the year, Robert Browne and Robert Maynard. Maynard was all too willing to comply with Catholic authorities, which brought him a rebuke from twenty-year-old prisoner Elizabeth Folkes. Folkes, "a tall, well-favoured young wench" who had refused to deny her beliefs, touched the heart of Dr. Chedsey, and as he read the sentence condemning her to death, tears

---

66. Foxe, 8:383, 387; Davids, *Annals,* 48.

trickled down his cheeks. After hearing the sentence, Folkes knelt in prayer, then urged her judges to repent, especially those, such as Robert Maynard, who had brought her to prison. In relating the story, Foxe indignantly mentioned that Maynard's sleeping as he sat in judgment on the bench was an indication of his callousness and indifference.[67]

In July, an itinerant gospel preacher, George Eagles, was apprehended in Colchester, an act that gained praise for the bailiffs from the Privy Council. Eagles, often called Trudgeover-the-World because he wandered about the country preaching, was considered such a threat that an edict was proclaimed throughout four shires promising a £20 award to his captor; years later it was revealed that Alderman Benjamin Clere was responsible for his arrest. Eagles was subsequently executed for treason, because he prayed that God would turn the heart of Queen Mary.[68] If Robert Maynard and Benjamin Clere were fully cooperating with the officials, others seemed quietly to be delaying the harsh measures in store for the heretics. Elizabeth Folkes was allowed to stay with her uncle rather than in prison, and she was openly offered escape, but she refused. Over a month passed after the sentencing of the heretics imprisoned in the castle, and they had still not been executed, so the Queen's Privy Council, on July 28, asked the town authorities why they had not carried out the sentence. Five days later, the five Colchester residents were burned in the early morning just outside the town wall, with a large crowd, estimated in the thousands, shouting in encouragement for the heretics, "The Lord strengthen them; the Lord comfort them; the Lord pour his mercies upon them." Just before the execution, the heretics kneeled down to say their prayers, and Elizabeth Folkes tried to give her petticoat to her mother, but one of the authorities did not want such a show from the prisoners. In his 1570 edition, Foxe identified the man as Master Benjamin Clere, described as having previously been a "gospeller," which accords with his father's early adherence to reform. On the afternoon of the same day, four Essex people "suffered their martyrdom with . . . triumph and joy" in the castle yard, again surrounded by crowds of encouragers. Bailiffs Browne and Maynard delayed the execution of one of the women who was supposed to burn; they explained in a letter to Bishop Bonner that Agnes Bongeor was saved at the last minute because the writ authorizing her execution had used the wrong

---

67. Oxley, 233, 236–37; Foxe, 8:301–3, 390.
68. *APC,* 6:129–30; Byford, "Religious Change," 227–28; Foxe, 8:393–97 (though Foxe says that a Ralph Lardin was responsible for the arrest of Eagles).

name. Nevertheless, Bongeor, who had a suckling infant, was burned six weeks later.[69]

More examinations were held in April of 1558, again with the officials of Colchester having to cooperate; in fact, two of Bishop Bonner's officials were gloating that the officers of Colchester were "very diligent with us." Three more people were burned in Colchester on May 27, the last Protestants to suffer that fate in Essex; there is evidence that at least two of them were from Colchester. As they burned, they "triumphantly praised God . . . and offered up their bodies a lively sacrifice." Officials were beginning to see that the persecutions were counterproductive and that even nonreformers had become sympathetic to the martyrs because of the harsh measures used against them.[70]

The count is uncertain, but from thirteen to fifteen Colchester residents were executed under the heresy laws. All were of a lesser social standing, a fact noted by the bishop's scribe John Boswell, who wrote to Bonner about Colchester:

> I do see by experience, that the sworn inquest for heresies do, most commonly, indict the simple, ignorant, and wretched heretics, and do let the arch-heretics go; which is one great cause that moveth the rude multitude to murmur, when they see the simple wretches (not knowing what heresy is) to burn. I wish, if it may be, that this common disease might be cured amongst the jurats of Essex; but I fear me, it will not be, so long as some of them be, as they are, infected with the like disease.

Seven of the martyrs were women (see table 6), which probably accounts for Commissary Kingston's suggestion to the bishop that if "the householders" of Colchester "might be compelled to bring every man his own wife to her own seat in the church in time of divine service, it would profit much." The seven women were not to be intimidated. Sixty-year-old widow Agnes Silverside (alias May, Smith, Downes) seemed to be a leader among Essex Protestants, and Foxe recorded a letter written to her

---

69. Oxley, 233–34; *APC*, 6:135, 144; Foxe, 8:387–90, 392, 421–23; Davids, *Annals*, 49, 54. In 1575 Clere's action was still remembered against him; see Byford, "Religious Change," 224–25.

70. Oxley, 237; Foxe, 8:420–23, 467–68; BL, Harley MS 416, f. 74; Byford, "Religious Change," 124; Brigden, *London*, 619. One of the martyrs was Christian George, the second wife of Richard George; the 1524–25 lay assessments show a William Harris in St. Nicholas's parish and one in St. Botolph's.

from a London prison by an Essex heretic who referred to her "constant faith." Foxe described her as a "good old woman" who answered her interrogators with "sound judgment and boldness." The bishop's official had a different view: "she is a froward, obstinate heretic, and willing to burn her old rotten bones." Most of the women seemed to be literate, as they spent their time in prison in reading and prayer, and they were all very knowledgeable of Scripture.[71]

Almost six months later, Queen Mary's death on November 17 brought the burnings to an end in Colchester. The wheel of fortune had turned. Protestantism was again in the ascendancy, but the years of conflict had taken their toll, and Colchester would reap the harvest, both good and bad, for years to come.

---

71. Foxe, 8:306, 388, 391, 414, 416, 423. Silverside was the widow of a priest, proba-bly Thomas Silverside (CR116/22d). Her first husband was possibly William Downes, who had died by 1517 (CR88/22).

Part 3
The Uneasy Alliance of Piety and Secular Power

7

Defenders of the Faith, 1558–62

"Lady Elizabeth, by the Grace of God, Queen of England, France, and Ireland, Defender of the Faith," exulted the Colchester court record on November 28, 1558,[1] a few days after Elizabeth's accession to the throne. Mary's reign had too often unleashed the acrid fumes of the burning of the flesh of condemned heretics, and Bishop Bonner's unwavering zeal had brought three more people to suffer at the stake in Colchester only six months before, so for those with Protestant sympathies it must have been clear that Providence had brought Elizabeth to the throne. The Reformation had come to England through King Henry's efforts to bring Anne Boleyn to his marriage bed, thus supplanting the Catholic Catherine of Aragon; in 1533 Henry's machinations had produced both the baby Elizabeth and the Protestant Church of England. Now, twenty-five years later, the daughters were repeating the experience of their mothers, that of a Catholic queen being replaced by a Protestant; and ardent reformers intended for the replacement to endure this time.

In Colchester the upheavals of Mary's reign produced an acrimony that would haunt the borough for years to come. Though there were many committed Protestants by 1558, traditional Catholicism still had its devoted adherents, so Colchester was not yet a wholly Protestant town. But the long reign of Elizabeth would eventually make it so. The courage and bravery of the martyrs had engendered much sympathy—as well as hostility against the local perpetrators of the executions, especially since the influential managed to evade punishment. In the first elections after Elizabeth's accession, three of the town leaders were replaced by Protestants, and thus began a new chapter in the history of Colchester. Town officials slowly began to experiment with the role of the Calvinistic godly magistrate, eventually taking the initiative to hire a town preacher to provide the preaching not found in the parish churches, and

---

1. CR124/7.

beginning an intensive campaign to direct the lives of the people toward godliness. The cohesion of the community had been sorely tried, not only by the traumatic events of Mary's reign, but by the forcible elimination of parish ceremonial and long-held beliefs. Town officials were trying to fill the gap. In many ways they were successful, but not all of their efforts were appreciated, so it was a time both of promise and hope and of disappointment and conflict. This chapter examines, first, the clergy and the institutional church at the beginning of Elizabeth's reign, which had been weakened both by the religious upheavals and by the effects of inflation on the value of the livings; and, second, the Protestant reformers and the influences on them, as well as their efforts beginning in 1562 to emphasize preaching and church attendance and to provide poor relief and a haven for Dutch refugees.

The Church in Transition

By the time Elizabeth succeeded to the throne, the church had been buffeted for twenty-five years by drastic reforms and then by the attempted reversal. Only two years before Elizabeth's succession, a priest friendly to Bishop Bonner reported: "the ministers of the church are hemmed at in the open streets [of Colchester], and called knaves. The blessed sacrament of the altar is blasphemed and railed upon in every house and tavern."[2] Now, with the Protestant Elizabeth as queen, the old mass was gone again, and in its place was a service centered around the Communion table and a new Prayer Book. With the Word, rather than the priest, as the ultimate authority, the new emphasis was on preaching, putting a new demand on the clergy. Even the private lives of the clergy were affected, since reformist thinking permitted clerical marriage. Yet, with all the changes, the basic ecclesiastical structure was still in place, with the parish system and parish churches in Colchester remaining the same, and with a church hierarchy still overseeing it all.

Though Elizabeth had a high stake in maintaining a Protestant England, her appointment of Matthew Parker as archbishop of Canterbury in 1559 signified that she was hardly a Protestant zealot. Parker, who had once been Anne Boleyn's chaplain, was certainly Protestant, but he was a moderate, having chosen to remain quietly in retirement in England during Mary's reign, rather than opposing Mary's religious policies and pos-

---

2. Foxe, 8:383.

sibly burning at the stake as Archbishop Cranmer had done. He had not even tried to flee to the Continent as so many did. The problems of changing back from a Catholic to a Protestant Church of England were many, with Parker's elevation to the archbishopric being one example. Though Parker was elected on August 1, four sympathetic and qualified bishops could not be found to consecrate him until December 17. With one exception, Mary's Catholic bishops had refused to take the oath of supremacy acknowledging Elizabeth as "Supreme Governor" of the realm in matters spiritual, as decreed by the Supremacy Bill passed by Parliament on April 29. To get conforming Protestant bishops in place, the Crown had to take a more direct role in church governance than was usual and so began nominating men who were then duly elected by church officials.[3]

Archbishop Parker's consecration was only one of the changes during the month of December, 1559, that affected the church in Colchester. A new bishop of London was needed, since Bishop Bonner, the notorious persecutor of Protestants in his diocese, which included Colchester, was among those refusing to take the oath of supremacy. For his defiance, Bonner was imprisoned in the Marshalsea prison, where he remained until his death ten years later. On December 21, Edmund Grindal officially became bishop of London. Having been a protégé of Nicholas Ridley, the former bishop of London who had burned beside Hugh Latimer at the stake in Oxford in 1555, Grindal had worked among the English churches in exile in Strasbourg and Frankfurt, so he was sympathetic to the reforming ideas that would come to be known as Puritanism during Elizabeth's reign. The church that had formed in exile would have a profound impact on England and on Colchester.

One of Grindal's first actions was to designate John Pullen, an Oxford graduate, as the new archdeacon of Colchester, an appointment that spoke volumes about Grindal. Pullen's ardent reformist views had deprived him in 1555 of the rectory of a central London parish, St. Peter's Cornhill, and Pullen had defiantly stayed in London for at least a year, where he had celebrated Communion at his own house at Easter and had gone out to preach in Colchester and probably to take part in the dissemination of the religiously seditious literature coming through the port of Colchester. Finally being forced to flee from England, he and his family traveled to Geneva, where they were received into John Knox's

---

3. For history of the Elizabethan church, see Cross, *Church and People;* Edwards, *Christian England.*

congregation. While there, Pullen collaborated on the new English translation that would be known as the Geneva Bible. Remarkably for a bishop, Grindal was not threatened by Pullen's more radical nature and beliefs. Grindal, who had tried to be the peacemaker between the disputing English Protestants in exile, would continue in that role as he struggled to maneuver the London diocese between the forces of Protestant zealots and the moderates.[4]

The first order of business for the Elizabethan church was to insure the loyalties of the clergy to the new ruler and the church over which Her Majesty, Elizabeth, was "Supreme Governor." After passage of the parliamentary bills again establishing the Protestant Church of England, local clergy were asked to subscribe their names, and about forty gathered in Colchester to do so. Most of them were from the surrounding area, with surprisingly few of them, only five, connected with the sixteen parish churches in Colchester.[5] It had not been a happy period for the established church in Colchester. Needing information about the state of the church, the new archbishop sent out a questionnaire in 1560, and the resulting information about the borough of Colchester was startling. Only one beneficed incumbent was active: William Lyon, at the village church of Mile End. Lexden's parson, a pluralist, had been absent from Lexden for at least twelve years and probably longer, as one of the suspected heretics in 1556 reported that the parson had been absent "these fourteen years." The indebtedness of the rector of St. Mary's, Thomas Browne, had resulted in his imprisonment and subsequent appeal to Westminster early in 1560. St. Leonard's rector, Peter Walker, was excommunicate; and all the other benefices were either vacant or had a curate serving in place of an incumbent. On the positive side, the curate at St. James's Church, Lawrence Agar, was said to be able to "preach truly."[6]

The incumbents at St. Leonard's, the parish that included the port area, were a good illustration of the pitfalls besetting the clergy in the 1550s and into the Elizabethan reign. Though Thomas Audley had pre-

4. Barrett L. Beer, "London Parish Clergy and the Protestant Reformation, 1547–1559," *Albion* 18 (1986): 386–91. On the Elizabethan church settlement, see Cross, *Church and People,* 124–136; Norman L. Jones, "Elizabeth's First Year: The Conception and Birth of the Elizabethan Political World," in *The Reign of Elizabeth I,* ed. Christopher Haigh (London: Macmillan, 1984), 27–53.

5. From a transcript of Lambeth Cart. Misc., vol. 13, pt. 2, no. 57, kindly supplied by the late Miss Hilda Grieve.

6. Grieve transcript of Corpus Christi College MS 122; Foxe, 8:305; CR125/5, 14d, 16.

sented the first new rector to St. Leonard's after the Reformation (William Wright, alias Smythe), the right of presentation was in the possession of the Crown by 1550, when Nicholas Davye, at the age of fifty-two, was appointed rector by King Edward. Davye had been a chantry priest at St. Leonard's, described as a man of small learning but of "good conversation," but the policies of Queen Mary deprived him of his post early in her reign. Former rector William Wright was restored to the position, but he died in 1557 and was replaced by Thomas Gale, the master of the Hospital of St. Mary Magdalen. Gale held the rectory only briefly, resigning after three months and dying shortly thereafter; the preamble to Gale's will, illustrating the confusion of the time, was a curious mixture of Catholic and Protestant expressions, with Gale beseeching the "blessed lady virgin" to intercede for his soul while at the same time stating that his only hope was in the mercy of Christ. Gale's brief tenure at St. Leonard's was followed by the appointment of Peter Walker, presumably a good Catholic, so it did not take Walker long to get in trouble with Elizabeth's officials. On March 20, 1559, the Privy Council ruled that Walker should be pilloried in the marketplace on the next market day, "for uttering lewd and untrue reports." His punishment was carefully prescribed by the Privy Council. The words "for false seditious tales" were to be inscribed on a label on his head while he was in the pillory in the Colchester market. Then, he would be freed if he found guarantors for his good behavior; otherwise he would go to the castle prison. Not surprisingly, Walker soon signed the subscription agreeing to conform to the Book of Common Prayer, although by the next year he was excommunicate for some unknown reason. Later, Walker conformed and was even appointed archdeacon in another diocese.[7]

Though he was not resident, Peter Walker continued holding the benefice at St. Leonard's until his death in 1570, so the port church was served by curates who seemed to be loved by the people and were much more in tune with the Protestant leanings of the parish, which included mariners who had long served the Protestant cause. The first curate to serve in the place of Walker was the former rector Nicholas Davye, whose life and service had spanned the changes from Catholicism to Protestantism. Nothing could be more Catholic than his earlier service as a chantry priest at St. Leonard's, but he had obviously adopted Protes-

7. See appendix 6; Newcourt, 2:173; Guildhall MS 9531/12, pt. 2; PRO E301/19; ERO D/ABW16/128; *APC*, 7:71; Grieve transcripts of Lambeth Cart. Misc., vol. 13, pt. 2, no. 57, and Corpus Christi College MS 122.

tant ways, including marriage. The succeeding curates, Thomas Upcher (by 1562) and Michael Goodeare, who was finally made rector on Walker's death in 1570, also had wives and children, thus pointing up one of the changes that was very noticeable and sometimes upsetting to parishioners accustomed to a celibate clergy. On the positive side, the presence of wives and children meant that the Protestant clergy was less set apart and possibly more accessible than the Catholic clergy had been. Clerical marriage had been defended by the earliest Protestant apologists, and in 1559 the Elizabethan settlement of religion returned to the Edwardian acceptance of clerical marriage; however, the ideal of clerical celibacy remained even beyond the Tudor period.[8]

Correcting the ills of the past was difficult, with one continuing problem being the nonresident, pluralist clergymen, such as Peter Walker, who left parishes with curates or even with no clergy whatsoever. The poor value of the Colchester benefices was at the heart of the problem. A survey from 1574 shows that the benefices had remained almost the same as they were in the 1535 survey known as the *Valor Ecclesiasticus,* and the steep inflation that had hit Tudor England made the benefices of less actual value than they had been in 1535, so it was almost impossible to survive on a benefice alone, especially with the additional needs of a family. As the 1560 returns lamented about the Colchester parishes, "All these will not make three men's livings if they were joined together."[9] It is no surprise that the clergy resorted to pluralism, the practice of holding more than one cure at a time, although Protestants often railed against the practice. When a 1563 report was made to the Privy Council by the bishop of London, Grindal found that in Colchester, ten parish churches still had no incumbents, but William Lyon, who had been described in 1560 as one who "keepeth hospitality, and doeth his duty diligently" as rector of Mile End, had also become rector of Holy Trinity and curate at Berechurch, the combined value of which would have been close to £14, with a little additional income from the curacy.[10] Even so,

---

8. Carlson, "Clerical Marriage," 27–30; Byford, "Religious Change," 138; Guildhall MS 9531/13, pt. 1, f. 156; will of Davye (1560), ERO D/ACR5/100; will of Goodeare (1572), ERO D/ACR6/319. See also the wills mentioning Goodeare's ministry at St. Leonard's in 1561, 1567, and 1568: ERO D/ACR3/180; ERO D/ACR6/42; ERO D/ACR6/87.

9. Newcourt, 2:172, 388; Grieve transcript of Corpus Christi College MS 122.

10. Grieve transcript of Corpus Christi College MS 122; BL, Harley MS 595, no 24, f. 69v. Morant's copy of an undated (probably seventeenth-century) Lambeth manuscript (D/Y2/2, p. 283) gives higher valuations.

it was not a plush living for Lyon. Throughout the Elizabethan period, pluralism continued in Colchester, and it was not usually condemned unless a clergyman failed to have services and do his duty in the church.

The established church, then, was in poor health in Colchester, but more vitality could be found among the zealous reformers, led by the new archdeacon of Colchester, John Pullen, who apparently lived, at least some of the time, in Colchester.[11] Pullen was in trouble for preaching in Colchester shortly after his return from his exile in Geneva,[12] and his continuing connection with Colchester seems to have stemmed partly from his marriage just before he went into exile to a Colchester woman, widow Joan Fawkon, the daughter of committed Protestant Nicholas Wilbore.[13] Though the parish church was greatly weakened by the ups and downs of the last few decades, many were heartened by the presence of John Pullen, which portended change, representing as he did both the church hierarchy and zealous reformers. Around the time of his appointment as archdeacon on December 13, 1559, John Pullen was admitted to the freedom of the borough, with the usual fine excused. It was a most unusual step for the corporation to take and was indicative of the intent and influence of the newly constituted body of leaders elected in the autumn of 1559, in the first election after Elizabeth's accession to the throne.[14] A reformist town governance was emerging.

Reform and a Profile of the Reforming Aldermen of 1560

Caution was the order of the day for the bailiffs in the first weeks of the new reign, and Elizabeth's new Privy Council inquired in late December as to why the bailiffs had not released eight persons in the castle prison who had been put there by Mary "as persons suspected in religion." Head bailiff Benjamin Clere was apparently still clinging to the position

11. Byford, "Religious Change," 137, found that Pullen bought a house in Colchester in 1561, although the 1563 certificate from the bishop of London said that he "lyeth at Thurrington [Thorrington], six miles from Colchester" (BL, Harley MS 595, no. 24).

12. *APC,* 7:87–88.

13. According to Garrett, *Marian Exiles,* 262–63, Pullen had a wife and a daughter, Faith, when he went into exile. It appears that he had married Joan, whose husband, Robert Fawkon, had died in 1554 (ERO D/ABW14/77), leaving three daughters, the youngest being Faith. See the wills of Joan's parents, Nicholas Wilbore (1557; ERO D/ABW39/196) and Margaret Wilbore (1566; ERO D/ACR5/136); Margaret's was written after Pullen died. See also CR136/3, which mentions a boy named John Pullen whose parents, John and Joan Pullen, were both deceased by 1568.

14. CR126/1d.

of tyrannical suppression that he had adopted during Mary's reign, and three weeks later the Privy Council ordered the bailiffs to release the prisoners. Just such reluctance must have helped to inspire the reformers to begin a concerted effort to alter the shape of town governance by electing new men to the aldermanic bench at the next election, due in the autumn of 1559. To put more reformers on the bench, however, meant that some of the old hands had to go. The political changes came at a cost, and tensions were high, reflecting the acrimonies of past years. In the summer before the election, William Beriff, the brother of Alderman John Beriff (who would be ousted), was summoned by the JPs of Colchester to be tried for his troublemaking, to which Beriff replied by attacking first Alderman John Beste and then William Sympson, whose wife had been tagged as one of the nonconformists during Mary's reign. Beriff was especially rude to Sympson; he called him " 'villain' in the hearing of several worthy persons, and constantly shouted and published it and struck [Sympson] with his fist."[15] Nothing else is known about the conflict, but the results were clear when three aldermen were ousted: John Beriff, William Strachye, and Robert Maynard, the sleepy bailiff who had roused the condemnation of two of the martyrs, Ellen Ewring and Elizabeth Folkes. Remarkably, Benjamin Clere stayed on, a tribute to his power in the town. Three new men were elevated from the common council: Robert Lambert, Robert Middleton, and Robert Northen. Five new men were brought onto the common council, and each, without exception, was a reformer or had close reformist connections. For example, Richard Alfeld's sister married Stephen Holt, the uncle of the twenty-year-old Elizabeth Folkes who had burned at the stake.[16]

Retaliation against William Beriff, who represented the opposition to the changes, was swift. At the lawhundred just after the election, Beriff, the brother of the alderman who had just been replaced, lost his freedom

---

15. *APC*, 7:26, 44; CR122/4; CR125/2.

16. Also gone from the council were Edmund Troman, who had been a trusted servant of the abbot of St. John's Monastery (*VCH Essex*, 2:98), and John Damsell, who had died in 1558 (ERO D/ABW12/95). On Alfeld, see Holt's will (1590), ERO D/ACW3/395. Among the other new councillors, Nicholas Clere was the youngest son of the alderman who had written the first Protestant will in Colchester (1538; PRO 25 Dyngeley). Richard Collett was one of the five signers of a 1559 presentment asking for stricter regulation of church attendance and for the reestablishment of St. Anne's almshouses (D/Y2/2, p. 65; Byford, "Religious Change," 134). Matthew Browne was a relative of Alderman Robert Browne; see William Browne's will (1566), ERO D/ACR6/20. John Luson and the new alderman, Robert Middleton, married the Reynolde sisters; see ERO D/P245/1/1 and ERO D/ABW31/100.

and was charged with the July assault on Beste and Sympson. At the next lawhundred in January, 1560, another Beriff brother, Thomas, lost his freedom for using a court outside the town in a dispute he was having with the Christmas family.[17] In 1560 the same reforming aldermanic group was elected, though political tensions must have continued, since an ordinance was passed in 1561 decrying "corrupt elections."[18]

The 1560 group of aldermen was the backbone of the conscious change toward a godly magistracy, so that group will now be examined for comparison to the 1530 group that was analyzed in chapter 1. By 1560, the wealthy Christmases were no longer active in borough affairs, but the Cleres provided one direct link with the 1530 set of aldermen, as Benjamin Clere was the son of John Clere from the earlier group. Two others, and probably a third, were also sons of aldermen,[19] and, as a whole, the 1560 group had noticeably fewer nonnative aldermen—two, compared to five in 1530—reflecting the hard economic times that had made Colchester less attractive to outsiders than it had been earlier. Clothiers still dominated the aldermanic group, with five in 1560, the same number as in 1530; in addition, one of the two merchants, John Beste, started out as a clothier and probably still dealt in cloth as a merchant. Three other trades were represented: Robert Browne was a grocer who had begun as a baker; haberdasher William Mott had once been a wax chandler; and Thomas Dybney, being in the less socially respectable trade of butchery, was accomplishing a lot just to be among the aldermen, as he was the first of his trade to reach that exalted status in Colchester. As far as wealth was concerned, George Sayer, already the owner of several manors,[20] was probably the wealthiest, followed by John Maynard.

The aldermen of 1560 were slightly less experienced in town governance than had been the group of 1530, with the average years of service for the group down from 12 to 10.7 years. Some men had extensive experience; Sayer, with 21 years, was senior in terms of service, having been elected shortly before the execution of the abbot of St. John's.[21] These leaders were men whose civic experience developed along with the Refor-

---

17. CR124/9; CR125/2–3, 9–10.

18. *RPB*, 31.

19. George Sayer was the son of Alderman John Sayer, and John Beste was the son of Alderman Robert Beste. Robert Browne was probably the son of Robert Browne I.

20. *Essex Fines*, 4:285, 297; 5:2.

21. *LP*, 14 (2): no. 43.

mation. Robert Browne II and Benjamin Clere were just a year behind Sayer in experience. During their first term as bailiffs in 1541, a case of blasphemy came before their first session of the peace, for which George Sayer and the experienced John Christmas were sitting on the bench as JPs. The case involved a carpenter's refusal to do reverence to the cross of Christ, and it seemed to be a matter more of strong disbelief than of Protestantism. Nevertheless, it is significant that the young borough court officials were active in taking up matters that had usually been the province of the ecclesiastical court;[22] later, as the experienced aldermen in the Elizabethan period, they would frequently do so.

The reformist connections between some of the 1560 aldermen pre-dated even King Henry's reforms of the early 1530s. In 1527, a circle of active Lollards came to the attention of the church hierarchy, and it was revealed that the household of Thomas Matthew was a center of the non-conformist teaching. Matthew had married a committed Lollard widow, Marion (or Maryon) Wesden, the mother of three daughters, Agnes, Maryon, and Jane Wesden. Matthew died in 1534, but, surprisingly, three of the 1560 aldermen were mentioned in his will written twenty-six years before. George Sayer had married Agnes Wesden, and William Mott had a close, though undefined, relationship as well, so Sayer and Mott were coexecutors of Matthew's will. Robert Lambert was also mentioned; possibly Lambert's first wife was a daughter of Robert Matthew, Thomas's brother. Years later, when William Mott wrote his will in 1562, he made Lambert the supervisor of his will, and Lambert, in 1590, made Mott's son, Robert, supervisor of his will.[23] Those early ties were lasting.

Others of the 1560 group had ties to early nonconformity or to English Protestantism; among those were cousins John Beste and Benjamin Clere. Implicated in the investigations into nonconformity in 1527–28 was "known man" Robert Beste, the brother of John, the 1560 alderman; and Alderman John Clere, the father of Benjamin, wrote the first openly Protestant will in Colchester, in 1538.[24] Three of the 1560 aldermen—Thomas Dybney, Robert Lambert , and Robert Middleton—were among the churchwardens or their assistants who, during the Edwardian

---

22. CR111/3. A case of usury was also before the court.

23. CR88/22d; Strype, *Memorials,* 1 (1): 116, 121, (2): 53–54, 64–65; will of Matthew, ERO D/ABW25/35; will of Mott, ERO D/ACR5/75; will of Lambert, PRO 69 Harrington.

24. Strype, *Memorials,* 1 (1): 117, 121, 124–27, 131; will of J. Clere, PRO 25 Dyngeley. Robert Beste was probably the Protestant exile in Frankfurt; see Bindoff, *House,* 1:426.

Protestant Reformation, sold church plate used in the Catholic mass or whitewashed walls to remove images.[25]

With such tendencies toward reform, Mary's Catholic reign had been a hazardous time to be a governor of Colchester. Seven of the 1560 group were already in office at the beginning of Mary's reign; of those men, five, as noted earlier, had a vested interest in or connection to the Reformation,[26] but those same men found it prudent to trim their sails of Protestantism, even though a number of Colchester Protestants died for their faith or fled into exile. The die was cast early in the reign, when the Colchester aldermen opted for the legitimacy of Catholic Mary, rather than being lured by the attempt to make a queen of Protestant Lady Jane Grey. Contacts with the central government during that time often proved to be intimidating. Some of the aldermen had the perilous duty of serving as MPs in Mary's Parliaments, and in Mary's first Parliament in late 1553, which stripped away the Edwardian ecclesiastical settlement, Alderman John Beste took the discreet course, not being among those who "stood for the true religion," that is, for Protestantism. Beste probably took a cue from his social superior and fellow MP John Lucas, the Colchester town clerk who had become rich by helping the government sell former monastic lands. It was probably with some relief that Colchester turned after that to local gentry for representation, except in Mary's third Parliament, in which resident members had to serve. George Sayer and Robert Browne had the dubious honor that time, and Browne was one of the members who walked out in protest against Mary's policies. Other aldermen had the frightening experience of being called before the Privy Council. Benjamin Clere and John Maynard went in early 1554, but Thomas Dybney's appearance in May, 1555, was more traumatic. To save his life, Dybney had to confess his "evil behavior in matters of religion" and do penance in Colchester.[27] Though often dragging their feet, town leaders had to give the appearance of being in league with Mary's policies, and by 1556 some were actively implementing the suppression of heretics.

Protestantism, however, won in the end in Colchester. The 1560 group of aldermen, though not the stuff of which martyrs were made, had taken the pragmatic course of survival for themselves and the bor-

---

25. Dickin, "Church Goods," 166–67.

26. George Sayer owned former priory lands; Beste, Clere, Sayer, and Mott had close relatives who were early reformers; and Dybney was churchwarden.

27. Bindoff, *House,* 1:426 and 2:555; Davids, *Annals,* 29; *APC,* 5:9, 134, 137.

ough, though they must have appeared lax and cowardly to the radical Protestants who brooked no compromise and who even gloried in dying for their faith. Since the aldermen had to help pass judgment on the radical Protestants and then carry out the sentences imposed, they must have keenly felt the dilemma of being in the middle. Though sympathetic to reform, they also had a strong sense of obedience to the Crown, the authority above them. After all, they could justify their actions to their Protestant critics by referring to the biblical injunctions to obey the ruling powers, though their actions were probably also motivated by a strong desire for self-preservation.

The aldermen of the 1560s would prove to be a formidable force in making Elizabethan Colchester a Protestant town, and the six extant wills from the group reflect their commitment to reform, although, at first glance, the 1562 will of William Mott seemed to be a puzzling exception. Mott had none of the Protestant phrases about Jesus Christ in his preamble, yet he mentioned friends from the early Lollard group of the late 1520s and early 1530s and even named John Pykas, a teacher of that early group, as coexecutor.[28] John Maynard, whose brother, Robert, had been labeled by Foxe as "a special enemy to God's gospel," asserted his Protestant, and even Calvinistic, beliefs in his 1568 will by affirming to be among the elect of God: ". . . trusting that through the death and passion of Jesus Christ I shall be partaker of the heavenly felicity among the elect and chosen people of God." In this period the language used in wills became much more expansive in its expression of a personal relationship with God. For example, in his preamble, John Beste (1573) commended his soul "into the hands of Almighty God . . . and of Jesus Christ his son, who by his most precious bloodshedding became my most merciful redeemer and savior, and of the Holy Ghost, my most sweet and eternal comforter." The six wills from the 1560 group showed a much higher concern for personal piety and pious deeds than was found in the 1530 group, with four of the 1560 aldermanic wills being far above average in their indications of piety, while the wills of Mott and Browne showed only a moderate concern. Every one of the aldermen gave to the poor, with John Beste giving £200 to "the sick, diseased, impotent, aged and most needy persons."[29] Both Sayer and Browne remembered the poor prisoners in the castle and in the moot hall, while Beste, Maynard, and

---

28. Mott also provided a house for Widow Cowbridge, whose son had burned at Oxford in 1538: see ERO D/ACR5/75; Foxe, 5:252–53.

29. Foxe, 8:387; will of Maynard, PRO 15 Sheffeld; will of Beste, PRO 2 Martyn.

Lambert supported the preaching in the town. From other sources, it is known that Clere's daughter successively married two of the town preachers and that Sayer established almshouses for the poor.[30]

Even with all the evidence of piety, charges of wrongdoing were occasionally leveled against the aldermen. A presentment in 1559 said that Robert Northen had withheld money from the poor in his capacity as farmer of St. Anne's Chapel,[31] and Benjamin Clere was at the center of more than one continuing dispute in Colchester. Clere was a complex person. Many apparently regarded him as being dependable and honest, since he was named as executor of two wills and supervisor of six others,[32] an unusually high number; yet there was a contentious side to him. In 1556 he balked at paying taxes; a long suit in the Chancery Court in London was initiated against him in 1558 on charges of malpractice as the master of the Hospital of St. Mary Magdalen in Colchester; and in 1560 he was sued by George Dybney for a debt of £250, beginning a long dispute between them.[33] Yet Clere had the backing of the town leaders, indicating their cohesion in that period; in 1577, when Clere was almost overwhelmed with lawsuits, the town assembly supported him, and the next year, his son-in-law, town preacher Nicholas Challoner, publicly defended him and refuted certain rumors about him.[34]

All but one of the 1560 aldermanic group served for long years or until death,[35] so they formed close bonds, probably a result of their shared experiences in times of troubles, as well as of a common Protestant approach to religion and the sense of mission that seemed to develop after hearing the preaching of the returned exiles. Their wills revealed a heightened sense of camaraderie; five of the six testators named other

30. D/B5 Sb2/3, f. 123; ERO D/ACA9/219; CR154/23d; Morant, 3:9.

31. D/Y2/2, p. 65; also see D/B5 R5, f. 75v, for another complaint about Northen.

32. Executor to the will of his father, John Clere (1538), and to that of widow Elizabeth Mytche (1563); supervisor to the wills of Alderman John Colle (1536), John Mytche (1540), Thomas Ryche (1553), brother-in-law William Bonham (1557), John Damsell (1558), and Alderman John Beriff (1566).

33. Bindoff, *House*, 1:650; CR126/5d. Clere somehow persuaded the Crown to install his minor son as master of the hospital for life, in what was apparently an ill-judged attempt to take over the hospital and its lands. The case of malpractice was not completely resolved until 1579: see *Calendar of Patent Rolls: Elizabeth I*, 9 vols. (London: HMSO, 1939–86), 2:415; Byford, "Religious Change," 226–27.

34. D/B5 Gb1, f. 3; D/B5 Sb2/3, f. 123. Clere's aldermanic career did not survive the lawsuits: he served until the 1576 election, though he lived for a few more years. In 1584 his son was in the Colchester prison for a £100 debt (CR145/7).

35. Thomas Dybney was the exception; he left after completing his service for the borough year of 1560–61 and apparently moved to nearby West Bergholt (CR136/5).

aldermen as executors or supervisors,[36] a remarkably high number in contrast to the 1530 group, only one of whom did so. The aldermen also formed marriage alliances, such as the marriage of Clere's daughter with Lambert's son.[37] Even with the close bonds, there were still some unholy disagreements among them, though the differences were few compared to the number among the 1530 group. For example, George Sayer sued Robert Middleton and another man in 1564 for a £200 debt.[38]

Forged in the fires of religious changes and refined by the common goal of promoting Protestantism in Colchester, the cohesion of the aldermanic group was made stronger by alliances of blood and marriage. All of those factors worked together to form a pride in being an alderman, as illustrated by the 1573 will of John Beste. In a boon to historians and genealogists, Beste carefully detailed the relationships of his cousins the Cleres and proudly noted each one who was an alderman. Significantly, Beste identified himself as merchant and alderman. Such self-identification in the wills indicated pride in being an alderman, but less than half (three out of seven) of the men in the 1530 group had so named themselves, whereas four out of the six aldermanic testators in the 1560 group did so, and the two who did not had already ceased to be aldermen before they died.[39] A unified leadership was essential for effective reform.

1562: Reformers Taking the Initiative

With reformers in the ascendancy in town governance, measures were gradually taken to insure a Protestant agenda in the town. The leaders seemed to be feeling their way along. They were already used to active involvement in the promotion of religion, and John Pullen, having just come from Geneva, no doubt influenced them to adopt the Calvinistic approach, with the godly magistrates being partners with religious leaders to create a godly community. Calvinism thus gave town leaders a mission in the town, a task made more urgent by the losing struggle of the institutional church to maintain its role in the urban parishes. On Pullen's part, it was consistent with the Genevan approach for him to be made a burgess of the town and even to serve as an elector, while also being an archdeacon and part of the church hierarchy. The first two

---

36. The exception was George Sayer (PRO 25 Daughtry).
37. ERO T/R108/2.
38. CR128/12d.
39. George Sayer (1574) and Robert Lambert (1590).

official town preachers, William Cole and George Withers, would also become burgesses of Colchester, and, like Pullen, they did so without the usual entry fee. Significantly, three reformist attorneys, William Ram, William Markaunt, and Richard Putto, were also admitted gratis to the freedom of the town in 1559, and each of them would play a part in the emerging reformist policies.[40]

By 1562 reformers were ready to take the initiative; by that time, other reformers had joined the town assembly, making it easier to pass reformist measures. One of the new aldermen was Nicholas Clere II, in whose house martyr Elizabeth Folkes had been a servant. New members on the common council included Stephen Holt, uncle of the same Elizabeth, and Thomas Symnell, a churchwarden who sold church goods in the 1540s and was a signer of a 1559 presentment asking for stricter supervision of church attendance. In the borough year of 1561–62, reformer Robert Middleton served his first term as bailiff, and during his tenure in the spring of 1562, new measures began to be taken. The year of 1562 was pivotal, with measures being taken by town leaders in four major areas: church attendance, regular provision for preaching, invitation to Dutch refugees, and poor relief.

Church Attendance

The first effort was aimed at church attendance. The Act of Uniformity, passed in 1559 by Queen Elizabeth's first Parliament, had mandated diligent and faithful church attendance by every inhabitant of the realm on every Sunday and on all holy days, to hear common prayer from the Edwardian Prayer Book of 1552 and to hear preaching. Any offenders who had "no lawful or reasonable excuse to be absent" were each to be fined 12d., which was to be levied by the churchwardens of the parish, with the money going to the use of the poor.[41] On April 16, 1562, Colchester town leaders passed an ordinance requiring church attendance, but it was notable for its emphasis on attendance at sermons, rather than at divine service. One person from each household was required to attend

---

40. Cole became burgess in 1564 (CR129/1d), Withers in 1569 (CR133/3); on the attorneys, see CR125/6, 7d.

41. G. W. Prothero, ed., *Select Statutes and Other Constitutional Documents Illustrative of the Reigns of Elizabeth and James I*, 4th ed. (Oxford: Clarendon Press, 1913), 17. Emmison, "Tithes," 193, notes that there were still about twenty-nine holy days, in addition to Sundays, in Elizabethan England.

a sermon every Friday, and at least two persons from each parish were to be chosen to monitor the streets on Sunday and feast days, especially during sermon time, to be sure that no one was violating the strictures against work, play, or ill rule. Offenders were to be punished with twenty-four hours in the jail of the moot hall. Included also was a list of overseers of church attendance for each parish, with each parish having two overseers except for St. Leonard's, which had three. Many of the overseers were on the common council, and many, perhaps most, were also churchwardens.[42]

The usual procedure for regulating church attendance was for churchwardens to report offenders to the periodic archdeacon's court, so the new ordinance and its enforcement meant that Colchester authorities were taking over some of the work of the ecclesiastical court. Before the 1562 ordinance, presentments for nonattendance were rare in the borough court, but in the 1540s, barbers, especially one Robert Donnyng, were charged several times for shaving or cutting men's hair on holy days, as well as for drinking when they were supposed to be at church.[43] Behavior on holy days had begun to have political implications in Marian Colchester; in the first lawhundred after Mary's accession to the throne, the perennial barber offender Robert Donnyng was cited, along with three persons who opened their shops on feast days. At least one of them, and possibly others, was a Protestant. Presentments for nonattendance at church followed, with six persons, all followers of reformist preacher Thomas Putto, being mentioned.[44] In turn, the accession of Elizabeth found Catholics absenting themselves from church, and the court roll pointedly cited Geoffrey Golerd for failure to attend church "from the time of the Coronation of the new Queen."[45] After the 1562 ordinance, butchers were frequent offenders. Six months after the ordinance was passed, four butchers were fined for selling meat on Sundays in times of divine service; ironically, two of those butchers were overseers for

42. D/B5 R5, f. 86. Palliser, "Parish," 21, believes that the church and state probably thought of households, rather than all individuals, as being represented at services. Byford, "Religious Change," 150, 153–54, notes that the 1562 ordinance was an echo of the unique 1559 presentments about church attendance signed by five lesser men, three of whom were on the second council by 1562; see D/Y2/2, p. 65.

43. Donnyng presentments: CR119/2; CR112/2d; CR119/23d; CR120/2d. Other presentments of barbers: CR120/2, CR141/4, CR142/7d, CR143/2d. Other presentments for nonattendance: CR112/3d; CR113/16d; CR120/2d.

44. The wife of Hawkes the shoemaker, who was charged, was a follower of Putto: see CR120/2d; CR122/4; CR117/10d.

45. CR124/4. See also CR125/3; CR126/3.

church attendance in St. Martin's parish, where the butchers lived. It would not be the last time that the Sunday work of butchers would be noted in the borough court rolls.[46]

Emphasis on Preaching

Nothing was so representative of Protestantism as the emphasis on the preaching of sermons. English culture in the mid–sixteenth century was still largely oral, and in the eyes of the reformers, people needed to be educated and made knowledgeable about the Word of God so that lives could be amended. In their view, preaching played a crucial role in that process. Only two pre-Reformation Colchester wills mentioned sermons, with both wanting preaching by the Grey Friars, so there seemed to be little preaching in the parish churches of early Tudor Colchester.[47] The next reference to sermons came in 1538, in the first clearly Protestant will in Colchester, written by Alderman John Clere, who gave two reasons for preaching: for "the laud, honor and praise of Almighty God and to the true setting forth of His Word." The Word of God was the final authority for the Protestant, but that Word needed to be made relevant and understandable to the ordinary person, and that was where preaching came in. As Essex Puritan preacher Arthur Dent later remarked, "Preaching is the food of our souls." For the Protestant, the key to reform, both of the individual and of the community, lay in preaching.[48]

Elizabeth's injunctions, issued in 1559, emphasized preaching, stipulating that every parson should preach in his church at least once every month, which was a contrast to the earlier Catholic requirement of once every three months. The injunctions said that the duly licensed parson should "purely and sincerely declare the word of God," and on the days when there was no sermon, the Lord's Prayer, the Apostles' Creed, and the Ten Commandments should be recited to the people. If a parson was not a licensed preacher, and many were not, then he was to read a homily on Sunday.[49]

There were few clergymen in Colchester at that time, and there were even fewer who were qualified and licensed to preach, so the failure of

---

46. CR127/2. For some other examples, see CR127/3d; CR140/2; CR141/4; CR142/2d.
47. PRO 17 Milles; PRO 28 Ayloffe.
48. PRO 25 Dyngeley; William Hunt, *The Puritan Moment: The Coming of Revolution in an English County* (Cambridge: Harvard University Press, 1983), 93–94, 113.
49. Prothero, *Statutes*, 185, 187.

the established church to supply even the minimal preaching enjoined by Elizabeth's injunctions was an opportunity for town leaders to take a major lead in the religious affairs of the town. With the 1562 Colchester ordinance on church attendance insisting that people come to hear sermons, regular preaching had to be supplied. A document made shortly after the ordinance on church attendance was passed shows that money was being collected from townsmen to pay for regular Friday sermons set up by the corporation, though an official "common preacher" was not on the scene for another two years. Many of the sermons were probably given by Archdeacon Pullen, according to the evidence from a vocal critic, who mentioned that Pullen spoke at St. Peter's on Sunday. The impact of Pullen's preaching was felt by apothecary Simon Smyth, probably because Pullen had criticized Smyth's behavior, which later included some ungodly gambling and adultery.[50]

Gradually, the practice of regular town sermons evolved into the hiring of a "common preacher of the town" in 1564, with all the bailiffs, aldermen, and common councillors monetarily supporting the effort, according to a list of contributors made in October, just after energetic reformer Robert Middleton was elected bailiff for his second term. Six weeks later, the first common preacher, Master William Cole, was made a burgess of the town. The system of hiring their own preacher obviously found approval in the town, as another role of contributors, made four years later, was again headed by all the leaders of the town; their names were this time followed by the names of forty-eight other inhabitants, including two local gentry, a gentleman lawyer resident in the town, and even the curate of St. Leonard's Church.[51] Colchester's hiring of a "common preacher" also had a seal of approval from the established church. George Withers, who replaced preacher Cole, was appointed to the post of archdeacon of Colchester, an office he would not have received had the bishop of London disapproved of his preaching in the town.[52] For Colchester it was a happy state of affairs to have Edmund Grindal as head of the London diocese, since he was entirely sympathetic to the reformist cause.

Just as significant as the hiring of preachers was the type of men

---

50. BL, Stowe MS 829, f. 84; Byford, "Religious Change," 143, 146, 148.

51. W. J. Sheils, "Religion in Provincial Towns: Innovation and Tradition," in *Church and Society in England: Henry VIII to James I,* ed. Felicity Heal and Rosemary O'Day (London: Macmillan, 1977), 175; D/Y2/2, pp. 115, 117; CR129/1d. Among the contributors were the gentry Thomas Lucas and Richard Aberford, the lawyer Edmund Markaunt, and the curate Michael Goodeare.

52. CR133/3; *VCH Essex,* 2:39.

selected. Clere's first Protestant will back in 1538 had made the connection between preaching, piety, and learning when he asked that five sermons be made "by the most discretist, wisest, and best learned men that can be gotten." The Catholic priest had derived his authority from the role given him by the church as the instrument through which God and mankind met in the sacraments, whereas the Protestant preacher's personal sanctity, learning, and preparation permitted him to be an instrument of divine grace through his preaching. By bringing the Word, the preacher dispensed salvation to those in need and was, in that way, a mediator between God and mankind, which was a role both like and unlike that of the Catholic priest. Both roles brought God and mankind together, but the altar had been replaced by the pulpit.[53]

The first three "town preachers," Pullen, Cole, and Withers, were not only zealots for their faith but notably learned men, setting a high precedent for their successors. Moreover, each brought the influence of Calvinistic Geneva to Colchester. John Pullen, B.D., educated at New College and Christ Church, Oxford, used his learning while in Geneva to translate a small part of the Geneva Bible.[54] Like Pullen, William Cole was also of Oxford (Corpus Christi), was one of the translators of the Geneva Bible, and married the daughter of a Colchester widow, Ales Agar. Cole, however, had chosen to remain on the Continent after Elizabeth's accession to the throne, preaching to the Merchant Adventurers in Antwerp until 1564, when he returned to England and to Colchester, perhaps partly drawn there by his marital connection to the town. Cole began preaching as Colchester's first official town preacher, though Archdeacon Pullen had unofficially served in that capacity. Attesting to Cole's learning was his later role as the head of his Oxford college, Corpus Christi, being its first married president.[55]

---

53. PRO 25 Dyngeley; see Hunt, *Puritan Moment,* 114; John Morgan, *Godly Learning: Puritan Attitudes towards Reason, Learning, and Education, 1560–1640* (Cambridge: Cambridge University Press, 1986), 82–83; C. John Sommerville, *The Secularization of Early Modern England* (New York: Oxford University Press, 1992), 167.

54. Garrett, *Marian Exiles,* 262–63. Though Pullen was not an official "town preacher," he was serving in that capacity.

55. Patrick Collinson, *Puritan Movement,* 48–50; Byford, "Religious Change," 162. I have not found any references to an Agar family, but a Lawrence Agar, who was able to "preach truly," was the curate at St. James's Church in 1559 (Grieve transcript of Corpus Christi College MS 122). At the same time, a Thomas Aunger was curate at St. Giles's, but his name was given as Ager in the 1562 episcopal visitation (Guildhall MS 9537/2, f. 65). Also, the 1572 will of Emme Smarte of Greenstead (ERO D/ABW34/132), whose long preamble indicated Protestant zeal, mentioned cousins named Agas, one of whom lived on East Street. In 1580 a Margaret Ager from Holy Trinity parish was cited in the archdeaconry court (ERO D/ACA9/123).

Like the two men before him, Dr. George Withers was newly returned from a sojourn on the Continent when he became Colchester's town preacher, but Withers, having been earlier in exile in Geneva, had been more recently studying at Heidelberg. Withers was not behind the other Genevan exiles in zeal, being known for having been deprived by Archbishop Parker in 1565 for not wearing the proper cap while preaching at Bury St. Edmunds, for having denounced painted windows in a sermon at Cambridge, and for successfully promoting the establishment of the Calvinist discipline in the Palatinate. An appeal that Withers and a London preacher made to Elector Palatine Frederick III also indicated the thinking of Withers; the appeal described the English church as being "on the brink of destruction," with little ministry or discipline, and with the bishops being little regarded by the godly. While in Heidelberg, Withers's earlier education at Oxford and Cambridge was supplemented by study at the University of Heidelberg, where he entered into a famous debate with the German doctor Thomas Erastus. Out of that disputation grew the concept that would grow in importance in Jacobean England, that is, Erastianism, which advocated the supreme authority of the state, at least of the godly magistrate, over church affairs. Consistent with his extreme Calvinistic views, Withers had taken the Presbyterian position in the debate. This, then, was the man who became Colchester's town preacher in early 1569. No doubt his aggressive Calvinism recommended him to the town leaders who hired him, but they were also impressed by his learning, as he was proudly described as a "Doctor of Sacred Theology" when he was made a burgess of the town on February 14, 1569. Ironically, Withers later became more moderate, probably a result of a new perspective acquired as a part of the church hierarchy after he was appointed archdeacon of Colchester in 1570. Even in his moderation, however, Withers later defended the Presbyterian ministers under him, though he was not in complete sympathy with them. Following in the footsteps of his predecessors in Colchester, Withers, shortly before his appointment as town preacher, also married a Colchester woman, Priscilla Shelbury, granddaughter of Alderman Ralph Fynche, and Withers continued living in Colchester for a time after he became archdeacon, as he was still living in St. Nicholas's parish in August, 1572.[56]

---

56. Davids, *Annals*, 73–74; Collinson, *Puritan Movement*, 81, 110–11; *VCH Essex*, 2:39; Newcourt, 1:92; CR134/3; ERO TR108/2; *Boyd's Marriage Index, Essex* (n.p., n.d.); CR120/13, 13d; ERO D/Y2/10, p. 40; D/B5 R7, f. 314v.

Colchester was in the forefront religiously, not only in having zealous reformers, but in having learned men, such as Pullen, Cole, and Withers, to preach for them. Not until the early seventeenth century was the Anglican ministry fully university trained, so graduates were rare in the early years of Elizabeth's reign. Indeed, the 1559 injunctions recognized the problem, citing the many priests who were "utterly unlearned" at that time.[57] When a replacement was sought for Withers, who was named to the rectory at Danbury in late 1572, the services of "a learned man of Cambridge," presumably Nicholas Challoner, were obtained, but this time a significant change occurred in the funding. At the end of 1573, the town leaders decided that the rent of £20 a year from Kingswood Heath would go toward "a learned preacher for the town." The records are not entirely clear, but it seems that the first year of the new arrangement, apparently beginning sometime in 1574, was a probationary year for Challoner; in July of 1575, the position was upgraded when the town assembly agreed that Mr. Challoner would "have his patent sealed for rent of £40 as his stipend."[58] The office of town preacher was thus changed from a tenuous position supported only by voluntary, and probably erratic, contributions, to one of permanence and stability. The office of town preacher was thus fully institutionalized by 1575, resulting in a change of relationship between the preacher and the town, which is explored in chapter 8.

From the uncertain steps taken at the beginning of Elizabeth's reign, the town leaders were moving forward confidently, shouldering the responsibility to provide not only justice and order but godly teaching as well. In the spring of 1562, the ordinance requiring church attendance passed and the first voluntary contributions for preaching were given, and in the autumn of the same year, the assembly of the town took two other significant steps: to invite the Dutch to live in Colchester and systematically to collect money for the poor after every town sermon.

Invitation to Dutch Refugees

After the election of Benjamin Clere and reformer Robert Lambert as bailiffs in the autumn of 1562, Bailiff Clere was designated by the assembly to appeal to the queen's Privy Council to gain permission for Col-

---

57. Patrick Collinson, *The Religion of Protestants: The Church in English Society, 1559–1625* (Oxford: Clarendon Press, 1982), 94; Prothero, *Statutes,* 188.
58. D/B5 R7, ff. 242v, 269.

chester to take in some of the Dutch "now banished for God's word" (the Flemish refugees fleeing from Spanish persecution).[59] In noting that the action involved "the establishing of [the refugees'] church in this town," Colchester leaders were seeing the sheltering of the Dutch as a holy project. Protestant sympathy was evident; town leaders had no way of knowing that eventually the Dutch would bring unprecedented economic prosperity to Colchester. The first Dutch settlers, about fifty people, did not arrive in Colchester until 1565, but five years later a larger group of about two hundred people was requesting permission to move from Sandwich and settle in Colchester. The town authorities wrote to the Privy Council in 1570, explaining that the foreigners came to England for protection, "to save their lives, and keep their consciences," having been driven from Flanders, "for that their consciences were offended with the Masse; and, for fear of the tyranny of the Duke of Alva." The town leaders reported that they had found the Dutch to be "very honest, godly, civil, and well ordered people," but this time they also added the economic argument that the Dutch were skilled in "such sciences as are not usual with us," thus combining by 1570 the religious, charitable, and economic reasons for welcoming the Dutch.[60]

Poor Relief

The November, 1562, assembly that invited the Dutch also made new provisions for the poor. Six men of the common council were designated to be responsible for having two or three of them at every Friday sermon, to "gather and collect the charitable devotion of well disposed people toward the needful relief of the poor and impotent people within this town," after which they were to distribute the money on the following Sunday for the "sustenation" of the poor. Though this was a new system for caring for the poor, it had some precedence. Parliamentary legislation in 1536 suggested the collection of voluntary alms for the poor by churchwardens or two other persons, thus beginning the practice of having someone responsible for poor relief. The 1538 will of Alderman William Becket probably referred to those "officials" when he gave varying amounts to the poor in several Colchester parishes, with an additional sum to go "to those that are to deal to the poor folk in every

59. D/B5 R5, f. 2v.
60. William John Charles Moens, ed., *Register of Baptisms in the Dutch Church at Colchester* (Lymington: Charles T. King, 1905), ii.

parish."[61] The early poor legislation also mentioned the use of "common boxes," and references to the "poor box" or the "poor men's box" can be found in Colchester wills beginning in 1550. The Elizabethan injunctions of 1559 likewise insisted that each parish should provide "a strong chest" for the collecting of alms.[62]

Other national legislation had elements that contributed to the practice instituted in 1562. A 1547 act had suggested weekly collections in the parish church after a preacher had exhorted the congregation, thus connecting sermons and almsgiving; and a 1552 statute took the process further by saying that local authorities should name two collectors to gather alms every Sunday in each parish, with uncooperative persons to be chastised by the minister and even by the bishop if the person proved to be recalcitrant in his or her giving. Each parish was to make a list of the legitimate poor within its boundaries, as well as a list of contributors. Though the almsgiving was voluntary under the 1552 legislation, the pressure to contribute was strong; in effect, more power was given to local authorities to collect for poor relief so that they could take over part of what had earlier been the work of the church.[63]

The problem of poverty deepened acutely in Colchester in the mid-1550s, so the more drastic measure of compulsory poor rates was instituted. Norwich had compulsory poor rates as early as 1547, York in 1550. So Colchester was following their lead in 1557 when a system of assessment of "every house, warehouse, or shop" was developed, with the owners paying 8d. for every noble of the assessed value of their property. The document is damaged, but it is clear that the persons designated in each parish to make the assessments and the list of rates had their authority from the bailiffs. No one had to pay if his house was rated at less than 3s. 4d. or if it was empty. Though the priests collected the money, any refusal to pay would be punished by the bailiffs. Not only was the new system compulsory for all who could afford to pay, but the civil authorities had ultimate oversight, rather than the church.[64] There is

---

61. D/B5 R5, f. 94v; A. L. Beier, *The Problem of the Poor in Tudor and Early Stuart England* (New York: Methuen, 1983), 23, 39; ERO D/ABW3/59.

62. Beier, *Poor,* 23; PRO 4 Bucke; Prothero, *Statutes,* 187. The poor box at St. Martin's was mentioned in a 1548 visitation of the church (see Dickin, "Church Goods," 167), though C. Dyer, *Standards of Living,* 248, says that churchwardens were keeping a parish box for donations to the poor by the mid-fifteenth century.

63. Beier, *Poor,* 39–40; Marjorie Keniston McIntosh, "Local Responses to the Poor in Late Medieval and Tudor England," *Continuity and Change* 3 (1988): 229.

64. McIntosh, "Local Responses," 228; D/Y2/2, pp. 37–38.

no evidence that Colchester's system lasted beyond the emergency period of the 1550s, and possibly the lapse of the compulsory rates prompted the new system of collection at sermons in 1562, when collections for the poor at town sermons must have seemed a logical and efficient step to take, especially since attendance at the weekly sermons was mandated. Nothing was said about compulsory giving in the 1562 measure, but the need was not quite so acute as it had been in 1557.

In 1563, the year after Colchester initiated the collections of alms after the town sermons, Parliament passed a new Act for the Relief of the Poor that, for the first time, made the giving compulsory on a national level. Within each parish, householders were called by the town officials to meet together after divine service in the church so that each householder could commit himself or herself to a certain amount to be given weekly. Collectors were appointed to list the contributors and the amounts to be given and then to gather the "charitable alms" every Sunday and distribute them to the poor. Penalties were set up for any officials or collectors who refused to do their duties, and anyone refusing to pay the alms was to be exhorted, first by the parson and churchwardens, then by the bishop or his representative, and then, if the person still refused, by the justices of the peace, who had the authority to imprison the reluctant contributor. Thus, both the sacred and secular authorities had a part in the process, though the secular officials had the ultimate power to force compliance. Colchester had initiated this same kind of cooperation between the town and ecclesiastical officials in its own 1557 ordinance, but this instance was a first for national legislation in the area of poor relief. The bailiffs, then, were taking over part of what had usually been a work of the church, and they were doing it with the approbation of the central government. Another Parliamentary act, in 1572, empowered the justices of the peace—after surveys of the poor to determine needs—to set the size of the contributions to the poor and, in the process, to assess the richer for greater amounts, thus making it an imposed tax.[65]

It is unclear when Colchester subscribed fully to the 1563 legislation, but it was certainly doing so by the summer of 1572, perhaps in response to another recently passed statute, which had come out of the May–June session of Parliament. A long document, recorded in August in the Monday Court Book of Colchester, listed two to five men from each parish

---

65. Prothero, *Statutes*, 41–45, 67–72; Paul Slack, "Poverty in Elizabethan England," *History Today* 34 (1984): 6.

who were to determine both those poor needing help and those people who would contribute to their relief. Then, names of the contributors and the poor in each parish were carefully listed. For example, in St. Mary's parish, thirty people were giving from 1d. to 4d. weekly, and nine people, seven of them widows, were receiving 3d. per week. St. Botolph's had the most contributors (forty-six), but they also had the greatest number of poor people listed—sixteen, who received from 3d. to 12d. weekly. Alderman George Sayer in St. Peter's parish gave the most, 12d. weekly, but some people in his parish only gave ½d. per week. A year later, another list of one-year appointees appeared in the records. This time there were only two collectors listed for each parish, but each parish also had one or two other men designated as overseers of the poor, an office that had been mandated by the 1572 statute.[66]

The 1572 legislation had also, for the first time, mentioned housing for the poor, suggesting that town leaders, if need be, should provide such. This issue had already been a matter of concern in Colchester, where the three old houses for the poor, St. Anne's, St. Mary Magdalen's, and St. Catherine's, had either disappeared or fallen onto hard times during the Reformation years. One of the changes requested early in Elizabeth's reign by Colchester reformers was the reestablishment of hospitality at St. Anne's. This old chapel on the road leading to Harwich had once supplied beds "for the poor traveling by the way." As an appendage of St. Botolph's Priory, it had been transferred into private hands with the dissolution of the priory in the 1530s, so the reformers of 1559 pleaded that "the poor, lame impotent may be restored to their own again, which is a work of mercy." But their plea apparently fell on deaf ears.[67] The old Hospital of St. Mary Magdalen, seemingly overlooked, survived the Reformation's dissolution of many similar establishments and continued sporadically in its role as a residence for five poor old men, but it was the old St. Catherine's Hospital on Crouch Street, near the center of town, that was apparently refounded by the town leaders.[68] In January, 1563, just two months after the collection for the poor at town sermons was

---

66. D/B5 R7, ff. 306v–317v, 321; Prothero, *Statutes*, 70.

67. Morant, 2:44–45; ERO D/Y2/2, p. 65.

68. In 1556 the bishop of London's commissary included the Hospitals of St. Mary Magdalen and of St. Catherine in a list of hospitals that he thought had been overlooked by ecclesiastical supervisors. He also referred to St. Catherine's as a chapel, reporting that a crowd, upset over the sitting of a Crown commission to deal with heretics in Colchester in 1556, had been so large that it took him two and one-half hours to get from the castle to St. Catherine's Chapel. See Foxe, 8:305–6; Morant, 2:21–22.

instituted, a John Samer was made the new keeper and governor of the hospital for "poor and impotent people." Simply designated as the "poor house," it was sustained by the weekly contributions, and under the auspices, of the town leaders.[69]

Caring for the poor continued to be a concern of the town leaders, and in September of 1565 the assembly resolved to sell some common land, the "June Commons," and use the money for a hospital, or a dwelling, for poor children. It must have been in existence by early 1572, when testator John Medcalf gave 3s. 4d. to the "poor children of the new hospital" in Colchester. In early 1571 the assembly was considering setting up a local Bridewell house, in imitation of Bridewell, the house of corrections set up for the poor in London in 1553, but as a temporary measure the bailiffs provided 10s. yearly to the poor of St. Botolph's and St. Mary Magdalen.[70] A hospital was being erected in April, 1572, according to the will of Alderman John Fowle; however, the hospital project seems to have stalled temporarily by the time Alderman John Beste, in October, 1573, bequeathed £200 "to the relief of such diseased, impotent and needy persons as shall be kept" in the new hospital, "if the hospital which the bailiffs and commonalty of the town have gone about to establish shall be erected within a year after my decease." Beste's money must have hastened the erection of the hospital, for children from the poorhouse were baptized in that parish in 1574.[71]

The Colchester authorities, then, especially beginning in 1562, were taking an active religious lead in the town, in requiring attendance at town sermons preached by ardent reformers hired by the town leaders, in inviting religious refugees to the town, and in supplying leadership in the work that had traditionally been the role of religion, the caring for the poor. The balance between the part played by laity and clergy had shifted, with the laity increasingly taking much of the initiative. The town leaders had themselves become reformers and, as such, would gradually take on the task of trying to reform the lives of individuals. Not all of

---

69. D/B5 Sb2/1, f. 20; CR128/12. In housing the poor, almshouses were increasingly being set up, and at least in the case of the four established by brewer and alderman Ralph Fynche in the 1550s, the bailiffs were to have ultimate responsibility for the houses; see Morant, 3:7.

70. D/B5 R5, f. 106v; ERO D/ACR6/321. A possible Bridewell was mentioned in the will of Joan Dybney, ERO D/ACR6/219. See also Slack, "Poverty," 6; Morant, 3:5.

71. PRO 17 Draper; PRO 2 Martyn; Morant, 1:75; *VCH Essex,* 9:90.

those efforts were welcome. Two elements could be potentially hostile: the established church, since the town was developing a competing institution in the office of town preacher; and the inhabitants of the town, both the poor and the better-off, many of whom liked the old ways and therefore resisted reform. Chapter 8 investigates the effects of reform on these two groups, and their responses toward the reforms of the leaders of the borough.

8

The Church and the Laity, 1562–75

On her deathbed in 1571, widow Joan Dybney trusted to be received by God "in peace out of this world into eternal life."[1] Dybney had already traveled far in her lifetime, having been in exile in Switzerland during Mary's reign, and her continuing commitment to the Protestant cause was never in doubt. Her first legacy to her eldest son was her Geneva Bible, and she gave generously of the cloth from her shop to several favorite ministers and their wives, making one of the ministers the supervisor of her will. Joan gave to promote learning, but, ironically, the young baker's son for whom she supplied books, Samuel Halsnoth, would grow up to be a bastion of traditional Anglicanism, who became known as Samuel Harsnett, the archbishop of York. Dybney and Harsnett were representative of two streams of Protestantism in Elizabethan Colchester, the moderate and the more radical, whose different agendas regarding needed reforms in the church often failed to blend compatibly. The result was a period of tensions, trials, and conflicts that saw the emergence of a Puritan movement, first defined by its stand against clerical vestments. This chapter describes the continuing problems in the church and the reactions among the laity to the Puritan agenda. The Puritan emphasis on learning, preaching, and Scripture had its effects on the laity, but the zeal of the Puritans to direct personal behavior brought out a resistance that culminated in a long and unpleasant dispute in 1575 involving the influential alderman Benjamin Clere and creating a split on the aldermanic bench.

The Church in Need of Reform

The church was uneasily finding its way. Two main problems were in need of attention: the most obvious was a lack of clergymen, especially

---

1. ERO D/ACR6/219.

those who were well educated in Protestant theology; the other was the need, perceived by the more radical, for the church to further reform its practices so as to rid it completely of its Roman ways. Colchester certainly needed more clergymen. The two working incumbent clergymen in Colchester in 1562 must have felt overwhelmed by the needs around them, as, between them, they were in charge of five of the sixteen parish churches.[2] Bishop Grindal, highly sympathetic to reform, wanted to install more clergymen, but the problem was finding men who were able. Education was the key, but it was a slow process. In the meantime, the town leaders had stepped into the breach by hiring preachers to deliver sermons to the town, and Bishop Grindal was certainly not opposed, since well-qualified preachers had been chosen. Learning, however, was not the only basis for approval; the right kind of reformist preaching must be done, the kind that would later be called "Puritan."

Grindal also took steps to fill in the gaps in the ministry in Colchester, though there was a certain risk involved, well illustrated by the career of Thomas Upcher, whom Grindal ordained deacon in 1560, after which Upcher became a curate at St. Leonard's. Upcher's connection with the town would last for many years and would make quite an impact, not all of it salutary. Upcher's zeal was undisputed. Originally a weaver in Bocking, an Essex village near Braintree, Upcher early came to the attention of government authorities, even being brought before the Privy Council when England was Protestant during Edward's reign. The charge was holding an illegal conventicle of about sixty people at his house at Christmastime in 1550, at which "things of the scripture" had been discussed, especially "whether it were necessary to stand or kneel, bare head or covered, at prayer." A man who considered such ideas was bound to be noticed during Mary's reign, and an "Upchear," probably Thomas, was one of the prisoners who took part in a hot dispute over predestination before the Court of King's Bench. After his release, Upcher went into exile and was among those leading the move to erect a new English

---

2. The two incumbents were William Lyon at Mile End, Holy Trinity, and Berechurch; and Hugo Allen at St. Mary-at-Wall and, by 1563, at St. Mary Magdalen's, according to Guildhall MS 9537/2, 63v–65, and the Grieve transcript of BL, Harley MS 595/24, f. 69. The rector of Lexden was absent; Thomas Harvie was listed as vicar of St. Peter's in 1562, but a 1560 return said he was a curate, which was probably correct, since he was gone by 1563. Rosemary O'Day, "The Anatomy of a Profession: The Clergy of the Church of England," in *The Professions in Early Modern England,* ed. Wilfrid Prest (London: Croom Helm, 1987), 40–44, discusses the difficulties of the clergy.

church at Aarau in Switzerland, so Upcher's leadership qualities were also evident.[3]

Grindal's approval of Upcher, manifested in his ordination of Upcher to the diaconate so that he could become a curate in Colchester and then a rector in nearby Fordham, brought a reproval from Archbishop Parker, who urged Grindal "to forbear ordaining any more artificers, and others that had been of secular occupations that were unlearned."[4] Parker thought Grindal to be too lax, but Grindal, though aware of the problems that could come through the ministry of a man like Upcher, was willing to take the risk. Not surprisingly, a controversial issue emerged: the wearing of the surplice when administering Communion. Predictably, Upcher the reformer refused to wear the clerical vestments. The 1559 injunctions had ordered that the clergy "wear such seemly habits, garments and such square caps" as were used in the last year of Edward's reign, but Grindal, knowing the intensity of Upcher's beliefs, wrote that he "was contented to bear with Mr. Upchire for the surplice." In contrast, Grindal warned Archdeacon Pullen in 1560 "not to suffer ministration of the communion in gowns without surplices to spread and creep forward," adding, "You may not relent at every persuasion in this matter."[5]

Upcher was not the only Colchester minister to take a stand in the vestment controversy. Town preacher William Cole was on a list prepared for Lord Robert Dudley of godly preachers who were described as having "utterly forsaken Antichrist and all his Romish rags." George Withers, too, had refused to wear the square cap at Bury St. Edmunds, before he came to Colchester; the year was 1565, and the issue of clerical dress had become devisive. Early in the same year, the laxity of clerical attire had alarmed the queen, and she wrote a letter to Archbishop Parker urging corrective action to deal with the growing problem of the "diversity of opinions and specially in the external, decent, and lawful rites and ceremonies to be used in the churches." Parker consequently took action against the unfortunate Withers, depriving him of his benefice, but the entreaties of the people of Bury persuaded Withers to submit to the dress requirements and be restored to his post. A few months later, in March,

3. Jay Pascal Anglin, "The Essex Puritan Movement and 'Bawdy' Courts," in *Tudor Men and Institutions: Studies in English Law and Government,* ed. Arthur J. Slavin (Baton Rouge: Louisiana State University Press, 1972), 174; *VCH Essex,* 2:31; Cross, *Church and People,* 98; Garrett, *Marian Exiles,* 316–17.

4. Quoted in Garrett, *Marian Exiles,* 317.

5. Prothero, *Statutes,* 188; Collinson, *Puritan Movement,* 67.

1566, Parker issued his *Advertisements,* which insisted that the clergy conform and wear the prescribed clerical dress. The Parker document was not constitutionally valid, since it had not passed a convocation of the clergy, but it did serve to draw lines between the two sides. The matter came to a head immediately, when 110 London clergymen were summoned to Lambeth Palace and ordered to conform to the prescribed dress. Thirty-seven refused and were suspended, but some of the suspended clergymen defied the archbishop and proceeded to preach sermons attacking the queen, the Privy Council, and the bishops. It was a turbulent time in London,[6] and the turmoil spread to Essex. In August, the Spanish ambassador to England, Guzman De Silva, wrote to his king to report a disturbance among the Essex clothworkers that resulted in a death sentence for six of them. He noted the economic concerns of the clothworkers but added: "They are also offended at the regulations with regard to the ministers wearing a decent clerical habit as formerly, and also as to wearing surplices in churches. Everywhere heretics take advantage of religion to disturb the people for their own ends."[7]

The issue of clerical dress would not go away, as it had become a clearly visible symbol of the conflict within the church between those wanting further reform—the Puritans, as they came to be called—and those who thought reform had gone far enough. The court records from the archdeaconry of Colchester show a number of cases having to do with clerical dress beginning in 1569; in 1577 the court ordered the redoubtable Thomas Upcher to confess his fault before his two congregations, one being St. Leonard's in Colchester, for not wearing the surplice and for not making the sign of the cross in baptism.[8]

For the Puritan, or "hotter Protestant," public worship focused on the sermon rather than on sacraments and ritual, so the order of service set forth in the Prayer Book was downplayed; in fact, one of the attractions of the town sermons was the freedom from the restraints of the Prayer Book.[9] The act of preaching was one criterion for judging whether a cler-

---

6. Collinson, *Puritan Movement,* 48, 69–70, 75–77, says Puritanism was given definition at this time. See also Davids, *Annals,* 74.

7. *Calendar of State Papers, Spanish* (London, HMSO, 1862), 1558–67, 1:570–71.

8. *VCH Essex,* 2:42, 46; Anglin, "Essex Puritan Movement," 195. On Puritanism, see Collinson, *Puritan Movement,* 26–27, 50, 67, 87–88.

9. Before Cole's stint as the Colchester town preacher, he had preached for the English merchants at Antwerp, during which time he received a letter from Bishop Grindal suggesting that he shorten some of the Prayer Book service so as to leave reasonable time for the sermon. Grindal's liberalism was also showing when he told Cole that he need not wear the surplice, since many of the Continental churches did not do so; see Collinson, *Puritan Movement,* 50, 67.

gyman was a Puritan, especially if he was one of those called a "painful" preacher, that is, one who could graphically paint a picture of the consequences of sin and bring the sinner to regeneration in Christ. Both of the curates at St. Leonard's in the 1560s, Thomas Upcher and Michael Goodeare, were preaching, probably without license to do so; in fact, not until 1577 was Upcher licensed to preach by his mentor, Edmund Grindal, who by that time was archbishop.[10] Even though preaching ministers were few in Colchester, the town probably had more than did most places. Throughout the 1560s, there were few licensed preaching ministers in England, a fact lamented by George Withers in an undated letter addressed to Frederick III, the prince elector Palatine, written probably around 1567, just before Withers became Colchester's second town preacher and, later, archdeacon of Colchester. Withers yearned for a "more complete reformation of the whole church" and decried the poor state of the ministry, "for those persons . . . can do nothing according to the principles of the word, but are obliged to act in every respect at the nod of the Queen and the bishops." He claimed, "Most of them are popish priests . . . and the far greater part of the remainder are most ignorant persons."[11]

By 1570 the parish churches of Colchester were still in the doldrums. An ardent reformer and trained Cambridge graduate, Oliver Pigge, was appointed to the rectories at St. Peter's and All Saints' in 1569, but his stay in Colchester seemed to be brief. After becoming rector at Abberton, just south of Colchester, in 1570, Pigge moved there and then later to Rougham in Norfolk, but his later activity indicates that his heart was in the organization of the Presbyterian movement in Suffolk, where his radical convictions landed him in jail in 1583.[12] For Colchester, then, apart from that of the faithful William Lyon at the village church of Mile End, the only continuing parish ministry in the borough was at St. Leonard's, where Michael Goodeare was made rector in 1570, after serving as a curate there with Thomas Upcher for several years. Upcher replaced the ailing Goodeare as rector in 1571, giving the fearless reformer the bless-

---

10. Hunt, *Puritan Moment*, 92; Anglin, "Essex Puritan Movement," 174. Evidence that the curates were preaching includes W. Hamond's request that Goodeare preach his burial sermon (1567; ERO D/ACR6/42) and Grace Cock's request that Upcher preach a sermon (1572; PRO 18 Daper).

11. Davids, *Annals*, 74.

12. *VCH Essex*, 2:38; Guildhall MS 9531/13, pt. 1, f. 151; Collinson, *Puritan Movement*, 127, 218–19.

ing of the church as expressed by Archdeacon Withers and Bishop Sandys, Grindal's replacement as bishop of London. Withers and Upcher had a personal connection, as Upcher performed Withers's marriage ceremony to a Colchester woman in 1568, but Upcher's talent, even though he was not formally trained, must have commended him in a time of scarcity of preaching ministers.[13]

Another minister, Jan van Migrode, appeared in Colchester in the early 1570s, but he brought his own church with him. Following the granting of a formal license for settlement in 1571, a large influx of Dutch and some French refugees came to Colchester, so that by 1573 there were 474 "strangers" occupying eighty houses. Migrode, the Dutch minister, made possible the establishment of a formal congregation, which was allowed to worship at St. Giles's and later at All Saints'. This was not the Church of England, though, but a Calvinist reformed church, and the Crown was intent on order and uniformity of religion in the kingdom. Since the "stranger churches" were a special case, they were tolerated, but they were to be under English civil and episcopal rule. As stranger churches were told, they were not to permit Englishmen to attend their services, nor were they to proselytize among the English.[14]

The presence of the strong Dutch congregation and their minister must have made even more apparent the paucity of trained preaching ministers in the Colchester churches. With so little progress having been made in the institutional church by 1573, it is not surprising that the aldermen turned to a more permanent plan for supporting a Cambridge-trained man to be Colchester's town preacher. Still, there had been a lot of sermons preached in Colchester in the decade and a half of Elizabeth's reign, and some of the effects of those sermons could be seen in the laity.

Tensions and Transformations among the Laity

The years of religious transition had been unsettling in Colchester; as testator Robert Saunderson remarked in 1540, the result was an "unstable

---

13. *CPR: Elizabeth I*, 5:188 (which mistakenly gives the name of the church as St. Lawrence's); *Boyd's Marriage Index, Essex*.

14. Moens, *Dutch Church*, ii; J. E. Pilgrim, "The Rise of the 'New Draperies' in Essex," *University of Birmingham Historical Journal* 7 (1959–60): 46; Goose, "The 'Dutch,'" 166; *VCH Essex*, 2:39; G. W. Bernard, "The Church of England, c. 1529–c. 1642," *History* 75 (1990): 188; Eric Kerridge, *Textile Manufactures in Early Modern England* (Manchester: Manchester University Press, 1985), 229.

and mutable world."[15] During Mary's turbulent reign, committed Protestants faced the dilemma of whether to resist and possibly be burned, to flee, or to submit to insure survival. There were possibilities for conflict between those whose relatives had courageously burned for their faith and those who chose to flee, between the families of the martyrs and the leaders of the town who collaborated in the executions, between radicals and moderates, and between Catholics and Protestants. In the first years after Elizabeth's ascension to the throne, the town records were full of legal battles and even charges of assault among leading citizens, though the true causes of the quarrels were rarely explained. Those tensions would continue to surface over the next few years to challenge the town governors. In their eyes, the answer to the problem was to make the townspeople into committed Protestants; they knew that the principles of Protestant belief needed to be taught, that the church was unable and partly unwilling to do so, and that they themselves would have to take the initiative.

They had a strong base from which to start, as some strong pockets of Protestantism remained intact during Mary's reign. The Wilbore family was one of those. Nicholas Wilbore had been admitted as a burgess in 1522, coming from Yorkshire, and by 1533 he was a co-fee with men who were already connected with, or would later be known as, reformers in Colchester, one of whom, John Mace, was burned at the stake in Mary's reign.[16] Wilbore's son-in-law, Robert Fawkon, was obviously Protestant; dying in 1554 in Mary's reign, Fawkon left money to Thomas Putto, the man whose preaching out in the field was termed heretical two years later. Joan, Fawkon's widow and Wilbore's daughter, then married John Pullen, the reformist preacher and later archdeacon of Colchester, and went into exile with him.[17] Wilbore, who died while his daughter was in exile, commended his soul, in good Protestant fashion even though Catholic Mary was on the throne, "to the tender mercy of . . . Jesus Christ," rather than to Mary and the saints. When Wilbore's wife, Margaret, lay on her deathbed nine years later, the town preacher, reformer William Cole, was at her side. When their son died in 1577, he made a tantalizing reference to "the gold ring that Master Latimer gave

---

15. ERO D/ACR4/80.

16. *OB,* 152; CR102/15 (which listed other co-fees, William Buxton and Thomas Dybney); Foxe, 8:138–39.

17. ERO D/ABW14/77; CR122/4; Garrett, *Marian Exiles,* 262–63; ERO D/ACR5/136; CR136/3.

me," possibly referring to Hugh Latimer, the bishop preacher and reformer whose convictions brought him to death by burning with Bishop Nicholas Ridley in 1555. Wilbore's sister-in-law, Alice, mentioned owning a "Bible of the great volume" in her will. They were truly a family dedicated to Protestant reforms, and they were not alone.[18] Strong solidarity among the Protestant reformers who survived Mary's reign can be traced in the records. Their families often intermarried, and many of the same family names repeatedly emerged together in wills and other legal documents, a testimony to the fact that persecution produced closeness among the persecuted. Even with the early forsaking of Catholic practices and the strength of Protestantism, however, the majority of the population in Colchester did not share the strong reformist views, and some were quietly hoping for a return to the Catholic mass.

Even the inns had taken on a partisan flavor, with the King's Head favoring Protestantism. As early as Edward's reign, the King's Head had housed reformist preachers, among them John Pullen, the future archdeacon; and during Queen Mary's reign, the King's Head became a meeting place for "the afflicted Christians." The prosperous innkeeper, William Peverill, profited from the Reformation, buying former chantry property, and his words in his 1561 will showed him to be a committed Protestant, "trusting that . . . I shall be . . . amongst the chosen and elect people of God."[19] On the other side of the fence was the White Hart, where in 1557 the heretics were examined and condemned. The innkeeper, Richard Cosen, was known for his Catholic sympathies, which probably explains why he was charged with blasphemy in the borough court in 1560.[20] He was in trouble again in 1562 for a conversation with William Blackman, who was helping Cosen cut some hay. Praising the French Catholic duke of Guise, Cosen lambasted William Cardinal, the Protestant recorder of Colchester and JP of Essex, for wrongfully taking away Cosen's goods. Blackman later related the conversation to Protestant Richard Wilbore, who passed the information on to Alderman Nicholas Clere. The bailiffs arrested and imprisoned Cosen, and in the investigation, Cosen's maid reported that Cosen and his wife often spoke long-

---

18. ERO D/ABW39/196; ERO D/ACR5/136; ERO D/ACR7/173; ERO D/ACR6/309.

19. PRO 12 Chayre; Foxe, 8:305, 384; Strype, *Annals*, 2 (2): 282. Collinson, *Birthpangs*, 107, notes that Protestantism at that time was still "at ease with the culture of the streets and of other public places."

20. Foxe, 8:390; CR125/4d; Ward, "Reformation," 91. Scarisbrick, *Reformation*, 136–61, discusses the survival of Catholicism among the people.

ingly of the old religion and disparagingly of the Genevans now in their midst. Several years later, nuns from Brabant were staying at the White Hart, so its Catholic reputation lived on.[21]

There is no indication that many inhabitants of Colchester were yearning for the Catholic mass, but not everyone fell into line with the radical reformist preaching being offered by John Pullen. Apothecary Simon Smyth, in a conversation in his house in early 1562, railed against Pullen's preaching, and a butcher's wife loudly proclaimed her distaste for Pullen's forceful and uncompromising style.[22] Furthermore, an apparent indifference to religion had reared its head. Beginning in the 1530s, the wills showed a marked increase in the percentage of people who seemed to be only nominally religious, with the figure rising to a high point of 53 percent in the 1550s (see chapter 4, table 2). The percentage went down in the 1560s, to 33 percent of the testators who seemed to be totally indifferent or only nominally interested in religion, but that was still high compared to 9 percent in pre-Reformation Colchester. Perhaps some were timid Catholics, but the number from the 1560s possibly reflects an increasing secularity. As the well-known Maldon preacher George Gifford later remarked, "Even in the best and most religious towns the greater part have very little zeal."[23] In any case, the reformist leaders knew that they had work to do. Transformations in thinking and practices do not come quickly or easily, but the sermons of the Genevan reformers would gradually have an impact on townspeople. Quiet changes were also occurring in funeral practices, education, and ownership of Bibles.

Burial Sermons

One of the effects of the reformers' emphasis on preaching was the new use of burial sermons, which began to be requested in wills in 1563. The influence of the preaching ministers was obvious; in the first two decades, almost every testator specified a certain preacher, usually the common preacher, for his or her burial sermon. For example, Alderman John Beriff requested Master William Cole "to make a sermon to preach the glad tidings of the gospel at my burial." The burial sermon was a kind of

---

21. Byford, "Religious Change," 158–61; D/Y2/6, p. 61.
22. Byford, "Religious Change," 143–46, 148.
23. Quoted in Hunt, *Puritan Moment,* 124–25.

Protestant substitute for prayers for the dead; whereas the Catholic prayers were for the purpose of bringing one more quickly to the felicities of heaven, the Protestant burial sermon was primarily to help others gain the joys of heaven. However, only the more prosperous could afford sermons. In the 1560s the usual fee for a burial sermon was 6s. 8d., and that price rose to 10s. in the 1570s, when a burial sermon seems to have become something of a status symbol. There were fewer requests for burial sermons than one might have expected—only sixteen in Elizabethan Colchester—probably because the burial sermon came under fire from some radical reformers, who condemned the practice as unscriptural, of pagan origin, and subject to misconstruction as a Catholic ritual.[24]

In addition to the sixteen testators who requested burial sermons, five others left money for sermons after their deaths, but again with specific instructions. Alderman Thomas Turner asked Master Challoner, the town preacher, to preach four sermons "besides his ordinary sermons, at such time as he shall think good." The widow of an alderman, Alice Maynard, had a heart for those people who rarely had preaching; her executor was instructed to "appoint some godly or learned preacher to preach four sermons in some country towns where the Gospel is not usually preached."[25]

University Education

Another effect of reformist preaching was the greater number of sons sent to study at the University of Cambridge. Only a few had been sent earlier, with William Gilbert being an outstanding example. Gilbert graduated from St. John's in 1560 and eventually became a physician and the most distinguished man of science of his generation through his work on electromagnetism. In the 1560s more Colchester sons began to be sent to university, in the beginning phase of what some historians have called the educational revolution, when "matriculations at Cambridge rose from 160 a year in the 1550s to more than 340 a year in the 1570s and

24. Will of Beriff, PRO 17 Crymes; Frederic B. Tromly, " 'According to Sounde Religion': The Elizabethan Controversy over the Funeral Sermon," *Journal of Medieval and Renaissance Studies* 13 (1983): 293–312.

25. Wills of Turner, PRO 15 Carew; Maynard, PRO 18 Watson. Other testators, such as Alderman J. Maynard (1565; PRO 15 Sheffeld), J. Jerman (1577; ERO D/ABW21/168), and J. Harvye (1584; ERO D/ACR7/274), left 6s. 8d. or 10s. to certain ministers or preachers, suggesting that the testator was wanting a sermon preached.

1580s."[26] Puritan teachings in some of the Cambridge colleges must have had a strong drawing power,[27] as at least some of the Colchester fathers sending their sons to Cambridge were committed Protestants. William Daniell, for example, provided at his death in 1567 for the continued maintenance of his son, Samuel, who had been a pensioner at St. John's for one year; and in 1573 the son of Alderman John Beste was at the university.[28] Cambridge had served as a center for Christian humanist learning early in the sixteenth century, both through the pious Lady Margaret's establishment of new colleges to promote the new learning and spirituality, and through the influence of Erasmus, who taught Greek at Cambridge from 1511 to 1514. With that background, Cambridge became the early center of Protestant thinking in the 1520s and 1530s. Later, the three largest Cambridge colleges of the time, St. John's, Trinity, and Christ's, all played a role in the development of Puritanism among the clergy and schoolmasters, and in the controversy over vestments that began in the universities in the 1560s, almost all of the members of St. John's refused to wear the surplice. Oxford, which came later to Protestant thinking, also produced some outstanding reformers, such as John Pullen and William Cole.[29]

To support learning at the universities, then, was consonant with strong Puritan views. Alderman John Fowle bequeathed £50 in 1572 to both Cambridge and Oxford "towards the relief of poor scholars." Fowle's Puritan sympathies were obvious from his other legacies to the common preacher and to the Puritan minister Thomas Upcher, and the

---

26. Cressy, *Literacy,* 168.

27. O'Day, *Education,* 77–131, describes the type of education given at the universities; J. T. Cliffe, *The Puritan Gentry: The Great Puritan Families of Early Stuart England* (London: Routledge and Kegan Paul, 1984), 92–103, discusses the influence of Puritanism in the various colleges of Cambridge.

28. ERO D/ACR6/21; PRO 2 Martyn; John Venn and J. A. Venn, eds., *Alumni Cantabrigienses: A Biographical List of All Known Students, Graduates, and Holders of Office at the University of Cambridge from the Earliest Times to 1900* (Cambridge: Cambridge University Press, 1922), pt. 1, vol. 2. Also, Alderman Benjamin Clerc said that he intended to send his son to Cambridge (Bindoff, *House,* 1:650), Richard Collett provided for a son at Cambridge in 1583 (CR145/16d), and in 1584 Alice Maynard left 40s. to the son of the deceased minister of St. Leonard's, Samuel Goodeare, a sizar at St. John's, Cambridge (PRO 18 Watson; Venn and Venn, *Alumni,* pt. 1, vol. 2).

29. Cross, *Church and People,* 49, 54, 58, 137; Collinson, *Puritan Movement,* 127–28; Cliffe, *Puritan Gentry,* 92–98. Later in Elizabeth's reign, two colleges were founded at Cambridge with the express purpose of promoting Puritan learning: Emmanual (1584) and Sidney Sussex (1596).

same concern for Puritan godliness was evident in six out of the eight Colchester wills that left money to Cambridge. William Markaunt's legacy to Cambridge was explicit in its connection between learning and preaching; Markaunt left £40 for the buying and distribution of "very good books of divinity" to poor theology students, with the legatees to be decided by four of the "most godly and discreet learned ministers that shall then be preachers of the same Divine Doctrine." Thomas Hopper went further and named four preachers who were to determine how his legacy to Cambridge was to be spent, with one of the four "preachers of God's holy Word" being the famous Puritan divine Master John Knew-stub, himself a graduate of St. John's, Cambridge.[30]

Knewstub and Oliver Pigge, parson of St. Peter's and All Saints', had been students at St. John's together, and increasing numbers of Cambridge alumni became preachers in Colchester. When the bailiffs were seeking a common preacher to be in Colchester on a more permanent basis in 1573, they "covenanted with a learned man of Cambridge," Nicholas Challoner of Clare Hall. Challoner's two successors were also Cambridge men, George Northey of Clare Hall and Richard Harris of St. John's. Likewise from St. John's was Robert Lewis, vicar of St. Peter's from 1579 to 1589, who later, with his wife, set up a scholarship at the college.[31]

Ownership of Bibles

Puritan preaching instilled a desire for a knowledge of the Word of God, and wills show that a few more people were owning Bibles, which had been made much easier with the publication of the new Geneva Bible in 1560. That relatively inexpensive English version had been translated by reputable scholars who had been Marian exiles together—among them William Cole, Colchester's town preacher—and it was printed in the readable roman type and, for the first time, in a size that one could hold easily. Archbishop Parker, having little sympathy for Bible reading among the laity, had in effect suppressed the Geneva Bible, refusing to

---

30. Wills of Fowle, PRO 17 Draper; Markaunt, PRO 12 Rowe; Hopper, PRO 112 Cobham.

31. Collinson, *Puritan Movement*, 127; D/B5 R7, f. 242v; D/B5 Gb1, ff. 21v, 94v; on Harris, *DNB*, 9:22; Davids, *Annals*, 114; BL, Stowe MS 841, f. 45; Venn and Venn, *Alumni*, pt. 1, vol. 1 and pt. 1, vol. 2.

issue a license for its publication in England, so it had been published abroad at first. But Grindal quickly issued the printing license after becoming archbishop.[32]

Two women, both testators in 1571, were among the earliest known lay owners of the printed Bible in Colchester. Alice Wilbore, of the Protestant Wilbore family, bequeathed "my bible of the great volume," probably denoting the 1539 translation, and Joan Dybney left her Geneva Bible to her eldest son, Thomas Firefanne.[33] Dybney's family illustrates the role of Scripture in the life of one Protestant family. In mentioning in her will a "chest that I brought from beyond the sea," Dybney must have been referring to her exile during Mary's reign.[34] Her eldest son, Thomas Firefanne, stayed behind in Colchester, and he was among the twenty-two indicted of heresy and taken as prisoners to London to be examined by Bishop Bonner. On the way, they were cheered through the streets of London by about a thousand persons, as Bonner himself reported in a letter published by Foxe in his *Book of Martyrs*. Foxe also published a part of the confession of faith and doctrine of the twenty-two prisoners, which showed a thorough acquaintance with the Word and made a strong appeal to the authority of Scripture.[35] Firefanne, managing to escape execution, lived for decades in Colchester, and the wills of several committed Protestants show a close relationship with Firefanne. Alderman Richard Thurston called Firefanne "a loving friend and neighbor," and the widow of Puritan preacher Thomas Upcher bequeathed Upcher's gown to Firefanne.[36] Other members of Joan Dyb-

---

32. Edwards, *Christian England*, 146; David M. Palliser, *The Age of Elizabeth: England under the Later Tudors, 1547–1603* (London: Longman, 1983), 332; Collinson, *Puritan Movement*, 164–65. The Geneva Bible was very popular, going through some sixty editions before publication of the King James Bible in 1611.

33. Wills of Wilbore, ERO D/ACR6/309; Dybney, ERO D/ACR6/219.

34. In 1556 Dybney was among those who, with Thomas Putto, were charged in the borough court as being obstinate and fugitive heretics (CR122/4), and Dybney was reported as having gone away. Among those listed as exiles in Aarau in Switzerland was a widowed Margaret Dybney from Colchester—probably Joan—with her two children (Oxley, 204, 217). Joan was the widow of John Dybney, whom she had married on June 30, 1547, when she was widow Joan Reve, according to the parish records of St. Nicholas's (ERO T/R108/2). John was probably the son of Alderman Thomas Dybney, who had to confess his evil behavior in religion before Mary's Privy Council; see the will of the alderman's father-in-law, John Mace (1533), ERO D/ACR2/158. Joan mentioned a "Father Dybney" in her will.

35. Foxe, 8:306–10; Thomas's surname is given variously as Feersanne and Firefanne.

36. PRO 30 Darcy; PRO 46 Kidd. Firefanne witnessed the will of Katherine Plaistow in 1600, ERO D/ABW29/278; her husband, R. Plaistow, had died in 1571 (ERO D/ACR6/314) and was the third person in that year to mention owning a Bible, along with Joan Dybney and Alice Wilbore.

ney's family valued the Word of God. Dybney's son through her second marriage, Adam Reve, and his wife, Bridget, both died twenty years after his mother's death. Bridget, dying last, left their Bible to their son, Israel, carefully providing that an older stepson keep it until Israel was twenty-one years old.[37]

Only ten testators in Elizabeth's reign bequeathed Bibles, but Bible ownership was a mark of genuine commitment and probably of literacy, as Bibles were too valuable to be passed on to someone who could not read them. Significantly, half of the Bible-owning testators were women, and two of the five male testators bequeathed their Bibles to women, attesting to women's literacy and to the place that they had found in the reformed church. A Dutchman, Francis Van Pradeles, was obviously impressed with the ability of his cousin Ellen to whom he left "seven great books to exercise herself therein," including a Bible, works by John Calvin and Heinrich Bullinger, and Foxe's *Book of Martyrs*.[38]

The increased preaching and Bible ownership in Colchester were a measure not only of the depth and endurance of the earlier change from Catholicism to Protestantism but also of the more subtle transformation from Henrician and Edwardian reform to Calvinistic Puritanism's stricter reliance on the Word. Puritanism had the potential of being both more inclusive in its use of the laity in leadership roles and also more exclusive in its stern moral expectations, which excluded and punished those who were not willing to live the godly life. This newer emphasis in Colchester Protestantism eventually met firm resistance, a negative tribute to the success of the Genevan reformers.

Trials and Tribulations: Resistance to the Puritan Agenda

The teachings of Geneva had given a central role to the godly magistrate, including the regulating of the behavior of individuals, but one George Dybney was not inclined to accept such interference from magistrates or ministers. Libels thrown around the town in the spring and summer of 1575 and an attempt to stop a perceived case of adultery one night in June of that year precipitated a lengthy and painful period in the religious and corporate life of Colchester, which pitted most of the town leaders

---

37. ERO D/ABW32/24; ERO D/ABW32/33. The giving of Bible names was another mark of the commitment of the Reve family; the sons were Samson and Israel, unusual names in Colchester at that time. Parson Thomas Upcher named his son Isaac (PRO 4 Arundell).

38. ERO D/ACW2/36; see also will of T. Hopper (1597), PRO 112 Cobham.

and preachers against George Dybney and his friends, among them the supposed adulterer John Lone, who disliked the strict Puritan teaching. In the end the feud, which was carried into the Court of Star Chamber, was primarily between Dybney and Alderman Benjamin Clere. Not only did the case pose the basic problem of the limits of religious and secular authority in the town, but it also created tensions among the town leaders, revealed corrupt behavior, and opened old wounds from the Marian years.

Central to the case was George Dybney, who had a mixed record as town official and troublemaker. A native of Colchester,[39] Dybney first appeared in the Colchester records in 1560, when he sued Benjamin Clere for a debt of £250. His first recorded conflict with church officials was in 1567, when Bishop Grindal directed Archdeacon Withers to bring Dybney into the archidiaconal court to answer information "laid against him" by town preacher William Cole.[40] At that time Dybney was already elected as one of the four sergeants at mace, a position he held for two years in the late 1560s. During the borough year of 1570–71, when Benjamin Clere was senior bailiff, some sort of trouble with town authorities resulted in Dybney's imprisonment for forty days, although by Dybney's account, "there was no cause to charge me with." The problem apparently resulted in the loss of Dybney's rights as a burgess, but he was readmitted in 1572 and thus again eligible to serve as sergeant in 1573–74, even though he was under suspicion in the ecclesiastical courts for withholding 6s. 8d. of the goods of the Bradfield church.[41] At the end of May, 1575, Dybney was under suspicion for libels against the government of the town, and at his examination, he charged that "that knave, prelate Upcher" was behind it all and in collusion with the bailiffs.[42]

A few days later, a midnight arrest of a friend of Dybney's accelerated the tensions. When constables went to the house of the absent William Collyns and found together mariner John Lone and Margery Collyns, William's wife, they arrested and imprisoned the couple. Lone protested his innocence, but the town authorities ordered a punishment used fre-

39. As noted in CR136/8, when Dybney was readmitted to the freedom of the town. It is uncertain whether Dybney was a relative of the Protestant Dybney family mentioned earlier.

40. CR126/4, 5d; D/Y2/6, p. 59.

41. D/Y2/2, pp. 69–76; CR136/8; D/ACA6/197. Dybney was buying and selling property in 1570, at which time he was a clothier in St. Peter's parish (CR135/8).

42. D/Y2/2, pp. 69–76.

quently for adultery: riding in the tumbrel through the high street of the town. Lone's resistance resulted in his being carried farther than usual, but then he was released into the custody of beer brewer William Reade, whose daughter Lone was engaged to marry. Lone and the Reades lived in St. Leonard's parish, and their parson, Thomas Upcher, demanded that Lone take Communion before the marriage ceremony; to take Communion, Lone had to submit first to Upcher by entering into a bond agreeing never to slander Upcher. Dybney had not been silent through all of this, muttering that Upcher was again behind it all and that the town leaders had punished Lone far too harshly.[43]

Dybney was correct in his perception that the town leaders and Genevan reformers were in agreement about the need to regulate behavior in the town. Shortly after the Lone incident, archdeacon and former town preacher George Withers preached a sermon against whoredom and against any who would "mislike of the punishment of it."[44] Resistance quickly developed in the form of anonymous written statements of opposition circulated in the town, or libels, as they were called. Such writings were viewed as a threat to order in the town; back in 1539 the borough court heavily fined two men who had made "a writing, or written matter to cause discord between their neighbors," and who had "placed this writing on 'lez posts' in the night." The targets of the 1575 libels were Parson Upcher and other ministers from the area. Later investigations revealed that about fourteen such libels were produced, several of them originating with Christopher Johnson, servant to gentleman lawyer Edmund Markaunt. Some of the libels were clever verses referring to Sir John Lacklatin, an old term for the unlearned clergy, so Thomas Upcher, with little or no formal education, was obviously vulnerable. In fact, Johnson admitted that the verses were directed at Upcher for three reasons: because Upcher did not know Latin, for his treatment of Lone, and for his flaunting of the law of the church in not wearing the surplice.[45] The criticisms of Upcher reflected the conflict in England between

---

43. Byford, "Religious Change," 194–209, has a full account of the case.

44. Quoted in Byford, "Religious Change," 208.

45. CR109/2d; Byford, "Religious Change," 211–12, 214, 219; *APC,* 9:105. Christopher Johnson was probably a relative of Markaunt, as the three Markaunt brothers, all living in St. Giles's parish, each mentioned a Johnson in their wills, and Johnson was possibly reflecting their views. The Markaunts were well-educated, committed Protestants: see wills of Edmund (1579), PRO 28 Darcy; William (1582), PRO 12 Rowe; John (1583), PRO 49 Brudenell.

moderate Protestantism and the Geneva reformers, with the latter most consistently represented in Colchester by the uncompromising Parson Upcher, who was viewed as an upstart lacking in compassion.

The identification of Upcher's goals with those of the majority of the aldermen was not unfounded, as there were certainly some close connections between Upcher and several of the aldermen, notably the two from Upcher's parish of St. Leonard in the early 1570s. In 1572 Upcher was a supervisor, along with Alderman Robert Lambert, of the will of merchant and alderman John Fowle, who had taken as his second wife the daughter of Lambert. Shortly afterward, Upcher was a co-fee with the Lamberts to buy land for Fowle's son. Several years later, when Robert Lambert died, still an alderman in 1590, his continuing respect for Upcher was evident in his legacy to Upcher as a preacher "of God's holy words." There were other ties; Upcher was also close to the Cock family of St. Leonard's. Widow Grace Cock asked Upcher to preach a sermon after her decease in 1572, and her son-in-law, also named Cock, became alderman in 1575.[46]

Upcher was not the only clergyman who was a target; several area clergy also suffered from the arrows of the libelers. The libel "A choke peace for A pigg" was no doubt aimed at former Colchester clergyman Oliver Pigge, who was residing at nearby Abberton, and "Wilton and Skilton" must have been directed at John Wilton, who lived at Aldham. Alarmed by the continuance of the libels, town leaders backed Upcher by calling on neighboring clergy for help in a preaching campaign against the libels, with the bailiffs writing that the libels had "defaced" all ministers of the Word of God and that some of them had been slandered "by the name of Comon bull, Man slear, Wedlock breaker, proud prelates and many other the vilest and most shameful and scandalous words, terms, and names." The libels continued, becoming even more scurrilous, and the bailiffs complained that the libelers had hung copies "upon church doors and cast them into church porches and churchyards where the people should assemble themselves to hear sermons, but also set some of them openly upon posts and cast many of them abroad in the streets."[47]

In mid-August, the libelers shifted tactics and began concentrating on

---

46. PRO 17 Draper; PRO 69 Harrington; PRO 18 Draper; CR137/2d. Upcher's second wife, Joan, spoke in her will (PRO 46 Kidd) of her "very good friend" Mistress Anne Lambert, Robert Lambert's wife.

47. Byford, "Religious Change," 215, 220–21, 223.

the town leaders because of their opposition, with the special target being the powerful alderman and Upcher supporter Benjamin Clere. George Dybney marshaled some telling accusations against Clere, and Christopher Johnson formulated them into a libel called "The Buryall of Clere." In the missive, Clere was accused of corrupt practices when he was deputy custom comptroller in Colchester, of ruining the Hospital of St. Mary Magdalen, and of bribing a jury that was trying a case in which Clere was involved. Furthermore, in the trial that eventually came before the Star Chamber in London, Clere's activities during Mary's reign were brought into question. Christopher Johnson reminded the court that Foxe's *Book of Martyrs* had identified Clere in the 1570 edition as the alderman who acted harshly toward the heretics who were about to burn in Colchester, and Johnson also accused Clere of being responsible for the capture of the Protestant preacher George Eagles.[48] These were harsh judgments against the senior alderman of the town who had already served as bailiff eight times and who was, by that time, the only alderman left from Mary's reign.

The town leaders responded to "The Buryall of Clere" by writing to the Privy Council about "the casting around of libels" in Colchester; Matthew Stephens's house was searched, and he was imprisoned, as was Christopher Johnson. The Privy Council examined George Dybney on September 25. The libels were said to be "seditious," for in the council's view any undermining of the proper civil authority was sedition. Dybney was imprisoned at Woodstock but was released three months later under a bond of £100 for his appearance in the Star Chamber, which fined him £20.[49]

The situation in Colchester was not so easy to discharge, as the libels had polarized the town and had even affected the unity of the leadership. Elections were approaching in the early autumn of 1575, when "The Buryall of Clere" was being cast about and the leaders were beginning their appeal to the Privy Council. In the Michaelmas elections at the end of September, the town's electors showed their support for Clere by electing him to a ninth term as bailiff. Perhaps more significant was that John Hunwick, who had served only one year as alderman, was not reelected, which was unusual. The official reason given was that Hunwick had been

---

48. Byford, "Religious Change," 224–28.
49. *APC*, 9:25, 61, 105; Emmison, *Disorder*, 46; Byford, "Religious Change," 238–43. The Privy Council had suggested that the corporation take the case to the Star Chamber, which they did, with deputy town clerk, William Ram, representing Colchester.

elected without being of the full livery of the town, but if historian Mark Byford is correct, Hunwick's dismissal was more likely a result of Hunwick's belief that Upcher was too severe in his judgments. Hunwick was the only alderman who did not sign the order of punishment for John Lone in the adultery case, thus signifying his disapproval, an attitude that was perhaps even more unacceptable given Hunwick's residency in St. Leonard's, Upcher's parish.[50]

Under Clere's term as bailiff, then, the case against the libelers went before the Star Chamber. Clere was fighting back, both on the local level and in the central court system, and he had won, at least for the moment. It was a pyrrhic victory, though, as it was Benjamin Clere's last year as alderman, even though he lived on for another few years.[51] Perhaps he was getting too old, perhaps he had spent too much money in litigation, or perhaps the accusations brought against him had too much truth in them. An opponent, William Reade, John Lone's father-in-law, took Clere's place in 1576, and in 1577 Hunwick was restored as alderman. It was not to be the last upheaval in town governance, though, as the borough authorities soon found themselves in the middle of new problems resulting from the mixture of politics and religion. They had always taken a part in the religious life of the town, a tradition that had made them compatible with the Genevan teachings regarding the lay magistrate's involvement in producing a godly society, but the intensity of the Puritan teachings called the magistrates to an even greater role both in the religious life of the town and in regulating the behavior of its inhabitants. As they were learning, it was "painful" teaching, and not all of it was to the liking of the townspeople.

---

50. Byford, "Religious Change," 204, 237, 268; Davis, "Colchester," 122.
51. At least until 1584, it seems; see CR154/23d.

9

Tightening the Reins of Governance, 1575–80

By 1575, all but one of the town leaders from the early Reformation and Marian years were dead, and that one alderman would soon be out of office, so a new generation was taking over. It was a watershed year, a turning point affecting both the governance and the religious life of the town. Conflicts that had been simmering were brought to a full boil in 1575. The scathing criticism directed at the preachers and town leaders that was spread by the libelous missives only strengthened the resolve of the governors to root out evil behavior in the town. A part of the solution was to put the position of town preacher on a solid basis, so that he could live in the town and give his undivided attention to his job as common preacher, a measure made all the more necessary since the parish churches were still struggling with inadequate staffing. With the heightened tensions in the borough, it became obvious that the gentry was split between Catholicism and moderate Protestantism, with both religious groups looking with disdain on the Puritan zeal of the preachers and the corporation leaders.

There were other conflicts in 1575. The Dutch were becoming so numerous that complaints were lodged against them and an agreement had to be worked out whereby the Dutch paid hefty sums to the town, which may partially explain why some of them moved to Halstead the next year.[1] Wider conflicts in England set the stage for those in Colchester. The Catholic threat was becoming more real as priests from the new training center at Douai began entering England; at the same time, Calvinists were continuing their aggressive attempts to purify the church, and the Anglican hierarchy began reacting against extremism, whether of Catholics or Puritans. Social conditions produced another kind of conflict as poverty and vagrancy rose to levels unprecedented in Tudor

---

1. Moens, *Dutch Church*, iv.

England. This chapter and the following one look at the years from 1575 through 1580, during the tenure of Nicholas Challoner, when religious and social conflict was at a peak in Colchester, and examine the counter-measures taken by the town authorities: tightening the procedures of town governance, obtaining influential advocates in Westminster, and, especially, regulating the behavior of townsmen.

A Resident Town Preacher amid Troubles and Tumult

The bailiffs had turned to Cambridge in late 1573 when they were seeking a "learned preacher," a replacement for George Withers, who had other commitments as archdeacon of Colchester and rector at Danbury. Payment of Withers had been through voluntary contributions, but the town assembly thought the need for a town preacher was important enough to hire the next preacher on a more permanent basis through corporation funding, for which they allotted £20 a year from the rent of Kingswood Heath. The man was Nicholas Challoner, B.D. His first year and a half were probably probationary, but he obviously proved satisfactory, as in July, 1575, the assembly agreed that Master Challoner would "have his patent sealed" as common preacher of the town. It was probably no coincidence that the permanent agreement came during the weeks when libels against the preachers were being circulated in the town and when the arrest and punishment of the supposed adulterer John Lone was still a hot topic. According to the agreement, Challoner was to receive a generous £40 annual stipend.[2]

The parish churches in 1575 continued much the same, with the faithful William Lyon out at Mile End. John Price and John Walford (or Welfare) were rectors of Lexden and All Saints', but apparently neither man preached or made much of an impact, unlike the rector at St. Leonard's, Thomas Upcher, who was the subject of the anti-Puritan libels being spread abroad in the town, which continued into early 1576.[3] Challoner's preaching was probably included in some of the libels against the

2. D/B5 R7, ff. 242v, 269. In contrast, the town preacher in Rye was paid £10 a year in the 1570s, which rose to £20 in 1589 and to £26 13s. 4d. in 1591, according to Mayhew, *Tudor Rye,* 77; but the Ipswich town lecturer in the seventeenth century received £120 and a house rent-free, according to Michael Reed, "Economic Structure and Change in Seventeenth-Century Ipswich," in *Country Towns in Pre-Industrial England,* ed. Peter Clark (Leicester: Leicester University Press, 1981), 112.

3. *Calendar of State Papers, Domestic: Edward VI, Mary, Elizabeth, and James I,* 12 vols. (London: HMSO, 1856–72), 1547–80, p. 520.

preachers, but because he was a university man, he commanded more respect than Upcher could. That Challoner's preaching was held in high regard is apparent from the wills: four testators requested sermons or left money to a cleric during Challoner's time in Colchester, and every one of them mentioned Challoner by name. The two testators from St. Leonard's, however, also referred to their parson, Thomas Upcher, so they were not rejecting Upcher but acknowledging Challoner's greater status as a preacher.[4]

Upcher continued to be a lightning rod for conflict, while at the same time commanding loyalty from such people as mariner John Firley, who called him "friend" and left money to Upcher's son.[5] The church hierarchy was ambivalent about Upcher. In 1577 Archbishop Grindal licensed Upcher to preach, but in the same year the intrepid Puritan was ordered by the archidiaconal court to confess his fault before his two congregations for not wearing the surplice and for not making the sign of the cross in baptism. Again in the same year, the same court backed Upcher when a woman who had slandered him was commanded to revoke her words and ask his forgiveness before five or six neighbors.[6] The greater authority of Nicholas Challoner, in comparison to Upcher, was evident in the role of disciplinarian and instructor given him by the archdeaconry court in 1576, when Richard Spenser, a curate at Greenstead, was summoned to the court to answer a charge of drunkenness. On Spenser's failure to appear, he was excommunicated; however, he submitted and was ordered to do penance. He was instructed "To stand up before the preacher at the end of sermon in St. James's church and openly confess his faults, and [he] shall write without the book such places against drunkenness as Mr. Challener [sic] the preacher shall instruct him, desiring the people there present to pray to God for his amendment."[7]

Any Calvinist preacher who was both encourager and guide to the godly magistrate was sure to get involved in the civic affairs of the town, and Challoner was no exception. That he had married Benjamin Clere's daughter Sarah put him squarely on the side of the older ruling group that had taken the lead in hiring Genevan preachers. The senior member of the town governors, Clere was not reelected in 1576, which was no small happening, as he had served since 1540. His failure to be elected

4. PRO 15 Carew; ERO D/ABW21/168; PRO 25 Bakon; PRO 4 Arundell.
5. PRO 4 Arundell.
6. Anglin, "Essex Puritan Movement," 174, 195; Emmison, *Morals,* 289.
7. Quoted in Emmison, *Morals,* 226–27.

again was the result not only of the charges of corruption brought against him by George Dybney but also of the heavy expense of continuing litigation in the London courts against the libelers, which was being borne by the people of Colchester. They blamed Benjamin Clere for spending the town's money, especially after a general aid was assessed on the citizens. Most of the town assembly continued to support Clere, though there were a few highly vocal critics, with Thomas Barlowe forcing his way into the assembly and shouting that "the town was worse three hundred pounds for Master Clere." Barlowe had lost his place on the common council in the 1575 election, at the same time that Alderman John Hunwick was forced out. Barlowe did not stint on his criticism of Clere, having noted in the spring that Clere was "a dishonest man" and a robber, both of the prince and of the poor. Barlowe's latest bold outburst gained him an indictment for attempting "to deface and deprave" Clere. Another opponent, John Symcott, was imprisoned for his refusal to pay the aid. In July, before the election process began at the end of August, complaints about Clere had reached the ears of the Privy Council "about certain injuries to the inhabitants," and a royal commission was appointed to investigate. The matter was serious enough for the commissioners to suspend the courts of the town for a few weeks in the latter part of the summer of 1576. In late September, when the annual election would have been in its final stages, the Privy Council was still concerned about "a certain controversy" among the Colchester town leaders.[8]

In that strained atmosphere, dissident William Reade, the father-in-law of supposed adulterer John Lone, was elected alderman in 1576, taking over Benjamin Clere's seat; in addition, the relatively new gentleman in town who had refused to pay the aid for the litigation, John Symcott, was elected chamberlain. The election represented a split among the reformers, with some of the long-standing reformers, such as Nicholas Wilbore, opposing Clere and his authoritarian approach. An attempt was made to bypass the usual procedures and elect John Hunwick as bailiff, but the Privy Council, who had to help solve the matter, ruled that Hunwick was not eligible since he was no longer serving as alderman. The Privy Council chastised the aldermen, however, for the "factions and quarrels among you, which we could wish were removed," and they threatened Colchester with the revoking of its charter if the troubles continued. The assembly moved to tighten up the election procedures, but

---

8. *APC*, 9:153, 199, 208; CR139/22d. Byford, "Religious Change," 244, 247, 249–51, 254, has a lengthy account of the situation.

they still showed their support of Benjamin Clere a few months later. In January, 1577, the town assembly noted that Clere had some serious court suits being brought against him, one of them by John Symcott, the new chamberlain, and that the corporation itself would defend Clere if the suits were not dropped, thus indicating the majority of the assembly's support for Clere in the midst of conflict.[9]

The political divisions dating from 1575 continued, with the minority group that opposed the Calvinistic preachers and magistrates bringing Hunwick back into office in the 1577 election. Barlowe was also brought back to the common council, and John Symcott was elected to the council for the first time. Sharp divisions emerged again in the 1578 election, and just before the first phase of the election, preacher Nicholas Challoner, speaking from the pulpit after giving a sermon, noted that rumors were circulating that his father-in-law, Benjamin Clere, and his brother-in-law, John Clere, were seeking office. Challoner's statement, as recorded, is enigmatic, but there was no mistaking the conflict between Alderman William Reade and Puritan preacher Thomas Upcher. In the same week that Challoner spoke about the election, Reade sued Upcher for trespass, a charge that could cover a multitude of offenses. Reade defaulted in his prosecution of Upcher, but the tenacious Upcher was not going to let the matter go away. Upcher demanded damages, and when Reade failed to pay the 28s. 11d. mandated for damages and costs, Upcher persuaded the bailiffs to order the sergeant at mace to apprehend Reade, who by that time had lost his post as alderman after having served for only two years.[10]

The libels, which had been such a sore point in 1575–76, continued sporadically throughout the late 1570s, but they became more than a mere nuisance in the spring of 1579, when the town authorities appealed for help in dealing with them. In the examination of the matter, one

---

9. D/B5 Gb1, f. 3; Byford, "Religious Change," 253–57; Davis, "Colchester," 122. Symcott was admitted in 1574 (CR138/2d).

10. D/B5 Sb2/3, f. 123; CR140/31; CR141/53. The records show that the feisty Reade was in a serious quarrel over fishing nets in 1580 and was imprisoned in 1582, perhaps the result of a debt owed to Alderman John Hunwick (CR142/13d, CR144/7d). Upcher also excluded Hunwick from Communion; see Byford, "Religious Change," 259–63. Another possible casualty of the long conflict was Alderman Robert Middleton, who was not reelected in 1580 after having served since 1559, when he was among the first reformers brought in after Elizabeth's accession to the throne; a possible explanation is that Matthew Stephens, who wrote some of the libels in 1575, was Middleton's son-in-law. See Stephens's will, PRO 42 Kidd. Middleton was still alive in 1603 when Robert Mott wrote his will, PRO 32 Harte.

Robert Younger gave some interesting details, reporting that in 1577 a libel, which was sewn up in brown paper, was thrust into his shop window. Immediately carrying it out to the Hythe, to the bailiff Master Hunwick, Younger returned to town to attend the sermon being preached at St. Botolph's. The sermon had already started, so he had to wait outside the church, during which time he saw two women talking and laughing together and pointing their fingers at him; he was convinced that they were responsible for the libel.[11]

Turbulence was not confined to Colchester alone, which was one reason why the Privy Council was so concerned about the conflicts in Colchester. In the summer of 1576, two men named Newton and Petloe, supposedly from Colchester, were being examined by a royal commission concerning a commotion in Essex; they were confined to the Tower but were released on bond in June, 1577.[12] In January of 1578, an Edwardian pretender, Robert Mantell, was committed to jail in Colchester Castle; when he escaped eighteen months later, it was revealed that he had been aided by some women followers, who were accused of "lewd practices of sorceries and conjurations."[13] The upheaval of the late 1570s brought out all sorts of strange accusations.

Social and Religious Divisions among the Gentry

In the atmosphere of heightened conflict in Colchester, evidence suggests that social and religious differences were contributing to the political divisions in the town. A well-documented fight in April, 1576, between members of the local gentry, John Christmas and Richard Southwell, and their followers, heralded a conflict that went deeper than the alleged cause, an insult at a jousting tournament. The matter was first examined by Sir Thomas Lucas and the bailiffs of Colchester; in May, Southwell was brought before the Privy Council on a charge of "certain lewd and inconvenient speeches used of the Queen's Majestie." Southwell was released, however, because some persons who were supposed to have heard his disloyal speech would not confirm it.[14] The immediate issue may have been sale of land that the Southwells and Katherine Audley

---

11. D/Y2/2, p. 113. Byford, "Religious Change," 269, thinks it possible that the women were merely gossiping about Younger's infidelities.

12. *APC,* 9:188, 263, 373.

13. *APC,* 10:146; 11:194, 214–15; 12:29.

14. *APC,* 9:112, 117, 125, 129; Emmison, *Disorder,* 105–6.

bought from John Christmas,[15] but there were deeper issues troubling the disputants. John Christmas was the descendent of Colchester aldermen and clothiers who, during much of the first half of the sixteenth century, were part of the richest family in Colchester. The Christmases' wealth had permitted them to buy manors so that their sons could be gentlemen. John's grandfather, also named John, was the last Christmas alderman, and John's father, George, had been the first Christmas gentleman, but George did not prosper as his forebears had done. To maintain his gentle status, George gradually began selling the lands that his fathers had so carefully accumulated.[16] John was fifteen when his father died unexpectedly in 1566, so it was a twenty-five-year-old John who, with his mother, Bridget, and her new husband, George Darrell, was selling lands to the Southwells and widow Katherine Audley. Whatever the immediate problem in 1576, John must have also felt resentment at having to sell family property, which lessened his wealth and status, and he was the aggressor in the quarrel in April when he led about thirty men against Southwell and brandished a caliver, a light musket, as if he were going to shoot Southwell.

Katherine Audley was a key player in the dispute between Christmas and Southwell. Katherine was the "bastard daughter" of Sir Richard Southwell, a wealthy landowner from Norfolk and court official who benefited from the dissolution of the monasteries. Nevertheless, his staunch Catholicism made him a firm supporter of Queen Mary, and he lost his seat on the Privy Council when Elizabeth became queen. Southwell had more than one illegitimate child, and the Richard Southwell who fought with John Christmas seems to have been the bastard Richard Southwell of Horsham St. Faith's. The bastard Richard had a son, Robert, today known as one of the minor poets of the late Tudor period, who would arrive in England in 1586 and later suffer martyrdom as a Jesuit priest.[17] Katherine Audley was the aunt to the Jesuit martyr-to-be, and she was no less a committed Catholic than he was. Through Katherine, the Audley household became known as a center of Catholicism in the Colchester area, an ironic development since Thomas Audley, Colchester town clerk and later lord chancellor of England, was one of the architects of the Protestant Reformation under Henry VIII. Just two

---

15. *Essex Fines,* 5:195, 200, 202.

16. *VCH Essex,* 9:77–78; *Essex Fines,* 5:22, 27, 33, 39, 40, 50, 69, 96, 113.

17. Joseph Foster, ed., *London Marriage Licenses 1521–1869* (London: Bernard Quaritch, 1887); *DNB,* 18:700–703.

weeks after Lord Chancellor Audley's death in April, 1544, Katherine had married Thomas, a brother of the lord chancellor, who had bequeathed the manor of Berechurch to his younger brother and namesake. Thomas was probably somewhat older than Katherine, who seems to have been a second wife; Thomas died in 1557, but Katherine lived until 1611.[18] Katherine was, therefore, head of the Audley household for many years; she was obviously a strong woman, and her Catholicism repeatedly brought her into conflict with Colchester authorities and with Elizabeth's Privy Council.

Fear of Catholics had intensified over the past decade, beginning with Catholic Spain's invasion of the Netherlands in 1567 and the creation of a college to train English Catholic priests at Douai in Flanders in 1568. Also in 1568, Mary, queen of Scots, fled to England, thus providing a focus for Catholic hopes for restoring a Catholic to the English throne, making Catholicism potentially treasonous. The 1569 rebellion of the Catholic northern earls, an attempt to restore Catholic worship, was followed the next year by the pope's excommunication of Queen Elizabeth and a call for Catholics to depose her. Such threats motivated Parliament to pass, in 1571, the Treasons Act, which was aimed at Catholics, though Elizabeth would not allow extreme measures against them. Stern measures seemed warranted when the Ridolfi plot, a plan to kill Queen Elizabeth, was exposed and when the foremost French Protestants were murdered in the bloody St. Bartholomew's Day Massacre, which was instigated by the French queen, Catherine de Medici. Such actions made everyone in England nervous, and the pope's Te Deum in thanksgiving for the death of the French Protestants seemed especially callous to the English. By 1574 anti-Catholic feelings had just begun to lessen but were stirred up again by the arrival in England of the first three priests from the Douai seminary. The identification of Catholicism with foreign and treasonous powers probably helped to lessen the attachment of ordinary Englishmen to Catholicism, and other forces had been at work to make many people of England into Protestants by the mid-1570s. They had been attending the English church regularly as law required and had slowly begun to identify with it, and Elizabeth's policy of benign toleration had helped the transition in that it did not make an issue of individual beliefs and so had not polarized the people. Also, many of the older partisans had died and Protestantism was persuasive, so Catholicism, at

---

18. Foster, *London Marriage Licenses;* Morant, 2:30; D/ACA21/465; *VCH Essex,* 9:338.

least in Essex, was being kept alive not by ordinary people but by gentry, such as Katherine Audley. Gentry in other areas were likewise serving the same function and providing refuge for the incoming priests.[19]

The year of 1577 was hardly a year of peace for either Catholics or Puritans. The government ordered a return to be made of the Catholic recusants in each diocese, and sixty Essex names were reported. Among the "papists dwelling in Colchester," the state records listed Mistress Audley, describing her as "a very wealthy and dangerous woman," who had twenty to thirty people at a time to mass at her home.[20] It was becoming much more dangerous to be a Catholic in England; some of the incoming Catholic missionaries had been imprisoned, and in 1577 one man was executed for treason under the Treasons Act of 1571. Even so, most lay Catholics were not seriously threatened, especially if they were willing to conform by attending church occasionally. But they were certainly watched.[21]

There was no doubt about the sympathies of the Colchester authorities. In late October, 1578, the bailiffs reported the presence in the town of "men very obstinate in the Popish profession and religion, who refused to attend sermons." The accused men were not interested in hearing the Word of God from Master Challoner, and three of them slipped away to London, seemingly their original destination. Apparently traveling on the same ship as these men, which landed at Harwich, were some gentlewomen from Brabant, three of them "professed nuns" of Sion Abbey in Mechelen. Colchester authorities detained the Catholic women, for which the Privy Council praised the bailiffs and instructed them to question the women and try to get the names of friends. The examination by the bailiffs showed the women to be part of the English colony of Catholics that had been living abroad, and they seemed to be part of the

19. Cross, *Church and People*, 143–44; Powell and Cook, *Historical Facts*, 94, 121–24; Edwards, *Christian England*, 139; Christopher Haigh, "The Church of England, the Catholics, and the People," in *The Reign of Elizabeth I*, ed. Christopher Haigh (London: Macmillan, 1984), 203.

20. Powell and Cook, *Historical Facts*, 124; Emmison, *Morals*, 93; *CSPD*, 1547–80, p. 576; M. O'Dwyer, "Catholic Recusants in Essex, c. 1580–c. 1600" (Master's thesis, University of London, 1960), 34–35. The 1577 document is transcribed in *Essex Recusant 5* (1963): 41–42.

21. Bindoff, *Tudor England*, 237; John Guy, *Tudor England* (Oxford: Oxford University Press, 1990), 299. One Rooke Green of Great Sampford was imprisoned in Colchester Castle in early 1579 "for matters of religion" after he had refused to be brought "to conformity" by local ministers, but he was released "because of bodily weakness" and the death of his father-in-law (*APC*, 11:174; Emmison, *Morals*, 94).

Catholic missionary effort to heretical England. The bailiffs were also admonished to get "a learned preacher to try to bring them to conformity," and Master Challoner's services were called on. The bishop of London had also been notified, and he ordered that those "lewd women" then staying at the White Hart be kept apart from everyone except designated keepers, "persons to you known of that fidelity as is requisite." A week later, on November 11, 1578, the bailiffs wrote to the bishop reporting that they were trying "to win the Papists from the blindness they have been fostered in, and to that intent they were severed then into godly and honest houses, procuring the town preacher and other wise and godly persons to repair unto them to confer in religion." The bailiffs went on to remark that they would gladly have the papists "rooted from" the town, so that "the number of them should be the less and thereby the infection."[22] Feelings against foreign Catholics were strong, and to the Colchester bailiffs, the presence of Catholic missioners was like a spreading cancer among them.

With such intense religious feelings in the late 1570s, it is no surprise that conflict, both political and religious, should arise, since the two were so intermingled. A disagreement between local gentry, including Sir Thomas Lucas, over the muster of the militia in Colchester in 1580 brought Mistress Audley's political loyalty into question in the Privy Council, as it was charged that she was influencing others around her manor at Berechurch to refuse to muster in Colchester, which in turn brought up the question of whether she was conforming to the Church of England by attending divine service at her parish church. The whole matter ended lamely over a question of where she was to pay taxes.[23] Though state politics and religion were in close harmony, one's dissonant beliefs were tolerated as long as there was political loyalty and a measure of outward religious conformity.

The conflict between John Christmas and Katherine Audley's Southwell brother in 1575–76, then, probably had religious as well as social implications. The transfer of land from Christmas to Audley and Southwell must have been galling for Christmas, as it represented not only a social comedown for his family but a victory for the Catholic Audleys.

---

22. D/Y2/5, p. 19; D/B5 Sb2/3, 104–5; *APC*, 10:355; D/Y2/6, pp. 61, 65, 69. Haigh, "Church," 202, writes that, by 1580, half of the missioners were working in Essex, London, and the Thames Valley.

23. *APC*, 12:51, 126, 131; 13:78, 262–63.

The earlier Christmases and Lord Chancellor Audley were cousins, and Lord Audley had made sure that the Christmases benefited from the Reformation, just as he did. Later, the Christmases had formed alliances with the Protestant Lucases and the earl of Oxford, and George Christmas had proven his Protestant sympathies when, as vice admiral of Essex, he prevented the Catholic Lady Waldegrave's daughters from escaping overseas.[24] The Christmases, who were firmly in the Protestant camp though not under the banner of Puritanism, were among the moderate Calvinists, along with Sir Thomas Lucas and Edmund Markaunt, the lawyer from whose house the anti-Puritan libels had spread through Colchester in 1575–76.[25] The moderates were generally educated people from the gentry or the professional class and often took their religion seriously but were not in the radical camp of Puritan preacher Thomas Upcher or in the Catholic camp of Katherine Audley. This middle group in Colchester seemed to be behind many of the libels in 1575–76 and was probably behind many in 1577, when two women from the gentry, Elizabeth Christmas and Mistress Sampforthe (or Simpcote), were thought to be the instigators of the libel thrown into the shop window of Robert Younger.[26]

Conflicts between social groups were nothing new, but the religious differences provided an added dimension that made the divisions stark indeed, with Katherine Audley and the town leaders representing the two extremes of Catholicism and Puritanism, and with most of the gentry, and probably a number of the townspeople, in the middle. The gentry had the power to disrupt the doings of the town leaders who were their social inferiors, but Puritanism, with its sense of purpose and rectitude, had a power of its own.

---

24. For the relationship of the Audleys and Christmases, see chapter 2 n. 13; Bindoff, *House*, 1:647. George Christmas's daughter married town clerk John Lucas (Morant, 2:17). Robert Christmas, younger son to Alderman John Christmas and servant to the sixteenth earl of Oxford, was one of Oxford's executors; see F. G. Emmison, ed., *Elizabethan Life: Wills of Essex Gentry and Yeomen* (Chelmsford: Essex County Council, 1980), 1–4.

25. Markaunt had once served as lawyer for George Christmas, and both Edmund and John Markaunt seemed to be serving Sir Thomas Lucas, perhaps as stewards: see *Essex Fines*, 5:27; Markaunt wills, PRO 28 Darcy and PRO 12 Rowe.

26. D/Y2/2, p. 113. Christmas was possibly the daughter of Alderman Thomas Christmas, who died in 1520 leaving a young daughter, Elizabeth (PRO 28 Ayloffe). If so, Elizabeth would have been around sixty years old or more in 1577. Simpcote was possibly the wife of the Tymdott (or Symcott) who was tried in the Star Chamber for throwing libels in 1576 (*APC*, 9:105); a John Simpcote, a gentleman, was suing Benjamin Clere in 1577 (D/B5 Gb1, f. 3).

Local Puritans Take the Offensive

Just as the Catholics were feeling the intensification of pressure on them, so were the Puritans. In 1575 Archbishop Matthew Parker died and was replaced, with the queen's consent, by the friend of the reformers Edmund Grindal. The elevation of Grindal was a happy situation for the reformers, but their rejoicing was short-lived. The queen, adamant about keeping the Church of England in the middle-way settlement already agreed on, the *via media,* opposed extremes on both sides: Catholic mission efforts and the attempts of the Puritans to "purify" the church. The issue of "prophesyings" brought the queen and Archbishop Grindal to an impasse.

Prophesyings, conferences of preachers and would-be preachers in the market towns, were part of the attempt to inform the ill-educated clergy so that they were better able to preach the Word. The name for the events was taken from an early conference in Zwingli's Zurich that engaged in "exercises of prophesying," which we would call preaching, by following the apostle Paul's instructions to "let two or three prophets speak, and let the others weigh what is said . . . . so that all may learn and all be encouraged." Prophesyings, not officially condoned by the Church of England, were initiated by preachers themselves, but by the 1570s they were often conducted before a lay audience, many of whom sat with their Geneva Bibles in hand to follow the scriptures cited by the preacher. Two or three sermons were often preached on the same text, followed by a more private conference of the ministers, frequently over a collegial dinner, where they could critique the sermons and thus improve their preaching. The prophesyings did much to promote reformist thinking, both among the clergy and the laity. By 1574, a prophesying was being held at Colchester, probably moderated by the new town preacher, Nicholas Challoner.[27]

The spread of what Queen Elizabeth considered to be extreme views began to be actively checked in 1577. She had already ordered specific prophesyings to be suppressed whenever she heard of them, and in the summer of 1576 a prophesying at Southam in Warwickshire came to her

27. William Harrison, *The Description of England,* ed. Georges Edelen (Ithaca, N.Y.: Cornell University Press, 1968), 25–27; Collinson, *Puritan Movement,* 51, 127, 159–60, 168, 174–75, 182; 1 Corinthians 14:29, 31, Revised Standard Version; Patrick Collinson, "The Elizabethan Church and the New Religion," in *The Reign of Elizabeth I,* ed. Christopher Haigh (London: Macmillan, 1984), 189–90; Morgan, *Godly Learning,* 223–26.

attention, probably because the bishop was opposed to it. Puritan friends at the court scrambled to save the rest of the prophesyings while obeying the queen in suppressing the one in Warwickshire. They warned Archbishop Grindal of the danger, but there seems to have been a political conspiracy at work to embarrass the Puritan friends at court, Leicester, Walsingham, and even Burghley. In a few months, Elizabeth called in Grindal and ordered him to suppress all learned exercises and conferences and to restrict the number of preachers to three or four for each shire. Grindal tried a reasoned approach to change the mind of Elizabeth, getting evaluations from bishops about the prophesyings in their dioceses, showing precedence from biblical and patristic sources, and suggesting that prophesyings be subject to the oversight of the church to prevent abuses. Grindal defended the need for preaching and even went so far as to suggest that there were limits to royal authority in matters spiritual. Elizabeth was not persuaded, and Grindal would not compromise what he considered to be matters of conscience. The queen suspended Grindal from office without formal process in July, 1577, and royal letters were sent to all bishops directly ordering them to forbid prophesyings. Grindal languished in virtual imprisonment in the archbishop's palace until his death in 1583.[28] Not only was Grindal incapacitated, but a new bishop of London had come on the scene in 1576. This new bishop, John Aylmer, was no friend of the Puritans, as the men of Colchester would learn all too well.

It was a precarious time for the reformers of Colchester, yet Archdeacon Withers, a moderate Puritan, was still in place, and a strong alliance between reformist aldermen and preachers continued. Although faced with numerous problems and factions within the town, the reformist aldermen finally managed to retain their political dominance, with the active support and encouragement of common preacher Master Challoner and the Puritan rector of St. Leonard's, Thomas Upcher. George Dybney, instigator of many of the 1575 libels, was correct in his charge that the bailiffs and preachers of Colchester were in collusion, which was just the way that a good Genevan would want it. It was a powerful combination. When the libels had been cast about the town, the town officials called on neighboring preachers for a preaching campaign. The cooperation of Upcher and the bailiffs against their opponent Alderman William Reade was evident, and the local ecclesiastical court and secular authori-

---

28. Collinson, *Puritan Movement*, 191–97.

ties were cooperating in the regulation of immoral behavior. For example, in late 1579 the troublesome case of an adulterous Dutchman was finally resolved in a compromise in which the man was ordered by the archidiaconal court to confess his wrong before the bailiffs; the town preacher, Master Challoner; and others at the house of Robert Mott, the senior bailiff.[29]

Town leaders found various ways to take the offensive against the factionalism that had been heralded by the 1575 libels. One tactic was to tighten the procedural rules of governance and insist on the dignity and decorum of the town assembly. The 1577 rules said that no councillor was permitted to "announce his opinion to the bench being sitting but [he] shall rise with reverence and come before the bailiffs and so declare his opinion standing." Councillors were warned not to interrupt fellow councillors nor to reveal "secrets of the council house," and they were later admonished that they would be fined if they did not wear their gowns of office for the meetings of the assembly.[30] The concern about proper procedures was evident in late 1577 when Bailiff Pye, Alderman Robert Mott, and Chamberlain William Dybney were sworn in as burgesses, and in early 1578 Alderman Nicholas Clere and a number of common councillors were also sworn. They were all born in the town and so had to pay nothing for the privilege of becoming burgesses, but their formal swearing in, which should have occurred well before they became town officers, had apparently been neglected.[31] A technical lapse of procedure had been the excuse for excluding John Hunwick from office in the 1575 election, and it is quite possible that both sides were using such omissions against their opponents. A memo in the spring of 1578 noted that William Turner, who had represented himself as a burgess of the town at the preceding autumn lawhundred, was not a burgess by birth and had not been created one, thus probably explaining why Turner had not been reelected as alderman in the 1577 election.[32]

While getting their own governing house in order, the aldermen recognized that solving their problems was sometimes impossible without the influence, advice, and aid of people familiar with the ways of the

---

29. Emmison, *Morals,* 3. Byford, "Religious Change," 164, notes that in May, 1566, Archdeacon Calfhill sat with the town officials in a case of fornication; Smith, "Social Reform," chapter 4, pp. 29, 38, stresses the cooperation of the archdeaconry court and the town officials.

30. D/B5 Gb1, ff. 9v, 11.

31. CR140/5d, 13.

32. CR140/13.

royal government in Westminster but also sympathetic to the Puritan point of view. Their lack of influence had been brought home to them in the summer of 1576 when the Colchester courts were actually suspended for a time so that a commission appointed by the Privy Council could look into complaints against Benjamin Clere. Giving up their right to hold court, even briefly, was a serious indignity that moved the aldermen to seek influence where they could. In a letter to the earl of Leicester in September, 1579, the bailiffs, notifying him that their recent election had been held peacefully, were quite straightforward in asking that Leicester might "have us in remembrance when any Commission shall proceed for any affairs within our town." The bailiffs thought that they and the town's justices should be included on any commission, "the want whereof here of late hath been great discountenance to the bailiffs," and they claimed that they were "hardly dealt withal by the Commissioners, to the . . . great prejudice of our liberties." The bailiffs had previously appealed to Leicester, the friend of the Puritans, as early as 1573, but as helpful as the earl could be, he was hardly at the beck and call of the burgesses of Colchester.[33] The realization that they needed more permanent friends in London was the mark of a newly honed political consciousness.

A new strategy, then, seems to have developed in the election of 1576, that of hiring as town clerk and recorder men who could be sources of wise counsel and help when needed, as well as advocates at the court for the Puritan leaders of Colchester. In 1572 William Cardinal, a Puritan whose family seat was at Great Bromley, about seven miles east of Colchester, had already been retained as town clerk, and in the 1576 election, he replaced Sir Thomas Lucas as recorder. The change was significant. Sir Thomas's father had earlier served the town faithfully and well as town clerk, while at the same time serving the Reformation and his own pocketbook, thus establishing the family wealth in Colchester and a mansion on the site of St. John's Abbey, just outside the town. It was natural for the town leaders, beginning in 1566, to turn to the son for legal services, but Thomas, who was knighted in 1571, was probably not a very effective servant of the town. He had an "imperious and violent" temper, which twice landed him in prison, and he got the bailiffs in trouble when he instigated their attack against East Donyland fishermen in 1567. Lucas was working in tandem with the Clere faction in the 1575

33. *APC*, 9:153; CR139/22d; Morant, 3:35 (appendix to book 1); *APC*, 8:123.

libel case, and those difficulties may have been the reason for the termination of Lucas's official connection with the town, but one can only speculate on whether the severing of the relationship was the decision of Lucas himself or of the town leaders. It could have been instigated by the corporation, motivated by a desire to hire someone more able to serve their interests in their time of trouble, or it may have been that Lucas was unhappy with the radical tendencies of the town leadership, perhaps having been influenced by his stewards, the Markaunts, who were influential among the moderate Protestants in the town. In any case, the severing of Lucas's official connections was probably the beginning of the bad feeling that continued off and on between the town and Sir Thomas, who continued living there until his death in 1611.[34]

In 1576, then, William Cardinal became Colchester's recorder, the town's chief legal counsel, and James Morice was hired as town clerk. The association with Morice would continue until his death twenty years later, though he continued residing in London, where he worked as a lawyer whose abilities were later rewarded by the post of attorney in the court of wards and liveries. Morice, like his father and uncles before him, was an active reformer, but he also had the expertise and connections that Colchester needed. The Morice seat was at the Essex town of Chipping Ongar, so Morice was already a JP of Essex when selected as town clerk. His ability was confirmed in 1578 when Morice had the honor of being selected bencher and autumn reader at the Middle Temple, which by that time had been purged of recusants and was fully Calvinistic. Morice was a learned man, owning books in Latin, Greek, and French, but he also knew the English common law thoroughly. The bailiffs called on his services whenever needed, as was the case in 1579 when the bailiffs conferred with Morice about several libels "cast about this town." Morice gave reasoned and judicious advice in 1583 to the bailiffs who had imprisoned Catholic Thomas Debell, counseling that, though Debell was "a notable papist and a lewd and busy fellow, yet the thing wherewith he is charged, be not in my opinion of such moment, nor so offensive to the laws of this realm, as that by ordinary way of justice he may be indicted or brought in question for the same." Morice would not allow Puritan zeal to outrun the law, and he thus served as a needed brake on the sometimes radical measures taken by the bailiffs. Morice would not yield when he thought he had the law behind him, but he also

---

34. Bindoff, *House,* 2:555–56; Emmison, *Disorder,* 104; Davis, "Colchester," 163 n. 132.

considered extremist measures counterproductive, serving only to stir up the wrath of the opposition. In the 1593 Parliament, while serving his fourth term as MP for Colchester, Morice became the spokesman and advocate for the common law in the Puritan battle against the new Court of High Commission with which Archbishop Whitgift was trying to impose religious conformity, using methods that, in Morice's view, were contrary to the common law. His courageous stand for religious liberty resulted in a brief imprisonment, though he apparently retained the respect of Queen Elizabeth, who regarded him "both an honest man and a good subject." Morice had well-placed friends in Westminster, a valuable asset in Colchester's eyes; among them was Sir Francis Walsingham, who had first proposed that Morice be elected as MP from Colchester in 1584.[35]

Colchester's continuing need for influence in Westminster brought an even greater change in 1578, when Cardinal was replaced by Sir Francis Walsingham as recorder. Later, Cardinal's appointment to the Council in the North would take him away from Essex altogether, but it is unclear why the change was made in 1578 in Colchester, unless it was due to an even greater awareness of the need for influence in Westminster, since more serious factionalism had again erupted. Walsingham had no previous connection with Essex or Colchester, as Colchester officers normally had, but Walsingham's recommendation was his ardent Puritanism and his influence at court as privy councillor. Walsingham served as Colchester's recorder until his death in 1590, so by 1578 Colchester leaders deemed that they had in their recorder, Walsingham, and in their town clerk, Morice, the men best suited to serve their needs.[36]

The bailiffs made use of Walsingham's services. In May, 1579, the bailiffs appealed to him on behalf of the man who had earlier fought one of the Catholic Southwells, John Christmas, who was ordered to appear before the Privy Council. Christmas's troubles may have been related to the "libels and slanderous rhymes" that were thrown about the town in the spring of 1579, which needed "some good light for the finding out of the evil disposed libellers."[37] In any case, disorder again broke out in the

---

35. Hasler, 3:98–100; George Rickword, "Members of Parliament for Colchester, 1559–1603," *ER* 4 (1895): 241; J. Ewing Ritchie, "James Morice, M.P. for Colchester, 1586–1593," *ER* 2 (1893): 166–67; CR140/28; D/Y2/8, p. 323. Morice's 1596 will is in Emmison, *Wills of Essex Gentry and Yeomen*, 10–11.
36. Hasler, 1:537; 3:571–74.
37. D/Y2/9, p. 293; *APC*, 11:78; D/Y2/2, p. 105.

town in 1579, provoking, it seems, another royal commission to impose order, as in 1576. Peaceful elections were finally held, providing an occasion for almost identical letters to the earl of Leicester, noted earlier, and to Walsingham, acknowledging their help in bringing the town back into "our liberties, which others heretofore have fought to deprive us of," and asking that Colchester leaders be included on any future royal commissions. Walsingham replied by cautioning that town leaders should guard against alienating the Crown by being too quick to take a firm stand on their rights and privileges: "Touching your liberties, for that in other Incorporations I have seen sometimes so much standing upon charters and privileges that her Majesty's necessary service hath thereby been hindered; I would not wish you, except it be in some great point that may touch your town deeply, to stand upon them." Like Morice, Walsingham saw dangers in uncompromising extremism that often produced division, whether it was in civic affairs or in religion. For example, there was no more committed Puritan than Walsingham, yet he counseled Puritans in England to be thankful that "God's word [is] sincerely preached and the sacraments truly administered." He advised, "The rest we lack we are to beg by prayer and attend with patience." Both Morice and Walsingham, then, had sound advice for a town sometimes given to extremes.[38]

As well as making concerted efforts to exert more influence at high levels and to unify the town leadership, the town leaders also made a newly intense effort to regulate behavior more strictly and to punish wrongdoing, motivated partly by the desire to root out ungodly behavior and partly by the problems of increasing population and economic hard times in the late 1570s. The bailiffs tightened the reins of governance, but it was a precarious business; rebellion and disruption might result if the reins were either too tight or too loose. As the bailiffs noted in the 1579 letters to Leicester and Walsingham, the temporary takeover of the borough courts by the royal commission had promoted "the animating of the inferior sort of our town."[39] In the thinking of the aldermen, it was imperative that they keep tight control over that "inferior sort" of people. Just as the Crown demanded outward conformity from Catholic recusants in the matter of religion, so the town leaders demanded conformity to a certain standard of behavior. It was an activist approach that even then, as it does now, stirred up controversy, and it requires some detailed analysis.

---

38. Morant, 3:34–35 (appendix to book 1); Hasler, 3:572.
39. Morant, 3:35 (appendix to book 1).

Regulation of Behavior

Though moral reform reached a new intensity under the reformist town government in the late 1570s, it should be noted that attempts at community control of behavior were hardly new in the Tudor era. L. R. Poos has cited several cases found in the Essex courts leet beginning in the fourteenth century, a manifestation of an "activist moral stance" in the community.[40] The endeavor to direct moral behavior in early Tudor Colchester is examined in this section, as those attempts shed some light on the thinking that considered moral reform to be a part of town governance, even before Puritanism.

Much of the personal moral behavior that was cited in the Tudor courts through Mary's reign either was of a sexual nature or involved the playing of illegal games, so in looking at those two prevalent offenses, four specific reasons for the regulation of personal behavior emerge. Sexual offenses, which were regularly brought into the borough court, were often reported as being disruptive or as being hurtful or offensive to others. For example, during the first six years of the reign of Henry VIII, court records gave several reasons why a sexual offense was improper; for example, widow Isabella Morice, reputed to be a prostitute, caused quarrels and disputes.[41] Thomas Crane was presented because he frequented a house of bawdry, "to the great injury of his neighbors." A later jury ruled that Crane lived "in open adultery to the nuisance of his neighbors and of other lieges of the Lord King." Such acts were often referred to as "ill rule"; that is, they did not accord with proper order in the town. For example, blacksmith John Elyott was cited *pro mala regula* in his house, which the record noted was often called "bawdry." Proper sexual behavior was seen as a part of the good order in the town, which the leaders were expected to impose. In a 1531 assault and rape case, nothing was said about the offense to the victim, Joan Feks, but the act was "against the King's peace."[42]

---

40. Poos, *Essex,* 273–76. Brown, *Popular Piety,* 244, 261, notes that the direction of personal behavior was a continuation from the past in the diocese of Salisbury; Margaret Spufford, "Puritanism and Social Control?" in *Order and Disorder in Early Modern England,* ed. Anthony Fletcher and John Stevenson (Cambridge: Cambridge University Press, 1985), stresses that "godly discipline" was not a new phenomenon in the sixteenth century.

41. CR84/16d; on prostitution, see J. A. Sharpe, *Crime in Early Modern England, 1550–1750* (New York: Longman, 1984), 110.

42. CR85/5, 9; CR86/5; CR100/9d. In a rape case in 1543, the "grievous damage" was to the woman's husband (CR112/5).

The first reason, then, for the regulation of personal behavior was to keep good order in the town—to keep down the quarrels, disputes, and raucous behavior that could result from sexual impropriety. In the thinking of the time, private behavior was not separated from the morality of society as a whole. Communal needs were always uppermost, so the regulating of civic, economic, and even private moral behavior was thought to be necessary for the good order of the community. Any personal moral behavior thought to be detrimental to society was monitored and punished if need be.

Improper sexual behavior not only led to disruption in the town but also involved an improper use of one's time. The blacksmith kept ill rule in his whorehouse, "at improper time." Robert Collingwood, who slept with his mistress, also his employer, and "got her with child" in 1536, also played at games and walked "abroad in the nights." In the same year, the rector of St. James's was said to keep ill rule with the wife of his parish clerk, "at unlawful hours in several nights." Night activities were always suspect, as dire deeds could occur under the cover of darkness, and certainly some of the most disorderly brawls occurred at night.[43]

Idleness was always questionable. A session of the peace in 1526 ruled that laborer William Cok was a "comon vagabond" and had no occupation. The next year a charge against John Blaksall, who "maintained his wife in ill rule with priests and other knaves," was that "he goeth up and down and doeth nought," and a presentment in 1559 simply charged that Ringer of Lexden "lives an idle life." More complex was the charge in 1553 against William Mulling, "an idle person exercising no labor whereby he may honestly and truly make a living; nor does he attend his church on Sundays; whence his neighbors, moved by suspicion against him are asking that he be examined as to whence he gets his livlihood."[44] Idleness, seemingly a simple matter, stirred up all sorts of complex feelings in others. Idleness was seen as a prelude to serious mischief, and it could detract one from doing what one ought, such as attending divine service, but more than that, it had social implications. In a society that valued order, the aimless way of life of the idler represented disorder, and in many cases the idler was shirking his duties and responsibilities within the family. Since the shirker was economically unproductive, he and his family could become a financial burden on his neighbors. Economically, the right use of one's time was needful for economic prosperity, not only

43. CR85/9; CR105/5; Emmison, *Morals*, 114, 123.
44. CR96/8; CR97/19; CR124/4; CR120/2d.

of the individual, but of the whole town. Indeed, in the thinking of the time, the community that neglected its moral health was sure to suffer economic ills.[45] Encouraging the proper use of time, then, both for good order and for economic prosperity, was a second reason for the regulation of personal moral behavior.[46] Just as it was thought necessary to regulate excessive prices or poor quality of food or goods as offenses against the community, so it was considered necessary morally—and economically—to monitor idleness.

The attitude toward idleness was most apparent in some of the frequent charges regarding the playing of games, considered a form of idleness. Certain games were prohibited, and from the fourteenth century onward the bailiffs restricted the playing of games, especially among the apprentices.[47] Some of the games, such as the popular tennis and bowling, seemed to be innocent enough, but they were "against the statute." Those who permitted "other people's servants in unlawful and inopportune times" to play the games on their property were subject to fines, and an even heavier penalty was often exacted from those playing during the time "of divine service."[48] Predictably, playing with dice was unlawful; in 1520 Bland, the schoolmaster, was fined 12d., which was twice the usual fine for playing illegal games. Presumably, he should have known better. The next year, a barber "played with false dice with the servant of Robert Brown and deceived the same," for which he was given the comparatively stiff fine of 3s. 4d. Along with the Reformation's curtailing of the celebrations of saints' days, a parliamentary act of 1541, repeating some previous prohibitions, forbade such popular games as "tables, tennis, dice, cards, bowls." Most of the charges of the illegal playing of games were directed at "the inferior sort" of people, but a Colchester session of the peace in 1544 held masters responsible for their servants; four men were charged with allowing their servants to play for money on feast days. Furthermore, the senior bailiff for the year, Benjamin Clere, was presented for allowing servants to play at unlawful games.[49] One was particularly accountable not merely for one's own behavior but for the

45. Hunt, *Puritan Moment*, 79; David Underdown, *Revel, Riot, and Rebellion: Popular Politics and Culture in England, 1603–1660* (New York: Oxford University Press, 1985), 35.

46. See MacCaffrey, *Exeter*, 96, on idleness.

47. R. H. Britnell, "Bailiffs and Burgesses in Colchester, 1400–1525," *EAH* 21 (1990): 107.

48. CR86/22; CR89/2; CR90/2.

49. CR91/3; CR93/2; Underdown, *Revel*, 47; CR114/2.

behavior of others if one was in a position of authority or was enticing others to misbehave; thus there was a communal need for regulating the proper use of one's time. Idle gaming had a double peril; it led to mischief and promoted economic laziness. Both effects were unacceptable.

Good order and proper economic behavior were two strong reasons for the regulation of personal behavior by the town authorities, but the underlying principle was obedience to God's law. As the jurors at the 1515 lawhundred noted, the keeping of a whore by the miller Robert Milles was "against the Law of God Almighty and in evil example to others." Obedience to the law of God was not mentioned frequently—it was a principle understood by all. Instead, the most common reason given for presenting sexual impropriety was that it was an evil example to others. Such a pattern of behavior could lead others into mischief and thus bring disruption and harm to the life of the town, but at bottom such behavior was evil because it was against God's law as found, for example, in the biblical injunctions against adultery, fornication, and idleness. Many instances could be cited of the use of the phrase "in evil example"; for example, the wife of William Lynwoode was a procurer between various persons and thus an evil example. Sexual misconduct by the clergy was a particularly reprehensible example; the rector of St. Mary Magdalen was said to be in evil example for keeping a prostitute in 1542. Two years later, he was charged with "ill rule of his body," in "pernicious example." The evil of resisting God's law, and its connection to good order in the community, was aptly summarized by the record of the session of the peace held in October, 1534, when a woman named Webbe was charged as one who "commonly harbors and receives common prostitutes and other evil persons who resort to her against divine and human law so that great tumult and discord and homicides and other evils and numerous dangers . . . result therefrom."[50] Increasingly, a consciousness of God's law would play a part in the town's regulation of personal moral behavior, as the town leaders began to be prompted by Puritan preaching.

Urban officials were not alone in their attempts to regulate behavior; they were, to a large extent, reflecting a trend in England and, indeed, in Protestant Europe toward a closer monitoring of personal moral behavior. A fourth reason for regulatory measures in Colchester, then, was the legislation emanating from the central government, though this reason became important only as parliamentary regulatory legislation increased

---

50. CR86/22; CR82/10d; CR111/13; CR112/3d; CR104/5.

in the later Tudor period, particularly beginning in the 1570s. However, an early example comes from 1540 when William Parker, who had until recently been a friar, was said to be consorting with Margaret Fysshe, a woman of ill repute with whom he had illicitly lain two years before. A session of the peace, therefore, charged Parker "under the Statute of the Lord King lately issued thereon," a reference to the Act of Six Articles (1539), the fourth article of which stated that ex-religious persons—that is, those formerly associated with the recently dissolved monasteries—were not permitted to marry.[51] Of course, the Act of Six Articles was concerned only with the moral behavior of a special group, but the very fact that Parker was a cleric and would normally be under the jurisdiction of an ecclesiastical court points up one of the complexities of the regulation of morality in the Tudor period. The overlapping jurisdictions of the secular and the ecclesiastical courts could be confusing, but the fact that both kinds of courts were involved heightens the sense of the intertwining of all facets of Tudor life. Personal morality was both a sacred and a secular concern, so the role of the ecclesiastical court needs to be considered.

The Ecclesiastical Court in Colchester

The disciplinary arm of the church at the local level was the archdeaconry court, which must be understood to get a full picture of the regulation of personal moral behavior and the community values that prompted such supervision. The extant records, which list the business and cases brought before the court of the archdeacon of Colchester, date, for the most part, only from 1569, but they are fairly complete after that, thus providing another source of information about life in Colchester.[52]

Since the bishop seldom appeared at the local level, the archdeacon of Colchester—Dr. George Withers for much of the Elizabethan period (1570–96)—had direct control over the ecclesiastical structure in Colchester and the surrounding northeastern area of the county of Essex. The diocesan courts, not having been reformed, continued to operate much as they had before the Reformation, although parliamentary statutes were beginning to modify canon law by the end of the Tudor

---

51. CR109/10d; CR107/13; Powell and Cook, *Historical Facts*, 111–12.

52. The records are housed in the Essex Record Office in Chelmsford; see F. G. Emmison, ed., *Guide to the Essex Record Office*, 2d ed. (Chelmsford: Essex Record Office Publications, 1969), 75–76.

period. The archdeacon of Colchester conducted the two annual visits to Colchester, which were primarily inquisitory and administrative, but the regular sessions of the ecclesiastical court, usually at St. Peter's Church and with the archdeacon's appointed assistant, the Official, presiding, might be held as often as every three weeks, handling litigation and administering routine business, such as the granting of marriage licenses and the probate of wills. A third purpose of the court, which is of most interest to this discussion, was to serve as an agency of discipline "for the reformation of morals and the soul's health."[53]

Disciplinary prosecutions involved a broad range of activities, with a mixture of those having to do with theological beliefs and practices and personal moral behavior. Blasphemy, witchcraft, failure to attend church, and violations of the Sabbath were intermixed with cases of sexual incontinence, maintaining bawdy houses, fighting, defamation, and drunkenness. Disciplinary cases were often initiated by the judge, who had already been notified of suspicious behavior by court officers, parish clergy, or other informants; the judge would then summon the suspect for examination and might order an inquiry in the parish. Most of the disciplinary actions, however, were initiated by the obligatory reports of the churchwardens and their deputies, who were required by oath to provide "presentments" four times annually on the physical condition of church buildings and on the behavior of the incumbent and parishioners. If the wardens failed to make reports, they were themselves subject to excommunication. The unpaid churchwardens, usually two from each parish, were chosen annually around Easter time by consent of the minister and the parishioners, but they were sworn in by the archidiaconal court, so they were subject to the court and were a key link in its disciplinary function. Because two wardens had "not given in their accounts" in 1584, the parishioners lamented, "Therefore, we cannot do things we would, neither reform things that be amiss."[54]

Reporting on the behavior of one's neighbors had its hazards. As presented by a churchwarden of St. Nicholas's in 1591, parishioner John Culpack had, in the words of the warden, abused "one of the churchwardens and one of the sidesmen and one of the constables because,

---

53. Ingram, *Church Courts*, 42–43; Anglin, "Court," 11, 31, 59, 65–67; D/AZ2/26; Emmison, *Morals*, xi–xii, 43, 319; Palliser, *Elizabeth*, 334; Cross, *Church and People*, 135–36; and see chapter 3.

54. Ingram, *Church Courts*, 43–44; Anglin, "Court," 19–20, 58, 290; Emmison, *Morals*, 231, 234; Edwards, *Christian England*, 87; D/ACA11, f. 73.

finding him not at church, we came home to him and told him that we were sorry to find him in such fault." The warden continued, "presently he burst forth in words and said that we came to assault him and said that we had blackbirds in our breast." Culpack was further reported to have said that "the court was well occupied to make such lord's officers as we were and that the churchwarden was a blasphemous knave."[55] Sixteenth-century people were hardly shy about stating their displeasure with officials, but there was surprisingly little criticism of the system itself. The work of the churchwardens as moral policemen for the church court seemed to be reflecting the views of the community regarding the proper discipline of misconduct.[56]

The archidiaconal court could not make arrests, and a defendant had to be summoned to appear by a citation, which had to be served personally. The only penalty available against those who failed to appear was excommunication, but the judge often delayed that pronouncement for several sessions, hoping for compliance; and when excommunication came, it was often discharged through payment of a fine. Those charged with misconduct might try to clear themselves through purgation, the sworn testimony of friends as to good conduct. Those adjudged guilty of moral offenses often had to pay a penalty, though in proved cases of slander or incontinence in the diocese of London, the offender had to do penance, such as standing in church in a white sheet during divine service and confessing one's sin. Sometimes a like penance occurred in the public marketplace; for example, a woman from St. Leonard's who had committed fornication had to stand in the open market before the door of the moot hall on a Saturday between eleven and twelve in the forenoon, dressed in a sheet, bareheaded and barefooted, with a white rod in her hand.[57] Since the courts had little coercive power, the acts of penance were a mark of the offender's voluntary submission to the court and to the accepted standards in society.

Both the ecclesiastical and the secular courts in late-sixteenth-century Colchester, then, were regulating personal moral behavior, but the blurring of jurisdictions, especially in the matter of sexual offenses, could

---

55. Quoted in Emmison, *Morals*, 64. Seventy-one years earlier, a Richard Culpak was said to be spying on the jurors at the lawhundred and calling them "false jurors and knaves . . . to the disquiet of the same jurors" (CR83/1d). Not surprisingly, there were several instances of men trying to evade the office of churchwarden (Emmison, *Morals*, 231–33).

56. Keith Wrightson, *English Society, 1580–1680* (London: Hutchinson, 1982), 210–11; Sharpe, *Crime*, 85.

57. Ingram, *Church Courts*, 47–48; *VCH Essex*, 2:41–42; D/ACA6/162.

produce clashes. Although the spiritual courts were the primary keepers of sexual morality, sexual offenses had been consistently handled in the Colchester borough courts. The overlapping jurisdiction was not always clear; for example, rape and the keeping of whorehouses were offenses against the common law, but the ecclesiastical courts punished the unlawful acts that resulted. Justices of the Peace also had the right to deal with obvious cases of adultery or fornication, but, on the whole, punishment of such offenses seems to have been left to the spiritual courts.[58] The extreme reaction against the punishment imposed by the bailiffs on presumed adulterer John Lone in 1575 may have been, in part, triggered by the feeling that the borough court was overstepping its bounds.

Another case of sexual misconduct in the late 1570s was a source of tension with the church authorities. In mid-June, 1579, the bishop of London's top official wrote to the bailiffs, warning them not to interfere in a case of the marriage of a Dutchman, Francis deBlocke, "with his wife that now liveth with him." The chancellor, mentioning that he had already criticized the bailiffs of the previous year for interfering, suspected that the two men who had brought the charges against deBlocke were jealous of his prosperity rather than being interested in his reformation. Chastising the bailiffs, the chancellor wrote, "The examination of matrimonial causes is mere ecclesiastical and belongeth by the laws of the realm to our examination"; nevertheless, he ended his letter by desiring that God "bless your good government." Some of the facts of the case were recorded in the archidiaconal records; it seems that deBlocke had been intimate with Barbara Vanderheyden "before she was divorced" from her husband. The case was finally concluded, in an apparent compromise, under the next bailiffs, the third set to deal with the problem, when deBlocke was commanded to confess his sin before the two bailiffs; the town preacher, Master Challoner; and four other witnesses at the home of Bailiff Mott. It was a slow but effective conjunction of secular and ecclesiastical authority.[59]

A recent study has charted the relationship between the ecclesiastical and the secular authorities in Colchester, finding that, especially after 1580, there was close cooperation between the two courts.[60] For the detection of wrongdoing, each court depended largely on the presentments brought either by the jurors to lawhundreds or sessions of the

---

58. Ingram, *Church Courts,* 150–51.
59. D/Y2/6, p. 75; Emmison, *Morals,* 3.
60. Smith, "Social Reform," chapter 4, p. 25.

peace or by churchwardens to the archdeaconry court. Those presentments often reflected popular attitudes, local concerns, and community
values, as was evident by the comments of the jurors at a lawhundred in
1553. Charging Richard Markes for frequenting a house of ill rule, the
jurors remarked that Markes had "often been admonished thereon by his
neighbors [but] he nevertheless does not purpose to mend his ways."[61]
Both sacred and secular courts in Colchester essentially dealt with the
same clientele. The gentry and upper classes, subject only to superior
ecclesiastical courts, were exempt from the archdeacon's jurisdiction,[62]
and the town bailiffs usually had to appeal to higher courts whenever
they had a quarrel with the elite. The regulatory efforts of both courts,
then, were aimed at the inferior groups. Any attempts by the bailiffs to go
beyond that social boundary met with resistance. Just as the archdeacon
and his officials were subject to the church hierarchy, so were the bailiffs
subject to the national political hierarchy, but the bailiffs also had from
within the borough various political pressures that placed limits on their
power. Pressures on the bailiffs came both from above and below, making their position somewhat precarious; for example, the activities of the
bailiffs might be checked by the lesser people through insubordination or
riots, or members of the professional or gentry class might "publish"
libels and stir up the lesser folk against the bailiffs. Though the bailiffs
were especially vulnerable when they attempted to regulate personal
behavior, the intensification of such measures, discussed in chapter 10,
became one of the offensive tactics taken in the late 1570s against the turbulence of the decade.

61. CR120/2d; CR118/8d.
62. Anglin, "Court," 289.

10

Tightening the Reins on Behavior, 1575–80

Disciplinary measures against misconduct were not new in Colchester in the 1570s, yet beginning in 1577 and 1578 there was a new intensity in the regulating of certain offenses, such as working on Sundays or feast days, adultery, idleness, and vagrancy. Drunkenness, which had rarely been noted in the borough records, began to be targeted as offensive behavior in the courts. Moreover, rather than the usual money penalties for wrongdoing, public punishments became harsher and more frequent, and it also seems that more rigorous searches were being made for evildoing. In some areas of personal conduct, the town was only following the lead of Parliament, for example, in identifying the fathers of illegitimate children, but they were not always quick to enforce parliamentary legislation. It took them over twenty years to decide to start enforcing an act mandating the licensing of alehouses; their choosing to do so in the late 1570s adds to the picture of alarm over the increased numbers of poor and vagrants in the town. Though the increased disciplinary measures appear to be a part of the aggressive Puritan push for a godly society, it can also be argued that they were, in part, a reaction to the unusually severe social problems of the late 1570s. True reform, though, could only take place in the heart, and the town continued its support of the common preacher, Nicholas Challoner, believing that preaching was the key to reform.

The Intense Regulation of the Late 1570s

Sexual wrongdoing had been consistently and frequently noted in the Colchester court records, but a curious and unexpected change occurred in the second half of the Tudor period: presentments of sexual offenses fell dramatically, both at the lawhundreds and at the sessions of the peace. Table 7 shows that the change was slowly beginning even before Elizabeth's accession to the throne, making it appear either that the people of Colchester were losing their libido or that the borough courts were letting the ecclesiastical courts handle most of the cases. Of course, human passion continued to pursue its ends, and the archidiaconal court was especially busy with cases of fornication in the late 1570s,[1] but so were the borough officials. Prosecution of sexual offenses appeared to fall in the borough because JPs were initiating the action as needed throughout the year at petty sessions and by special juries, rather than waiting for the leisurely process of presentments at the thrice-yearly lawhundreds or sessions. For example, in May, 1576, a jury was trying to decide the case of Rose Lawrence, who had borne a son the month before. She was married, but her husband had apparently been away for some time,[2] and the jury learned that a butcher had "corporal knowledge of her" in the summer before. Special juries had begun to be used to investigate particular offenses; by 1584 a jury was regularly impaneled to inquire about "harlots and fornicators," or, as the record termed them in 1592, "loose women."[3]

Not only were the town officials initiating prosecutions more frequently and speedily, but they seemed to be quite active in searching out sexual wrongdoing or at least in having the constables do it. The charge of adultery in 1575 was brought against John Lone and Margery Collyns by constables who had gone to the Collyns' house just before midnight to see if there was any untoward behavior. The constables obviously had

---

1. Byford, "Religious Change," 364–65, 372, 374, 382, has charted the moral offenses in the archidiaconal court, and he shows that an unusually large number of sexual offenders were presented in 1578–79. Byford concludes that borough courts were as important, or more so, than the archdeaconry court in dealing with immorality and that both secular and ecclesiastical courts saw a rise in the number of moral offenses, particularly those of a sexual nature.

2. CR139/8. A William Lawrence, probably her husband, was in Rome in 1581, CR143/28d.

3. CR145/7; CR145/23; CR147/10; CR153/13d. Twenty-four names were on the jury list of 1584, but there were only twelve names in 1591 (CR152/14d). Smith, "Social Reform," chapter 2, p. 36, speculates that "fornication juries" appeared in the spring of 1576 as part of the reaction to the difficult Lone affair of 1575 and that they were an attempt by the town leaders to distance themselves from the judgments rendered. Unfortunately, the borough court records in the early 1570s are incomplete, so it is impossible to know exactly when the special juries began to be used. However, Byford, "Religious Change," 384–87, says that the juries came to be used after passage of the 1576 statute dealing with idleness. Juries had earlier been used for the more serious offenses handled by the borough court.

some power to search. In the early 1540s town constables were checking on activity in an alehouse during the time of divine service, and in the 1590s constables searched a certain house for a couple engaged in the act of fornication, but the pair was too quick for them and escaped out the back door. In another case, the churchwardens and constables worked together to check on a man known to skip church.[4]

The eagerness of town officials got them in trouble in 1567, when the bailiffs and commonalty were charged in the Court of Queen's Bench for imprisoning men and women in the moot hall, without bail, for adultery. The punishment of sexual offenses changed in the Elizabethan period; paralleling the greater involvement of town officials in searching out and prosecuting sexual wrongdoing was the more severe and more public punishment meted out to offenders. In the earlier Tudor period, when sexual offenses were initiated by presentments, a fine was invariably

TABLE 7.   Sexual Offenses in the Borough Courts

Years	Number of Lawhundreds Recorded	Presentments of Sexual Offenses	Average per Lawhundred	Number of Sessions of the Peace Recorded	Number of Sexual Cases	Average per Session
1510–29	40	104	2.6	16	4	0.25
1530–46	38	153	4.03	39	63	1.62
1547–49	4	5	1.25	3	9	3
1550–52	7	8	1.14	8	3	0.38
1553–55	7	1	0.14	7	0	0
1556–58	6	6	1	6	2	0.33
1559–61	8	0	0	8	5	0.63
1562–64	5	0	0	5	1	0.2
(Gap in the records)						
1577–79	6	0	0	6	2	0.33
1580–82	7	1	0.14	7	0	0
1583–85	9	0	0	9	1	0.11
1586–89	8	0	0	8	1	0.13

Note: Does not include five incomplete or undated sessions of the courts. Cases of "ill rule" were included only if the context clearly showed them to be of a sexual nature. No more lawhundreds or sessions of the peace were recorded after 1589.

---

4. Byford, "Religious Change," 194; Oxley, 145; Emmison, *Morals,* 8–9, 64. See Mayhew, *Tudor Rye,* 231, for the charge to the constables of Rye in 1574.

imposed, but a variety of punishments, most often the tumbrel, came to be used in the Elizabethan period, possibly following the urging of some of the educated people for more severe punishments against sexual offenders. The movement for harsher penalties actually began before the Reformation but came to be associated with the advanced reformers and, finally, with the Puritan thinkers, who believed that a fine was too light a punishment.[5] In Colchester, the earliest mention of the tumbrel seems to have been in 1563, when an adulterous couple was to ride in the tumbrel, a two-wheeled tipcart used for hauling dung.[6] The riders were intended to feel the ignominy of being hauled around the marketplace in a dung cart, with a sign on the cart that gave their names and their sin.[7] Furthermore, the designated day for the ride in the tumbrel was often on Saturday, a day when a crowd was assured in the market area.[8] Usually the couple rode together, even in the three cases when the fornication seemed to be a matter of rape.[9] In 1579, two rulings of a session of the peace revealed the different punishments given to men and women; spinster Ann Forde was put into the stocks for being a "common instigator of quarrels . . . and a common prostitute," but carpenter Robert West, who kept a "house of bawdry," was fined 2s. The bailiffs were also given the task of being the agent of punishment for county officials; in 1579 Sir Thomas Lucas sent an order to the bailiffs about Anne Goddard, who "by reason of her incontinent life lately had a bastard child within the parish of Much Birch." Lucas added: "before that time she hath been delivered of three or four bastards. . . . for her folly . . . this Anne Goddard [is] to be at the market day within your town to be severely whipped at a Cart's arse."[10] In contrast to the tumbrel rides, whippings, confinement in the stocks, and fines meted out by the secular officials, the ecclesiastical court often required, as they did of Richard Austen in 1576

---

5. "Calendar of Queen's Bench Indictments Ancient Relating to Essex, 1558–1603, in the Public Record Office" (typescript, Essex Record Office, Chelmsford, n.d.), no. 617, pt. 1, 7 (original numbering); Ingram, *Church Courts,* 151. Whiting, *Devotion,* 141, relates how the mayors of Exeter began to assume oversight of sexual offenses in the early Elizabethan period. Hunt, *Puritan Moment,* 76, found that punishments for sexual offenses in the Essex quarter sessions began to be harsher in the 1580s.

6. D/B5 Sb2/1, f. 19v; Emmison, *Home,* 54.

7. A rare tumbrel sign from 1583 was found by Mark Byford in the Colchester records. Byford says ("Religious Change," 399) that the ride in the tumbrel seems to have been accompanied by the ringing of a basin to call attention to it.

8. CR145/23; CR152/14d.

9. CR141/13; CR146/23, 31d.

10. CR141/4, 4d; D/Y2/8, p. 208.

for the sin of "incontinent living" with his niece, that the offender "walk through Colchester market in a white sheet, bare-headed and bare-footed, a white rod in his hand, and so stand openly in the place appointed for an hour's space, likewise in church next Sunday and on the second Saturday following in Colchester market."[11]

Not only was the punishment becoming more public, but the language used to describe the sexual offenses became more theologically graphic in the court records. In 1578 acts of fornication were said to be a "danger to [the participants'] souls."[12] By 1579 the devil had entered the picture, especially in rape cases. Plumber Dan Balle broke into the home of Helen Highnoone and assaulted her when her husband was away; the record said that Balle, "not having God before his eyes, but seduced by instigation of the devil, procured and incited Helen to consent to have copulation with him." Though Helen had been "in the peace of God," she had apparently come under the influence of the devil as well, since Richard's devil-inspired seducement was so effective that she consented, or at least the record said that she did. At least four other cases of rape afterward used the same terminology.[13] To the modern reader, the supposed consent of the women seems unlikely, but the consent phrase may have been inserted to protect the men against an act of 1576 that made rape by clergy a felony punishable by death; previously, felonies were sometimes avoided by claiming the right of clergy if one could read.[14]

The new terminology used to describe some of the sexual offenses might lead one to conclude that all the different handling of sexual wrongdoing in the borough courts was a result of Puritan preaching, but in 1576 a new focus began to suggest conjunctive economic concerns. An act of Parliament passed in the February–March session in 1576 gave justices of the peace the power to examine cases of bastards who might become a public charge and to punish the guilty parents. Beginning in May in Colchester, specially selected juries or the bailiffs began to try to determine the father of illegitimate children, and the efforts became increasingly successful and sophisticated. On January 13, 1578, Katherine Beriff and sailor Thomas Foster were reported to have committed fornication; ten days later the bailiffs judged that Foster was the probable

---

11. Emmison, *Morals*, 39; *VCH Essex*, 2:42.
12. CR140/10d, 31d.
13. CR141/13. See also CR144/13d; CR145/23; CR150/32d.
14. Prothero, *Statutes*, 74.

father of the yet unborn child.[15] By April of that year, the court, after ordering a couple to ride in the tumbrel, recorded for the first time a recognizance promising specific child support. Laborer Henry Heydon agreed to pay the queen £20 if he did not fulfill his obligation to support his illegitimate child by paying 4d. weekly for six years to the collectors of St. Nicholas's parish, for the "education and bringing up of a woman child by the said Henry Heydon begotten of the body of one [blank] Jackson."[16] An account of a similar case in 1580 was frank about the reason for insisting on child support from the father, that is, so that the town not "be charged with the child." Locksmith Richard Younger, who had raped Thomasine Butcher, was expected to pay more than laborer Heydon; Younger was ordered to pay 12d. weekly until the child was twenty-four years old. Another reputed father was commanded to pay 12d. weekly for seven years and 8d. for another five years.[17] The 1576 act of Parliament had not been mandatory, so the fact that the town officials were enforcing it is another clue that the town was experiencing economic stress from the increased poverty and vagrancy in the late 1570s. Not only did the more aggressive tactics used to combat wrongdoing reflect a Puritan desire for discipline in the town, but economic conditions made discipline more urgent.

Sunday Behavior

Along with the continuing regulation of sexual immorality, Sunday behavior was more closely monitored. Table 8 shows that the number of charges for not attending church were not particularly high in the 1570s and 1580s. Of course, the archdeaconry court was always active in the matter of church attendance, but the borough's involvement, which had been systematized in 1562, was apparently effective enough so that absence from church was not considered a problem in the town. The borough system of checking on church attendance seemed to be continuing as late as 1583, when a note from two men of the parish of St. Mary Magdalen reported that they had "made diligent search for all such persons as have neglected their going to church within our parish." The men reported, "we warned them sharply . . . and in so doing we found them

---

15. Ingram, *Church Courts*, 152; CR139/8; CR140/9, 10d; D/B5 Sb2/3, f. 21.
16. CR140/13d, 14.
17. D/B5 Sb2/3, ff. 4, 134; D/B5 Sb2/4, f. 23v, 76; CR144/13d.

afterward more diligent."[18] Of more concern to the town in the 1570s and 1580s were the people who insisted on working on or who were unruly or played illegal games on Sundays or feast days. Even with the unfortunate gap in the recording of the thrice-yearly court sessions in Colchester, table 8 clearly shows that Sunday work was of particular concern in the earlier Elizabethan period, with charges against such work reaching a peak in the early 1580s. The butchers and barbers were, as usual, continuing to violate the prohibition against working during time of divine service, but in 1578 an ordinance was passed that indicated that a new attitude toward Sunday was developing. The town assembly agreed that the biggest fair in Colchester, St. Denis's Fair, which lasted for eight days in the autumn, was not to be held on Sunday as it had been for years "to the dishonor of Almighty God." If any traders at the fair were found guilty of selling on Sunday, all their wares were to be forfeited, and no booths for the fair were to be built on Sunday.[19] In the same year, an influential preacher, Lancelot Andrewes, was giving sermons at Cambridge on the Ten Commandments and insisting on a strict observance of the fourth commandment, "Remember the Sabbath Day, to keep it holy."[20] Though the Colchester assembly would not have heard that sermon, they seemed to be a part of the thinking that produced it.

In 1579 a comprehensive Sabbath ordinance passed, stating that no one "shall sell, show, or set forth to sell any manner of wares" on the "Sabbath Day, called Sunday."[21] This occasion seems to be the first use of the term *Sabbath* in the Colchester records. Using the term *Sabbath* for Sunday was increasingly a mark of Puritanism, which wanted to emphasize that Sunday was a day of rest and so adopted the term for the Jewish

---

18. D/Y2/6, p. 104. See *RPB*, 139–40, for Edwardian ordinances against work on the Sabbath or principal feast days.

19. D/B5 Gb1, f. 10v; Morant, 1:77. Sommerville, *Secularization*, 34–37, discusses the effect of Protestant Sabbatarianism on English culture.

20. Hill, *Society and Puritanism*, 169.

21. D/B5 Gb1, f. 17. The concern with Sunday behavior resulted in a curious flurry of presentments about the wearing of caps. In 1571, an act of Parliament, apparently to benefit the wool trade and the cappers, ruled that all "citizens, artificers and labourers" above the age of seven were to wear woolen caps on Sundays and holy days. Furthermore, Puritans believed that the head should be covered during worship. For whatever reasons, the May, 1579, lawhundred presented nine men for not wearing on the head "a cap, according to the form of the statute," for which they were fined from 4d. to 12d. each. In the same lawhundred, however, two men were each presented for wearing "his hat on Sunday against the form of the statute." Nothing else about Sunday headgear appeared in the records. See Emmison, *Home*, 274–75; Collinson, *Puritan Movement*, 367; CR141/3d, 4.

TABLE 8. Behavior on Sundays and Feast Days

Years	No. of Sessions of the Peace & Lawhundreds Recorded	Failure to Attend Church				Working on Sunday or Feast Day				Games or Unruliness; Encouraging Others*			
		LH	SP	Total	Average per Court Session	LH	SP	Total	Average per Court Session	LH	SP	Total	Average per Court Session
1510–29	56	0	0	0	0	0	0	0	0	0	4	4	0.07
1530–46	77	1	2	3	0.04	1	0	1	0.01	4	5	9	0.12
1547–49	7	0	0	0	0	0	0	0	0	0	0	0	0
1550–52	15	0	0	0	0	2	0	2	0.13	3	0	3	0.02
1553–55	14	1	0	1	0.07	8	0	8	0.57	2	1	3	0.21
1556–58	12	6	2	8	0.67	1	1	2	0.17	0	0	0	0
1559–61	16	12	0	12	0.75	1	1	2	0.13	0	1	1	0.06
1562–64	10	3	0	3	0.3	0	14	14	1.4	0	0	0	0
(Gap in the records)													
1577–79	12	0	0	0	0	10	9	19	1.58	2	1	3	0.25
1580–82	14	3	2	5	0.38	19	18	37	2.64	20	1	21	1.5
1583–85	18	9	0	9	0.5	1	5	6	0.33	7	9	16	0.89
1586–89	16	4	0	4	0.25	2	0	2	0.13	7	0	7	0.44

Note: Includes all presentments in the lawhundreds (LH) and the sessions of the peace (SP).

*Includes "harboring servants for unlawful games," permitting one's servants to play illegal games, fishing and hunting, and keeping public drinking houses open.

day of rest, even though it was Saturday rather than the Christian Sunday. The Jews had been very strict about observing the strictures against work on the Sabbath, so the use of the term was significant; the emphasis had shifted from regulating behavior during worship services to the belief that the whole day was sacred. After the 1579 ordinance against Sabbath trading was passed, several people were fined from 6d. to 8d. for trading on Sunday.[22]

Idleness and Vagrancy

The stricter prohibitions against work on Sunday had a converse side in that failure to work on weekdays, or idleness, likewise was coming under the scrutiny of town officials with a new intensity in the late 1570s. Like the charges against Sunday work, charges of idleness and vagrancy reached a peak in the early 1580s (see table 9). Unlike Sunday behavior or sexual immorality, idleness and vagrancy were not handled by the ecclesiastical courts, so such charges in the borough court are a good measure of conditions and thinking in the town. With every able person having to contribute weekly to the support of the poor in the parish, any idleness was surely going to be noted by neighbors, who would resent giving their hard-earned money to support laziness. The parish listings of the poor and the contributors to the poor from 1572 noted a William Herywood in St. Mary's parish who had a wife and three children and "liveth idly and the presenters know not how."[23] The poor had continued to be a problem in Colchester, and in 1574 the officials found a creative way to care for some of the poor, usually orphaned children. The boy Thomas Watson was taken into service for twelve years by John Baker, who was then admitted to the freedom of the borough. Gradually other craftsmen began doing the same, taking poor orphans for as long as twelve years and in return being made burgesses without the usual payment.[24] The borough was willing to find ways to care for the helpless

---

22. CR142/2d; CR143/2. *VCH Essex*, 9:125, notes the early development of Sabbatarianism in Colchester. Not until 1591–92 was there any frequency of charges against Sunday trading in the manorial courts at Chelmsford and Moulsham, according to Emmison, *Home*, 304.

23. D/B5 R7, f. 307.

24. CR138/10d. See also CR139/5d, 7d; CR140/15, 31; CR141/26d, 27; D/B5 Gb1, f. 153v. McIntosh, "Local Responses," 232, notes that an earlier practice was to pay poor widows to board poor children.

poor, but poverty caused by one's behavior was another matter. In this period the fathers of illegitimate children began to be coerced into paying for the support of those children, and the same mentality behind such coercion moved the officials to crack down on vagrancy and the harboring of vagabonds in 1578.[25]

In the September lawhundred in 1577, Thomas Warde was appointed beadle of vagabonds. His appointment is the first time that the records mention such an office in Colchester. On the next law day, January 20, 1578, presentments against harboring paupers or against vagrancy suddenly emerged. Margaret Symson, widow of a former alderman, was presented for "receiving" two paupers "to dwell in her houses"—rental houses, it seems—without license from the bailiffs. Such presentments would become a familiar refrain in the records. On the same day, a session of the peace found that four men, who had been "wandering against the peace" three days earlier, had "neither land nor masters, and [were] not exercising any lawful merchandise, arts, or mysteries by which they can acquire their living." One of them was branded on the same day, probably as an example to others.[26] This penalty, the first instance in the Colchester records of public punishment for vagrancy, corresponded with the stricter policy of punishment for sexual immorality, and, likewise, the appointment of a beadle of vagabonds was similar to the policy of using constables to search out sexual misdoing. Both idleness and sexual offenses were examples, in the eyes of the magistrates, of problems stemming from one's own perverse behavior. To the Elizabethans, vagrancy denoted social displacement; the wandering, unemployed, masterless person fell under grave suspicion, as he or she was not conforming to the usual pattern of order and hierarchy in society.[27]

Thus began in early 1578 the rise in presentments of idleness, harboring vagabonds, and vagrancy as charted by table 9. In June two men were whipped for vagrancy, and, again, they were said to be idle men and without any occupation. The next month, a man and his wife and child were granted permission to live in the town for one year, provided that

---

25. Since the records are incomplete in the late 1560s and early 1570s, the spurt of such presentments could have begun earlier, but there was not a single presentment for idleness or vagrancy in the incomplete 1574 or the September, 1577, lawhundreds; nor was there one in the May, 1576, or September, 1577, sessions of the peace.

26. CR140/2d, 3d.

27. MacCaffrey, *Exeter*, 92–97.

TABLE 9. Idleness and Illegal Games

Years	No. of Sessions of the Peace & Lawhundreds Recorded	Idleness; Unemployed; Vagrancy; Harboring Vagabonds			Average per Court Session	Playing Illegal Games; Encouraging Games or Unruliness*			Average per Court Session
		LH	SP	Total		LH	SP	Total	
1510–29	56	9	1	10	0.18	46	27	73	1.3
1530–46	77	20	13	33	0.43	79	25	104	1.35
1547–49	7	0	0	0	0	5	0	5	0.71
1550–52	15	2	0	2	0.13	28	6	34	2.27
1553–55	14	1	0	1	0.07	4	1	5	0.36
1556–58	12	2	0	2	0.17	19	2	21	1.75
1559–61	16	5	1	6	0.38	4	9	13	0.81
1562–64	10	0	2	2	0.2	3	2	5	0.5
(Gap in the records)									
1577–79	12	5	6	11	0.92	1	5	6	0.5
1580–82	14	9	14	23	1.64	17	6	23	1.64
1583–85	18	5	6	11	0.61	8	3	11	0.61
1586–89	16	10	5	15	0.94	18	5	23	1.44

Note: Includes all presentments in the lawhundreds (LH) and the sessions of the peace (SP).
*Includes offenses on Sundays or feast days.

they did not become "chargeable to the town." They were ordered to "be of good behavior."[28] In 1580, shortly after seven unemployed laborers between the ages of twelve and forty years were brought before a session of the peace, the assembly ordered no more "strangers" to inhabit the town, arguing that Colchester already had "more than the town can sustain."[29] The decree had little effect; women traveling with men and whole families began to appear as vagrants in the town, and residents were fined heavily for housing vagrants without license from the bailiffs. Some of the vagrants were noted as being "able bodied and fit for labor." A comment in a 1582 lawhundred had an almost frantic quality: it was noted that Charles Bell "lives idly and does not work for a living and he is ordered to work." Some wanderers were ordered to "quit the town" or pay a heavy fine; others were whipped.[30] Town leaders, being inclined to think that the vagrants were themselves responsible for their plight, had no patience with unemployed vagrants. They did not understand the demographic and economic forces that made it harder, given the increase in population during Elizabeth's reign, for those at the bottom of the economic scale to obtain employment in hard times. So, being blind to the circumstances and fearful of the social dislocation, town leaders felt that the ruthless punishment of offenders was necessary.

Contiguous with the problem of continued vagrancy was the appearance of moral judgmental language. According to the court record, the seven unemployed laborers previously mentioned were "in evil example" to others, but gentleman William Markaunt articulated moral judgment most clearly in his will of 1582. Markaunt bequeathed money to be distributed to the poor in every parish on the day of his burial, but he charged that it was not to be bestowed on "any idle lubbers, common rogues, beggars, vagabonds; sturdy queens, common drunkards or such like, but upon the halt, the lame, the blind, the sick." Markaunt also noted that those whom God has blessed should "help to relieve our poor Christian brethren to the glory of God."[31] The distinction was clear between "the well disposed needy poor" and the not so well-disposed

---

28. CR140/30; D/B5 Sb2/3, f. 25. A 1547 law, quickly repealed, authorized even harsher punishment, that is, branding a V on the chest with a hot iron; see McIntosh, "Local Responses," 229.

29. CR142/2d; D/B5 Gb1, f. 20.

30. CR143/3, 3d, 4d; CR145/31d. See also CR142/7d; CR147/34d.

31. CR142/2d; PRO12 Rowe.

poor who were "likely to burden the parish,"[32] and the latter continued to receive the most common punishment for vagrancy, that of being whipped around the marketplace.[33]

The view of idleness as a moral problem helps to explicate the Puritan view of sin—that a sin, if unchecked, invariably led one down the slippery path to greater transgressions, so it was generally assumed that refusal to work connoted dishonesty and immorality, as well as laziness.[34] Those beliefs, though, do not fully explain the sudden rise in presentments of vagrants and idlers in 1578; instead, the unrelenting pursuit of idle persons by the town authorities occurred in answer to a mixture of moral and economic pressures. The reputation of the Puritans in modern times has suffered because of their zeal in searching out immoral behavior,[35] but such a harsh view of them often fails to appreciate the social and economic pressures of the time. Furthermore, it should be noted that the attempt to control moral behavior was not just a Puritan concern; as historian of Tudor poverty Paul Slack has noted, Puritan social attitudes and objectives "hardly differed from those of other members of the social, political and religious élite."[36] More regulation was often seen to be the answer in periods of economic distress; for example, beginning in the difficult 1550s, Parliament wanted heightened control over alehouses. An analysis of the debates in Parliament over the numerous attempts to legislate personal conduct shows that in addition to religious and moral reasons for the regulation of conduct, most of the bills and speeches gave other justifications, such as concern about public order and economic and political considerations.[37]

32. PRO 49 Brudenell; CR150/31d.

33. CR140/2d, 30; CR145/31d; CR149/16. Whipping about the town, usually at the rear of a moving cart, was the most common punishment for vagrancy in Rye; see Mayhew, *Tudor Rye,* 205.

34. Cynthia Herrup, "Law and Morality in Seventeenth-Century England," *PP* 106 (1985): 109.

35. For a summary of the work of historians on the moral discipline imposed on communities, see Martin Ingram, "Religion, Communities, and Moral Discipline in Late Sixteenth- and Early Seventeenth-Century England: Case Studies," in *Religion and Society in Early Modern Europe, 1500–1800,* ed. Kaspar von Greyerz (London: George Allen and Unwin, 1984), 177–93. Also in the book edited by Greyerz, see Bruce Lenman, "The Limits of Godly Discipline in the Early Modern Period with Particular Reference to England and Scotland," 124–45. See also Hunt, *Puritan Moment,* 79–84; Wrightson, *English Society,* 150–78; Underdown, *Revel,* 44–72.

36. Slack, "Poverty," 12.

37. Joan Kent, "Attitudes of Members of the House of Commons to the Regulation of 'Personal Conduct' in Late Elizabethan and Early Stuart England," *Bulletin of the Institute*

However, Puritan beliefs did make a difference in the view toward godly discipline. As far as the bailiffs were concerned, correction would go a long way toward alleviating the fear of social disorder and relieving the economic strain that the town was experiencing; hence, the town leaders insisted that fathers support their illegitimate children. The correction of wrongdoers had practical value for the community, since to do less was to incur the possibility of divine punishment. As an order against various sins in Hull in 1563 stated, any sinfulness in the town was "to the great provocation of God's wrath against this town," and therefore offenders must "be punished and made an example of to warn others."[38] At bottom, then, godly discipline had a religious origin, stemming from a deep sense of the need to create a better community, that is, one that valued godliness. Anglicans and Calvinists agreed on the need for godly discipline,[39] but Calvinist town leaders had an additional sense of mission, believing it to be their and the ministers' duty to create a society where truth, goodness, justice, and order prevailed.

Colchester bailiffs were not the only town leaders to wage a systematic campaign to reform conduct; they were actually part of a broader national trend. By the 1580s a number of English towns were engaging in the same battle, and the increasing number of bills introduced in the House of Commons regarding personal conduct (even though most failed to pass) indicated a definite impetus toward regulation of moral behavior in the later Tudor period.[40] In 1586 some of Her Majesty's privy councillors wrote to the bailiffs about restraining the killing and eating of meat during Lent; as they saw it, the "great disorders" needed to "be reformed."[41] Not only were the bailiffs following the lead of the national government in regulating conduct, they were also pressured from the people of Colchester. The presentments in the lawhundreds representing the concerns of the people were often ahead of the bailiffs in wanting controls placed on personal behavior. For example, the lawhundred presentments of unruliness or game playing on Sundays far outnumbered the

---

of Historical Research 46 (1973): 42–46. Slack, "Poverty," 11–12, has a good discussion of the connection between poor relief and social regulation.

38. Edward Gillett and Kenneth A. MacMahon, *A History of Hull,* 2d ed. (Hull: Hull University Press, 1989), 120; McIntosh, *Havering,* 250–57, stressed that in the borough of Havering, social control usually stemmed from practical concerns.

39. Lenman, "Godly Discipline," 132.

40. Clark and Slack, *English Towns,* 150; Kent, "Attitudes," 63–71 (appendixes).

41. BL, Stowe MS 150, f. 67.

cases brought before the sessions of the peace in the early 1580s (see table 8), so the JPs were apparently responding to pressure from below.

Imposing discipline was a difficult task that took time and commitment; evidence of the strain felt by the bailiffs was the recording of a unique list in the court rolls in 1578–79 of a rota of aldermen who were to sit for a week at a time with the bailiffs to preside over the courts and find an appropriate punishment for wrongdoers.[42] Presiding over courts and imposing punishment was not the only solution pursued by the town leaders. Their strategy included two other measures: trying to control some of the root causes of behavior problems and continuing to promote positive teaching, especially through the town sermons.

Ax at the Root of Wrong Behavior

A root cause of ill-judged and improper behavior identified by the Elizabethans was the alehouse, and increasingly they began to apply the ax to the root. During Mary's reign, Colchester inns and alehouses had been centers of religious discussion, but Elizabethans began to see them in a new light. As some of the preachers stated, alehouses were considered to be "nurseries of all riot, excess and idleness," and rooting out such disorders was the "foundation of reformation."[43] A 1574 notation in the records of the town of Hull showed the town leaders and clergy to be in full agreement about the sins spawned by alehouses.

> The learned, zealous and godly preachers of the most holy name of God within Kingston upon Hull do with one consent most earnestly and vehemently exclaim and cry out against the blasphemy of the most holy name of God, drunkenness, disorder, and infinite other abominable and detestable sins which do abound by reason of the great number of alehouses, the unreasonable and excessive strong ale by brewers there brewed and the continual and disorderly repair of people to these lewd houses. They also do thunder out the manifold, grievous and terrible plagues of God hanging over this town if a speedy reformation be not had.[44]

Not only did the alehouse promote idleness and consequent wrongdoing, but it also kept the customer away from the positive influence of church

---

42. CR141/24.
43. Quoted in Wrightson, *English Society*, 169.
44. Gillett and MacMahon, *Hull*, 122–23.

services. As the bishop of Durham remarked in 1560, "For come into a church on the sabbath day, and ye shall see but few, though there be a sermon; but the alehouse is ever full."[45]

The alehouse was indeed popular in England, perhaps partly due to the alehouse being given a new prominence with the Protestant proscription of feasts, ales, and games in the parish church. In Elizabethan Rye, by a conservative estimate, there was one tippling house for every fifteen to twenty households. A single return to the Privy Council from Colchester, dated October 12, 1577, listed the number of different establishments that provided drink and hospitality in Colchester. At that time, Colchester had nine taverns that sold drink, including wine, but that did not take in lodgers; five inns; and thirty-eight alehouses.[46]

Alehouses were not just a local concern. An act passed in one of Henry VII's Parliaments had permitted JPs to reduce the number of alehouses, but it was an Edwardian act in 1552 that set the operative standards for the Elizabethan period, with the stated purpose of preventing "hurts and troubles . . . abuses and disorders." JPs could issue licenses for alehouses if the applicant entered into a bond to maintain good behavior in the alehouse.[47] Before the Edwardian statute, only two lawhundred presentments and one case in the session of the peace that were about alehouses have been found in the Colchester records, and two of those spoke of "blind" alehouses, probably meaning a secret alehouse that promoted unruliness. For example, Richard Brampton's sister was fined 3s. 4d. in 1532 for keeping "bawdry and a blind ale house." The church courts were certainly aware of the problems in that earlier period; a fragment of the record of the visit of the archdeaconry court in the early 1540s mentioned a Colchester alehouse, "the resort of light persons, who, though warned by the constable, spend the time of Divine Service in 'bowling and gulling.' "[48] But the secular authorities were not overly concerned at that time.

After the Edwardian legislation, a few cases found their way into the Colchester courts; in 1556 William Peverell was fined 2s. for selling wine in his house, "against the form of the Statute lately issued thereon." Colchester, too, had an ordinance from the 1550s that insisted inns and taverns be closed during divine services on the Sabbath and feast days.

---

45. Quoted in Collinson, *Religion*, 203.
46. Sommerville, *Secularization*, 139; Mayhew, *Tudor Rye*, 50; Emmison, *Disorder*, 215.
47. Quoted in Wrightson, *English Society*, 167; Emmison, *Disorder*, 202–3.
48. CR101/16; CR93/20d; CR114/2; Oxley, 145.

Some of the reasons for wanting to control alehouses emerged in the presentments of those years: Richard Markes was said to be frequenting the house of William Frauncys at unlawful times, and a report states that "though he has often been admonished thereon by his neighbors, he nevertheless does not purpose to mend his ways."[49] It was difficult to control unlicensed houses, because selling ale had long been an established secondary employment of the poor.[50] Whether for that reason or for others, there seems to have been no concerted effort to control alehouses in Colchester until September 30, 1577.[51] On that day, eight presentments showing the people's concern came before the lawhundred, and the session of the peace dealt with three cases. On the same day that the first beadle of vagabonds was appointed, bakers had to enter into a recognizance to bake "wholesome bread in sufficient quantity so that there is no lack thereof," and a new crackdown began on the butchers who were selling meat on Sundays.[52] Economic regulation and moral reforms were inseparable. In the case of the alehouses, the statute had been in place since 1552, but the economic conditions of the 1570s provided a new urgency for enforcement of the statute. Local enforcement of government acts was often notoriously lax in Tudor England, so the very act of choosing to begin strict enforcement was significant. Though a number of the presentments against alehouses in the 1570s and 1580s came from the representatives of the people at the lawhundreds (see table 10), an even greater number of charges came through the sessions of the peace, indicating that the town authorities were focusing on the alehouses as basic to the reform of behavior. Over the years, connections between unlicensed alehouses and unruliness was noted in the records. For example, in 1586 Richard Lyes was presented for keeping a tippling house without license, for ill rule, and the record noted of Lyes, "he harbors suspect persons." On the same day, nine other people were fined by the JPs for keeping illegal alehouses.[53] The presenters at the lawhundreds were not particularly concerned about the licensing, as the JPs were, but they quickly took note if disturbances and unruliness were present.

---

49. CR122/3; *RPB*, 140; CR120/2d.

50. Wrightson, *English Society*, 168.

51. The effort may have come a few years earlier, as there is a gap in the records from 1565 to 1576.

52. CR140/2.

53. CR147/36, 36d.

TABLE 10.   Illegal Alehouses and Drunkenness

Years	No. of Sessions of the Peace & Lawhundreds Recorded	Illegal Alehouses			Average per Court Session	Drunkenness			Average per Court Session
		LH	SP	Total		LH	SP	Total	
1510–29	56	1	0	1	0.02	0	0	0	0
1530–46	77	1	1	2	0.26	0	0	0	0
1547–49	7	0	0	0	0	0	0	0	0
1550–52	15	0	0	0	0	0	1	1	0.07
1553–55	14	2	0	2	0.14	1	0	1	0.07
1556–58	12	4	0	4	0.33	0	0	0	0
1559–61	16	0	0	0	0	0	5	5	0.31
1562–64	10	2	0	2	0.2	0	2	2	0.2
(Gap in the records)									
1577–79	12	9	15	24	2	8	5	13	1.08
1580–82	14	6	30	36	2.57	7	2	9	0.64
1583–85	18	8	14	22	1.22	2	4	6	0.33
1586–89	16	2	17	19	1.19	3	0	3	0.19

Note: Includes all presentments in the lawhundreds (LH) and the sessions of the peace (SP).

Drunkenness

Along with the spotlight on alehouses came a new emphasis on drunkenness. The connection with alehouses was clear; in the September, 1577, lawhundred, Thomas Gladwyn was presented for keeping an alehouse contrary to the form of the statute and for "allowing drunkards."[54] As table 10 shows, charges of drunkenness were almost nonexistent in the earlier Tudor years, indicating a high level of toleration for tipplers. Drunkenness regularly received attention from the church courts, so secular courts had not usually been dealing with the problem unless it led to unruliness and disorder. However, charges of drunkenness emerged with the first group of reformers elected in Elizabeth's reign; in the October, 1559, session of the peace, Thomas Bell was charged with being a common "potater," which in English, the record noted, would be called "a

54. CR140/2.

common drunkard." Two other men were charged with him, one of whom, Robert Dunnyng, had been coming before the court since 1542 on charges of cutting men's hair on Sundays during divine service.[55] The charge of overindulging in drink was made in the same month in which preacher John Pullen, fresh from Geneva, was made a burgess of Colchester. Whether because of Pullen's influence or not, the early charges were made in the official sessions of the peace (see table 10), indicating a concerted attack by town authorities on the moral degeneration of which drunkenness was a sign. Drunkenness was often linked with other moral wrongs. For example, in the May, 1560, session of the peace, the same one in which a known Catholic, innkeeper Richard Cosyn, was charged with blasphemy, William Jurdon of "le spitalhouse" was said to keep "ill rule in his house," and it was noted that he "harbors or encourages persons who are drunk or not sober, and blasphemers and dice-players." A 1563 session of the peace noted that drunkard William Symnell was "an intemperate man."[56]

In the late 1570s, along with the crusades against Sunday work, illegal alehouses, and vagabonds, drunkenness was being brought before the borough courts, but the records displayed a new kind of judgmental language about drunkards. In the lawhundred of September 30, 1577, Edmund Ryche of Lexden was reported to be "a common drunkard, breaker of the peace, and blasphemer of the name of God," an accusation connecting drunkenness with the major sin of blasphemy.[57] In the next session of the peace, in January, 1578, more new phrases were used in connection with drunkenness when three men were said to be "common drunkards and topers, to the danger of their souls, and against the peace." Previously, the usual punishment for drunkenness had been a money penalty or the stocks, but one of those men was ordered by the JPs to confess his sins publicly on the following Sunday before "the Assembly," presumably the assembly of the saints gathered to hear the town preacher.[58] Thus, the JPs, at least in this case, adopted the methods of the church courts, which was not inconsistent with their increased role as arbiters of moral conduct. The next year, a miller was said to be "a com-

---

55. Emmison, *Disorder*, 212; CR125/2. On Dunnyng, see CR112/2d; CR119/23d; CR120/2d.

56. CR125/4d; CR128/2d.

57. CR140/2.

58. CR140/9; it could be referring to a meeting of the town assembly, but no other instances of Sunday meetings have been found.

mon drunkard and disturber of the peace of God and the Queen's peace"; William Mason was charged with the same, and he was optimistically ordered "to amend." In 1581 drunkard Simon Cock was also called a "blasphemer of the name of God."[59]

Not only was there a new certainty about the danger of drunkenness, but, as table 10 shows, drunkards were presented not just at the sessions of the peace but at the lawhundreds, indicating that the people were considering intoxication a problem. One wonders if the preaching of Nicholas Challoner and his predecessors had helped to form in the minds of the people and town officials the thinking that excessive drinking was a sin that led to greater sins and that it was too serious a problem to leave merely to the church courts. An incident in 1576 shows how some of the attitudes toward drunkenness may have been formed; Challoner, on instruction from the archdeaconry court, was to hear a confession of drunkenness by the curate at Greenstead, Richard Spenser, who was to make his confession while standing before Challoner at the end of Challoner's sermon in St. James's Church. Challoner was then to instruct Spenser about the sin of drunkenness, and the people were to be asked to pray for the curate's amendment.[60]

Connecting blasphemy and drunkenness in the records was significant because, as William Hunt has noted, blasphemy was thought to bring "bad luck—both to the blasphemer and the community that tolerated it."[61] Because of the spiritual degeneracy that had come to be seen as attendant on persistent drunkenness, the problem of the individual had become a problem for the town and, as such, a possible cause of the town's social and economic ills. Colchester town leaders were obviously in accord with those who, between 1576 and 1628, made numerous efforts in Parliament to pass bills outlawing drunkenness, illicit sex, and blasphemy. In discussion of those bills, both preachers and MPs denounced sins that contributed to poverty; they condemned the propertied class for their greed and oppression of inferiors, and they condemned the poor as being susceptible to envy, laziness, and sensuality.[62] Since drunkenness was thought to lead to sloth, it became a tangible offense

---

59. CR141/3d; CR142/5.

60. D/ACA6/183.

61. Hunt, *Puritan Moment,* 79.

62. Hunt, *Puritan Moment,* 79. David Underdown, *Fire from Heaven: Life in an English Town in the Seventeenth Century* (New Haven: Yale University Press, 1992), 72–75, describes the problem of drunkenness in Dorchester.

that could be identified as a source of the problem of poverty; hence, the crusade against both unlawful alehouses and drunkenness heightened in the late 1570s and early 1580s. Though trying to strike down the root causes of misdoing, the bailiffs' views of social responsibility were not entirely negative, as they also took the positive steps of caring for the poor and, especially, of providing preaching through the town preacher, Nicholas Challoner.

Instilling Self-Discipline

The behavioral ills that were the subject of all the regulation were caused, at bottom, by a lack of self-discipline. Puritans thought it their duty to impose the negative discipline of punishment, if need be, until positive forces could instill self-discipline. The campaigns against drunkenness and unlicensed alehouses were not trying to eliminate drinking or alehouses entirely, but the reformers were calling for moderation and temperance, for self-discipline rather than self-indulgence. The sermon was the chief means through which new standards of personal conduct could be planted in the hearts of the populace until those standards became their own. As William Hunt noted in his work on Essex Puritanism, the "provision of more sermons was the key to reform," with the function of the preacher being that of linking "immiserating vice, especially drunkenness and lechery, with damnation, thereby enforcing the culture of discipline with the most frightful of sanctions."[63]

The town preacher and lay town leaders were a powerful combination. Town officials had generously provided by making the town preacher's position a permanent one, and Challoner's official funding signified an attempt to legitimize the Puritan position in Colchester. Though the town preacher's learning and position meant that he had quite a lot of independence and influence, still he was in the pay of the town, which meant that the two elements were working in tandem. Having the town preacher as a permanent resident made a difference, too. Challoner was involved in politics, particularly through his marriage into the Clere family, and it seems reasonable to assume that Challoner was active in encouraging the course pursued by the town leaders in the late 1570s as they attempted to meet the increased social and economic problems by a heightened regulation of personal conduct. His training at

---

63. Hunt, *Puritan Moment*, 83, 94.

Cambridge would have taken him in that direction, and the trend among Puritan preachers in Essex during that period was to try to inspire each civic leader to take on the vocation of a godly magistrate, ruling in accordance with the divine will. A student of the Essex archdeaconry courts has noted that Puritan preachers were often resorting to secular courts rather than to the Courts Christian when they wanted discipline imposed on offensive parishioners.[64] Evidence that the cooperation between Challoner and the bailiffs was encouraged by the sympathetic archdeacon of Colchester can be found in the 1579 case of a Dutchman who was ordered by the archdeaconry court to confess his adultery before Challoner and the bailiffs together. This same case resulted in the bishop of London's chancellor chastising the bailiffs, revealing the suspicion by which the official church sometimes regarded the combined work of the bailiffs and the town preacher.[65]

As Challoner was encouraging the imposition of godly discipline by the magistrates, he was also able to take the larger perspective in religious and economic matters. Under pressure of the war against vagrancy, the assembly passed a resolution in 1580 that without the consent of the bailiffs and aldermen, no more strangers were to inhabit the town, as Colchester already had "more than the town can sustain." The stress of the situation was evident, but three weeks later, Challoner led other ministers in writing to Sir Francis Walsingham on behalf of the Dutch congregation, expressing concern that the loud opposition of the "meanest sort" would drive the Dutch from Colchester. Both religious and economic benefits had accrued through the presence of the Dutch; according to Challoner and other letter writers, the Dutch had been "civil, honest, and godly," and as a result of their presence, many were now employed who formerly "were idle and miserable poor, into which state by the absence of these strangers they are like to return."[66]

The archdeacon, George Withers, also wrote a letter to Sir Francis Walsingham on behalf of the Dutch, and he spoke of the "good example" of the Dutch, "both for life and religion," which had been a real comfort "to all those that be godly minded." Withers, who had been associated with Colchester for at least ten years, spoke of the former decay in the town before the Dutch arrived. "I know," Withers affirmed,

---

64. Lenman, "Godly Discipline," 132; Anglin, "Essex Puritan Movement," 184.

65. Emmison, *Morals,* 3; D/Y2/6, p. 75.

66. D/B5 Gb1, f. 20; Pilgrim, "'New Draperies,'" 46–47; Moens, *Dutch Church,* vi; *CSPD,* 1547–80, p. 687.

"that a number of houses are now in very good reparations whereof no stick would have stood at this day if they had not come thither." The townspeople's attitudes toward these strangers in their midst were representative of the conflicting forces within the town. The Puritan town leaders and preachers respected the Dutch both for their industriousness and their godliness; in fact, they saw the two attributes as working together, so that to be godly was also to be industrious. In contrast, in Withers's words, were "the willfull men who will not see God's manifold blessings," who "do by their inhumanity towards poor afflicted strangers procure God's wrath upon themselves and others."[67] In Puritan minds, the "willful men" were shortsighted and godless, needing the example of the Dutch and the discipline of the godly magistrates and preachers of the town; otherwise, God's punishment would be inflicted, not just on the obstinate, but on the whole community.

The Dutch remained in Colchester, but within a month after the letters defending the Dutch were written, the town preacher, Nicholas Challoner, was dead. In a most unusual gesture, the town showed its respect for Challoner and his preaching by providing a £10 annual pension for his widow.[68] Challoner's tenure was a watershed period in the town, bringing a heightened intensity of regulation in the attempt to create a godly society, but it had also produced lamentable polarizations and divisions.

67. Moens, *Dutch Church,* vi.
68. D/B5 Gb1, f. 21v.

11

Master Northey and Religion in Colchester, 1580–93

Nicholas Challoner was hardly cold in his grave before the hiring of a new preacher, George Northey, M.A., of Clare Hall, Cambridge. A letter written by the bailiffs in 1583 explained how the unusually rapid decision was made.

> Master Challoner, the faithful servant of God and our dear preacher in his grievous sickness, looking for death and praying most earnestly for us, wished [Northey] to succeed in his place if he might be gotten, so well and of long time was he knowing unto him, being in the same college, and albeit we gave great credit unto his words, yet after ourselves had heard him preach . . . we sent our letters to the master and fellows of Clare Hall, suspecting our own judgment, desiring to have more certain knowledge from them. . . . [they] commended him unto us, and . . . [said] that we were to look for a great blessing with him.[1]

The stipend of £40 a year to be paid to Northey was the same as Challoner had received, but such wholehearted recommendations possibly resulted in an added clause that stated that Northey was to be the preacher for the town until either he or the council gave notice of one year. Thereafter, it was more difficult for either side to renege on their agreement.[2]

Northey replaced Nicolas Challoner not only in the pulpit but in the marriage bed as well, when he married Challoner's widow, Sarah, the daughter of former alderman Benjamin Clere. With that marriage, he not

---

1. D/B5 Gb1, f. 21v; D/Y2/6, p. 83. Challoner died in November, 1580, and Northey was hired on December 12.
2. D/B5 Gb1, f. 21v. Rickword, "Members . . . 1559–1603," 241, says that Northey was a relative of Richard Northey, who was an alderman from 1562 until his death in 1573, but I have not been able to confirm this.

only became stepfather to the young girls Marie and Anna Challoner but was suddenly related through marriage to several of the town leaders.[3] The bond between the learned preacher and his employers needed to be strong, as they had to work in close harmony to achieve their common goal of encouraging godliness in the community. Northey, later writing a letter of recommendation for a schoolmaster, stressed his commonality with the town leaders as his brothers in Christ. Though his words had a formal quality about them, they conveyed a respectful, even loving, relationship between Northey and the men whom he called his "dear brethren": "Right worshipful and beloved bretheren . . . I do unfeignedly love and reverence you, that be our governors and bear brotherly goodwill to the rest that be of the council."[4] For their part, the aldermen obviously respected Northey's preaching and work in the town, and when Northey's Presbyterian beliefs resulted in his suspension as a preacher, the aldermen worked long and hard for his reinstatement. The populace enjoyed Northey's preaching so much that the ministers found it difficult to draw an audience to their sermons in the parish churches when Northey was in his pulpit.[5]

Northey's preaching demonstrated that reformist beliefs were appealing to many of the people and town leaders, thus bringing a measure of unity, but other problems in the church did not go away. This chapter concentrates on the condition of the church and clergy in Colchester during the more than dozen years of Northey's tenure, until his death in the summer of 1593. Though Colchester had a few more preaching ministers in the parishes than before, many of the churches were still stagnant, especially those with a Catholic patron. At a higher level, lines were drawn in the religious controversies in England that resulted, among other things, in the development of separatism and the renewed conflict over the wearing of the surplice and conformity to the Book of Common Prayer. Conflict rocked the church once again.

Condition of the Church

The poor condition of some of the parish churches was evident to everyone: buildings were in disrepair, few of the clergy were able to preach,

3. See wills of Northey, ERO D/ACW3/14; Winkin Grynerice, ERO D/ABW16/275; Griffin Earnesbie, PRO 29 Sainberbe.
4. D/Y2/4, p. 193.
5. Davids, *Annals*, 106–7; Collinson, *Puritan Movement*, 382; D/ACA14, f. 136.

and most of the parishes were too poor to support educated clergy. The larger church, beset by its own problems, seemed to have little ability or will to correct the situation, so the town assembly agreed in 1581 to suggest to Parliament that the sixteen Colchester parishes be united into five or six, with the clerical appointments under the supervision of the bailiffs. As it was, the town leaders had little power over the workings of the parish churches in Colchester, but the right of presentation of the parish clergy would have given them a great deal of power, probably too much in the eyes of the church. Nothing came of the plan, but the bold scheme was indicative of the desire of the town leaders to shape the religion of the town.[6]

Certainly, all hands were needed in solving the many problems of the parish churches, not the least of which was the poor condition of most of the buildings as revealed by the records of the archdeaconry court. One of the worst was St. Martin's Church, in the parish of the butchers, who were the notorious violators of the restrictions against working on Sunday. Perhaps it was because the leading parishioners spent so little time in it that the church building was often said to be "in decay." Richard Spenser, the clergyman who had done penance for drunkenness before Challoner and the congregation in 1576, was the ineffective curate in 1581; the chancel, the part of the church for which the clergy was responsible, was said to be "ruinous." A year later, the wardens were apparently talking about Spenser when they reported, "Our parson hath carried away our glass . . . , and we cannot get it again, nor our chancel repaired."[7] By 1587 the church was reported to be "ready to fall down," and in 1588 the wardens tried to explain: "The windows and church [are] in great decay, and the parish is so poor that we are not able to make it and are behind in repair."[8]

St. Martin's was not the only church building with severe problems. In 1588, the walls and windows of Holy Trinity Church were "in decay," and being also in need of "a pulpit and a place for the minister to sit in to read divine service," the wardens were given a timetable for repairs. At the same archdeaconry court, St. Nicholas's Church was also said to be in decay and had unglazed windows. Five years later, Holy Trinity

6. D/B5 Gb1, f. 22v; Davis, "Colchester," 95.

7. D/ACA9, ff. 90, 127, 228; D/ACA10, f. 169. See also D/ACA10, f. 157; D/ACA14, ff. 126, 130, 148, 216, 290; D/ACA21, ff. 98, 385, 345.

8. Emmison, Morals, 243; D/ACA14, f. 290. See Davis, "Colchester," 85–86, for St. Martin's problems in the early seventeenth century.

Church was still "in decay," with the explanation that "the parishioners are so poor that they are not able to repair it," but by 1599 the church was being repaired.[9] Windows were also a problem at St. Botolph's, according to the account of the wardens in 1584: "The glass windows of church and chancel are so broken that the church is more like a dove-house than a place of prayer, for which cause both the preachers and others have made great complaint. The communion table is nought and certain stools are broken all a-pieces and thrown about."[10]

The picture seemed to be one of neglect and progressive decay, not just of the fabric of the church, but of the articles needed for divine service. For example, the reports about small St. Runwald's Church, situated in the middle of the market area on High Street, progressed from reports of broken windows to the 1596 statement by the wardens that they did not have "a communion cup with a silver cover, nor a comely pulpit." The same statement claims: "The surplice is so scant that the minister cannot wear it. Windows are broken and the stools in decay. And the pavement broken, and they want the tomes of homilies." By 1605, there were problems with the roof and tiles.[11] Completing the picture of neglect were the less than holy purposes to which some of the buildings were subjected. William Sympson was presented in the September, 1588, archdeaconry court for not removing his logs out of St. Runwald's Church, and at the same time, Stephen Casser of All Saints' was said to be "selling wares in the church and . . . making a dunghill in the churchyard and keeping hogs there."[12]

Some historians have surmised that the neglect and desecration of church buildings and the failure to build new church buildings in the later Tudor period signified a lack of religious commitment, but as Patrick Collinson points out, the Catholic belief in the sacredness of the physical resting place of the body of Christ, the Eucharist, in the church building gave way under Protestantism to belief in the sanctuary of God in the human heart. Protestants were builders, but Collinson notes that "the buildings they erected consisted of godly lives, their materials not bricks and mortar but hearts and minds literally 'edified' by the preaching of the

9. D/ACA14, f. 130; D/ACA21, f. 28; D/ACA24, f. 243; Davis, "Colchester," 85.

10. Emmison, *Morals*, 135, 246, from D/ACA11, f. 105.

11. D/ACA5, f. 88; D/ACA14, ff. 183, 291; D/ACA17, f. 267; D/ACA21, f. 376; D/ACA24, f. 32; Davis, "Colchester," 85.

12. D/ACA17, f. 72; Emmison, *Morals,* 270.

Gospel." The church they were concerned about building was of living stones; nevertheless, with the Protestant emphasis on preaching, the church building was to be maintained, as long as it was actually used for preaching. Both the parson and the wardens were responsible for the upkeep of the building, and the few Colchester churches that had strong preaching ministers were not usually subject to the neglect that was so obvious in many of the Colchester parish church buildings. St. Leonard's Church, which had the most consistently active ministers in the Elizabethan period, had only relatively minor problems; for example, at various times, they lacked a cover for a Communion cup, the church was disorderly and filthy, and they had a churchyard gate out of repair.[13]

In contrast, St. Martin's and other neglected churches had only sporadic curacies or incompetent ministers. In fact, much can be concluded about the condition of the ministry of a Colchester parish from the condition of the church building. For example, after the ruinous St. Martin's Church was partially denuded by the drunken curate Richard Spenser, it was then "blessed" with curate Robert Goode (or Golde, according to some of the records), who was later appointed rector at Holy Trinity. Goode, who was labeled as "sometime a mender of saddles and panels," was among those listed in a Privy Council report of September, 1584, as being one of the "ignorant and unpreaching ministers" in Essex. A 1586 commission examined Goode on his knowledge of the Scriptures and found him to be "insufficient." Some of Goode's parishioners at Holy Trinity thought him to be morally corrupt, accusing him of drunkenness and of keeping a whore at Harwich, and he was reproved by the archdeaconry court for not instructing the children in the catechism and for allowing persons suspected of bawdry to take Communion.[14] The same conjunction of poor clerical performance and the neglect of the building can be seen in the report of the wardens of St. Botolph's Church about William Kirby, who had not held a service in the church "since Michaelmas and but twice on Holy Days." He was not catechizing the youth, and all the windows of the church were broken. Later, Kirby was reported to be "a common alehouse haunter and a frequenter of a harlot's house."[15]

---

13. Collinson, "Elizabethan Church," 171–72; D/ACA5, f. 39; D/ACA14, f. 168; D/ACA21, f. 228.

14. Davids, *Annals*, 98; Guildhall MS 9537/6, f. 177; D/ACA14, f. 50; D/ACA17, f. 21; Emmison, *Morals*, 23, 143, 209.

15. D/ACA11, f. 15; Emmison, *Morals*, 221.

It was no coincidence that the values of the livings at St. Martin's, Holy Trinity, and St. Runwald's were among the lowest in Colchester (see appendix 5). The clergy could not do their duty in maintaining the part of the building for which they were responsible, and the poverty of the livings also meant that the bottom of the clerical barrel had been scraped to obtain someone to serve in those parishes. Even the conservative Archbishop Whitgift in 1585 was bemoaning the inability of most livings to support learned ministers; he found that only about six hundred of England's nine thousand benefices could adequately support a learned minister.[16] The inadequacy of Colchester livings was probably one of the reasons for the attempt, aborted though it was, to reshape the parishes in 1581; certainly, a consolidation of some of the poorer parishes would have permitted the securing of a better-educated clergy.

The problems of the institutional church in Colchester pointed up one of the endemic problems in Tudor church life—patronage. Patrons had the right of appointment to the benefice of a church; a conscientious patron might work hard to get a good cleric and insure that he had an adequate income, but not all patrons were so inclined. The Reformation had wrought radical changes in the patronage of Colchester churches, since most of them had been in the hands of either St. John's Abbey or St. Botolph's Priory. Most of the rights of presentation to the seven churches that had belonged to St. John's ended up under the aegis of the Crown, with mixed results for Colchester churches: the beloved Michael Goodeare at St. Leonard's and the suspected whoremonger Robert Goode at Holy Trinity were both Crown appointees.[17]

The situation of the churches that were formerly in the presentation of St. Botolph's Priory and had fallen into the hands of Sir Thomas Audley in 1536 was complex, since the Audley household, once a cornerstone of Protestantism, eventually became a bastion of Catholicism as a result of the marriage of Sir Thomas's brother, also named Thomas, to the Catholic Katherine Southwell in 1544. However, it seems clear that the bent of the Audley family in its presentations was toward Protestantism until the death of Sir Thomas's nephew in 1572. The one recorded presentation by Sir Thomas's brother and heir was that of Sir John Thorpe to St. Peter's Church in 1545, and Thorpe was apparently a Protestant,

16. Rosemary O'Day, "Clergy," 40; Wrightson, *English Society,* 207.
17. Guildhall MS 9531/13, pt. 1, ff. 156, 222. See Rosemary O'Day, "Ecclesiastical Patronage: Who Controlled the Church?" in *Church and Society in England: Henry VIII to James I,* ed. Felicity Heal and Rosemary O'Day (London: Macmillan, 1977), 137–55.

since he was the writer of several Protestant wills.[18] Sir Thomas's nephew, likewise named Thomas, was holder of the rights of presentation after his father's death in 1557, and he was quite active, making five presentations between 1559 and 1571 and concentrating his efforts on All Saints' Church and St. Peter's, which had the best resources to support clergymen.[19] One of the clergymen presented, Oliver Pigge, was a known Puritan. However, another appointee, John Walford (or Welfare), was listed in the 1584 report to the Privy Council as being among the "ignorant and unpreaching ministers,"[20] but Walford was respected by at least some of his parishioners at All Saints'. Tailor Richard Mason made Walford supervisor of his will, calling him "my well-beloved in Christ, . . . minister of the Word of God."[21]

After the 1572 death of Sir Thomas's nephew, there is no record of Audley presentations until almost twenty years later, when Mistress Katherine Audley presented to St. Peter's in 1590.[22] However, in those two intervening decades, the influence of the Audleys remained, and it is likely that the Audleys appointed Mr. Phillips as curate at Berechurch, who had the distinction of being called "a drunkard" in the 1584 survey, and Thomas Holland as curate of St. Botolph's, who had several conflicts over his practice of baptism with the wardens, probably a result of Holland's Catholicism. In 1586, Holland was labeled by an episcopal commission as "a rank papist."[23] Even if Holland's curacy at St. Botolph's was an indirect attempt to install Catholics, there is no evidence to indicate that Katherine Audley's single official presentation in 1590 to fill the vacancy at St. Peter's Church was such an attempt. On the contrary, one

---

18. See the information on the Audleys in Morant, 2:30–31; Guildhall MS 9531/12, pt. 1, f. 153. Some of the wills are ERO D/ACR3/80, 107, and D/ABW31/93.

19. Guildhall MS 9531/13, pt. 1, ff. 113v, 138, 151r and v, 163.

20. Davids, *Annals*, 98.

21. D/ABW25/315. Walford also seems to have been appointed later to the rectory of St. Mary-at-Wall; the 1594 will of Dorothy Rushbroke, ERO D/ABW32/59, shows him to be there, as does his 1596 testimony in the borough court as "minister of St. Mary" (CR158/16d).

22. Guildhall MS 9531/13, pt. 1, f. 248v. By that time, her two younger sons had also died; see Morant, 2:30. Morant mistakenly says that Katherine married Sir Thomas's nephew, rather than his brother.

23. Davids, *Annals*, 98; D/ACA14, ff. 140, 142; Guildhall MS 9537/6, f. 177. See Newcourt, 2:166; Morant, 2:30. The manor at Berechurch was held by the Audleys; Sir Thomas Audley had tried to separate Berechurch from Holy Trinity and make it a separate parish church, but the Audleys never funded it enough to do so. Sir Thomas had granted the tithes of St. Botolph's to the rector of All Saints', also in the patronage of the Audleys, so the rector of All Saints' may have been responsible for hiring the curate at St. Botolph's.

might argue that the new vicar, Edward Gutter, was probably a good Protestant, since he was a graduate of Clare Hall, Cambridge, which had produced the likes of Preachers Nicholas Challoner and George Northey, and he described himself in his will written early in 1593 as a "minister of the Word of God."[24]

Rather than many active attempts to bring Catholics into the churches, the Audley approach after 1572 was neglect, notable more for what might have been had the Audleys remained strong Protestants. With money to back up their commitment, they could have had a great influence on Colchester churches by installing Puritan preachers, which the Audleys after 1572 were certainly not going to do. The important church of St. Peter's was left vacant when Puritan Oliver Pigge departed for Suffolk, probably in 1571, and the Audleys neglected to appoint a new vicar, resulting in the archbishop of Canterbury stepping in to fill the vacancy in 1579, appointing Robert Lewis, a native of Colchester.[25] When Lewis departed almost a decade later, the Crown presented a Thomas Taverner to St. Peter's, but he did not stay long, so Katherine Audley's presentation of Edward Gutter in 1590 was probably prompted more by a desire to retain the family patronage and influence rather than an attempt to install a Catholic, which, by that time, would have been foolhardy anyway.[26]

The advent of Robert Lewis in 1579 reinforced godly preaching in Colchester. Lewis was a preaching minister educated at the Puritan St. John's College, Cambridge, and the archbishop appointing him was Edmund Grindal, a Puritan sympathizer. Grindal had been rendered largely ineffective by 1579, but the prosperous and influential parishioners of St. Peter's must have found a way to get Lewis appointed. Lewis's Calvinist sympathies were clear; he was a member of the Dedham conference of Puritan preachers, the group of preachers with Presbyterian sympathies who met regularly at Dedham, and he was later suspended from his ministry by the bishop of London for his opposition to the church courts. While still fairly new to his vicarage in Colchester, Lewis was one of the ministers who, with town preacher Nicholas Challoner, signed a letter to Sir Francis Walsingham in defense of the Dutch

---

24. Venn and Venn, *Alumni,* 2:276; ERO D/ABW16/361.
25. Davids, *Annals,* 114; Newcourt, 2:179. On Lewis's origin, see the wills of Lewis's uncle, Robert Barnes (ERO D/ACR3/180), and of Lewis's mother (ERO D/ABW23/176).
26. Guildhall MS 9531/13, pt. 1, ff. 244, 248v.

in Colchester.[27] The special status of Lewis and George Northey as learned preachers was evident when they were both appointed to a special commission in 1586 to examine clergy in their knowledge of Scripture.[28]

By the time George Northey arrived as town preacher in 1581, then, the Puritan push for preaching ministers had advanced somewhat. When Challoner had arrived in Colchester in the mid-1570s, Thomas Upcher at St. Leonard's was the only active preaching minister in town, and he did not have the desired educational credentials. When Northey came as town preacher, Upcher was still at St. Leonard's, though he left a year later, perhaps realizing that he was overshadowed by the preaching of the better-educated ministers. Not only was Cambridge-educated Lewis preaching at St. Peter's, but Robert Searles, another Puritan, had been at the Lexden village church since 1576, having been presented to the advowson by Thomas Radcliffe, the third earl of Sussex. The appointment of Searles was possibly influenced by the earl's wife, Frances, by whose will the Puritan Sidney Sussex College was founded at Cambridge in 1596.[29] Though Puritan preachers were now to be found in most of the churches attended by the influential and prosperous town leaders, Puritanism was not totally dominant in the town, where Catholics and even separatists could be found.

Religious Divisions in the Borough

In 1581, John Luson of Greenstead, the village church on the hill just east of the town of Colchester, was presented in the archdeaconry court for refusing to receive Communion from the minister of Greenstead. Luson's reply was that the minister "handleth the bread unreverently with filthy hands." In the church court, not receiving the Eucharist was a chargeable offense,[30] and the presentment of Luson, notable for his curious explanation, possibly represented an attempt by a Catholic recusant to cir-

27. Harold Smith, *Ecclesiastical History of Essex under the Long Parliament and Commonwealth* (Colchester: Benham, n.d.), 12–13; Davids, *Annals,* 114; Moens, *Dutch Church,* vi. Lewis's wife, Mary, was a Clere, the daughter of Alderman Nicholas Clere III, and she was a first cousin to Challoner's wife, Sarah; see Mary's will, PRO 109 Soame.

28. Guildhall MS 9537/6, f. 177.

29. Smith, *Ecclesiastical History,* 13; Anglin, "Essex Puritan Movement," 174–75; Addison, *Essex Worthies,* 151. Upcher moved to nearby Fordham, where he had held the benefice since 1561. Frances was the aunt of Sir Philip Sidney.

30. Emmison, *Morals,* 99, 107.

cumvent the demand that everyone attend church and receive Communion periodically. Charging the minister with improper administration of the sacrament would have been a convenient excuse for a Catholic who was willing to attend the Anglican service occasionally but did not want to partake of the Protestant Communion.

The situation of Catholic recusants—those who, for conscience's sake, did not want to participate in the Anglican services—became far more precarious in the 1580s, partly because of the increasing militancy of the Catholic priests, especially the Jesuits. The priests from the Catholic seminary at Douai had been arriving since 1574; about a hundred were in England by 1580, but in that summer the first two Jesuits, Robert Parsons and Edmund Campion, arrived. At a time when Catholic Spain was on the move again and when the papacy was encouraging revolt in Ireland, the presence of Jesuits was reckoned to be a real threat to England. The government was spurred into action, and in March, 1581, Parliament passed the Act to Retain the Queen's Majesty's Subjects in their Due Obedience, which, in effect, extended the Treasons Act of 1571 to cover anyone who converted to Catholicism or who persuaded anyone to convert. Anyone hearing a mass was to pay the stiff fine of 100 marks and be imprisoned for a year, and the fine for being absent from church for a year was raised to £20 a month, a considerable increase over the 12d. fine imposed in 1559. Strict enforcement of the penalties would have been devastating, but enforcement was selective and sporadic, and most lay Catholics were not seriously threatened.[31]

The Catholic priests were not handled so gently, and executions multiplied after the 1581 act. At the end of that year, Campion and two other priests were put to death in London for treason, and four months later the only Catholic priest executed on Essex soil was hanged in Chelmsford, also for treason. Campion vigorously denied treason against the queen, but in the age in which he was accused, religious conformity was equated with political loyalty. The secular powers, using a fourteenth-century law to execute Campion, were quite ready to link active Catholicism with treason, and they had some cause to do so. A conspiracy in 1581–82 to return Scotland to the Catholic fold and then conquer England had abundant support, including that of the pope; the Jesuits; the king of Spain; Mary, queen of Scots; the French Guise family; and Bernardino de Mendoza, the Spanish ambassador in London. In Novem-

---

31. Cross, *Church and People,* 144; Guy, *Tudor England,* 285, 299.

ber, 1583, Francis Throckmorton revealed under torture a Guise plot to invade England, and he implicated the queen of Scots, Mendoza, and some Catholic noblemen and gentlemen.[32]

It was a traumatic time for lay Catholics. The increasingly polarized climate did not allow for the tolerant connivance of the priests who had turned a blind eye to the "occasional conformity" of lay Catholics, and the incoming Jesuit priests forbade any measure of conformity to the Anglican religion. Most of the Catholic laity were loyal to their queen and accorded her the right to determine the type of worship they participated in, but the priests entering England championed defiance of authorities, even at the risk of severe penalties. The Catholic recusants were not united among themselves; some were anti-Jesuit, and many were anti-Spanish. The habits of obedience to the sovereign were strong, and most lay Catholics remained loyal to the queen, though they were under pressure to do otherwise. Many found a way around their dilemma by making infrequent visits to their parish churches to show their loyalty to the queen. The queen, trying to be sensitive to the Catholic position, had vetoed an earlier attempt to legislate the forcing of Catholics to receive Communion. Thus John Luson, the Greenstead man who refused Communion, could be charged in the ecclesiastical court, but as long as he attended his parish church now and then, he could not be tried in the civil courts.[33]

The traitorous conspiracies of the early 1580s provoked alarm among the subjects of the queen, including those in Colchester, who were ever vigilant about their resident Catholics in the Audley household. In February, 1584, the bailiffs of Colchester notified the Privy Council of the apprehension of one Thomas Debell, a servant to Mistress Audley. Debell, who had uttered words about the queen of Scots and the late traitors, was said to be "very dangerous." A letter written to Walsingham on the next day, certifying Debell's arrest for seditious speeches, charged that Debell was "greatly inclined to Papistry."[34] The Privy Council's reply suggested caution, saying that more proof would be needed before Debell could be charged and that the bailiffs should take the advice of their town clerk, attorney James Morice. Morice wrote to the bailiffs

---

32. Guy, *Tudor England,* 284–85; J. E. Neale, *Queen Elizabeth I* (Garden City, N.Y.: Doubleday, Anchor Books, 1957), 272.

33. *VCH Essex,* 2:44; Cross, *Church and People,* 145–46; Powell and Cook, *Historical Facts,* 94; Guy, *Tudor England,* 298–99.

34. D/Y2/7, pp. 199, 201.

and, as an ardent Puritan, noted that Debell was "a notable papist and a lewd and busy fellow," but he warned, "Yet the thing wherewith he is charged, be not in my opinion of such moment, nor so offensive to the laws of this realm, as that by ordinary way of justice he may be indicted or brought in question for the same."[35] The rule of law was uppermost, and the civil law, though it imposed difficulties, also afforded a measure of protection to lay Catholics, such as the Audleys and their household. Though the church courts occasionally charged Thomas Debell with failure to receive Communion and for absence from his parish church, Holy Trinity, Debell continued in Colchester; in 1596 he explained to the archdeaconry court that, being attendant on Mistress Audley, he was conforming to the Communion requirement by accompanying his mistress to the evening service in Berechurch.[36]

Catholic priests had no such protection from civil law; in fact, a new law, the Act for the Queen's Safety, was passed by the Parliament of 1584–85, which had been stirred up by the assassination of William of Orange by a Catholic fanatic in the autumn of 1584. The new law declared that anyone knowingly receiving or aiding Catholic priests was guilty of a felony and that any Catholic priest ordained since 1559 could be convicted of treason. Since treason garnered the penalty of death, the execution of priests from 1585 increased under the new statute. Under Elizabeth, no Catholics were executed for heresy; those executed were instead charged with treason against the state. For Catholics, caution was the order of the day. The Spanish ambassador, writing to the king of Spain around 1586, reported: "The counties of Essex and Kent I have been unable to investigate for fear of discovery. There are some Catholics and schismatics, but the whole population of these counties is infected with heresy."[37]

From the bailiffs' point of view, the borough of Colchester continued to be "infected" by Catholics, largely because of the Audley influence.

---

35. BL., Stowe MS 150; D/Y2/8, p. 323.

36. ERO D/ACA21, f. 465; see also ff. 28, 50. There was a network of gentry around the Audley household who probably had Catholic sympathies, including Master Doctor William Drury, who was married to Katherine Audley's sister and resided at Brett's Hall, Tendring, in Essex. Also, the wife of Jerome Gilbert, Jane, was possibly another sister. Jerome was a recorder of Colchester during Mary's reign, and his son was the famous scientist Dr. William Gilbert, who produced the early work on electromagnetism. See wills of William Gynes, PRO 15 Tirwhite; Jerome Gilbert, PRO 38 Rowe; Jane Gilbert, PRO 83 Leicester. On the Drurys, see *DNB*, 6:62–63.

37. Guy, *Tudor England*, 301, 332; *CSPSp*, 1580–86, p. 609. Under Elizabeth, four persons were burnt for heresy, but none were Catholic; see Bindoff, *Tudor England*, 241.

The need for vigilance continued. In 1587, a letter to Sir Francis Wal-singham reported the presence in the town of a certain Thomas Smith, a teacher of French and Spanish who had been "brought up in the Papist religion at Douay." When the bailiffs examined Smith, he agreed "to reform himself and resort to the church to the divine service and sermons, upon which he was bound to his good behavior." He attended the town preacher's sermon the very next day, but Smith's reform was cut short by the arrival of two men from France, Englishmen who had probably stud-ied at Douai, who were suspected to be "great papists." A letter to Wal-singham written on July 14, 1587, reported that one of the travelers, William Atkinson, was "a very obstinate and contemptuous person and like to do much hurt in the commonwealth if he may have liberty." The bailiffs had also garnered information to relay to Walsingham about four Catholic priests in London who were able to hear mass at the Marshalsea prison whenever they liked. From other, undated letters, it appears that Thomas Smith and the two travelers, William Atkinson and Edward Parker, were taken prisoner in Colchester, as a later letter from Parker, whose real name was Edmund Shelley, requested assistance from rela-tives for himself and the others who were prisoners "for religion's sake." A messenger was employed to take the appeal to relatives, and among the planned recipients was Mistress Audley, who probably had a connection to Shelley through mutual relatives.[38] Anti-Catholicism reached a peak in England in the next year, with the threatened invasion of the Spanish Armada, but even with the English victory over the Spanish, the cam-paign against Catholics continued in Colchester, though in a less hysteri-cal manner.[39]

Separatists

The borough had accommodated to living with the Catholic Audleys, but having separatists, or independent small religious groups, in their midst could be more disturbing. In towns like Colchester, which had a tradition of being on the outer boundaries of religious conformity, there had

---

38. D/Y2/6, pp. 15, 113, 121, 125, 127. Katherine Audley was an illegitimate daughter of Sir Richard Southwell, and one of the Southwell men married the daughter of Sir William Shelley, so Katherine Audley and Edmund Shelley were probably connected through mutual relatives, rather than by a blood relationship: see *CSPD*, 1547–80, p. 576; *DNB*, 18:700–702.

39. A Scotsman was examined in Colchester in February, 1589, about a certain Robert Bruise, a Jesuit and suspected papist agent (D/Y2/5, p. 63).

always been those who had gone over the edge. In the early Tudor
period, there had been the Lollards; then the Reformation spawned more
than one group of independent thinkers, such as the Family of Love,
whose teachings were brought to Colchester during Mary's reign by a
joiner from Delft, Christopher Vitells. The Marian period also produced
independent preachers, such as Thomas Putto, whose preaching in
unlawful gatherings at Mile End heath kept people away from their
parish churches. In every period, there was the odd person with the
extreme ideas, such as the bricklayer from Langham who unwisely
expressed his beliefs publicly in Colchester in 1581. Not only was he
against infant baptism and the taking of oaths, but he thought that war-
fare was unlawful for a Christian and that it was impossible for one to be
a magistrate and a Christian as well. His inclusion of the queen herself in
the latter belief landed him in the assize court in Brentwood for his "seditious words."[40]

Potentially more serious to a state church was the development of a
separatist church. As early as 1567, a separatist group in London began
out of opposition to the attempt by church authorities to impose a certain
mode of clerical dress for divine services. The more lasting separatist
movement began a little later, with Robert Browne's arguments in Cambridge against the episcopal system of the licensing of preachers; according to Browne, anyone inspired of God should have the freedom to
preach. Browne's move to Norwich in 1581 really launched the movement to separate deliberately from the established church. After being
forced into exile, Browne published in the Netherlands in 1582 his theological justification for separatism, *A Treatise of Reformation without
tarrying for Any.* For Browne, the separatist did not need to wait for the
aid of magistrate or monarch to shape his church, with the church being
the gathered congregation of the elect and being completely separate
from the state and any state church.[41]

The separatist views spread rapidly among the lesser folk in the early
1580s, and there is a fascinating account of an illegal conventicle in a
thick woods on Midsummer Day near Ramsey, some twelve miles east of
Colchester. The people feasted on roast beef and goose and then heard
William Collett, a keeper of hawks for Master Lucas, read from the third

---

40. Strype, *Annals,* 2 (2): 282–86; CR122/4; J. S. Cockburn, ed. *Calendar of Assize
Records, Essex Indictments: Elizabeth I* (London: HMSO, 1978), no. 1277; Martin, *Radicals,* 179–226.

41. Collinson, *Puritan Movement,* 88–91; Cross, *Church and People,* 147–48.

chapter of the Gospel of John while standing on a ladder. Around the same time, three separatists were hanged at Bury St. Edmunds, and there was a report of separatists in Colchester, though nothing is known about their identity or activities.[42]

The separatist movement had a traumatic effect on Puritans. The lord chief justice, in his report about the hanging of the separatists at Bury St. Edmunds in 1583, also mentioned five ministers convicted of disparaging the Book of Common Prayer. One of those ministers was the ardent Puritan Oliver Pigge, who had previously been the incumbent at St. Peter's and at All Saints' in Colchester, and who was in jail in 1583 for altering the baptismal service to suit his Puritan views. Pigge was incensed at being linked in any way with separatists, and he quickly wrote a letter averring that he detested from the heart the "evil proceedings" of Browne and the other separatists. In his treatise, Browne had condemned Presbyterians even more than Anglicans, since the Presbyterians, in Browne's view, knew the truth but did not follow it. The Presbyterians were deeply stung by Browne's attack. Thomas Cartwright, the Calvinist apologist, quickly emphasized that the Church of England included the whole nation and, despite past criticisms, was a church of Christ, imperfections and all. One of the results of this new stress on the inclusiveness of the church was that, in the eyes of the Presbyterians, the godly monarch and godly magistrates became even more important, since they were essential instruments for shaping the coterminous society and church.[43] The Puritans could gladly cooperate with the state in denouncing Catholics, but the separatist beliefs were a little too close to their own views for comfort. Puritans wanted it known that they were a part of the Church of England, whereas separatists were the outsiders.

Puritans at Work

There seemed to be only a few separatists and Catholics around Colchester, but the two groups generally attracted entirely different social levels. There were probably a few of the lesser folk who remained Catholic, especially in the outlying, rural areas of the borough, but the continuance of Roman Catholicism in Colchester was led by gentry with high connections, the Audleys. In contrast, separatism appealed to the craftsmen and laborers who had little stake in maintaining the hierarchi-

---

42. Emmison, *Morals*, 97; *VCH Essex*, 2:38; Collinson, *Puritan Movement*, 227.
43. *VCH Essex*, 2:38; Cross, *Church and People*, 148.

cal society. Puritanism, however, had an appeal for people at all social, economic, and educational levels, though the pull was strongest on the middle groups that wanted change to occur within the boundaries of order that were already in place in society. This section of this chapter examines Puritanism's mature development, its repression by Archbishop Whitgift, and its decline as an organized movement, all of which happened to coincide with the tenure of town preacher George Northey, in the 1580s and early 1590s. The educated clergy provided much of the leadership of the Puritan movement, and a look at the activities of the Puritan clergy in Essex and at the national level is needed to understand the workings of Puritanism in Colchester.

Some of the Puritan clergy had formed associations by the early 1580s, with areawide meetings to coordinate their approach to doctrine and practices. One such meeting, to be held secretly on May 16, 1582, at Cockfield near Bury St. Edmunds, was reported by Oliver Pigge, who, in addition to his Colchester connections, was a leader of Suffolk Puritans. About sixty ministers, including some from Essex, went to discuss the Book of Common Prayer, to try to determine which practices could be tolerated and which should be rejected.[44] Town preacher George Northey and Colchester clergyman Robert Lewis possibly attended the meeting in Suffolk, for both of them were a part of the Dedham conference of Puritan preachers, which has gained fame among historians of Puritanism because its detailed minutes are the only minutes of such a group to have survived. The Dedham group, which was strictly for clergy only, was a part of a network of conferences that was loosely led by the London group, headed by John Field. To avoid suspicion, the Dedham conference met secretly at various places from 1582 to 1589 under the leadership of the Dedham lecturer, Dr. Edmund Chapman, who was the brother-in-law of William Cardinal, former Colchester town clerk and recorder.[45] In their weekly meetings, the Dedham group, which never had more than sixteen active members at any one time, discussed doctrinal matters, as well as the practical problems of their ministries. They also looked at procedures in the wider church, as they did in a meeting held in Colchester on May 6, 1583, when they discussed the archidiaconal court system and made proposals for changes. Of the twenty clergy who belonged to the Dedham conference at one time or another, seventeen of them were university graduates, with all but one coming

44. Collinson, *Puritan Movement*, 218–19.
45. Hunt, *Puritan Moment*, 96; Hasler, 1:537; Collinson, *Puritan Movement*, 223–24.

from Cambridge. The conference, which some have called a Presbyterian classis, or local synod, had no official status, so it could only offer advice to its members, although the decisions were expected to be followed by the ministers and their congregations. In other cases, conference members put pressure on secular authorities to act, and in some instances of disputes between a minister and his congregation, the conference tried to negotiate between them.[46]

The more radical of the conferences were Presbyterian in nature, though the members of the Dedham conference were not all thoroughgoing Presbyterians. Church government had not been an issue with the Elizabethan settlement of religion in 1559, but the opposition of bishops in the controversy over clerical dress in the 1560s had led some of the Calvinists to question the whole system of episcopacy. Thomas Cartwright, in his lectures in Cambridge in 1570, was not the first to advocate a church governed by ministers and elders rather than by bishops, but he was the first university teacher to do so, and he became the primary spokesman for the Presbyterian system of governance. From the New Testament book of the Acts of the Apostles, Cartwright proposed a system of congregations governed by pastors and elders, overseen by area assemblies (or classes) made up of representatives from local congregations, in turn overseen by provincial and national synods.[47] By the 1580s, the Presbyterian versus the episcopal system of church governance was the hot topic, and some have assumed that Presbyterianism was synonymous with mainstream Puritanism, but that was not universally true. Colchester's George Northey was a dedicated believer in the Presbyterian system, but not all members of the Dedham group were ready to overthrow the episcopal system completely. As a whole, the Dedham conference was less radical than the London group under John Field, which would have aggressively eliminated bishops. More than once, Chapman expressed regret at the forwardness of the London classis, and the Dedham group did not always obey the rulings of the London general assembly. Most of the Dedham men were more exercised over matters with which they often had to deal, such as the three subjects that they proposed for discussion at a Cambridge conference: how extensively the Prayer Book should be followed, the problem of separatism in their com-

---

46. Anglin, "Essex Puritan Movement," 183–86; Collinson, *Puritan Movement*, 225–27.

47. Hunt, *Puritan Moment*, 97; Collinson, *Puritan Movement*, 226; Cross, *Church and People*, 140–41.

munities, and whether the godly minister should appear before the ecclesiastical court.[48]

Though not all Puritans were hot Presbyterians, it was that issue that finally stirred up the repressive policies of the established church, which felt very threatened by the Puritan attacks against the episcopal system. The man who was mainly responsible for the expulsion from Cambridge of Thomas Cartwright, the promoter of the Presbyterian system of governance, was John Whitgift, who became the apologist for the episcopal system in the mid-1570s. Whitgift, as a man willing to defy the Puritans, caught the queen's eye, and she groomed him to take the place of Edmund Grindal, the archbishop of Canterbury whose Puritan sympathies had quickly brought him into opposition to the queen. Grindal, who had been rendered impotent by suspension from his duties since mid-1577, died in the summer of 1583, and on September 23 Whitgift was elected archbishop. A measure of Whitgift's influence with the queen was that he was the first prelate to sit on the Privy Council since Cardinal Pole had during Mary's reign.

Whitgift's elevation set off a revival of Presbyterianism. Many reformers were quite willing to be under the episcopal system as long as the bishops were sympathetic to their desire for reform, as Grindal certainly was, but having John Whitgift in the highest episcopal office was sure to increase demands to eliminate the episcopal system entirely. John Field, the London coordinator of the Presbyterian movement, found new recruits, and several new groups of Presbyterian classes developed, recreating what the Dedham group and a few others had already established. Representatives of the local groups came together at the time when university degrees were given and met in London during Parliament, so that, for a time, an embryonic alternative to the established church existed.[49] The opponents of reform saw Presbyterianism as a logical progression in the demands of the reformers: arguments about caps and surplices led to denying the authority of the bishop to enforce such regulations and, so the argument went, finally to the elimination of bishops altogether and to the denial of the Crown's authority in ecclesiastical matters. However, most Puritans generally accepted the connection between church and state. They would retain the bishop, but his primary

---

48. William Haller, *The Rise of Puritanism* (New York: Harper, 1957), 16; Collinson, *Puritan Movement*, 228–29, 261, 288, 305–6, 319.

49. Collinson, *Puritan Movement*, 243; Cross, *Church and People*, 148–49.

function was as a minister and preacher of the gospel. Any power to govern that the bishop had derived from the queen, not from God, and he worked in conjunction with, not above, the secular governors of the land. The more radical members of the classical movement did want to remove bishops entirely, but not until the late stages of the movement was there talk of severing completely the relationship between church and state.[50]

Whitgift wasted no time in demanding obedience to the higher powers. Only a few weeks after his election, Whitgift, with the queen's approval, promulgated "divers articles touching preachers and other orders for the Church" to which all clergy must subscribe, else they would not be allowed to continue any churchly functions. A new Court of High Commission was established to enforce clerical conformity to twenty-four articles, which were a set of interrogatories aimed at Puritans. Not only was the content of some of the articles offensive to Puritan beliefs, but the interrogatories had to be answered with a kind of oath, *ex officio mero,* which had the effect of forcing one to incriminate oneself. The sticking point for Puritans was the article proclaiming that the Book of Common Prayer "containeth nothing in it contrary to the word of God" and that the form prescribed in the book, and no other, was to be used in public prayer and in the administration of the sacraments.[51]

Whitgift's bold move was sure to trouble even the moderate reformers who had conscientious qualms about some of the demands of the Prayer Book. About forty-three Essex ministers were suspended for noncompliance, and the Dedham conference initiated a new strategy, a survey of the ministry in the county. The survey, compiled in mid-1584, showed that many of the beneficed clergy in the county were incompetent, so that, with many of the godly preachers being unable to assent conscientiously to all of the practices in the Prayer Book, the people were bereft of their best ministers. The Privy Council was convinced by the argument that implied that the social order was in jeopardy, and a compromise was arranged. In the face of all the petitions and protests, Whitgift backed down, demanding that subscription to all the articles be given only by new ministers rather than by all the clergy. All of the members of the Dedham conference subscribed, though some of them were in trouble

50. Bindoff, *Tudor England,* 227–28, 242–43; Collinson, *Puritan Movement,* 188–89.
51. Collinson, *Puritan Movement,* 244–46, 266–67.

again when John Aylmer, bishop of London, visited in 1586 and suspended forty ministers, most for failing to wear the surplice.[52]
The battle was taken up in the Parliament that met in late 1586, when
a radical Presbyterian bill, along with a revised edition of the Geneva
Prayer Book, was presented to the House of Commons. The strategy was
developed by the London Presbyterians, but not all reformers were in
favor. Dr. Chapman, leader of the Dedham conference, thought that the
demands for all or nothing were too extreme, and the Dedham group
rejected the Genevan Book of Discipline, even though they were in
agreement with much of it. Although most of the House was sympathetic
to a moderate Puritanism, the proposals put forth by the Presbyterians
were too radical, and the bill was defeated in 1587. However, the events
at the end of 1588 presaged the end of the Elizabethan Puritan movement. The political base of Puritanism began to crumble when one of the
defenders of Puritans, the earl of Leicester, died in September. In late
1588 some satirical tracts that caustically ridiculed the bishops and were
supposedly written by Martin Marprelate appeared. The investigation of
the tracts set off a search for the actual authors, which uncovered evidence leading to the prosecutions of some of the principal Presbyterian
ministers and the imprisonment of Thomas Cartwright. The classical
organization was broken up, and Puritanism, as an organized movement,
declined until its revitalization under the Stuarts.[53]
When the Parliament of 1592–93 met, James Morice, Colchester's MP
and town clerk, valiantly tried to denounce Whitgift's articles by charging that the oath required of the clergy was in violation of the common
law and was infringing on the liberties of the queen's subjects. For his
efforts, Morice was imprisoned, Whitgift having persuaded Elizabeth
that Morice was trying to institute the kind of church governance that
Scotland had. Whitgift was so much in control that an act of the House
of Commons was directed against Protestant nonconformists in much the
same way that the earlier laws had been directed against the Catholic
recusants. According to the preamble of the fierce new act, it was
intended to prevent the "perils as might . . . . grow by the wicked prac-

---

52. Collinson, *Puritan Movement,* 263–65, 271–72, 280–81; Hunt, *Puritan Moment,*
97–99; Davids, *Annals,* 76–77; Cross, *Church and People,* 148. Many parishes in England
were eventually surveyed, and those surveys became the basis of presentations in the Parliament of 1586–87.

53. Collinson, *Puritan Movement,* 303, 315, 319–20, 386–87, 391–96, 437.

tices of seditious sectaries and disloyal persons." Anyone who refused to
come to church for a month or who was "present at any assemblies, conventicles, or meetings, under color of . . . exercise of religion" would be
imprisoned without bail until that person conformed; refusal to conform
resulted in exile or death. Two separatist leaders who had been arrested
in 1587, Henry Barrow and John Greenwood, were finally executed in
1593, and following them to the scaffold was one of the presumed perpetrators of the Marprelate tracts, John Penry.[54] The triumph of the con-
formists in the Church of England was complete.

The clergy and people of Colchester could not escape the force of the
religious events swirling around them. To get a picture of the effect of
Puritan beliefs in Colchester, three areas that were of varying consequence to the clergy, the people, and the town leaders will now be examined. First, affecting only the clergy and the institutional church was the
Puritan dilemma over how much jurisdiction the church courts had over
godly ministers; second, the parish clergy and many of the parishioners
were exercised over the usage of the Book of Common Prayer, especially
in its prescriptions to wear the surplice and to use certain procedures in
baptism; third, the radical belief in the Presbyterian system of church
governance held by the town preacher resulted in his suspension, to the
dismay of the town leaders, who worked diligently to alter the bishop's
ruling.

Jurisdiction of the Church Courts

One of the topics taken up by the Dedham conference was the matter of
how far the godly minister should submit to the summonses of the
archidiaconal court, to which the parish ministers were subject. Dis-
mayed that the ecclesiastical courts had not been reformed, the reformers
believed that the power of the courts should be curtailed and distributed
to the pastors in their congregations, to assemblies of preachers, and to
bishops acting in conjunction with ministers and magistrates. They
thought that the church courts had failed miserably in the essential task
of true godly discipline, but the more important point in their minds was
that the bishop and his archdeacons had usurped the disciplinary role,

---

54. Hunt, *Puritan Moment,* 105; Davids, *Annals,* 86–87; Collinson, *Puritan Movement,*
428, 431.

which properly belonged to the officers of the local church, the pastor and elders.[55] The Dedham group of ministers discussed for a whole year the desired reformation of the local ecclesiastical court system. They believed that the parish clergy should not be at the beck and call of the inferior court judges, and they suggested that discipline start in the local congregations and only be moved into the church court to correct obstinate offenders who had refused to submit. They wanted to revive an old, disused practice of the English church that would have the effect of changing the practice of visitations to a synod of ministers. The effect of their suggested reforms, as historian Jay Anglin has noted, would have been to reverse the roles of the clergy and the inferior court judges, so that the clergy had the primary role. The proposals were submitted to Archdeacon Withers in the form of a petition in early September, 1584. The Dedham conference had started working on the proposed church court reforms before Whitgift's ascension to the archbishopric, but by the time the document was finished, the issue of subscribing to the Prayer Book was uppermost, and reform of the church courts gave way to more pressing matters. Even so, the church courts were still a target. In their petition to the Privy Council in 1584, the Puritans struck at the ecclesiastical court system when they charged that the suspensions and excommunications levied against them by inferior judges were illegal, since those judges had failed to meet the proper qualifications of office, especially a doctor of laws degree. At bottom, though, was the vexed question of whether Scripture taught that the inferior judge had the authority to impose discipline on the "godly learned minister" who, according to his interpretation of Scripture, was not subject to that kind of hierarchical supervision.[56]

The question of the authority of the church courts revealed the strong Puritan leanings of one Colchester clergyman, Robert Lewis, who, as a member of the Dedham conference, had helped draw up the proposals for reform. Lewis, vicar of St. Peter's, obviously felt strongly on the matter; in several instances, he refused to obey the summonses of the archidiaconal court, until finally he was suspended for contempt of court. Both

---

55. Collinson, *Puritan Movement*, 189, 346. For the relationship between the archdeaconry court and the clergy within its jurisdiction, see Anglin, "Essex Puritan Movement," 180–83. For reforms of the ecclesiastical courts suggested by the Puritans at the Hampton Court Conference, see Collinson, *Puritan Movement*, 457.

56. Anglin, "Essex Puritan Movement," 184–85; Collinson, *Puritan Movement*, 271; Byford, "Religious Change," 390.

the offense of contempt of court and the penalty of suspension for that offense were rare. In January, 1588, the archdeaconry records noted that Lewis had already been suspended by the bishop of London for three quarters of a year; a year later he moved to Suffolk, probably deciding that the diocese of London was too incompatible with his own views. Lewis, along with several other Colchester clerics, had suffered lesser penalties for Prayer Book violations, but Lewis was the only one who was willing to go so far with his beliefs about the church court's lack of authority over him. Two years earlier, Lewis had represented the Dedham conference at a Cambridge meeting where a discussion centered around the practical question of what ministers should do if they had to choose between conformity and the loss of their income.[57] Lewis apparently made his decision; he was either very stubborn or a man of high principle.

Use of the Prayer Book

The second issue for examining Puritanism in Colchester, the use of the Prayer Book, was the most important at the local level, for it was a way for the clergyman to make known his belief so that it was obvious to all parishioners. Offenses related to the Prayer Book found their way into the records far more than any other issue of the 1580s and are a help in determining the beliefs of the people, as well as of the clergy. The use of the vestments prescribed by the Prayer Book had been a devisive issue starting back in the 1560s, but it had gradually died down, and the issue was not pressed again until Whitgift's insistence on the clergy's total conformity to the Book of Common Prayer. One of the first to be suspended was doctrinaire Robert Lewis, the previously mentioned vicar of St. Peter's who was so thoroughly committed to Puritan principles. Carrying out Archbishop Whitgift's demand for diligent enforcement was John Aylmer, the bishop of London, and on Aylmer's triennial visitation to his London diocese, held at the end of 1583 shortly after Whitgift's articles were promulgated, at least forty-three Essex ministers were suspended for their refusal to comply. Twenty-seven ministers and supporters, among them Thomas Upcher, who had been the minister at St. Leonard's until 1582, wrote to the Privy Council, appealing to the council as the "only sanctuary next to Her Majesty which we have," and they noted

---

57. Anglin, "Essex Puritan Movement," 175, 198; ERO D/ACA14/290; Emmison, *Morals*, 173; Collinson, *Puritan Movement*, 321.

their scruples against accepting the Prayer Book as being totally in accord with the Word of God. The survey of ministers in Essex, first compiled by the Dedham conference in the summer of 1584, was initiated to give the secular arm some ammunition to use against the church hierarchy. The emphasis was on the number of clergy who could not preach, who lived scandalous lives, or who did not serve their cures adequately because they either did not live in the parish or held more than one cure. In addition, the "painful and careful preachers and ministers . . . who have been sundry times molested and vexed" were listed, to emphasize that the few diligent, learned clergy were the very ones being hampered by the church hierarchy. As the Privy Council noted when they sent the survey to Archbishop Whitgift and Bishop Aylmer, the church in the county of Essex was in "lamentable estate."[58]

The list of Colchester ministers included in the survey (given in appendix 8) was later amended for the 1586–87 Parliament, thus resulting, it would seem, in the addition of two names, Cock and Holmes, who would not have been on the original list, since they entered their curacies in 1585. The list, therefore, gives a good view of the Colchester clergy in the mid-1580s, as it was seen by the Puritan compilers. All twelve of the Colchester clergymen were on the list, but the classification of certain men needs explanation. One might assume that none of the "ignorant and unpreaching ministers" had Puritan sympathies, but that was not true of Gerrard Shelbury, listed as parson of St. Nicholas, who also served the curacy at Greenstead from 1580 to 1585. Shelbury was the first to be charged in the Colchester archdeaconry court for not saying service "according to the Queen Majesty's Laws," thus putting him on the side of the Puritans. Shelbury's case was unique. A native of Colchester, Shelbury's father, Richard, was an immigrant from Gelderland, who prospered enough in Colchester as a haberdasher so that his widow, Gerrard's mother, remarried twice, both times to aldermen of the town. Gerrard became a haberdasher, married the daughter of an alderman, and served on the common council until 1577, when he apparently became a clergyman. By 1579 he was listed as a "clerk" in the borough records. Perhaps the fact that in 1568 his daughter, Priscilla, had married George Withers, archdeacon of Colchester, had something to do with Shelbury's elevation to the clergy, even though he was unlearned.[59] Shel-

58. Davids, *Annals,* 77–79, 98–114; Hunt, *Puritan Moment,* 97.
59. ERO D/ACA11, f. 11; *OB,* 150; ERO D/ABW31/63; T/R108/2; CR119/13; CR141/21; *Boyd's Marriage Index, Essex.* The second and third husbands of Gerrard's mother were Aldermen Thomas Reve and Ralph Fynche.

bury's lack of formal learning was a grave hindrance with anyone who valued the Puritan emphasis on learning and preaching; in 1585 it was reported that the parishioners of the urban St. Nicholas's parish were not coming diligently to church and, openly stating that they would not come "because of the simplicity of our minister," were finding instruction elsewhere. In the same year, Shelbury's other parish, rural Greenstead, which possibly had Catholic sympathies, charged that the divine service had not been "orderly" for five weeks and that Shelbury was "unable to deliver wholesome doctrine." However, Shelbury was examined in 1586 by an episcopal commission, which included the learned George Northey and Robert Lewis, and his knowledge of Scripture was found to be sufficient.[60]

In the same survey, two men listed as "double beneficed," Lowe and Holmes, who were not named elsewhere in the survey, revealed their proclivities toward conformity or reform by their stands on the surplice issue. Thomas Lowe, appointed as rector of St. Leonard's Church in 1582, was listed in a will of that year as being one of the preachers of Colchester, and he was initially a member of the Dedham conference, although he soon pulled out, apparently not having a stomach for controversy. He must have readily subscribed to Whitgift's articles, but his backsliding into conformity did not make him popular with the Puritan compilers of the survey, since, though he was a licensed preacher, he was not listed among the "painful and careful preachers . . . who have been . . . vexed." The makers of the survey did not include a category for conforming preachers like Lowe, since conformity hardly promoted their point of view, but they were probably happy to list him among the pluralists.[61] Lowe was unpopular with some of the parishioners at St. Leonard's. At the height of the tension over Whitgift's articles, Anna Lytlewood, possibly the wife of churchwarden Richard Lytlewood, "violently and without cause" (according to the archdeaconry court record) ripped the stole in St. Leonard's Church in 1584. The next year, another parishioner, John Sharp, ridiculed the minister for wearing the surplice, crying "that the fool had gotten on his fool's coat."[62] It is not surprising that "hot gospellers" were found at St. Leonard's, where radical reformer Thomas Upcher had preached for several years until he left for Fordham

---

60. ERO D/ACA14/50, 87; Guildhall MS 9537/6, f. 177.

61. In the will of William Markaunt, PRO 12 Rowe, Lowe was listed as preacher along with Northey, "our general preacher and pastor of our congregation"; Lewis was listed at St. Peter's, Searles at Lexden. See Smith, *Ecclesiastical History,* 12.

62. ERO D/ACA11/53; Collinson, *Puritan Movement,* 92.

in 1582. Something certainly stirred up parishioner Alice Allison, who, according to the wardens' report in 1587, publicly "uttered many slanderous speeches against our minister, Master Lowe."[63]

A contrast to the backtracking of Thomas Lowe was the new rector of St. James's Church and Greenstead, Robert Holmes, also listed as one of the "double beneficed." Holmes had not been around in the early phases of the controversy over subscribing to Whitgift's articles, but a new official in the archdeaconry court, Thomas Taylor, began a campaign in 1587 against Puritan views in the archdeaconry of Colchester. Until then the court had been fairly lenient toward Puritans. Holmes was cited for slack administration of Communion, for not catechizing the youth, and for absence from the archidiaconal court, all of which could conceivably be attributed to laziness; however, a public statement made in 1588 placed him firmly in the Puritan camp. During a service at St. James's, Holmes declared, "The surplice is a superstitious thing from the pope and it is pity the same is suffered in the church to the hurt of divers good men's consciences."[64]

The "painful preachers" listed in the survey of the mid-1580s were threatened at that time because of their violations of the Prayer Book, and the archidiaconal campaign against Puritanism in the late 1580s also touched most of them, again over failure to conform to the Prayer Book. Robert Searles of Lexden escaped the threatened deprivation in 1584 and seems to have conformed afterward, but the unyielding Lewis, in April, 1587, was not wearing the surplice or saying "Divine Service on the Holy Days as he is tried and bounden by the laws of the realm." In the same period, Lewis was refusing the summonses of the ecclesiastical court, for which he was eventually suspended.[65]

Cut in the persistent mold of Lewis was Thomas Knevett, who was new to the roster of Colchester preachers. So eager was he to preach that he did so shortly after his arrival to the rectory of his new church in Mile End, even though he was not licensed to do so. He held a master's degree from Jesus College, Cambridge, so obtaining a license was probably fairly certain, but going ahead and preaching was an unwise move, particularly with the forthcoming bishop's visitation. For Knevett it was the

---

63. ERO D/ACA14/225.

64. Anglin, "Essex Puritan Movement," 196–97; ERO D/ACA14/167, 200, 291; CR150/32; see also Guildhall MS 9537/7, f. 40v.

65. Davids, *Annals*, 113; ERO D/ACA14/135, 142.

characteristic beginning of a long career in Colchester, which was marked by zeal for preaching and Puritan principles, but with sometimes questionable wisdom. The archdeacon's official often charged him with failing to hold services on holy days, and he once alleged that Knevett "marryeth not with the ring, signeth not the cross, weareth not the surplice." No one was likely to mistake Knevett as a conformist.[66]

Another new clergyman in the borough, William Cock, was, like Knevett, appointed by the Protestant Sir Thomas Lucas, and was to have a long career in Colchester. While serving briefly as a young curate at St. James's Church, Cock was faulted for not instructing the children in the catechism, but the court noted that "he doth make exposition of some part of the Scriptures every Sunday." His friendship with preacher Thomas Upcher, which later resulted in Cock's being the recipient of Upcher's "best gown" after Upcher and his wife died, was further proof of Cock's reformist tendencies, and Cock, like the other reformers, fell under the disapproval of Official Taylor in 1587. Cock, though, seemed to be much less tendentious than Upcher, Lewis, and Knevett. After serving the church of St. Giles for thirty-four years, Cock died in 1619, and his will showed him to be a gentle, loving family man.[67] The wearing of the surplice during Communion had become a hot issue again, thanks to the uncompromising stand taken by Archbishop Whitgift. To the "painful and careful preachers," such matters as wearing the surplice, using the ring in the marriage ceremony, and making the sign of the cross in baptism were not simply matters of preference but were unlawful and thus could not be compromised.

Such high-mindedness did not last. Some of the Essex Puritans left the diocese because of their refusal to wear the surplice, but most seem to have quietly made concessions or found a way around the problem. Some of the neglected parish churches could argue that they had no surplice or that, as was reported about St. Runwald's, "The surplice is so scant that the minister cannot wear it."[68] On the whole, the archidiaconal court was not too hard on the Puritans, but one minister, Robert Holmes, had to submit officially, probably because of his public outspokenness. In March, 1589, it was reported that Holmes had not worn the surplice for

66. Davids, *Annals,* 111; Venn and Venn, *Alumni,* pt. 1, vol. 3; ERO D/ACA14/216, 227.

67. ERO D/ACA10/157; PRO 46 Kidd; ERO D/ACA14/189; ERO D/ACW8/245.

68. Davis, "Colchester," 86; ERO D/ACA24/32.

the past year, and the official demanded that he bring certification of compliance to the next court. The report in May was that Holmes "weareth the surplice." Perhaps it was more than mere coincidence that the last meeting of the Dedham conference was held in the following month.[69] The reformist movement, at least for the time being, was waning, though it was certainly not dead.

Belief in the Presbyterian System of Church Governance

Town preacher George Northey was not immune from Official Taylor's campaign against Puritans in the late 1580s for violations of the Prayer Book. As the record noted, Northey was cited "for not fulfilling the bishop's injunctions in not saying divine service and for not ministering the sacraments with the surplice." Northey's unique case needs to be examined. According to the survey of ministers presented to the Privy Council (see appendix 8), Northey was among the "painful and careful preachers . . . who have been sundry times molested and vexed," but Northey, unlike the others, had been suspended from preaching even before Whitgift's articles were promulgated at the end of October, 1583. On October 8 the bailiffs, William Turner and Robert Byrde, were already busy petitioning Sir Thomas Heneage, the lord treasurer, for help in obtaining Northey's reprieve from his suspension; two days later the bishop replied to Heneage, explaining that the articles from the new archbishop were forthcoming. Aylmer wrote that Northey should be prepared not only to subscribe to the articles but especially to agree to two things: to add to his preaching the administration of the sacraments and the saying of the service according to the Book of Common Prayer, and to assent to "the ministry of England and the lawful calling of bishops allowed by statute."[70] Several months later a letter from the former Colchester town preacher, William Cole of Corpus Christi College in Oxford, provided further insight into the reason behind Northey's suspension. Cole, at the request of the bailiffs, had visited his friend Bishop Aylmer but had not succeeded in changing Aylmer's mind. As Cole reported, "His [Aylmer's] answer was that he put Mr. Northey to silence, not for sub-

---

69. Anglin, "Essex Puritan Movement," 179, 196–97; ERO D/ACA17/163, 190; Hunt, *Puritan Moment*, 102.

70. Anglin, "Essex Puritan Movement," 196; D/Y2/6, pp. 81, 82, and see also 99; Collinson, *Puritan Movement*, 246.

scribing to the articles, but for affirming in his presence that there was no ministry in England."[71]

Northey's belief in the pastor-and-elders system of governance, which made him boldly but unwisely deny the episcopal system in front of the bishop, was reason enough for Aylmer to stop Northey's Presbyterian tongue. Even former Genevan Cole was "verily persuaded" that Northey's "opinion is very dangerous to the estate of the whole realm." To the established authority, nonconformity was hazardous; as Sir Thomas Heneage noted, "If Master Northey will not frame himself to be of one mind with the Church of England . . . I can have no reason to speak for him." Bishop Aylmer maintained that "the unity of the church must be sought of us all."[72] In November, 1583, after Whitgift's articles had appeared, Bishop Aylmer promised the bailiffs that he would consider allowing Northey to preach again if he would subscribe to the articles, and Aylmer testily explained, "[If Northey] for every small matter and upon every light occasion . . . can be content to single himself from the whole body of the church . . . then I may not yield to him nor you, in the violating of such laws." But subscription to the articles was not such a small matter to either Northey or the bailiffs. When the bishop suggested that the bailiffs replace Northey with "a grave learned man, one Master Stearne," he also belittled what the bailiffs had perceived to be the needs of the town. Aylmer noted, "And for my part I do think you have not such want of teaching among you, considering that you have Master Upcher and other great preachers among you."[73] Even Puritan radical Thomas Upcher had attained respectability in comparison to Northey and his antibishop views, but Upcher, having removed to Fordham, no longer had a pulpit in Colchester. The bailiffs had earlier explained that by Northey's "silence, our whole town is in great distress, having in the same but one minister left that is able to preach [Robert Lewis], so as the tenth part of our town have no instruction." They also argued that it would be foolish "to leave a kind man whom we know and to take another untried whom we know not." Furthermore, any man who would be so disloyal to the godly ministry as to take Northey's job under such circumstances would hardly be the kind of man that Colchester would want.[74]

---

71. D/Y2/6, p. 107.

72. D/Y2/4, p. 153; D/Y2/6, pp. 82, 107.

73. D/Y2/6, p. 91. Master Stearne was probably John Sterne, who was appointed suffragan bishop of Colchester in 1592.

74. D/Y2/6, pp. 81, 85.

In their numerous appeals on Northey's behalf, the bailiffs wisely did not touch the issue of church governance. As late as October 20, 1583, they did not know why Northey had been suspended, and earlier they had argued that choosing a new man might give the appearance of questioning "the truth preached before." Shortly after, on October 24, Heneage enlightened the bailiffs, and in December they explained to Ambrose Dudley, the earl of Warwick, that the bishop wanted Northey to "subscribe that the institution of the bishops and ministers in England is according to the Word of God which he [Northey] is loath to do." The bailiffs frequently emphasized Northey's influence; he has "done much good, both by his doctrine and life." They noted that Northey was "godly, learned, and in life unreproachable" and that he was a preacher "of the sincere Word of God" and gave "godly instruction." Moreover, he had preached against the papists from time to time, and his silencing was a matter for "great rejoicing to the Enemy of the Truth and state of this land (the papists we mean)." In contrast, Northey's silencing was "a great grief to the true professors of the gospel of Christ in this town."[75]

Another letter from eleven burgesses of the town to the town leaders certainly suggests that Northey was highly esteemed. Unfortunately, the top and a side of the letter are torn off, so the date and the name of the addressees are missing, but the letter urged a vigorous support of Northey by "your worships" and was apparently written to the bailiffs and aldermen soon after Northey was suspended. Five men from each of the two councils of the town and one other man signed the letter, which urged the town leaders to be courageous and not to "neglect the glory of God." Using the argument that "if good reason allowed you to choose him, you have greater cause to hold him," they cited the example of the men of Corinth who so loved the apostle Paul that, if it had been possible, they would have pulled out their eyes and given them to him.[76] It could be argued that Northey's relatives were behind the letter, as the first signer of the letter was Northey's brother-in-law, prosperous shoemaker Winkin Grynerice; nevertheless, the support behind Northey was obviously strong among the top leaders of the town, especially in view of the continued diligent attempts by the bailiffs on Northey's behalf. Northey's preaching appealed to the leaders of the town, who had a solid personal regard for "our general preacher and pastor of our con-

75. D/Y2/6, pp. 81, 83, 85, 89, 99, 105; D/Y2/4, p. 121.
76. D/Y2/6, p. 135. The letter was written before February, 1585, the date of the death of the first signer, Wynkyn Grenerice, Northey's brother-in-law.

gregation," as William Markaunt put it. Northey was called a "loving friend" by Alderman Robert Lambert and "a loving brother in law" by clothier Griffin Ernesbie. Northey himself, in his will of 1593, mentioned several "loving friends," all of them educated gentry or leaders in the town, and he named three of those "trusty and well beloved brethren and friends" as supervisors of his will. According to a letter written to Archdeacon Withers, there was also harmony between Northey and the town ministers. Many people considered Northey to be a warm and loving person.[77]

Perhaps the strongest argument offered by the bailiffs for the restoration of their town preacher was their conviction, as they wrote to the earl of Leicester, that Northey's preaching "of the sincere Word of God" had a salutary influence on the "good government of the people." Northey was a popular preacher; Robert Lewis of St. Peter's complained that his audience was drawn away by Northey's preaching, even when Lewis preached on the same text. The curate at St. Botolph's, William Kyrby, said there was no point in his preaching quarterly sermons or even in his saying the litany on Wednesdays and Fridays, because the people were all going to Northey's common sermons. When William Peryman and his wife were cited in the archdeaconry court for not attending their Greenstead parish church regularly and for refusing to pay toward the making of the surplice, it was noted that they sometimes went to hear Master Northey preach. With Northey's preaching being so popular, after he was suspended the bailiffs argued to Sir Thomas Heneage that Northey's sermons had contributed to orderliness in the town: without godly instruction, "we perceive the people not so well ordered as before they were."[78]

Northey was eventually restored to his pulpit in Colchester. Unfortunately, the details of the lifting of his suspension are lost, but the mid-1580s survey notes that Northey was suspended "for the space of a whole year," so he was probably restored in late 1584. Giving a clue as to the compromise that must have been worked out was the later archidiaconal charge against Northey "for not fulfilling the bishop's injunctions in not saying divine service and for not ministering the sacraments with the surplice."[79] Northey seems to have been restored on the condition

77. PRO 69 Harrington; PRO 29 Sainberbe; ERO D/ACW3/14; D/Y2/4, p. 117.

78. D/Y2/4, p. 121; Collinson, *Puritan Movement*, 382; Byford, "Religious Change," 324; ERO D/ACA14/136; D/Y2/6, p. 81.

79. Anglin, "Essex Puritan Movement," 196; see also Guildhall MS 9537/7, f. 41.

that he not administer Communion, and he was no doubt also prohibited against speaking in favor of the Presbyterian system of governance.

Northey's ministry in Colchester and the reaction to his silencing show the importance attached to the preaching of the Word in Colchester; to the town leaders always on the side of order, preaching instilled moral and religious principles that were good for one's soul and for society. Though reformist preaching offered benefit both to the individual and to the community as a whole, dangers were attached. Greater responsibility accrued to the individual, especially if he was a learned cleric; Robert Lewis thought he could not yield to the summonses of the archidiaconal court or wear the surplice, and he finally left Essex for less restrictive pastures. George Northey was convinced that the episcopal system was contrary to the Word of God, but in balancing the conflict between his beliefs and the needs of society, Northey must have finally decided that keeping quiet about his views was preferable to no ministry at all. A complex balancing act was required of those ministers committed to the reform of both church and society. The ministers were hardly the only ones affected, however, and the role of the magistrates is further examined in chapter 12.

12

At the Height of Godly Governance

Puritanism, unlike Catholic dissent, was not dependent for leadership either on the clergy or on the gentry. The emphasis of the Calvinist reformers on the collaboration of the ministry and the magistrates was one of the features that made Puritanism attractive to merchants, lawyers, and small landholders. When lawyer William Markaunt drew up his own will in 1582, he left a sizable amount to the poor of Colchester, requesting that the bailiffs and aldermen meet with the "godly learned preachers" of the town to "settle the bestowal" of the money.[1] The cooperation of sacred and secular authorities was evident in 1586 when, just a week after an episcopal commission certified that Thomas Holland, curate of St. Botolph's Church, was a "rank papist," the town JPs cited Holland with the vague charge of being a barrator (an instigator of disputes) and a disturber of the peace.[2] Many of the urban authorities did not need any urging to take an active lead in godly matters, and much of the strength of Puritanism was in lay participation and leadership. In Colchester, while they continued to care for the poor, to encourage good moral behavior, and to support the town preacher, the leaders began a new effort, the reestablishment of the town's grammar school. In the early years of George Northey's ministry, the town leaders were at the apex of their attempts to be godly magistrates in the Calvinistic mode. Working in conjunction with a congenial and talented minister, the civic officials were enjoying the fruits of their labors in the creation of the grammar school, but, ironically, circumstances at the time initiated a subtle tilt away from the extreme Calvinistic attitude toward local governance. Political developments undermined the experiment in godly governance, but both the worthy and the disruptive effects of the measures instituted would outlast the idealism that brought them about.

---

1. PRO 12 Rowe; Collinson, *Puritan Movement*, 93–94.
2. Guildhall MS 9537/6, f. 177; CR148/38d.

The Magistracy—Caring for the Poor

In the repeated crises of dearth and epidemic in the 1570s and 1580s, which reached their peak in the 1590s, the greatest challenge for the town leaders was how to care for the swelling numbers of the poor and destitute. The 1580s saw an increasing determination to prohibit any new poor from taking up residence in the borough: in 1580 the town assembly ordered that "no more strangers" were to inhabit the town without consent of the bailiffs and aldermen, as Colchester already had "more than the town can sustain." In 1582 a poor man named Bannester, who had lately "wandered to the town" and was dwelling with his wife and child in the house of a glazier, was ordered to "quit the town" or pay a fine of 20s., as he did not have a license from the bailiffs. Not even the clergy were immune from being taken to task for housing paupers; the parson of St. Leonard's, Thomas Lowe, was told to pay a penalty or remove from his house a man named Newman, who was deemed "likely to become a charge" to the parish. One Marcock was ordered to leave, being a poor man with many children who was considered "likely to burden the parish." The authorities were not completely heartless, however, as the people were usually given a grace period of several weeks before they had to depart, with Marcock and his many children being given five months.[3] The preceding cases were recorded in the records from the lawhundreds and sessions of the peace in the 1580s, and unfortunately such records are missing from the 1590s. Undoubtedly such problems continued, although formal attempts were made to stop the problem. As far back as 1388, Parliament had attempted to control migration of the poor by stipulating that they were to remain in the parish of their birth unless they already had work elsewhere. In 1591 the Colchester assembly ordered the constables to make a survey of the town to identify the poor who had not been born in the town and who had lived there less than three years, and those people were to be returned to their place of birth or to a place where they had resided for three years. Furthermore, no one was to receive any poor into the town unless a £20 bond with two sureties was posted, promising that those poor would not "become chargeable to the town."[4]

---

3. D/B5 Gb1, f. 20; CR143/4d; CR147/34d; CR148/39. See also CR148/38d; CR149/38d; CR150/31, 31d, 32d.
4. E. M. Leonard, *The Early History of English Poor Relief* (1900; reprint, London: Frank Cass, 1965), 4–5; D/B5 Gb1, f. 78v.

Keeping out additional poor people did not solve the problem of the poor who were already inhabiting the town, and the collections for the poor continued—both collections at the parish level and those taken after the Sunday sermons. Detailed listings for each parish had begun in 1572 and included the names of the two collectors and (usually) two overseers for each parish, as well as a list of the 102 poor people receiving relief and the 300 persons paying the poor rate.[5] In the 1580s a book began to be used solely for the purpose of recording the compulsory parish contributions.[6] Occasionally, the lawhundred jurors would present a reluctant giver; for example, Henry Herning did "not give to the poor as he ought," so he was ordered to give henceforth.[7]

The system for collecting contributions for the poor after the Sunday sermons by the town preacher had become more complex by late 1578, probably a result of the increased needs of the poor by that time. Rather than two collectors appointed for the year who reported directly to the bailiffs, which had been the case in 1575, the new system appointed two new men to collect money for the poor at the door of the church for four Sundays in a row. Their orders were to "receive and take the charity and benevolence of well disposed persons resorting from the sermon for the relief of the poor in this town," after which they were immediately to take the money to the two men appointed as distributors for the year. At the end of the month, the collectors were to submit a record of each week's receipts, and the orders to the collectors concluded by warning, "And hereof fail ye not." Records show that collections after sermons continued at least through the 1590s.[8]

The money from the collections for the poor in the parish and at the sermons was not enough to combat the ever increasing numbers and needs of the poor. Additional monies began to be allocated from fines, with the first fine, it seems, being connected with the new order in 1578 against selling on Sunday at the biggest fair of the year, the St. Denis Fair. Anyone caught selling was required to forfeit all his or her wares, with half of the proceeds going to help the poor and the other half going to the bailiffs and commonalty. The assistance to the poor, rather than being a

5. D/B5 R7, ff. 307–17; VCH Essex, 9:90–91.
6. ERO, Borough of Colchester, Contribution Book to the Poor (1581–82).
7. CR141/3d. See also CR141/2d; CR148/37.
8. D/B5 R7, f. 326; D/Y2/2, p. 42, and see also pp. 39, 42–59; D/Y2/7, p. 226. The back of the Contribution Book to the Poor also includes some of the records from the sermon collections in the 1590s.

planned response by the town leaders to the poverty around them, was probably an afterthought, inserted to make more palliative a law that defied the usual custom. By 1583, however, even the regular fines for poor quality of workmanship were beginning to include the poor as recipients of a portion of the proceeds. In that year, the inquiry into the proper tanning of leather resulted in fines equaling 17s., which was to be divided three ways, with the examiners of leather, the poor, and the bailiffs and commonalty each receiving a third.[9]

Even with all the voluntary and involuntary collections for the poor, the funds were still insufficient to care for the many poor children in the 1590s. The system that granted admission to the freedom of the town in return for the care of a poor child had begun in 1574 and continued through the 1570s, reaching a peak in 1578 and 1579, when a plague epidemic increased the number of poor orphans. Then the practice was discontinued until 1586, when food again became scarce, with dearth thus paving the way for death and more orphans. In December, a shoemaker from Sussex was admitted to the liberties of the town on the condition that he educate and maintain Elizabeth Lome and thereby "exonerate the town of the charge."[10] Bread was again scarce in 1589, and another orphan case appeared in the borough records: Thomas Stone of Manningtree was admitted gratis, provided that he take care of the children of the deceased Nicholas Alden.[11] In 1591, the year that a petition went to Queen Elizabeth from the poor inhabitants of Colchester begging for redress against enclosures and foreigners taking their jobs, the next case concerning a poor child appeared, but this one was different in that weaver William Sellowes was admitted for taking ten-year-old John West, the son "of a poor man of the town," as apprentice for fourteen years.[12] In previous cases, either it had been noted that the children were orphans or the circumstances had suggested such, but this case was the first that expressly noted that the child's father, who was obviously too poor to provide for training, was alive. As economic distress, food shortage, and epidemics proliferated in the 1590s, so too did the cases providing for poor children in the borough court; twenty cases were recorded in the 1590s, with the peak years of 1593 and 1594 having nine of those

---

9. CR144/18d. See also CR147/14, 25; CR150/2.
10. Emmison, *Home*, 182; CR148/5d.
11. CR150/14, 21.
12. *CSPD*, 1591–94, p. 153; CR152/16.

cases.[13] The character of the cases also changed. Beginning in 1592, some of the men taking the poor apprentices seemingly were burgesses (as admission to the liberties of the borough was not mentioned), and some daughters of poor people were taken into the homes of craftsmen for a specified seven years of service. Showing unusual initiative was Joan Alden, "a poor child" and the daughter of the deceased Nicholas Alden. In 1594, Joan, who had five years earlier been put into the care of Thomas Stone, contracted herself for a seven-year apprenticeship with Frances Loper, "a stranger," that is, a foreigner.[14]

Various expediencies for the care of the poor were explored; an example was the unusual case of William Ware, who was admitted as a burgess on the condition that he maintain and keep his father and mother "with meat, drink, and all necessaries during their lives."[15] The town governors also continued to be alert to the possibilities of child-support payments from the fathers of illegitimate children, whenever paternity could be established. John Fassekin, "the reputed father" of a "bastard child" born of Susan Viccars, was ordered by the JPs to pay for the upkeep of his child, paying 12d. weekly to the parish collectors of the poor for seven years, followed by another five years of paying 8d. weekly.[16] Even begging was officially controlled. In June, 1591, the assembly ruled that no poor person was to beg in the town without a license from the officials, and licenses were to be given only to those too old and infirm to work. Those begging without a license would be punished by imprisonment in the moot hall and whipping or would be "otherwise punished."[17]

The town took measures to correct the more basic problem of unemployment. The same assembly which imposed a begging license was, first and foremost, wanting to aim at "setting the poor on work and avoiding of indolence in the town." They noted that the town had "many impo-

13. Of the twenty men taking children, eight were admitted to the freedom of the borough.

14. CR155/6. In 1607, Alderman Richard Symnell left £50 to the corporation, the profits of which were to provide annually for the "putting forth to service . . . of three poor children," at £1 each (PRO 71 Windebanck).

15. D/B5 Gb1, f. 138.

16. D/B5 Sb2/4, f. 76.

17. D/B5 Gb1, f. 76v. An undated document, probably from the early seventeenth century, said that if any children begged, they were to be taken to the house of correction (D/Y2/2, p. 60).

tent poor" and that they were "exceedingly pestered with idle persons," resulting in "thefts, pilfering, and other lewd and ill vices."[18] Though the leaders condemned the illicit behavior that was, in their eyes, a result of idleness, they were also beginning to realize that they had a responsibility to try to help the unemployed find work. A partial solution was at hand in 1590, in a gift of £100 from a widow of Markeshall, Dame Mary Judd, a native of Colchester whose husband had been the wealthy London merchant Sir Andrew Judd.[19]

The town leaders were accustomed to handling charitable legacies,[20] but Lady Judd's gift was different in that it was especially for "setting on work such poor persons inhabiting" Colchester. Wool, yarn, flax, or whatever was available was to be bought to provide spinning and weaving for the poor. Parliamentary legislation in 1576 had authorized justices of the peace to provide a stock of wool or other materials suitable for providing work for the poor so that they would have no excuse for being idle. There is no evidence that Colchester JPs had followed the 1576 legislation, but the Judd gift, made formal in an indenture in early 1591, provided the impetus needed; by June of that year the town had decided to use the money by giving £50 each to clothiers Thomas Ingram and Robert Steven, who were fast rising on the ladder of prominence in Colchester.[21] As the "workmasters," Ingram was to provide work—spinning, carding, combing, and braking (breaking flax or hemp)—for the poor of the Head and North Wards, and Steven was to do the same for the poor of the East and South Wards. In this context of providing work for the poor, the concurrent decisions were made to limit begging only to those "too old and infirm to work" and to rid the town of any poor who had not lived in Colchester at least three years. In addition, "for the better avoiding of the mischief of poor in this town (if it shall so please God)," it was ordered that the constables make a survey of the poor artificers and laborers who were able to work, and those unemployed

---

18. D/B5 Gb1, f. 76.

19. On Sir Andrew, see John Scott, "Tudor Adventurer," *British History Illustrated* 1 (1975): 56–63. Addison, *Essex Worthies,* 114, mistakenly says that Sir Andrew was of Colchester, but he was from Tunbridge, in Kent.

20. An example is the £104 given in 1566 by London merchant Sir Thomas White to be used for loans to clothiers (D/Y2/10, p. 35).

21. Prothero, *Statutes,* 72–74; D/B5 Gb1, ff. 71v, 76, 76v; D/Y2/10, p. 34. Ingram of St. Peter's was, in 1590–91, the town chamberlain and on the second council, and he rose to the aldermanic bench in 1594; Steven of St. James's was already a member of the first council but was not reelected in 1595, perhaps a victim of the apparent Haselwood and Byrd controversy discussed in chapter 13.

were then to be placed with masters, thus replacing the foreigners who had been working for those masters. Any master who refused was to forfeit 10s. to the use of the poor.[22] This order requiring masters to take poor laborers probably accounts for the sudden appearance in 1592, noted earlier, of small craftsmen burgesses beginning to take poor children as apprentices.[23] The Judd gift, then, had been an impetus for an organized, concerted effort, beginning in 1591, to deal with the problem of the poor.

The administration of the Judd gift can be followed. A year after the initial appointment of two workmasters, four were appointed in 1592, with only Thomas Ingram continuing from the year before. That system must have had its problems, as the next year another strategy was used: the £100 was to be lent to "honest young clothiers" to buy wool to "set the poor on work." Those who borrowed £20 had to employ six poor people, while those who borrowed £10 had to employ three. By 1599 the money was apparently being loaned at 10 percent interest, "at £10 in £100 per year," and several names were listed as borrowing from £5 to £20.[24]

Others followed Lady Judd's generous example of compassion for the poor, and the task of administering the funds established again fell to the bailiffs. In 1593 Alderman John Hunwick, the Merchant Adventurer, bequeathed £300 to the corporation, with the profits to be used by "the bailiffs and commonality" for the poor, though Hunwick did not specify whether the annual income from the money was to be given outright to the poor or used in putting them to work. Apparently the £300 was loaned out at 10 percent interest, as it seems that £30 was available annually. Every fifth year, the £30 profit was to be given to the officials of Ipswich, who would then distribute it to the poor of Ipswich, Maldon, and Sudbury.[25] More closely following Lady Judd was clothier Thomas Ingram, the man who had been workmaster for Judd's money for at least

---

22. D/B5 Gb1, ff. 76v, 78, 78v.

23. In such cases (beginning with CR154/1d, 3), the taking on of an apprentice was without the former trade-off of receiving admission to the freedom of the borough.

24. D/B5 Gb1, ff. 84v, 92, 156v. The formal accounting of Lady Judd's gift continued into the Stuart era; see D/B5 Gb2, ff. 49, 55v, 60, 67, 83.

25. PRO 45 Dixy; D/Y2/5, p. 67; D/B5 Gb2, f. 4. The accounts of the Hunwick legacy can be found in D/B5 Gb2, ff. 25v, 44v, 53v, 58v, 65, 72, 80v, 99. The old alderman and clothier Thomas Lawrence left £100 in 1594, but his legacy was of a more conventional kind, with the money to be distributed by his executors to the "old spinsters and breakers" who had worked for him (PRO 80 Dixy).

the first two years. Ingram had apparently flourished and had moved on to Coggeshall by 1602, when his gift to the people of Colchester, formalized by an indenture, was said to be given out of his "love and affection to the town where he long dwelt." Intimately acquainted with the Judd poor relief, Ingram set up a system that both helped young clothiers and provided work for the poor. His £100, controlled by the bailiffs and five principal parishioners of Ingram's former parish, St. Peter's, was to be loaned to five clothiers at the relatively low rate of 5 percent, with the stipulation that the clothiers were to secure enough wool for the poor of St. Peter's to spin or work. Furthermore, it was stipulated that the workers were to be paid "at the common price," which indicates that equitable wages had not always been forthcoming in these arrangements.[26] In 1613 the corporation, deciding that a workhouse was needed, used the funds from the Judd, Hunwick, and other legacies to establish it.[27]

Town leaders were quick to follow suggestions coming out of Parliament. The 1597–98 Parliament passed a new poor law that brought together former legislation but added little that was new, except that it did transfer the main responsibility to churchwardens. Town leaders were obviously aware of the legislation that was making its way through the parliamentary process, probably being informed by MP Richard Symnell, a native of Colchester and the longtime deputy town clerk,[28] and at the end of November, 1597, the assembly adopted some of the provisions of the new parliamentary poor law then under discussion, although poor relief continued under the auspices of the town leaders, rather than being placed under the churchwardens. The new parliamentary legislation ruled that all begging was illegal, unless one begged for food within one's own parish and by permission of its wardens and overseers, so the assembly provided for the appointment of an overseer to insure against begging and to inform the bailiffs of any newcomers in the town. A beadle was also appointed, and for the first time, the overseer and beadle were to be paid. A house was designated as the place where the poor could fetch their work, and the responsibility for setting the poor to work was given to the churchwardens, so they did acquire a new

---

26. D/Y2/10, p. 34. Thomas Cutler made Thomas Ingram, alderman of Coggeshall, the supervisor of his 1603 will (ERO D/ACW4/287).

27. Martin, *Story of Colchester*, 55; Davis, "Colchester," 81; *VCH Essex*, 9:96. In 1607 Alderman Richard Simnell gave £50 to be loaned to "four honest shoemakers," with the profits to go to the poor (PRO 71 Windebanck).

28. Prothero, *Statutes*, 96–103. Symnell was town clerk briefly, in 1596–97, but he was replaced by Robert Barker, his fellow MP in the 1597 Parliament.

job. The 1598 Poor Law was reenacted with only a few additions in 1601, and the 1601 law remained in place as the basis for all English poor relief until 1834.[29]

Colchester authorities, occasionally ahead of the nation in responding to the needs of the impoverished, were willing to experiment with creative methods for dealing with both long-term problems and emergencies. An example of addressing the latter was their reaction to the scarcity of food in November, 1594, after heavy summer rains had brought on an agricultural disaster. Under senior bailiff Robert Mott, who had so often found ways to bring peace and solve problems, the assembly decided that they themselves would lend money to buy corn for the poor, with the aldermen each loaning £20; first councillors, £10; and second councillors, £5. Six men were appointed to receive the corn from the ship and sell it to the poor. Furthermore, one baker from each ward was appointed to bake bread two days a week to be sold to the poor, with the bread being delivered by two men appointed in each ward. Of course, it was the duty of godly magistrates to look to the needs of the poor; nevertheless, such concern was praiseworthy. Although town authorities could be harsh toward the wandering poor or those perceived to be lazy or guilty of misconduct, there also seemed to be a genuine interest in the well-being of their own poor, such as that expressed by town leader Christopher Langley in his 1601 will, in which he left money to the "poor, old, lame and impotent persons" in his parish.[30] No doubt, some of the concern for the poor was economic, but also spurring it on were such ideals as that expressed in a sermon in the late 1580s: "That is a good commonwealth that looketh to every member in the commonwealth, and those men are worthy of riches that look daily to the feeding of their poor neighbours."[31] Puritans, moderate Protestants, Catholics, and separatists could all agree on that.

Godly Magistrates—Discipline

Matters of discipline continued to exercise both the town leaders and the ecclesiastical courts, but records of the Puritan Dedham conference show

29. Prothero, *Statutes,* 96–97, 99; D/B5 Gb1, ff. 133v, 134; Leonard, *Poor Relief,* 73–80.
30. PRO 15 Montague.
31. Quoted in Martin Seymour-Smith, ed., *The English Sermon, an Anthology,* 3 vols. (Cheadle, Cheshire: Carcanet Press, 1976), 1:153.

that in disciplinary matters, most members preferred the help of secular officials rather than the local church court. Indeed, the borough was as active as the church in correcting moral wrongdoing in the Elizabethan period.[32] Discipline was considered to be medicinal, necessary for the reforming of the soul to bring it to health. As the records of the town of Rye noted about a man who spread libels, "It is thought good that discipline be ministered . . . , that he may be reformed and may be brought to live under law and government." Colchester leaders were serious about promoting godly behavior, and a 1587 ordinance stipulated that those burgesses eligible to participate in elections would not include any who had "received punishment or [had] been convicted of adultery, fornication, drunkenness, theft, or as common swearers."[33]

In the Colchester borough courts, the intense concern with the regulation of conduct in the late 1570s continued and even increased in the early 1580s against idleness and vagrancy, playing illegal games and unruliness (see chapter 10, table 9), and illegal alehouses (see chapter 10, table 10). Monitoring of Sunday behavior also increased. Church attendance and working on Sunday had already received a fair amount of attention, but not until 1581 did the charges for unruliness and playing unlawful games on Sunday become frequent. For example, in January, 1582, eight men were presented at the lawhundred for playing ball on Sunday, and four months later four men were playing "stoolball," which somewhat resembled cricket, for which two men were fined 4d. and two were put in the stocks.[34] Along with a new use of the term *Sabbath*, new descriptive phrases also entered the court records. In 1582, for working on Sunday, barber John Payne was said to be a "profaner of the Lord's Day," and blacksmith Darbye was proclaimed to be in "profanation" of that day.[35]

Not only was the borough concerned with games on Sunday, but charges suddenly increased in 1581 against the playing of illegal games at any time. The dramatic upsurge came in the court leet, the thrice-yearly lawhundred, and one wonders if the preaching of the recently arrived George Northey had anything to do with the sudden concern of the

---

32. As shown by Mark Byford in "Religious Change," 374–82.
33. Anglin, "Essex Puritan Movement," 184n; Byford, "Religious Change," 359; Collinson, *Puritan Movement,* 40; Mayhew, *Tudor Rye,* 204; Davis, "Colchester," 125; BL, Stowe MS 836.
34. CR143/4; Emmison, "Tithes," 200.
35. See chapter 10 n. 22; CR143/4d; CR144/21.

jurors with games. The occasion on which one of the players of unlawful games, Gosse the barber, was charged by the jurors as being a "blasphemer of the name of God" was the first time those two charges were connected.[36]

Vigilance regarding the behavior of inhabitants continued in the 1590s. In 1598 an ordinance against the "multitude of alehouses" noted not only that alehouses had "been harborers of thieves, harlots, and other lewd persons" but also that "much beastliness have been in them committed by drunkenness and other abuses of the good creatures of God to the high displeasure of almighty God, great trouble, and distress of this ancient borough and utter undoing of many of the poor inhabitants." At the national level, an unusually large number of bills were introduced in Parliament for the regulation of alehouses between 1601 and 1606.[37] The strong language in the Colchester ordinance reflected the bleak conditions of the 1590s, when England was racked by bad weather and poor harvests, with the resultant starvation and poverty made more difficult by the increased population and difficulty in finding work. In the thinking of the time, it was incumbent on the town authorities to do all that they could to keep sin out of the town, lest God's "heavy hand of correction" bring greater miseries on them.[38]

Godly Magistrates—Preaching

The attention given to inhibiting drunkenness and the playing of illegal games increased partly because those habits were keeping people from attending church and hearing sermons. The town leaders were so convinced of the salutary benefits of preaching that they went to great lengths to try to effect the reinstatement of their town preacher, George Northey, who was suspended from preaching by the bishop in the autumn of 1583. The bailiffs made full use of every influential contact they had, writing letters of appeal to their recorder, Sir Francis Walsingham, and to Bishop John Aylmer, Sir Thomas Heneage, the earls of Leicester and Warwick, and their former town preacher, William Cole.

---

36. CR144/21. The new terms may have been simply a manifestation of the national trend indicated by the introduction of six bills against profanation of the Sabbath in Parliament between 1584 and 1601 as Sabbatarianism came to be one of the main emphases of urban Puritanism; see Slack, "Poverty," 8.

37. D/B5 Gb1, f. 149; Underdown, *Revel*, 48.

38. The quoted phrase was used to describe a plague epidemic in Rye, according to Mayhew, *Tudor Rye*, 200.

To add to the array of names, an agent, John Harrison, was also contacting Walsingham, Sir Thomas Gawdie, and Sir Thomas Lucas.[39] Such a spirited campaign was conducted at some risk to the bailiffs; Heneage became impatient, and the bishop became upset with them.[40] Nevertheless, the mission was accomplished, and Northey again began preaching, probably in late 1584.

It had become a mark of honor for a town to have its own preacher, so a measure of civic pride was probably involved in the decision to wage such a persistent battle for Northey. More than that, however, the preaching of "the sincere Word of God" promoted the "good government of the people." Around the time that Northey was reinstated, extra efforts were made in the borough courts to insure attendance at church; seven men were cited for absence from church for about half a year, "in great contempt of the Word of God." Others were charged with being drunk on Sundays during the time of assembly, "in great offense against God."[41] Such concern about attendance at divine services bespoke a pride in having worked so diligently to provide preaching for the people, as well as a confidence that preaching would bring God's blessings and favor to the town. Perhaps that kind of thinking led the leaders to make town preaching a part of the ceremonial ritual of the town. On November 1, 1585, the assembly decided that in addition to the regular weekly sermons, there would be a general sermon attended by bailiffs, aldermen, and council in their livery on seven special days of the year.[42] Along with the mixture of preaching and civic ceremonial, the choice of days was also characteristic of the intermix of the sacred and the secular. Three days (Christmas, Easter, and Whitsunday) were primarily religious; one (the anniversary of the ascension of Queen Elizabeth, November 17) was important in the life of the nation and the church; one (Midsummer Day) was a traditional, almost pagan holiday; and two were important in the civic life of the town, with Michaelmas being the beginning of the new borough year and St. Denis's Day being the most important day of the trading fair in Colchester. The town leaders were obviously proud of their town and their preacher. As someone wrote to the bailiffs and the assembly in 1591, "To be seated in a healthsome place where there is an

---

39. D/Y2/6, p. 95. For the letters of the bailiffs, see D/Y2/4, p. 121; D/Y2/6, pp. 81, 83, 85, 87, 89, 105, 135. See chapter 11 for a detailed account of Northey's suspension.

40. D/Y2/4, p. 153; D/Y2/6, p. 107.

41. Collinson, *Religion,* 171; D/Y2/4, p. 121; CR146/28, 29d.

42. D/B5 Gb1, f. 39v; D/Y2/10, p. 100.

ordinary public sanctified ministry is one special point, and not the least to be regarded."[43] Connecting preaching with town ceremonial had its unhealthy aspects, however, as that very connection further institutionalized the role of town preacher. The danger lay in the possible politicizing and weakening of that very gospel message that was supposed to bring health to the soul.

Godly Magistrates—Education

In addition to continuing the care for the poor, the discipline of wrongdoing, and the maintenance of preaching, the town leaders were eager to promote the godly civic commonwealth by reestablishing the town grammar school, which was on a shaky foundation. Schools teaching elementary skills were certainly to be found in Colchester—mention of them was occasionally made in the records of Tudor Colchester, as were vague references to schoolmasters[44]—but Colchester leaders were most interested in the grammar school, which taught Latin and was the beginning of a higher level of education. Puritans were great promoters of education; the goal was to produce a learned preaching ministry, but more than that, Calvinists who wanted the Presbyterian system of church governance desired a learned laity as well, for a classical education was thought to equip one for leadership within the family, the church, and society.[45] The motives of the town leaders for wanting a solidly founded grammar school in Colchester probably reflected both religious and secular concerns. As men attempting to be godly magistrates, they wanted to encourage the development of both learned ministers and laity, but a grammar school would also enhance the town's image and would provide a means of social and economic advancement for their sons. The process by which the renewal of the school was brought about is a helpful gauge of the delicate balance that had to be maintained by the town leaders between their desire to continue their free exercise of Calvinistic

---

43. Quoted in Collinson, *Religion*, 171.

44. CR122/3d; D/B5 Sb2/3, f. 25v; CR137/9d; ERO D/ABW23/222; PRO 35 Scott; CR160/16d. The archdeaconry court, which licensed schoolmasters, noted several schoolmasters in the later Tudor period, both licensed and unlicensed (ERO D/ACA17/71; ERO D/ACA21/285, 293, 326, 391, 460; ERO D/ACA24/94, 243, 308, 335; ERO D/ACV3/94–96). On such schools, see Cressy, *Literacy*, 34–36.

45. Collinson, "Elizabethan Church," 185; Gerald Strauss, "Lutheranism and Literacy: A Reassessment," in *Religion and Society in Early Modern Europe 1500–1800*, ed. Kaspar von Greyerz (London: George Allen and Unwin, 1984), 116–18.

town governance and the need to satisfy an increasingly restrictive church hierarchy, particularly in regard to Presbyterian ideas, such as those held by Northey.

A grammar school, under the patronage of the bishop of London, had existed in Colchester as early as the twelfth century in the parish of St. Mary-at-Wall, but in 1539 Henry VIII granted two of the richest chantries to the corporation for the founding of a grammar school, apparently to be located in the tenement called Westons, in the parish of All Saints, where Alderman Thomas Christmas had founded a school by his will of 1520. King Henry's grant thus gave control over the school to the corporation, rather than to the bishop of London. The school seemed to be successful; records show that it produced eleven scholars for two Cambridge colleges, St. John's and Gonville and Caius, between 1561 and 1583. The school's foundation was in jeopardy in 1578, however, when the right to the chantries was disputed, since the original requirements of Henry's grant had not been fully carried out. At that time, the borough leaders asked their new recorder, Sir Francis Walsingham, "to be a mean" to the queen for issuance of a new patent.[46]

Nothing came of the initial attempt to refound the grammar school, but on October 20, 1583, in the midst of the concern over the silencing of preacher George Northey, the bailiffs wrote to Walsingham. Lamenting "the want of godly instruction," the bailiffs asked for Walsingham's help in Northey's restoration and asked that Walsingham also "have in remembrance our old suit for our school and school lands." The following March, the bailiffs renewed their suit to Walsingham on behalf of Northey, and they again beseeched him "to have in remembrance our suit for our school lands."[47] The silencing of Northey had possibly made the bailiffs feel that putting the grammar school on a solid foundation was even more urgent. In May, Alderman John Pye was in London on business for the corporation, and he had a busy time of it, seeing Walsingham at Greenwich and then back in London at the Black Friars the next day. After talking to the earl of Leicester the following day, he reported that "the business concerning the school went forward very well."[48]

---

46. *VCH Essex*, 2:502 and 9:352–54; Martin, *Story of Colchester*, 31, 39, 44; Jay Pascal Anglin, *The Third University: A Survey of Schools and School Masters in the Elizabethan Diocese of London* (Norwood, Pa.: Norwood Editions, 1985), 24–25, 42, 150; PRO 28 Ayloffe.

47. D/Y2/6, pp. 87, 89.

48. D/Y2/9, p. 19.

On July 6, a new charter was issued by Queen Elizabeth that refounded the free grammar school and again gave the corporation the important right to appoint the schoolmaster. However, Bishop Aylmer was to be the visitor and overseer of the refounded school, and the bishop and the renowned Puritan educator Alexander Nowell were to draw up the statutes. Since the advent of the Reformation, the conviction had grown that schools were essential to the political and religious settlement, and Queen Mary, realizing the validity of that idea, instituted a policy of episcopal oversight of schools whenever possible. Queen Elizabeth encouraged the practice, so letting Bishop Aylmer have the oversight of the Colchester school may have been a condition for getting the charter for the new foundation. Still, it was something of a conciliation to the bishop of London and, as such, may have been part of the compromise package that also restored George Northey to his pulpit. In August the corporation purchased Westons, the schoolhouse on Culver Street, from John Christmas, whose great-grandfather's will had first established a school at that location. Edward Watson, who had been the teacher at the school since January of the year before, was retained as schoolmaster. The school could have as many as sixty students, with sixteen being free scholars who had to be the sons of burgesses and were chosen by the bailiffs; the other students paid a fee.[49]

By January, 1587, the statutes for the grammar school were completed by Bishop Aylmer and Dean Nowell. They set up a classical curriculum. The schoolmaster was required to hold a master of arts degree and to be able to teach grammar, Latin, and Greek, in both verse and prose, "avoiding . . . those authors which be rather nurseries of looseness of life and filthy behavior, than meet for honest and chaste ears." The master was to be "of a sound and good religion, void of all papistry," and the bishop or his chancellor had to be satisfied as to the master's orthodoxy and learning. The Lord's Prayer, the confession of sins from the Book of Common Prayer, the Apostles' Creed, and the Ten Commandments, as well as short prayers for the scholars, the queen, and "the good estate of the town of Colchester," were to be said every morning and evening. On Sundays and saints' days, scholars and masters attended "the church . . . where the general sermon is made." Once a week, the master was to catechize the students, using Master Nowell's catechism, either in Greek or

---

49. Morant, 3:10–11; *VCH Essex*, 2:502–3; Nicholas Orme, *Education and Society in Medieval and Renaissance England* (London: Hambledon Press, 1982), 26; D/B5 Gb1, ff. 27v, 28, 37; Anglin, *University*, 42.

Latin. Every quarter, the master and students who were of sufficient knowledge and faith were to take Communion at the parish church; here Bishop Aylmer made a slight bow to George Northey when he did not require the rite of confirmation for the students before taking Communion, stipulating only that the scholars yield an adequate account of their faith to "the public preacher of the town." The students worked hard, beginning their school day at 7 A.M. in the winter and 6 A.M. in the summer, and ending at 5 P.M., with a two-hour break in the middle of the day. Examinations were held in March and October by the archdeacon of Colchester, "two public allowed preachers," and any other learned man brought with them, all in the presence of the bailiffs.[50] The grammar school was thus an instrument for disseminating the values of the society and for teaching classical knowledge within the framework of true religion, as well as respect for the queen, the church, and the town.

The grammar school had some distinguished masters. After Edward Watson, twenty-six-year-old Samuel Halsnoth (or Harsnett, as he was later called), a native of the town and educated at the grammar school, came from Pembroke College at Cambridge, where he was a fellow. The other fellows of Pembroke, including the great preacher and scholar Lancelot Andrewes, confirmed that Halsnoth was "of a good name and honest conversation" and was "very meet, able, and sufficient" to perform the duties of schoolmaster. Halsnoth stayed only about two years, however, and he returned to Cambridge to study divinity and eventually become the master of Pembroke, the bishop of Chichester, the bishop of Norwich, and the archbishop of York.[51] It was quite a career for a baker's son. Halsnoth, as Archbishop Harsnet, founded his own school at Chigwell, in Essex, in 1629, and his experience as a young teacher in Colchester probably influenced his specifications for a schoolmaster, who was to be a graduate of a university, at least twenty-seven years old, able in both Greek and Latin, of good behavior, and "above all, that he be apt to teach and severe in his government."[52]

Halsnoth's resignation in 1588 evoked numerous letters of recom-

---

50. Morant, 3:12–14; *VCH Essex*, 2:38, 503. David Cressy, "A Drudgery of Schoolmasters: The Teaching Profession in Elizabethan and Stuart England," in *The Professions in Early Modern England*, ed. Wilfrid Prest (London: Croom Helm, 1987), 129–53, outlines grammar school curriculum, the various levels of grammar schools, and the role of the schoolmaster.

51. Morant, 2:17–18 and 3:14; *VCH Essex*, 2:504; Addison, *Essex Worthies*, 96.

52. Addison, *Essex Worthies*, 96; Cressy, "Schoolmasters," 140.

mendation for a successor. Halsnoth persistently recommended a Master Sadlington of Peterhouse College, Cambridge, writing three letters to the bailiffs in which he highly praised Sadlington and even indulged in some uncharitable derision of the abilities of Sadlington's competitor, William Bentley. Though Sadlington also had the impressive support of Sir Francis Walsingham and the fellows of Peterhouse,[53] Bentley won the post. The bailiffs' rejection of Halsnoth's desired successor may have been, in part, a perception that Halsnoth's ambition was greater than his Puritan sympathies. Halsnoth's father had been Calvinistic, or at least he described himself as being "of the elect" in his will of 1574. While still a young man, Samuel, an obviously talented scholar, had preached a sermon at Paul's Cross in 1584 attacking double predestination. At the time, Calvin's theology, including his doctrine of predestination, was accepted even by the conservatives in the English church, so Halsnoth was hauled before the High Commission and rebuked by Archbishop Whitgift himself. Thirty years later, in a speech before the House of Lords, Halsnoth said that he had never forgotten that experience and that it had made him resolve to be silent on critical issues thereafter. Halsnoth's middle-of-the-road stance was reflected in his 1629 description of the schoolmaster that he wanted for his Chigwell school: the master was to be "of a sound religion, neither papist nor puritan."[54]

Bentley's qualifications were impressive. Like Sadlington, Bentley had a well-known person writing for him, Lord Darcy; and Bentley's former schoolmaster at Shrewsbury, having heard that "Master Harsnet" was leaving "the painful trade of teaching," wrote commending Bentley's learning, as did the masters of three Cambridge colleges and the fellows at Clare Hall and Emmanuel College. Unlike Sadlington, Bentley had the backing of several active Puritan preachers, such as John Knewstub, leader of the Puritans in Suffolk, and Thomas Farrar, vicar at Langham and member of the Dedham conference, who recommended Bentley "for his sound skill in true religion." Possibly swayed by the Puritan preach-

---

53. D/Y2/4, pp. 159, 163, 167, 187; D/Y2/9, p. 269. Mr. Brodwaye of Maldon was also recommended (D/Y2/4, p. 207).

54. The will of Halsnoth's father William, ERO D/ACR6/437. Halsnoth had been encouraged in his studies by ardent reformer Joan Dybney, who requested in her 1571 will that 40s. be used to buy books for the ten-year-old Samuel (ERO D/ACR6/219). See Collinson, *Puritan Movement*, 501n; P. G. Lake, "Calvinism and the English Church, 1570–1635," *PP* 114 (1987): 35; Cressy, "Schoolmasters, 140.

ers, the town leaders gave the nod to Bentley on November 12, provided that he be found fit for the job.[55]

Although it seems that some of the letters about Bentley before his appointment charged him with incompetency, he received a strong supportive letter from George Northey, which noted that he, along with the masters of some Cambridge colleges, had earlier recommended Bentley to the Dedham school. Northey did not deny that he had had previous disagreements with Bentley, but he noted that even the apostle Paul and Barnabas had disagreed. Northey's words also hint that opponents had thought Bentley's work to be unproductive: "We that be in the ministry think that we preach sincerely and diligently, and we do not always see such success and fruit of our labors as we do desire." Northey had known Bentley at Cambridge, both having been at Clare Hall, and Northey, addressing the problem of Bentley's poverty while at Cambridge, noted that although Bentley had been "very poor" at Cambridge, he had not fallen into debt.

The cautious bailiffs asked other reformers to give their opinion about Bentley. Laurence Newman, vicar of Coggeshall and member of the Dedham conference who also tutored selected students, replied, as did the noted Puritan diarist from Wethersfield, Richard Rogers.[56] Despite the reservations voiced by Bentley's detractors, he received the appointment to the grammar school, and his letter to the magistrates on December 3 was a model of schoolmasterly prose and proper deference to his new employers.

You have committed to my charge a matter of great weight and trust, even the training up of the younger scholars in the principles of good learning: which being now tender plants may hereafter grow to be fruitful trees in the Lord's orchard. For the which I give you humble and hearty thanks, having obtained that which I earnestly desired, to live under worshipful government in that calling. . . . I am very willing that my ability to teach prose, verse, Latin, and Greek be tried according to the orders of this school.[57]

---

55. D/Y2/4, pp. 113, 125, 131, 135, 143, 149, 173; D/B5 Gb1, f. 62v; Anglin, "Essex Puritan Movement," 174–75.

56. D/Y2/4, pp. 193, 203, 211; Anglin, "Essex Puritan Movement," 174–75; Anglin, *University*, 152.

57. D/Y2/4, p. 97.

The lengthy process of selecting Bentley revealed the importance of both the school and the position of schoolmaster in the minds of the bailiffs. This appointment was the first under the school's new statutes drawn up by Aylmer and Nowell, and the bailiffs were no doubt concerned to show the bishop that they could handle the precarious business of finding a man who was both godly and able. However, when doubts arose, they turned not to the bishop but to reforming preachers, such as Richard Rogers. Bentley's probation period proved that the corporation's trust in him was justified, and he was officially confirmed in March, 1590, "with all the duties and fees as were granted to Mr. Halsnoth." Bentley's acceptance was complete when he was admitted to the freedom of the borough in 1595 without the usual fine.[58] The pride that the burgesses had in their grammar school was evident in the 1593 will of wealthy Merchant Adventurer and alderman John Hunwick, who left money for drinks ("a potation") for the scholars, on the condition that "the said master, usher, free scholars, and other scholars do attend my corpse unto the grave."[59] Not only did the Colchester school educate the sons of the burgesses, but in helping create a learned ministry and laity, the school connected Colchester to the wider network of zealous Christians. The grammar school was the culminating work of a reformist magistracy and a mark of civic pride.

Godly Magistrates—A Move Away from Extremism

The restoration of preacher George Northey and the refounding of the grammar school in 1584 represented the height of the dedication of the

---

58. D/B5 Gb1, f. 69, 114v. Other distinguished schoolmasters were later chosen: Theophilus Field, briefly the master in 1598, later became a chaplain to James I and attained bishoprics at Llandaff, St. David's, and Hereford; and William Kempe, master from 1598 until his death in 1637, authored a notable treatise on education (*VCH Essex,* 2:504; Morant, 3:14; Anglin, *University,* 147, 150). Other schools flourished as well. Thomas Rigby, a scrivener who wrote many of the Colchester wills in the late Elizabethan period, had a writing school (PRO 45 Dixy; ERO D/ACV2/9). The archdeaconry records show a continuing school in St. Peter's parish and periodic schools in other parishes. Peter Wagner Ramus, who held a B.A. from Cambridge, was "schoolmaster among the Flemings," having a license "to teach boys in any language, Flemish, French, Roman or Greek." Some of the schoolmasters were in Colchester only briefly, but Brian Harding, teaching at St. Peter's at the end of the Tudor period, settled in more permanently, being admitted to the liberties of the borough in 1598–99 (Emmison, *Morals,* 316–17; ERO D/ACV2/10, 78, 95, 108, 130; CR160/16).
59. PRO 45 Dixy.

corporation to Puritan thinking, yet those same events, though the town leaders could not have known it at the time, initiated, it seems, a slow swing back to a moderate Puritanism. Though the details of the compromise bringing Northey back are missing, it seems obvious that tied to the process was the refounding of the school, which provided an opportunity for both sides to gain and for both sides to bend slightly. The bishop obtained at least tacit submission from Northey on church governance, and Northey was allowed to continue preaching. The corporation got its preacher back and the refounding of its school, but under the oversight of the bishop. Thus both the preacher and the town submitted to the authority of the bishop, while yet retaining the right to appoint their own preacher and schoolmaster.

On September 1, 1588, an event took place in St. James's Church that showed that the town leaders had moved to a limited tolerance of extreme forms of Puritanism. In some ways it was a rather ordinary event—another minister with Puritan views was railing against the use of the surplice, calling it an instrument of papistry. Ministers were still quietly finding ways to avoid the use of the surplice, but this case was different in that Robert Holmes, the rector of St. James's, loudly proclaimed his beliefs in the middle of the service. It was also unusual in that it was taken up in the next session of the peace. Surplice violations were handled in the archdeaconry court, so the borough courts normally had no interest in them, but this case was different in that Holmes injudiciously mentioned the queen in his tirade. The JPs found that the case was a true bill, meaning that it might be sent to a higher court. The account of the case as given in the court roll follows.

> Robert Holmes, clerk, not having the fear of God before his eyes, but moved and seduced by the instigation of the devil . . . intending divers of the Queen's subjects to conceive . . . an evil opinion against the Queen, on 1 September, 1588, in St. James's Church, in his service deliberately spoke with malicious intent, in a loud voice (and this in English): "The surplice is a superstitious thing from the pope, and it is pity the same is suffered in the church to the hurt of divers good men's consciences. If I were before the Council, I would say as much; if I were before the Queen's Majesty I would make her blush for shame."[60]

---

60. CR150/32.

The indiscretion of Holmes might have been ignored by the borough authorities in earlier years, but it came just after the defeat of the great Spanish fleet in the summer of 1588, and respect for the queen (or "Gloriana," as the literary men called her) was at a height. That the Colchester JPs took up Holmes's case suggests that a swing back toward a moderate Puritanism was underway, helped along by national events. Whitgift's suppression of separatists and Puritan extremists, especially Presbyterians, no doubt made an impact on burgesses who were occasionally willing to take risks, as they did in defending Northey so vigorously, but were hardly revolutionaries. Furthermore, the Catholic plots on Elizabeth's life and especially the fear of Spanish invasion had unified the people as Protestants and Englishmen.[61]

With the uncertainties imposed by the Catholic threat, it was time to get back to some of the old traditions, but as Protestants. In the same parish where Holmes had spoken so forcefully, the churchwardens of the next year complained that the perambulations had not been walked for thirty years, "by reason whereof our boundaries are lost."[62] Not only were the physical boundaries of St. James's parish lost, but many of the social and religious boundaries of the thirty years of Elizabeth's reign and of the Tudor years had altered. Chapter 13 looks more closely at the new generation of leaders in the 1590s and analyzes some of the effects of the merging of godliness and governance in Colchester toward the end of Elizabeth's reign.

61. Collinson, "Elizabethan Church," 175; Loades, *Politics,* 39–47.
62. ERO D/ACA17/298.

13

A New Generation

By 1590 it was obvious that a new generation of town leaders had emerged. The alliance of piety and civic power that their fathers had so keenly developed had become institutionalized and taken for granted, so that the attempt at being a godly magistracy had lost its fervor. Puritan zeal was replaced by civic pride and by compromise with church authorities. Perhaps town leaders felt that there was less need for religious ardor, since the effort to create a learned ministry had finally placed responsible preaching ministers in the Colchester parish churches. Certainly, the exercise of secular power for pious purposes in Colchester had already had its successes, for a large majority of the inhabitants of the town, who had been exposed to the town preaching for years, were fully Protestant in their thinking by the late 1580s. Conversely, that merging of piety and secular power also had its dangers. The greater power accumulated by town leaders in their control of town preaching and behavior had the potential of undermining their godliness. As it was always a temptation to desire more power, the quest for power too often replaced the pursuit of holiness. Disunity resulted, especially at election time, and, ironically, even the process of selecting a new town preacher to replace the deceased George Northey in 1593 exploded in controversy and made it clear that the purity of Puritan zeal had become sullied.

This chapter analyzes the group of men elected to the aldermanic bench in 1590 and compares them to the 1530 and 1560 groups that have been previously examined. It then explores two of the successes of Protestantism: the Protestantization of the majority of Colchester inhabitants as shown by the wills, and the condition of Colchester parish churches as revealed by an episcopal visitation in 1592. Ten months after that visitation, town preacher George Northey lay on his deathbed, and the animosity over the appointment of Northey's replacement revealed the extent to which the godly magistrates had found their unity in the person of Northey. This chapter examines the apparently inconsistent appointment of moderate Richard Harris, including one of its effects, the hiring of a rival preacher at St. Peter's. By the end of the Tudor era, the godly fellowship of earlier years had turned into bitter division.

The Aldermen of 1590

By 1590 a glorious new era seemed to be at hand under "Gloriana"; it was a welcome change after the difficulties of the past three decades, which had included epidemics, poor harvests, a puzzling increase in vagrancy and the poor, and even an earthquake in 1580, all adding to the burden of administration in the town. Protestant refugees from the war in the Netherlands had come to Colchester in such numbers that xenophobia had raised its ugly head, and some of the Dutch had departed for Halstead, although they had only recently returned to Colchester in 1589. Colchester did its part in the war against Catholic Spain, supplying a ship for the sea battle. Afterward, the bailiffs quickly sold off the goods that had equipped the ship but noted proudly in the court rolls that the naval action had been "in defence of the sea and kingdom of England."[1] A national spirit was alive, even in Colchester, and a new confidence was abroad, especially among the laity. Reflective of the new emphasis on secular learning in England was the refounding of Colchester's grammar school and the work of Colchester's native son Dr. William Gilbert, who was practicing medicine in London and writing his pioneering work on electromagnetism, *De Magnete*. Indeed, the beginning of the last decade of the sixteenth century was a time of change, as a look at the aldermen of 1590 reveals.

Several of the aldermanic family names remained among the ten aldermen elected in 1590, but one notable change had occurred eleven years earlier: the last aldermanic representative of the Clere family, Nicholas III, died in office in 1579.[2] Thomas Lawrence, who by 1590 was at least eighty years old,[3] was senior not only in age but in terms of service as well, having been an alderman for 21 years, but Robert Mott and John Pye were just behind him with 18 years each. The average years of service, 10.4, was down only slightly from the 1560 average of 10.7.

---

1. *VCH Essex*, 2:220; CR150/19d.
2. However, another Clere, Nicholas IV, became alderman in 1604.
3. Lawrence's age was revealed in a letter written in 1591 to the aldermen by a friend of Lawrence's, who complained that Lawrence should not have been chosen bailiff, since he was above eighty years of age (D/Y2/8, p. 157).

The 1590 aldermen were only moderately prosperous, not having the kind of wealth that had earlier led the Christmases and Sayers into the gentry, although Thomas Barlowe, a Merchant Adventurer cut off by death in the prime of his career in 1593, probably had the greatest potential. Five of the 1590 aldermen were merchants, in contrast to the dominance of clothiers in the 1530 and 1560 groups. Even so, four aldermen were involved in the cloth or clothing business, but only John Pye was engaged solely in the production of cloth. Although the making of cloth was still thriving in Colchester, the Flemings were handling much of the production. The change away from a majority of clothiers among the aldermen reveals that during the century, Colchester wealth had shifted from St. James's parish, where earlier clothmaking was centered around the fulling mills at the bottom of East Hill, to High Street, where the market, the Dutch Bay Hall, and retail shops were located. Seven aldermen lived on or near the High Street;[4] two of the merchants lived in the more traditional area for merchants, St. Leonard's near the Hythe; and only the aged woolen draper and clothier Thomas Lawrence still lived in St. James's parish. The shift in wealth would come to be reflected in the relative influence of the parish churches, and this chapter will show how parishioners of St. Peter's began to take a lead in religious matters.

The number of native-born aldermen in the 1590s group (seven) was higher than ever, and all ten men had close aldermanic connections, even those born outside the borough,[5] so the impression is one of solidly entrenched power within a few ruling families, certainly more so than in the past. The apparent closing of ranks among the governing families may have been simply the result of the accumulated power that had slowly been gathering in the Tudor era, and certainly the hard economic

---

4. One lived in St. Runwald's parish, three in St. Nicholas's, and three in St. Peter's.

5. Richard Lambert, Robert Mott, and Ralph Northey were sons of aldermen; Thomas Reynold was a grandson of one; John Byrde and John Pye were stepsons of aldermen; and the one other native-born alderman, Martin Basell, had worked under Alderman John Beste, probably learning the trade of merchant from Beste (see Beste's will, PRO 2 Martyn). Of the three aldermen born outside of Colchester, Thomas Barlowe, prosperous enough to be a Merchant Adventurer, was probably the grandson of former alderman Thomas Flyngaunt; see the will of Flyngaunt (1541; Guildhall MS 9531/12, pt. 1, f. 184), who named Thomas and William Barlowe as grandchildren, and the will of Thomas Barlowe (PRO 29 Nevell), who had a brother named William. The other two outsiders married into aldermanic families. Thomas Lawrence wed the daughter of Alderman Augustine Beriff: see *OB*, 169; CR131/4d. Thomas Cock, the son of Giles Cock from nearby Fingringhoe, married Margaret, the daughter Alderman Thomas Cocke: see the 1572 will of Grace, the widow of Thomas Cocke I (PRO 18 Draper), and Thomas Cocke II's will (1594; ERO D/ABW10/26).

times had not drawn capable new people to Colchester, with the exception of the religious refugees, the numerous Flemish immigrants, who by 1590 were making a mark on the town economically but were still politically excluded. Perhaps even more important in the development of a more closed aldermanic group was the sense of embattlement that many of the leaders had experienced in the attempt to promote godliness in the town. Some of the confrontations had been tense. As a young alderman, Robert Mott was bailiff with Benjamin Clere during the tense time when arrests were being made for libels against Clere and the Puritan clergy in the 1570s.[6] In 1585 a spinster of the town leveled strong words against Bailiff Thomas Cock and one of the JPs of the year, William Turner. Sarah Holbrigge was brought before a session of the peace for publicly charging, "Master Cock is a thief, a bloodsucker, and a black serpent, and so likewise is Master Turner."[7] One wonders what they did to provoke such graphic language, but it was possibly related to the fact that the bailiffs and JPs were especially busy attempting to regulate church attendance, proper regard for the Sabbath, and the playing of illegal games.[8]

By 1590 the character of Protestantism had changed, having become solidly entrenched in England, especially with the defeat of Catholic Spain's mighty navy. Colchester remained one of the more zealous Protestant towns and a bastion of Puritanism; nevertheless, religious zeal was on the wane, even in Colchester. The authoritarian Archbishop Whitgift was fully in control, and many leading Puritans were either dead or had been forced to submit. The Presbyterian Dedham classis ended abruptly in 1589, and Colchester itself had made its accommodation with the archbishop in 1584 so that its town preacher could continue his work among them. It is likely that the act of compromising initiated the slow tilt toward moderation that was evident in Colchester by 1590. That year saw the death of the great defender of Puritanism Sir Francis Walsingham; it was a loss both for Colchester and for Queen Elizabeth, as Walsingham had been Colchester's recorder for twelve years, as well as the queen's secretary of state. Colchester's choice of a new recorder was most revealing, as the man chosen, Sir Thomas Heneage, had never been mistaken for an ardent Puritan. The 1590 aldermen seemed to be

---

6. Byford, "Religious Change," 237–38.

7. Morant, 3:34–35 (appendix to book 1); Byford, "Religious Change," 279; CR147/34d.

8. CR145/31–31d; CR146/28, 29d, 30.

less on the cutting edge than the 1560 town leaders had been; though still committed to moderate Puritanism, the 1590 group as a whole was not of the most radical persuasion.

Even so, some of the town leaders had a piety that seemed to be more than a mere tool for public display or an excuse for public control. Of the seven extant wills of the 1590 aldermen, four showed a high concern for piety and pious deeds, and two showed a moderate concern (the seventh cannot be considered, since it was a hurried oral will given by Richard Lambert just before he died).[9] The six full wills of the 1590 aldermen were similar to the wills from the 1560 group, with each alderman bequeathing something to the poor, although some of the men were more concerned with the plight of the poor than others. Clothier Thomas Lawrence left £10 to be distributed before his burial, but his major interest was in those people who had worked under him. Lawrence wanted £100 to be distributed among "my poor old spinsters and breakers," with £10 being given each winter for ten years, all "to their most comfort."

A difference from the wills of the 1560 group emerged in the matter of preaching, that hallmark of committed Protestantism. The only member of the 1590 group expressing a belief in the power of preaching in his will was the old man Thomas Lawrence, who asked that "some godly preacher" give a sermon at his burial, "to the stirring up of those that shall be present to the amendment of their lives,"[10] a fitting phrase for a man who had, with other town leaders, spent his public career working for the "amendment" of lives. The will of another old man, former alderman Robert Lambert, likewise valued preaching. Lambert was of the 1560 group, having been brought in as a loyal Protestant after Elizabeth became queen, and in 1586 Lambert paid a fine of over £13 for the privilege of retiring as alderman. He made his will in 1590, with, as he said in his preamble, "full and perfect assurance through the death of Jesus Christ, [that my soul] shall be saved and my sins pardoned." Lambert left £5 for the poor, but his greater concern was to support, in his words, "my loving friends, the preachers of God's holy words," and he enumer-

---

9. The four wills showing highest concern for pious deeds are those of Thomas Barlowe (1591; PRO 29 Nevell), Thomas Cock (1594; ERO D/ABW10/26), Thomas Lawrence (1594; PRO 80 Dixy), and Martin Basell (1618; PRO 20 Swann). Moderate concern was shown in the wills of Robert Mott (1603; PRO 32 Harte) and John Byrde (1611; PRO 34 Wood). See also Lambert's will (1600; ERO D/ABW24/17).

10. PRO 80 Dixy.

ated five preachers—his own rector at St. Leonard's was not included—with amounts to be given to each of the preachers.[11] Town preacher George Northey headed the list, and also included was the aging Master Upcher, once the rector at St. Leonard's, whose pharisaical zeal against one John Lone had initiated great controversy in the mid-1570s. Significantly, Lambert and Lawrence were from an earlier generation. On the whole, the wills written by the 1590 aldermen were lacking in the partisan Puritan zeal so evident in Lambert's will, but they did manifest a moderate, conventional piety.

Such a religious position was consonant with the security that the ten aldermen of 1590 had found in entrenched political power, a power that had come not because they were closely related to each other—none of them were—but because they had a common heritage in their long and enduring ties to the town and its governing families. Pride in being an alderman, which had developed so strongly through the shared religious and governing experience of the men of 1560, remained with the men of 1590, with half of those men writing wills in which they proudly identified themselves as aldermen.[12] Yet, if the naming of fellow aldermen as executors or supervisors is an indication, there seemed to be a lessening of the "fellow feeling" that Alderman Mott yearned for as he made his will in 1603; only two of the 1590 aldermen testators—Mott being one of them—appointed fellow aldermen as executors or supervisors. Again exemplifying the values of an earlier generation was the old man Thomas Lawrence, who outdid all his colleagues when he named Alderman Martin Basell as one of his executors and named three aldermen, all "loving friends," as supervisors.[13] The fellowship of the governors was obviously important to a man who had chosen to remain in office, though he was aged.

Perhaps symbolic of the entrenched power of the late Tudor aldermen were their gifts of ornamental plate, a trend seemingly started by Mott with his gift of a piece of plate in 1603 to encourage unity. Richard Symnell, in his will of 1607, gave to the bailiffs and commonalty two great silver and gilt bowls, probably large beer cups, "to be made of the best fashion with my name to be set upon them, to be used at their feasts and meetings in the moot hall"; and in 1619 Thomas Haselwood left £20 to

---

11. PRO 69 Harrington.
12. Barlowe, Lawrence, and Mott.
13. Wills of Mott, PRO 32 Harte; and Lawrence, PRO 80 Dixy.

the town "to be bestowed in plate."[14] The bequests of ornamental plate denoted pride in the town and an individualistic pride in the aldermanic role, as well as an interest in promoting camaraderie. But if fellowship had been the only interest, a dinner or a drinking for the aldermen would have served as well.[15] Instead, these gifts of plate were permanent and were as much for ceremony as for function. Pride in being an alderman and the outward fellowship of the 1560 group remained, but it had become ceremonialized and possibly less personal.

The increasing ceremony signified the slow changes experienced by the men of 1590. Only the 1560 group had lived in a time of volcanic change. In contrast to the aldermen of 1530, who had no strong sense of camaraderie among themselves or of piety toward God, the 1560 group had changed dramatically, being both drawn to each other and to God through the trials faced during the tumultuous years of Mary's reign and by their sense of mission in the town. It was a zeal that could not be sustained indefinitely. By 1590 the quick pace of change had slowed and the new generation of aldermen were more restrained in their religious devotion. Ironically, the greater moderation of the leaders became evident just at the time when a majority of the people of Colchester had become true Protestants.

A Protestant People

The work of the godly aldermen in Colchester had not been completely in vain. By the time of the defeat of the Spanish Armada, the Protestant faith had been internalized by many of the people of England, and the same was true of Colchester, as illustrated by the wills, which provide a measure of the effectiveness of Protestant zeal and preaching. Especially notable were the changes in religious terminology in the preambles. Protestants stressed the faith within the heart of the believer; as early reformer Bishop Hugh Latimer had preached, "This faith must not be only in our mouth, in our tongue, but it must be in our hearts." Testator Margaret Boniure, possibly the wife of glazier William Bongeor, who

---

14. PRO 32 Harte; PRO 71 Windebanck; PRO 61 Parker. A 1670 list of corporation plate mentioned Symnell's gift; see Rickword, "Members . . . 1559–1603," 244.

15. Only two examples of such legacies are found in the wills: Thomas Cock I (1544) left 10s. to the aldermen, "to be employed upon an honest dinner for them" (ERO D/ABW8/83); and John Stone (1551) bequeathed 6s. 8d. "toward a drinking among all the aldermen" (ERO D/ABW33/199).

burned for his faith during Mary's reign, spoke eloquently of her private relationship with God when she commended her soul "to almighty God, my creator and maker, and to Jesus Christ, my redeemer and atonement maker for my sins, and to the Holy Ghost, my sanctifier, in private of my heart to call upon him in all my trouble."[16]

For Protestants, a person's relationship with God was within one's heart and centered on the person of Jesus, rather than being mediated through Mary or the saints or a priest. References to Jesus were not common in the Colchester wills before the Reformation, but the first Protestant will, by Alderman John Clere in 1538, affirmed that his salvation was by the "passion and blood shedding" of Jesus. As other Protestants gradually began speaking of the forgiveness of sins through the death of Jesus, the person of Jesus became the basis for Protestant confidence in one's salvation. Statements of faith began to be more fulsome in the 1570s, with adverbs abounding; example phrases include "assuredly trusting to be saved," "perfectly trusting to be saved," and "faithfully trusting." At the same time, the verb *believe* and its variations began to be used with some frequency, and in the 1580s and throughout the rest of the Tudor period, *believe* was the most common term used in the strong expressions of faith. Widow Joan Lewis, mother of future vicar Robert Lewis, stated in 1570 that she was "steadfastly believing to obtain and gain forgiveness of all my sins through the death and merits of my Lord and Savior, Jesus Christ." Other terms were also used to communicate one's convictions, particularly *assured* and *persuaded*. Gentleman George Sayer wrote in 1595, "Being undoubtedly assured that by the death of Jesus Christ [I] am pardoned of all my sins and that thereby I shall enjoy the heavenly felicity with the saints of God."[17]

In the 1580s, for the first time, the seventy-one testators who included Jesus in the commendations of their souls outnumbered those who commended their souls to God alone (forty-six testators),[18] indicating full acceptance of Protestantism by a majority of testators. References to the death and "bloodshedding" of Jesus were also at a high point in the 1580s, when 36 percent of the testators made such an allusion. In the same decade, 37 percent of testators made a strong statement of belief or trust in God. All but four mentioned Jesus by name, and those

---

16. Hugh Latimer, *Sermons*, ed. George Elwes Corrie (Cambridge: Cambridge University Press, 1844), 504; ERO D/ACR6/433.

17. ERO D/ABW23/176; PRO 73 Drake.

18. See chapter 6, table 4.

four were obviously referring to Jesus; for example, Elizabeth Clere spoke of "his precious bloodshedding."[19] Along with the word *believe*, the words *trust* and *hope* became fairly common in the wills, revealing an inner confidence missing in the earlier wills, about the state of the soul immediately after death. No longer was the testator dependent on someone else's prayers, whether those of the saints in heaven or of a priest on earth. The faith or trust of the testator made the sacrifice of Jesus valid for oneself. As Robert Baker asserted in 1578, he was "hoping and assuredly believing to have pardon and forgiveness of all my sins in, by and through the merits, death and passion of my Lord and Savior, Jesus Christ crucified, my only and alone and by none other means or manner."[20]

Along with the greater number of preambles expressing confidence of salvation in Jesus, testators began to speak of their hope of the resurrection and the joys of eternal life in heaven. None were more emphatic or insistent than humble weaver John Halle in 1559 when he echoed the words of the burial service in the Book of Common Prayer: "My body to the earth. Earth to earth, dust to dust, and ashes to ashes for I believe steadfastly that I shall arise again in the great day of the Lord and through the merciful design of our Savior Christ that I have and shall have remission of all my sins and to be annointed as one of the number of those that shall reign with Christ everlastingly in glory. This faith is fast in my heart." Increasingly in the later Tudor wills, the section of the preamble dealing with the disposition of the body after death came to be an occasion for affirming one's belief in the joining of the soul and body together in a bodily resurrection on the last day. The 1592 will of John Pullyn, probably the son of zealous reformer and preacher John Pullen, stated, "Believing verily . . . that by the power of His resurrection this my weak body shall in the last day rise again to immortality when body and soul being joined together I shall be made partaker of Christ's excellent glory and live and reign with Him forever in joys unspeakable."[21]

A source of the Protestant confidence in one's salvation and resurrection might also be the belief that one was among the number of the elect souls destined for salvation; in 1590 Jacques Tompson wrote of "assur-

---

19. ERO D/ACR7/262.
20. ERO D/ACW7/10.
21. ERO D/ACR5/36; ERO D/ACW2/147.

ing myself that by the death of Christ my sins are forgiven me and that thereby as one of His elect I shall inherit the kingdom of heaven."[22] Only twenty-three testators stated that they were among the elect or chosen.[23] Such statements indicated belief in the Calvinistic doctrine of predestination, but even conservative Protestants in the Elizabethan period adhered to the doctrine, so the few references may only mean that it was such a common doctrine that it did not get much attention. However, there is a record of a conversation in the late 1570s in which the old sawyer Francis Hunt complained of a sermon in which Nicholas Challoner had set forth the Calvinistic doctrine of double predestination, that is, that all people are predestined either for salvation or damnation. The milder form of predestination, that only chosen people were predestined to be saved, had been a part of Christian thinking for centuries and was the doctrine that continued to be a tenet of the Church of England during Elizabeth's reign.[24]

Much of the process that had brought about the internalization of the Protestant faith was a result of Puritan preaching,[25] and a number of the ordinary people of Colchester were eager for sermons and sound instruction. Richard Turner and his wife, of the neglected parish of St. Mary Magdalen, refused to come to church in 1585 unless there was going to be preaching. For Turner the absence of preaching was not merely an excuse for staying at home; he obviously had Puritan sympathies that made him impatient with anything less than good biblical instruction. The same archdeaconry court that charged Turner with nonattendance also noted that he was reported to have said that he doubted whether his minister preached sound doctrine. Turner's accusation was not the first one by ordinary people about the lack of sound doctrine; at St. Martin's, where they endured a succession of incompetent curates, the wardens in 1582 were prompted to comment, "Our minister doth not at no time deliver sound doctrine; but as for false doctrine [it] is very plentifully poured." The reference was to curate Robert Goode (or Golde), who was

---

22. ERO D/ACW2/45.

23. Six of those wills seem to have been written by one scribe, William Ram, who possibly influenced the terminology used.

24. The conversation is given in Byford, "Religious Change," 273.

25. Attitudes toward preaching separated Anglicans, who wanted divine service according to the Book of Common Prayer, from the hotter sort of Protestants who favored sermons and less liturgy.

known as a "mender of saddles."[26] As rector of Holy Trinity Church, Goode was shut out in 1590 by the wardens, who were charged with "keeping and shutting the church door against the minister," not wanting him "to say the service."[27]

Instruction in the Word could produce laymen who were quite independent in their thinking, though this was hardly to the church's liking. Some laymen had even dared, when they had a lax clergyman like Robert Goode, to take on the duties of the clergy. In 1587, when Goode was supposedly absent, a layman conducted a burial service for a child "without the form of burial in the Book of Common Prayer." Goode countered that he was at home but that his presence was not wanted. Around the same time, laymen in two other parishes buried the dead "without the prayers."[28]

If Puritanism had its ardent supporters among the ordinary people, it also thrived among the middle and upper urban groups. The widow of Alderman John Maynard of St. James's parish left 40s. in 1584 to "the general preacher of the town," George Northey, and also directed her executor to "appoint some godly or learned preacher to preach four sermons in some country towns where the Gospel is not usually preached."[29] Lawyer William Markaunt of St. Giles's parish was also a supporter of preaching, leaving legacies in 1582 to Northey, whom he described as "our general preacher and pastor of our congregation," and to three preachers within the borough. Markaunt, as shown by his will, which he wrote himself, was a model of the learned laity who was concerned about advancing the preaching ministry, though he was hardly extremist. He owned Calvin's *Institutes* and Beza's translation of Scripture, as well as a "great book of common prayer" which had "bosses and clasps." He left £40 so that books of divinity could be distributed among

---

26. ERO D/ACA14/19; ERO D/ACA10/169. Goode was listed as the curate at St. Martin's in 1584; see Davids, *Annals,* 98. Smith, "Social Reform," chapter 1, pp. 13–14, showed that by the mid-Elizabethan period, the Reformation had the full support of many tradesmen and craftsmen in Colchester.

27. Emmison, *Morals,* 125. At about the same time, the warden of St. James's took away the book from Master Miller in service time, but the situation is unclear. Goode had earlier been charged by some of his parishioners for drunkenness and keeping a whore at Harwich, and one parishioner was even accused of "calling Master Good, Pope." See ERO D/ACA17/21; Emmison, *Morals,* 209.

28. Emmison, *Morals,* 172–73; ERO D/ACA14/150.

29. PRO 18 Watson. Table 3, in chapter 6, charts the indicators of piety in the wills of this period.

students of divinity at Cambridge and Oxford, with the stipulation that the scholars be among "the godly learned."[30]

One of the results of the years of preaching was an appreciation for the effect that it could have on the lives of others. In 1583 John Markaunt wanted a funeral sermon by a "zealous and learned preacher," so that the hearers "may be taught and exhorted . . . to the amendment of life, preparation for death and to live so well that likewise they may die well and end their days in peace." Markaunt ensured an audience by instructing that 40s. be distributed to the "needy poor" who were present to hear the sermon. In 1593 Alderman John Hunwick requested that a learned man instruct the prisoners to the amendment of their lives, and in the following year, Alderman Thomas Lawrence likewise wanted a sermon "to the stirring up of those that shall be there present to the amendment of their lives," though Lawrence's sharp business sense emerged when he added that the payment of 10s. to the preacher was not to be made until "after the sermon ended."[31] Markaunt's deceased brother, William, had provided a model of such amendment of life in his 1582 will, in which he gave money "by way of restitution" to sixteen named people who had paid interest of 10 percent on money that had been borrowed from Markaunt. He also wanted to reward the righteous when he left money to be distributed "among the poorest of my kindred, especially those who are given to advance and further the Word of God and the Light of His most holy Gospel, and practices the same in life and conversation."[32] Contact with the Word of God could change lives, and the godly among the learned laity and the civic leaders felt that they had a responsibility to share that Good News and exhort others to live righteous lives.

Not everyone was so committed, though, and there is plenty of evidence for resistance to the godliness that the bailiffs wanted to impose. In 1583 when the bailiffs wrote to Sir Thomas Heneage about the restoration of George Northey, they mentioned the faithful, the weak, and the "many ungodly persons" in Colchester; ungodliness was a common complaint from the Puritans.[33] The reforming zeal of the preachers was also resented. Clothier Robert Gale of St. Peter's charged that vicar Robert Lewis did not wear the surplice or say divine service on the holy days,

---

30. PRO 12 Rowe. The three preachers in the borough were Lewis at St. Peter's, Lowe at St. Leonard's, and Searles at Lexden.

31. Hunt, *Puritan Moment*, 92; PRO 49 Brudenell; PRO 45 Dixy; PRO 80 Dixy.

32. PRO 12 Rowe.

33. D/Y2/6, p. 85; Collinson, *Religion*, 200.

especially on St. Matthew's Day, "as he is . . . bounden by the laws of the realm." Gale's sudden zeal for conformity was probably his retaliation for having to pay a penalty of 2s. in a previous court for working on St. Matthew's Day.[34] The wills show a persistent percentage, about one-third of the testators in the Elizabethan period, who were only nominally religious or had no religious concern whatsover (see chapter 4, table 2). Although the moral fervor of Puritanism brought division as well as unity, the reforming magistrates were nevertheless successful in that a large number of people had become active Protestants. The church, too, was enjoying the fruits of Protestantism in revitalized parish churches serviced by a stable and learned preaching ministry.

The Parish Churches in Colchester

In Colchester the church was in a far better situation than it had been for decades. The report of an episcopal visitation held at St. Mary's Church on September 8, 1592, shows that the Colchester parish churches were better served than they had been since at least 1554, the date of the first surviving records from a Tudor episcopal visitation. All sixteen parish churches had either a rector or a vicar or were served by a curate or a sequestrator, that is, someone who had "bought" the living. Nine parishes had incumbents, although pluralist John Walford held two of the livings, at All Saints' and St. Mary-at-Wall. With the continuing problem of the poverty of the livings, parishes were, in effect, being loosely combined to produce a reasonable living for the clergy and to provide worship services for all of the parish churches. For example, Thomas Lowe of St. Leonard's was curate of nearby St. Mary Magdalen's, and Thomas Farrer was curate of St. Botolph's and rector of St. James's. The earlier vicar of St. Peter's, Robert Lewis, had begun the practice of serving nearby St. Runwald's as sequestrator, and the practice was continued by Edward Gutter. Necessity had forced the practical solution by which most of the incumbents took on a curacy or a seques- tration to add to their income.[35]

Of the incumbents listed in the 1592 visitation, only three, Cock at St. Giles's, Searles at Lexden, and Knevett at Mile End, served a single

---

34. ERO D/ACA14/141, 142.
35. Guildhall MS 9537/8, ff. 51–53; Morant, 2:14; D/B5 Gb1, f. 22v.

parish, although Knevett occasionally roamed farther afield.[36] Significantly, the advowsons of those three parish churches were held by Protestant landed families, the only Colchester advowsons so held since the
Audleys had become Catholics (see appendix 5). Patronage thus continued to be a factor in the state of the parish churches. The earl of Sussex
appointed Robert Searles to the Lexden church, and Sir Thomas Lucas
presented both Thomas Knevett to Mile End and William Cock to St.
Giles's. All three incumbents were in the godly Protestant mold, since
each was a preacher and, because of the refusal of each to wear the surplice, a known Puritan.[37] Cock's incumbency at St. Giles's, which began
in 1585, was a new development, as St. Giles's Church had previously
been served only by curates; apparently Lucas, who lived in the former
monastic buildings of St. John's in the parish of St. Giles, decided to augment the living at his own parish church. Before being presented to St.
Giles's, Cock had served as a curate at St. James's and had a license to
preach from Bishop Aylmer, so Lucas undoubtedly assessed Cock's abilities before appointing him to St. Giles's. Cock served for thirty-four
years at St. Giles's, until his death in 1619, outliving his patron, who died
at the age of eighty in 1611.[38]

The 1592 visitation listed thirteen different clergymen. Of those, at
least six—and possibly seven—were preachers or held the license to
preach. Heading the list of preachers were two men, town preacher
George Northey, who was preaching at St. James's Church, and Master
Theodorus Hill (or Hilles, as given in the archdeaconry court records),
who was preaching at All Saints' Church.[39] Hill was the minister of the
Dutch church; his actual name was Theodorus van den Berghe, but he
wrote under the Latin name Montanus, which, meaning "mountain" or
"mountainous," may account for his English name Hill. Van den Berghe

36. Some of Knevett's parishioners complained in 1594 that they had no service on
Easter Day because Knevett was "preaching in the town" (ERO D/ACA21/252). Also,
Searles seemed to employ curates part of the time (ERO D/ACA14/254).

37. Davids, *Annals,* 111, 113–14; ERO D/ACA14/227; Anglin, "Essex Puritan Movement," 175, 178, 197.

38. Guildhall MS 9531/13, pt. 1, f. 217v; Morant, 2:20. The presentation of Cock is not
listed in the bishop's register, so technically he was probably a curate. But the 1592 episcopal visitation named him as a rector (Guildhall MS 9537/8, f. 51v), so I classify him among
the incumbents. On his memorial tablet at St. Giles's, he was called the "pastor of this
church" (Davids, *Annals,* 114).

39. Emmison, *Morals,* 158. Both churches also had rectors listed.

was a highly respected minister who was courted at various times by churches in Bruges and Delft. Even Prince Maurits wrote in 1596 from Delft, urging his return. A London preacher corresponded with a Delft preacher regarding that appeal, stating: "I know him [van den Berghe] very well, he is a learned man and a faithful servant of Christ, well-versed in learning, able in life and experienced in the administration of the church, who has served the community there [Colchester] for many years with edification and in peace." The London preacher added that he did not think van den Berghe would leave Colchester, for "he stands alone in his community."[40] The Dutch church in Colchester strongly protested against van den Berghe's leaving, noting, among other reasons, that his knowledge of the English language was of great use to the community. Though van den Berghe acknowledged to the prince that he had often desired to serve God "in our homeland, rather than to stay any longer here in a foreign land," he acceded to the request of his congregation, staying in Colchester, where he died in 1598, having served the Colchester Dutch church since 1572. That he was listed in 1592 in the Church of England records as a preacher at All Saints' (where the Dutch congregation met) is remarkable, since neither he nor his congregation were Anglicans. He had been listed in 1588 also,[41] and one wonders if he was, by that time, possibly preaching the occasional sermon in English, since he was fluent in the language.

Leaving aside the learned preachers Northey and van den Berghe, there were preachers and university graduates among the regular parish clergy in 1592. Four incumbents were certainly preaching,[42] and one other possibly was.[43] Two held M.A. degrees,[44] and another three had

---

40. Quoted in L. Roker, "The Flemish and Dutch Community in Colchester in the Sixteenth and Seventeenth Centuries" (Master's thesis, University of London, 1963), 150.

41. He is listed in Guildhall MS 9537/7, f. 42, under St. Nicholas's, as the "preacher at the other church."

42. Cock preached at St. Giles's, Lowe at St. Leonard's, Searles at Lexden, and Knevett at Mile End. See Anglin, "Essex Puritan Movement," 175, 178; ERO D/ABW5/318; PRO 12 Rowe; ERO D/ACA21/59.

43. Gutter, who had an M.A. from Clare Hall and served at St. Peter's, referred to himself as "minister of the Word of God" (Venn and Venn, *Alumni*, pt. 1, vol. 2:276; ERO D/ABW16/361).

44. Knevett held his M.A. degree from Jesus College, Cambridge, where he also obtained a B.D. in 1595 (Venn and Venn, *Alumni*, pt. 1, vol. 3); and Edward Gutter held his M.A. from Clare Hall (see preceding note).

B.A. degrees;[45] one had been a Cambridge matriculate;[46] and William Cock had some learning, though it is uncertain whether he had a degree.[47] The Protestant plan to develop a graduate preaching ministry had begun to affect even Colchester parish churches; of the seven incumbents, all except one had some learning or university training, and two had advanced degrees. The exception was John Walford, who in length of service was the dean of the group; typical of an earlier generation of clergymen, he had been described in 1584 as "ignorant and unlearned."[48] However, even with the more advanced training of the parish clergy in 1592, none had the combined intellectual and preaching credentials enjoyed by common preacher George Northey.

Bishop Aylmer perhaps felt a little uneasy with the continuing emphasis on "painful preaching" in Colchester. Two months after the episcopal visitation in Colchester, Aylmer consecrated the conformist vicar of Witham, John Sterne, B.D., as suffragan bishop of Colchester. The post had been established by Henry VIII, but only one man had ever held the position, and he had done so in Henry's time. So Sterne's consecration was an unusual move, probably an effort to insure conformity in the Colchester church, as well as an attempt by the bishop to vitiate the authority of Archdeacon Withers, with whom the bishop had been at odds.[49] However, there is no indication that Sterne had much influence on the Colchester church. More unsettling was the death of George Northey ten months after the episcopal visitation; the era in which the town leaders and town preacher had worked in happy conjunction had come to an end.

Controversy around a New Town Preacher

By the time of George Northey's death in the summer of 1593, Puritanism had suffered major setbacks. Influential Puritans were dead or

45. These three are Lowe, who held his B.A. degree from Clare Hall (Venn and Venn, *Alumni*, pt. 1, vol. 3); Farrar, who held his degree from Peterhouse (Venn and Venn, *Alumni*, pt. 1, vol. 2); and William Cole, the new curate at Berechurch (ERO D/ACA21/460).

46. William Banbrick was matriculated at Corpus Christi (Venn and Venn, *Alumni*, pt. 1, vol. 1).

47. In his will (ERO D/ACW8/245), Cock mentioned owning several books.

48. Davids, *Annals*, 98.

49. The earlier suffragan bishop was William More, who served from 1536 to his death in 1540. See Martin, *Story of Colchester*, 53; Guildhall MS 9531/13, pt. 1, f. 269; Morant, 1:77; Byford, "Religious Change," 366; Newcourt, 2:162.

were being neutralized. Early in 1593, Colchester's MP and town clerk, Puritan James Morice, was detained by the queen for two months for attacking the legality of some of the procedures followed by Archbishop Whitgift's Court of High Commission. The triumph of moderate Protestantism was heralded in the same year by the initial appearance of that great defense of conforming Anglicanism, Richard Hooker's *Of the Laws of Ecclesiastical Polity;* even the Puritan writers were being more irenic by beginning to emphasize personal piety rather than divisive issues.[50] Archbishop Whitgift and Queen Elizabeth had triumphed over the Puritan attempts to further reform the church.

The death of Northey in July of 1593 was keenly felt, as it was a blow to the viability of the preaching ministry in Colchester. The town leaders hastened to replace him as soon as possible. On July 24 Northey was buried at St. James's Church, where he had most often preached;[51] on August 27 the assembly of the town agreed that "there shall be one general preacher for the town as before," with the same yearly pension as Mr. Northey had received, which was £40. They planned to hear a man named Richard Harris, and if they liked him, he would be hired as preacher. The proceedings moved apace, and three days later Harris was appointed, at a pension of one hundred marks, or £66 13s. 4d., which was well above Northey's stipend. Of that amount, £50 was to be paid by the corporation, with the rest coming from contributions, "the benevolence of the inhabitants of the town." The decision was all too hasty, though, and problems quickly developed over the finances. By September 27 the decision to give Harris one hundred marks a year was restated, but if Harris could not come, anyone else coming would get only forty marks a year. The finances were still a sore point the next March, when the assembly agreed that no preacher was to receive more than £40 a year except Master Harris, who was to have one hundred marks a year.[52]

The majority of town leaders obviously wanted Harris very much, and one wonders if the sudden jump in salary was a result of Harris's playing hard to get. The record of the August 27 assembly had made provision in case "Mr. Harris . . . cannot be had," and his coming was still in doubt

50. Cross, *Church and People,* 150–51, 161; Hasler, 3:99.

51. However, some town sermons had been preached at St. Botolph's, and in 1597 the assembly agreed that St. Botolph's was "the most convenient and fittest place" for the Sunday and Wednesday town sermons (D/B5 Gb1, f. 136). Nevertheless, Dr. Harris was still listed as "predicator" at St. James's through March, 1600 (ERO D/ACV2, ff. 9, 41–43, 48–50, 77–79, 94–96, 107–9).

52. D/B5 Gb1, ff. 94d–96, 98d, 101.

at the end of September.[53] Harris seemed to be an ambitious man, though his ambition was never fully realized. He was already more advanced in his career than the two previous town preachers were when they came to Colchester; Harris had already proceeded beyond the M.A. to the B.D. degree, which he had received from St. John's, Cambridge, in 1590. He was also serving as chaplain to the earl of Essex, the queen's favorite and newly made privy councillor. Continuing his scholarly studies even after becoming the Colchester town preacher, Harris was created a doctor of divinity in 1595.[54]

Harris's election says much about the mind-set of the majority of the town leaders. First of all, the hiring of a town preacher had apparently become a matter of prestige for the town, and Harris's credentials were impressive. Also, many of the parish churches had their own preachers, so the town preacher's sermons were no longer quite so essential. Cultural changes must have played a part. The heightened concern with education had moved the cultural elite of England into what has become known as the English Renaissance, which valued the classical virtue of moderation and produced exceptional poetry and drama. The earl of Essex was a part of that milieu, and, to some extent, so was his chaplain, Richard Harris, who was known to have played a role in Dr. Legge's tragedy, *Richardus Tertius*, while a student at St. John's.[55] The town leaders probably assumed that Harris's coming from St. John's would guarantee that he and the town leaders shared a common approach to religion; St. John's, after all, was a center of Calvinist orthodoxy under its master, William Whitaker. Harris had moved steadily through the course of study at St. John's and was one of the college preachers. In June, 1593, he was elected a senior fellow of the college, so there was no reason for Colchester authorities to question his religious commitment, and perhaps without realizing it, some of the town leaders had shifted away from zealous Puritanism and so did not care to question Harris's thinking too closely. They were not alone, for by the end of the century, even St. John's had moved away from the Puritan camp.[56]

The controversy over Harris's stipend got him off to a bad start in the town. Obviously, not all were in agreement with his selection, and at the same assembly in March, 1594, when Harris's stipend was finally set at

---

53. D/B5 Gb1, ff. 95, 98d.
54. *DNB*, 9:22; D/B5 Gb1, f. 102.
55. *DNB*, 9:22.
56. Collinson, *Puritan Movement*, 235; *DNB*, 9:22; Morgan, *Godly Learning*, 233.

one hundred marks, there were attempts to provide for a Master Symes "so long as he preaches at St. Peter's," with a collection to be taken in the South and East Wards for £20 for Master Symes, with the chamberlain making up any shortfall.[57] It seems that the preaching of William Symes at St. Peter's was meant to replace the godly preaching that George Northey had supplied and that, in the view of Symes's supporters, was not being provided by the newly appointed Harris. The situation at St. Peter's was complicated, since the Audleys held the advowson. Catholic Katherine Audley had presented Edward Gutter, M.A. from Clare Hall, in 1590, but Gutter had died early in 1593. The Audleys did not bother to present anyone else—perhaps they were preoccupied by the charge in the same year against Thomas Audley for being a recusant—so, early in 1594, Bishop Aylmer appointed the curate at Berechurch, William Cole, as the vicar of St. Peter's.[58] Cole was not a happy choice. Many of Colchester's religious zealots lived in St. Peter's parish, and Cole was obviously not the man to deal with the situation, being neither very careful nor conscientious. Early in his tenure at St. Peter's, a churchwarden forbade him to say the service, because, for some unknown reason, he was excommunicate. But Cole, though admitting that the warden was right, said the service anyway. The parishioners at St. Peter's had obviously decided to take matters into their own hands, for at the same archidiaconal court that dealt with Cole's preaching while excommunicate, Master Symes, S.T.B. from Clare Hall, was listed as a curate at St. Peter's and was instructed to show his letter of ordination and his license to preach, which he did shortly thereafter. Cole, the new vicar, then had another and better qualified man preaching in his church. It was at that point that the town leaders voted to take a collection from the South and East Wards, no doubt to augment the monies collected in the Head and North Wards, both of which surrounded St. Peter's Church and would have been the area from which people would have been drawn to the sermons. Vicar Cole was understandably unhappy with the situation. In the archidiaconal court of September, 1594, several charges were leveled against him: he was not wearing the surplice even when it was laid before him; he baptized three or four children even though he was still excommunicate; and on September 2, a Sunday, he did not come to church until

57. D/B5 Gb1, f. 101.

58. Venn and Venn, *Alumni,* pt. 1, vol. 2; ERO D/ABW16/361; ERO D/ACA21/148, 243; Guildhall MS 9531/13, pt. l, f. 275v; Newcourt, 2:53.

midmorning, by which time the preacher was already in the pulpit.[59] The list of Cole's indiscretions continued until his resignation in 1600: he was being sued for debt by clergymen in neighboring villages; unlawfully serving as curate at East Doniland; trying to preach without a license; failing to say services at St. Runwald's, which he had sequestered; and teaching thirty to fifty children at St. Peter's who were so unruly that they were breaking windows in the church.[60]

It is unclear when Harris actually began preaching in Colchester. Symes was still preaching at the end of 1595, when gentleman John Christmas requested Symes to preach his funeral sermon; but Symes was gone by 1597, when the archdeaconry court noted that there was no preacher at St. Peter's. Of the Tudor wills written after Northey's death, only three requested sermons by specific preachers, those preachers being Symes, William Cock, and Thomas Knevett.[61] Sermons by Harris were never mentioned in the wills,[62] although he was listed in the archdeaconry records from 1597 to 1600 as being the preacher at St. James's. Harris never had the close links to Colchester that former town preachers had. A concession was made to Harris, probably a recognition of his attaining the advanced D.D. degree in 1595, that he was at liberty to take another ecclesiastical living. So in 1597 Harris became rector of Gestingthorpe,[63] about twenty miles from Colchester, a move prompted perhaps by the difficulties experienced in getting his pay from the corporation. A case involving the town chamberlain, Liberty Cranvyn, who refused to pay Harris, ended up in Chancery Court, and in 1597 the corporation wrote an embarrassed letter to their new recorder, Robert Cecil, asking that Harris be discharged from paying a government tax, and explaining that Harris had extra expenses recently that related to the granting of his D.D. degree and that he was receiving only "a small pension here," which had been detained "by the practice of some in our corporation." Their view of Harris was favorable: "[Harris] was drawn by our importunacy from his study, possession and possibility of greater

---

59. ERO D/ACA21/174, 179, 196; Byford, "Religious Change," 344. O'Day, "Ecclesiastical Patronage," 150, mentioned that some other churches—notably St. Botolph's, Aldgate, in London—were hiring a preacher when they had a nonpreaching clergyman.

60. ERO CR156/18, 23; ERO D/ACA21/460; ERO D/ACA24/113, 202, 220, 223. By 1596, Cole had an M.A., but no one would give him a license to preach.

61. PRO 73 Scott; ERO D/ACV2/9; ERO D/ABW5/318; ERO D/ACW3/80.

62. However, Alderman Robert Mott left Harris 40s. in his 1603 will (PRO 32 Harte).

63. ERO D/ACV2; ERO D/Y2/10, p. 119; Byford, "Religious Change," 345; DNB, 9:22.

preferment than can be expected within our poor town, and since his coming hath in his ministry among us employed his time very painfully, to all our great comforts."[64]

Harris obviously had his advocates as well as his detractors, which was made even more evident by a libel case in the Court of Star Chamber in 1604. Libels against Harris had circulated in the town and even as far out as twenty miles from the town after Harris preached a sermon against some Brownists (as the followers of separatist William Browne were called) and other separatists who were prisoners in Colchester Castle. Harris emphasized his conformity, saying that he had always been "careful to avoid and forswear all erroneous and schismatical doctrine and opinion whatsoever and to the uttermost of his power hath disproved and spoken against that schism of the Brownists and other factious spirits too much abounding in the said town." Harris later confirmed his traditional views in his only written work, published in 1614.[65] Harris was clearly out of tune with a substantial group of the townspeople, who had a history of sympathy with nonconformity extending back to the time of the Lollards.[66]

A widely distributed libel written after Harris's sermon against the Brownists did not wholeheartedly endorse the Brownists but noted that the separatists were "certainly nearer God than a covetous prelate exacting mightily upon honest men." The libel, condemning Harris as a nonresident and for harrassing godly people, viewed Harris as a too willing participant in the authoritarian, ecclesiastical establishment that preyed on the ordinary Christian. For his part, Harris was convinced that his enemies included the rectors of St. Peter's and Mile End, Stephen Newcomen and Thomas Knevett, as well as his "spiteful enemy" Alderman Martin Basell. Harris asserted that the two men charged with beginning the libel campaign, Thomas Dixon and Stephen Parson, had done so "with the good liking of the said Stephen Newcomen." In fact, Harris noted that Newcomen and Knevett had regularly attended Harris's sermons just to find fault and that Newcomen, the more formidable oppo-

---

64. Quoted in Byford, "Religious Change," 347–48.

65. Quoted in Davis, "Colchester," 91, 159n. Harris's work was titled "The English Concord, in Answer to Becane's English Jarre, with a Reply to Becane's Examen," according to *DNB*, 9:22.

66. The incongruity of Harris's appointment prompted Davis, in "Colchester," 102, to conclude that Colchester's "failure to appoint lecturers of a consistent theological bent" meant that there was no "consistent Puritan predilection on the part of members of the corporation," but I believe my explanation to be nearer the mark.

nent, had "personally and by notorious descriptions reviled and unjustly traduced [Harris]" and "had continued most contumely invectives against him."[67]

The tide had turned against Harris and the careful, moderate religion that he represented. In 1605 Harris was ordered by the corporation to deliver his patent, although he was to continue as preacher and receive his usual annuity. In other words, Harris was to serve only at the pleasure of the bailiffs and could be dismissed at any time. Without the patent, the job no longer had the same certainty that had been granted to the previous town preachers, beginning with Nicholas Challoner. Three years later, Harris was ousted as town preacher. He eventually became rector at Bradwell-on-Sea and apparently lived in London for a time; nevertheless, when he made his will in 1621, he was living back in Colchester, where he was buried in St. Nicholas's Church and was commemorated by a monument described by eighteenth-century historian Morant as "nonsensical." True to form, Harris requested a funeral sermon from Dr. Welland of Stanway, who must have been High Church, since Stanway had become the parish church of the Audleys.[68]

A Puritan Offensive at St. Peter's

Harris was probably correct in identifying Stephen Newcomen among his leading opponents; once again, a preacher at St. Peter's was competing with Harris. Newcomen was appointed vicar at St. Peter's in 1600 in what appears to have been an offensive move by the godly. After the incompetent William Cole resigned from St. Peter's, the Audleys again failed to present a replacement, so instead of waiting for the bishop to intervene, two parishioners, John Byrde and Henry Osborne, somehow obtained permission to take the very unusual step of presenting Newcomen.[69] Newcomen, with an M.A. from Corpus Christi in Cambridge, seemed to be of the Puritan persuasion. His son, Matthew, who was educated at the Colchester grammar school, became a well-known Puritan

---

68. D/Y2/10, p. 119; D/B5 Gb2, f. 68; *DNB,* 9:22; PRO 78 Dale. Morant's comment appears in Cromwell, *Colchester,* 1:203. Harris's successor as town preacher, William Ames, represented a return to more radical thinking, but Ames, who has been described as "a Puritan's Puritan," was in Colchester for only one year. Ames's strong views got him in trouble, and he fled to Holland, where he died after distinguishing himself as a leader of Puritanism; see Davis, "Colchester," 102.
69. Newcourt, 2:179. The Audleys resumed their presentations in 1629.

preacher and succeeded the famous John Rogers at Dedham.[70] It seems likely that the intervention of Byrde and Osborne in presenting Newcomen to St. Peter's stemmed from their unhappiness with Harris's preaching. It was perhaps significant that the signatures of the three aldermen from St. Peter's—John Pye, John Byrde, and Martin Basell—were missing from the first directive of the assembly (on August 27, 1593) that mentioned hiring Richard Harris,[71] so they may have had reservations about Harris from the beginning.[72]

Stephen Newcomen possibly came to the attention of St. Peter's parishioners through their schoolmaster, Brian Harding, who was related to Newcomen,[73] but Henry Osborne, who became an alderman in 1595, was probably the moving force behind the presentation of Newcomen. Osborne's wife was a sister of the ardent Puritan Robert Lewis, the former vicar at St. Peter's, and Osborne had a great respect for preachers, as shown in his 1614 will.[74] Newcomen's preaching was more respected than Harris's was, as a number of Newcomen's parishioners and friends bequeathed money to him in their wills, in contrast to so few mentioning Harris.[75] Osborne's backing of Newcomen possibly explains some of the difficulties experienced by Osborne in the years after the 1604 libel trial. Osborne was the victim of arson, was called a "maggot monger," and was charged with partiality as a magistrate.[76] According to his will, Osborne was a "loving friend" of Alderman Martin Basell, the man whom Harris declared to be a "spiteful enemy."[77]

---

70. Gordon Hewitt, *To Frame the Heart* (Chelmsford: Chelmsford Diocesan Print Unit, for the Trustees of Henry Batchelor's Gift, n.d.), 29.

71. D/B5 Gb1, f. 95. Thomas Cock's name was also missing, and Byford, "Religious Change," 342–43, links the choosing of Harris with the 1593 election in which Cock was replaced by John Hunwick. Another possible explanation is that Cock was merely ill, as he died a year later; see his will, ERO D/ABW10/26. Pye died in 1597 (CR158/6d).

72. However, Byrde served as bailiff in 1593–94, the year in which Harris was finally hired.

73. PRO 90 Byrde.

74. ERO D/ABW23/176; ERO D/ABW42/92. Osborne left 20s. each to Lewis and to "the particular ministers and preachers of the Word of God in Colchester": William Ayer, the town preacher by that time; Stephen Newcomen; and William Cock, the long-serving minister at St. Giles's.

75. Leaving money to Newcomen were Alderman Robert Mott (although the even-handed Mott left money to both Harris and Newcomen; PRO 32 Harte), Mott's widow (ERO D/ACW6/201), Henry Lumpkin of the first council (ERO D/ABW43/43), clothier John Wisby of the first council (ERO D/ABW43/236), Alderman William Hall (ERO D/ABW44/229), and schoolmaster and kinsman Brian Harding (PRO 90 Byrde).

76. Davis, "Colchester," 129.

77. ERO D/ABW42/92; Davis, "Colchester," 101.

Religious Colchester was deeply divided between the moderates and the godly radicals at the end of the Tudor period. The last decade saw the ascendancy of the moderates, as revealed by the choosing of Harris, but by 1603 some of the more zealous were asserting their position again. On the religious fringes, the Catholic Audleys continued to hold their own, but the greatest growth appeared to be among the separatists, or at least that seems to be suggested by the fact that Dr. Harris felt compelled to preach against them. A number of the separatists had found their way to Holland, and from there some of them later sailed to the shores of North America; among those sailing on the *Mayflower* in 1620 were John Crackston, originally from Colchester, and his son, also named John.[78] Some of the Colchester parish churches continued to be poor and ruinous. St. Runwald's, the small, old church in the middle of the market area, was one of the worst examples, but just around the corner from it was the flourishing St. Peter's Church, which had become the center of godly preaching. That position had been held by St. Leonard's during the time of Thomas Upcher, but Upcher's influence had been replaced by the resident town preachers, Nicholas Challoner and then George Northey, who preached their sermons at St. James's and St. Botolph's. The influence of godly preaching continued on.

The Magistracy: A Volatile Mixture of Religion and Politics

Religion could not be separated from the politics of the town, particularly in the selection of the town preacher, which had become a symbol of civic pride, as well as an indication of the way the religious winds were blowing. Religious concerns had always flowed through the stream of governance in the town, but at times they became the wind driving the stream, making the waters turbulent indeed. Back in the mid-1570s, the libel controversy swirling around preacher Thomas Upcher eventually produced an aldermanic bench that was skewed toward Upcher.[79] The

---

78. J. R. Smith, *Pilgrims and Adventurers* (Chelmsford: Essex Record Office, 1992), 22.

79. Political factions had centered around Aldermen Benjamin Clere and John Hunwick, with the latter being opposed to Upcher. In 1575 Hunwick was ousted, followed the next year by Clere's ouster, but there began what seems to have been a "packing" of the aldermanic bench with Upcher sympathizers from St. Leonard's to counteract the Hunwick forces, who managed to reelect Hunwick in 1577. By 1579 Upcher forces had won, even though Hunwick was back on the bench and Clere was not, for Upcher had four sympathizers on the bench from St. Leonard's, Aldermen Robert Lambert, Thomas Cock, William Turner, and Richard Lambert. That was the only time in Tudor Colchester that aldermen from St. Leonard's dominated.

1590s again erupted in a mixture of religious and political turmoil over the appointment of Richard Harris as town preacher. The records are not so clear about the situation as they were in the 1570s, but it appears that two factions grew up, one around Thomas Haselwood of St. James's, a supporter of Harris, and the other around John Byrde of St. Peter's, who helped fund the alternative preaching at St. Peter's. In a controversial election in 1595,[80] Aldermen Byrde and John Pye, both of St. Peter's, were surprisingly demoted to the first council. In the same year, Thomas Haselwood was elected first bailiff, an unusually quick reelection to that office, which he had held only two years before, when preacher Richard Harris was initially selected. An observer from Maldon, writing to Cecil about the 1595 elections, reported that "in the two towns of Colchester and Maldon I found great quarrels and contentions both in their civil bodies and among their ministers, the people divided and the priests taking part on both sides and at war with themselves as well as in matters of popular quarrels as points of doctrine."[81] In the 1596 election, Byrde returned as alderman to replace Thomas Haselwood, who remained out of civic office until 1603, when he was elected first bailiff in another controversial election.[82] John Byrde and the men of St. Peter's finally gained dominance on the aldermanic bench in the mid-1590 elections, thus making St. Peter's the politically dominant parish, though not overwhelmingly so.[83] Richard Harris remained as town preacher, but St. Peter's had its own preaching minister, first William Symes and later Stephen New-

---

80. *VCH Essex,* 9:114.

81. Quoted in Davis, "Colchester," 128.

82. Davis, "Colchester," 130.

83. The 1598 election was most unusual for two reasons. First, the two men elected as bailiffs, Richard Symnell and Robert Wade, were both new to the aldermanic bench. Occasionally one new alderman had been elected as junior bailiff, but never before in Tudor Colchester had two new alderman been elected as bailiffs. However, the senior bailiff, Symnell, had long been deputy town clerk and then, briefly, town clerk, so he was thoroughly acquainted with the business of the borough. Second, both new bailiffs were designated as gentlemen—not since the early Tudor years had many gentlemen served on the aldermanic bench—and that social distinction probably accounts for their skipping entirely any service on the second council and for their sudden elevation to the office of bailiff. (Robert Wade had been elected to the first council in 1595; Symnell, in 1597.) It may be that their election was part of a move by some of the gentlemen living in the town to take a more active role in borough governance, both to diffuse the religious and political conflicts and to advance their own agenda of social conservatism (gentleman Robert Christmas had been elected chamberlain in 1595, but he died in office). In November, just after the election, the assembly passed the restrictive alehouse ordinance, which mostly restricted the lower social groups.

comen. The intensity of the Calvinistic message and the ideal of the godly magistrate had brought into the political climate a volatile force that would not be stilled for many decades to come.

The merging of secular power and piety created a powerful force, either for good or ill. As long as motives remained pure, religion could bring unity even to political foes, but more often religion merely became another excuse for political controversy and division. In general, though, the merging of religion and politics in Elizabethan Colchester, though fraught with repeated controversy, had thrived until it came in conflict with what was going on at the national level. At the beginning of Elizabeth's reign, the town had the freedom to experiment with the concept of the godly magistrate, but that freedom gradually eroded as Elizabeth gained in power over the church. George Northey's tenure as town preacher was pivotal; in the early 1580s the godly magistrates were at the height of their power, but Northey's suppression by Archbishop Whitgift ended in compromising Northey's Calvinistic message. Town leaders tried to continue as if nothing had happened, but a vital change had indeed occurred. As in the rest of the country, Puritanism in Colchester had met its match in the combination of the queen and the archbishop, for Colchester leaders had never been willing to oppose their sovereign for long. For the time being, Puritan zeal was in decline, but its force was not yet spent.

Conclusion

In 1485, at the beginning of the Tudor reign, John Elys requested that the executor of his will commission statues to be made of St. Helen, St. Margaret, and St. John the Baptist and then have them placed on Colchester's east gate.[1] No one in Catholic Colchester could have even imagined that just over a hundred years later, the majority of Colchester's inhabitants would be fully Protestant in their thinking. Although political forces undoubtedly aided the process, the religious climate in early Tudor Colchester prepared the way for the town's comparatively rapid acceptance of the Protestant Reformation. Orthodox lay piety, with its emphasis on true commitment to God, had within it a seed for change and reform, but more important was the longtime sympathy with Lollard thinking to be found in Colchester, even at the upper levels of borough governance and society. Since borough governors had to be concerned about obedience and loyalty to the sovereign from whom their liberties came, there was in Colchester during the Henrician and Edwardian reigns a happy conjunction of reformist tendencies and the rulings of sovereign and Parliament. Most borough authorities were eager or at least willing to defy church authorities and adopt Reformation ideas and practices, so by the 1540s Catholic practices were left behind and the Reformation was well established in Colchester. Even so, borough governance was little touched by the Reformation, but new forces were unleashed during the short reign of Queen Mary.

During Mary's attempt to restore Catholicism, Colchester inhabitants began to suffer the martyr's death for their faith, but some of the more cautious town leaders eventually reversed their earlier support for the Reformation and cooperated fully with the Marian authorities, making the committed Protestants in the town realize the need to be more aggressive if given the chance. Colchester became a refuge for radical London

---

1. *RPB*, 102.

preachers escaping Mary's fires. Some of those preachers found wives in Colchester, thus forming connections that would later draw them back to the borough when their exile in Geneva ended. Through their teaching, Colchester was brought into the fold of Calvinist thinking, which included the influential Genevan model of the godly magistrate working in conjunction with godly ministers.

The Protestants seized their opportunity early in Elizabeth's reign, taking over Colchester's governance and gradually initiating a closer union of religion and civic rule, thus following the model supplied by King Henry for the merging of secular and ecclesiastical power. The parish churches were in poor straits after the upheavals of reforms and counter-reforms, so the town governors, influenced by the preaching of the returning Marian refugees, gradually developed their own innovative agenda. Beginning in 1562, the town assembly passed ordinances requiring church attendance and collections for the poor, issued an invitation to Flemish refugees to make their home in Colchester, and hired a town preacher. The problem of the poor, however, did not go away. The situation in the 1570s became urgent, as the problems of vagrancy and poverty were fueled by an ever growing population and a scarcity of work. Town leaders began an intensive campaign to regulate the moral behavior of individuals, seeing such regulation as necessary for good order in society. Keeping control over the community had long been a duty of urban authorities, but moral reform took on a new intensity, prompted first by the unprecedented economic and social problems but also by Puritan zeal. Authorities were concerned not merely with illicit pregnancy but with incontinence, with behavior not only during divine services but during the whole of Sundays and feast days. A new emphasis on the evils of drunkenness and the harmful effects of alehouses emerged. Since preaching was viewed as a vital ingredient in the correction of the ills of society, the hiring of the town preacher became fully institutionalized, with the preacher being paid by the corporation, rather than by uncertain voluntary contributions. So the preacher became a permanent resident in the town. It is hardly surprising that the changes were not to everyone's liking, and acrimonious debate periodically divided the town for the rest of the Tudor period. Even so, Puritan influence continued its dominance through the 1580s, but almost imperceptibly the zeal of the early years began to moderate, especially after Queen Elizabeth and Archbishop Whitgift began to suppress the Puritan movement. Ironically, just at that time, a thoroughgoing Protestantism was evident in the majority of the people of Colchester, as is shown by the last wills and testaments.

To the ordinary inhabitant of Colchester, life must have seemed simpler back in 1485, when the statues of saints could bless a town. The Reformation had brought both gains and losses to the average parishioner. The liturgy and drama found in the Catholic parish churches were missing, but new town rituals, often built around town sermons, attempted to take their place. Divine services were now in the language of the people, and the people had access to the Bible in English. With the Protestant faith's emphasis on the responsibility of each individual to God, there was the possibility of a closer relationship with God, but that possibility also made evident the fact that many failed to be godly and in fact did not even want to be. The sermon culture brought by Protestantism slowly taught the people that they could hope for the joys of heaven, even without the intercessory prayers of a chantry priest; as John Pullyn stated in his 1592 will, he expected to "live and reign with [Christ] forever in joys unspeakable."[2] The monasteries were no more, but the gentry created by the land acquired during the Reformation, such as the Lucases and Audleys, took the place of the monasteries, particularly of St. John's, as competing powers in the borough. There also seemed to be a heightened moral sense by the end of the Tudor period, a phenomenon that perhaps explains the more frequent charges of witchcraft[3] and that also produced a more judgmental attitude. Robert Browne's 1595 will exemplified the impatience with wrongdoing. Browne left annual rent money for the poor but specified that "no part of the rent shall be given to the maintenance of any bastard child or parent of any bastard child."[4] Protestantism also brought new international influences into Colchester, not only the Calvinistic ideas brought back by Marian refugees, but a horde of Flemings fleeing the religious wars. The "Dutch" eventually proved to be Colchester's economic salvation, showing that religious zeal sometimes had its earthly rewards, too.

The tenor of borough governance had undoubtedly changed, a result of both the influence of Protestantism and the increased social needs. Town rulers became more active in areas heretofore not in their province, such as in the hiring of a town preacher. At times they were quite creative

---

2. ERO D/ACW2/147.
3. BL, Stowe MS 840, f. 42; ERO D/ACA24/110; "Calendar of Queen's Bench Indictments," nos. 660 pt. 2, 267, 665 pt. 2, 223, 682 pt. 1, 152–54 (original numbering).
4. PRO 69 Scott.

in finding solutions to the problems of the town, but more often they merely seemed intrusive. It was a struggle to bring cohesion to a community that had lost much of the unity experienced through the parish churches and parish guilds, but town leaders, influenced by Calvinism, also had a new sense of mission to try to create a godly society and a heightened awareness of the importance of their role in the process. Indeed, the linking of godliness and secular governance gave the leaders increased power, and, correspondingly, a greater deference was given to them, for example, in the increased use of the deferential title *master* for aldermen in the Elizabethan period.[5] Their increasing sense of importance was fed by their attempts, often successful, of tapping into national networks of power, a process that for Colchester began early in the Reformation. The advancement of Thomas Audley formed a fortuitous connection with the royal government that brought a new awareness of the possibilities of influence in high places. Increasingly, Colchester's choices of town clerks, recorders, and representatives in Parliament were a barometer both of Colchester's religious proclivities and of a heightened consciousness of the need for a connection with wider networks of power; for example, the retention as recorder from 1578 to 1590 of Sir Francis Walsingham, a Puritan who was also a royal court official, reflected the dominance of Puritanism in Colchester. The opportunities for town leaders to change society seemed greater under Protestantism, but so were the attendant hazards, both for governance and for themselves.

As a group, the town leaders were generally quite committed to the town and were serious about their role as leaders. Moreover, they were well above average in performing deeds of piety, and a number of them seemed quite sincere in their religious convictions. Many of them truly wanted a godly society, but power and piety do not mix well. Believing they had the sanction of religion behind them, the civil governors were vulnerable to the temptation of adopting a self-righteous moral stance that too easily became an authoritarian abuse of power, both toward the people and among themselves. Moreover, the desire for power, which was revealed most starkly at election time, corrupted their efforts, and

---

5. The title began to be used even among the aldermen themselves; for example, William Sympson named fellow bailiff "Master Pye" to be supervisor over his 1573 will (PRO 41 Carew). In York, aldermen expected to be addressed as "master," and citizens were not to refer to them by their Christian names or use the familiar pronoun *thou* when speaking to them; see Palliser, *York,* 290.

they were often bedeviled by disunity among themselves. The election reforming ordinance passed in 1587 acknowledged that the new regulations were occasioned by "great troubles and disorders," which were "to the dishonor of Almighty God." It noted that "if some good order and remedy be not provided," it would be to the "hindrance of the estimation and credit of this ancient borough, and deprivation of the wealth, good estate, and prosperity of the same."[6] A chastened town leadership was recalling the ideal of dutiful leadership as an instrument for bringing right order to society and giving honor to God.

Thus, a new concern about the ideal of unity emerged, for the godly magistrates were supposed to form a fellowship that worked and ruled in brotherly accord. An ordinance in neighboring Maldon even forbade "strife or debate among [the] fellowship" of the corporation and urged "common amity and brotherly kindness and unity in and with the whole Company, society, body of this House, one member with another."[7] Colchester rulers tried to unify the town under their authority, using town ceremonials as occasions to exhibit and validate their power. They resorted to more elaborate ceremonial dress, some of it deliberately imitative of the clothing of London aldermen. In 1598 councillors were told to wear black gowns lined with lambskin and with a black-and-scarlet hood, all in keeping with the "fashions of the livery gowns used in the city of London."[8] It was a revealing gesture, for they had symbolically resorted to finding unity and power in the imitation of others.

In 1603, just two months after Queen Elizabeth's death, Alderman Robert Mott, who had been an alderman for thirty-one years, serving six times as bailiff, lay on his deathbed. The involvement of the Mott family in Colchester governance had spanned the Reformation years, and they had a solid interest in religious reform. Mott's father had been an alderman who in his early years had formed a strong connection with a known Lollard family.[9] Mott was known as a peacemaker; back in 1579, Mott, conceivably chosen as first bailiff in that contentious year because he had the needed spirit of unity, wrote to the earl of Leicester and Sir Francis Walsingham to inform them that unity had finally replaced the "division

---

6. BL, Stowe MS 836, f. 20. It may be that the diminishing of Puritan zeal among the town leaders partly stemmed from the election troubles.

7. Petchey, *Maldon*, 156–57.

8. CR148/1.

9. William Mott apparently married a daughter from the Lollard Wesden family, as he was mentioned in Lollard Thomas Matthew's will (ERO D/ABW25/35).

and controversy which have been among ourselves."[10] In his last will and testament, Mott revealed a matter dear to his heart, expressing concern about oneness among his fellow town leaders.

> As I have always heretofore wished well to the good estate of the corporation of Colchester and now being much grieved for some unkind dissension lately risen there, for as a fellow feeling member of that body, I do heartily desire their peace and unity, and to that end and as a token of my well meaning to them all, do give and bequeath to the bailiffs and commonalty . . . a piece of plate to be delivered unto them . . . , for as the delivery and receipt thereof there be by some good means a charitable reconciliation made among them.[11]

Mott's words serve as a reminder of the strong sense of obligation to the commonalty that had been a longtime ideal for town governors, while also acknowledging the problem faced by the rulers who had attempted to form a godly society in Elizabethan Colchester. The quest for power had corrupted the effort, and as a result, entrenched civic pride had replaced true piety, the church's simple gospel message was adulterated, deep divisions developed in the town, and by the 1590s the governors themselves were less united and their religious zeal had faltered. Colchester's tale was an early version of the story that would be repeated over and over in England until its climax in a bloody civil war in the next century. It seems that piety and earthly power are seldom compatible.

---

10. Morant, 3:34–35 (appendix to book 1). An example of Mott's evenhandedness is that in his will, Mott left 40s. to the leading two preachers of the town, Dr. Harris and Master Newcomen, who were actively opposing each other.

11. PRO 32 Harte.

Appendixes

Appendix 1

Officers of the Borough of Colchester

Bailiffs. Two men, chosen from the ten aldermen, who served for one year.

Aldermen (earlier known as auditors). Ten men, including the two bailiffs. Often served for life.

Justices of the Peace. Seven men, as provided by the charter of 1462: the two bailiffs, the recorder, and four men elected from the ranks of the aldermen. In practice, the recorder, often a nonresident, was not present for the sessions of the peace.

Recorder, or *legis peritus* (one skilled at the law). Legal consultant to the town. Usually nonresident.

Clerk of the town. Handled and made a record of the everyday legal affairs of the town. A lawyer; usually one of the gentry. Most were resident; if nonresident, had a deputy to do the work.

Coroners. Two men, who were also aldermen. Determined cause of death when not due to natural causes.

Claviers. Four men; two aldermen and two men from the common council. Keepers of the keys of the town chest; kept the common seal, records, money, plate, and jewels belonging to the corporation.

Council of sixteen, or the *primum concilium*. The highest group of the common council, elected by the bailiffs and aldermen. The town assembly, composed of the bailiffs, aldermen, and council, met at least four times a year, with the power to legislate for the borough.

Second council of sixteen (only after 1519, though the charter of 1462 had provided for it), or the *secundum concilium*. Supposed to be four men from each ward, but that requirement was not always met. Had no independent function, but joined the first group of sixteen to form the common council. Elected by the bailiffs, aldermen, and first council.

Chamberlain. Treasurer and chief financial officer of the borough. Usually from the common council. Term of service was only for one year, and the same man never held the office twice.

Sergeants at mace. Four men, one for each of the four wards. Assisted the borough court, executing processes and arrests and impaneling juries; supervised elections. A paid position; received a salary and livery.

Elections were held yearly. Lists of officers are found in the borough court rolls, and the Oath Book listed the bailiffs and often the chamberlain for each year.

Constables. At least twenty-four men, sometimes more, with at least five from
each of the four wards. The unpaid police force of the town.

Other officers mentioned occasionally: water bailiff; clerks of the market (supervisors of fish, of tanned leather, of the butcher's art, and of land); common
dredgerman of oysters; later, surveyors for the poor.

Appendix 2

The Aldermen of Tudor Colchester

Name	Origin	Occupation	Parish	Years as Alderman	Advantageous Alliances
Aleyn, George	?	Merchant	St. Leonard's	Inc 1509–11 (died 1511)*	Mr wid of Ford & John Barker; son mr dau of Ald Smalpece I
Bardfield, John	Prob Colchester	?	St. Leonard's	Inc 1490–1506 (died 1506)*	Son mr dau of Ald Cowbridge; dau mr mr Henry Barker
Barker, Richard	?	?	St. Leonard's	Inc 1489–1500 (died 1500)	
Barker, Robert	?	Clothmaker & merchant	St. James's	Inc 1493–94 (died 1503)*	Dau mr Ald John Clere
Barlow, Thomas	London adm 1565	Grocer (Merch Adv)	St. Nicholas's	1586–91 (died 1593)*	Prob grandson of Ald Thomas Flyngaunt

*a will is extant
adm = admitted to the corporation
ald = alderman/aldermen
b = born
BIL = brother-in-law
bro = brother

d = died
dau = daughter
depr = deprived
fath = father
Inc = incomplete records
Merch Adv = Merchant Adventurer

mr = married
prob = probably
r = resigned
ref = refused the office
sis = sister
wid = widow

Name	Place (admission)	Occupation	Parish	Dates	Notes
Basell, Martin	Colchester adm 1579	Merchant	St. Peter's	1586–1622 (died 1623)*	Apprentice to Ald John Beste
Beket, William	Ewarton, Suffolk adm 1522	?	St. Peter's	1529–36 (died 1538)*	Mr Clere widow
Benyght, William	Langenhoe adm 1492	?	St. Nicholas's	Inc 1505–11	
Beriff, Austin	Monks Eleigh, Suffolk adm 1513	Clothmaker	St. James's	1537–46 (resigned, ill)	Dau mr Ald Thomas Lawrence
Beriff, John	Colchester	Clothier	St. James's	1549–59 (died 1566)*	Fath was Ald Austin Beriff; sis mr Ald Lawrence
Beste, John	Colchester	Clothier; mercer; then merchant	St. Peter's	1547–74 (died 1574)*	Father was Ald Robert Beste; Byrde stepsons became ald; cousin to Cleres, Christmases
Beste, Robert	?	?	St. Botolph's	Inc 1502–03 (died 1508)*	Mr dau of Ald Nicolas Clere I; sis prob mr Ald Thomas Christmas II; sis prob mr Ald Swayne
Bradman, John	Walden Parva, Hert- fordshire, adm 1513	Merchant	Holy Trinity	1520–25	

Name	Origin	Occupation	Parish	Years as Alderman	Advantageous Alliances
Breton, John	Layer Breton, Essex adm 1486	(Gentleman)	St. James's	Inc 1498–99 (died 1500)*	Mr wid of John Vertue
Browne, Robert I	Shelland, Suffolk adm 1509	Innkeeper	St. Runwald's	1536–48 (died 1548)*	Prob mr sis of Ald Coksale
Browne, Robert II	Colchester	Baker; then grocer	St. Runwald's	1540–68 (died 1568)*	Fath was prob Ald Browne I; uncle was Ald Coksale
Bryan, John	Walton, Essex adm 1488	Clothmaker	St. Peter's	1511–16	
Buxston, William	?	Mercer	St. Runwald's	1540–46 (died 1546)*	
Byrde, John	Colchester	Merchant	St. Peter's	1580–95, 1596–1610 (died 1611)*	Fath, John Byrde, was councillor; stepfath was Ald John Beste
Byrde, Robert	Colchester	Linen draper; merchant	All Saints'	1581–89 (died 1589)*	Fath, John Byrde, was councillor; stepfath was Ald John Beste; mr dau of Jacques Tomson

Name	Place	Occupation	Parish	Dates	Notes
Christmas, John	Colchester	(Esquire)	St. James's	1515–49 (dead by 1554)	Fath & grandfath, Thomas I and II, were aldermen; cousin to Thomas Audley; sis mr gentry (William Tey & John Golding)
Christmas, Thomas I	Colchester	Prob clothier	St. Mary-at-Wall	1474–1500	Fath was prob Ald Richard Christmas
Christmas, Thomas II	Colchester	Merchant & clothmaker	St. James's	Inc 1497–1520 (died 1520)*	Fath, Thomas I, was ald; cousin to Thomas Audley; dau mr gentry (William Tey & John Golding)
Clere, Benjamin	Colchester	Clothier	St. James's	1540–76	Fath & grandfath were ald; cousin was Ald John Beste; son mr dau of Ald Robert Lambert; dau mr town preachers Nicholas Challonet & George Northey
Clere, John	Colchester	Clothier	St. James's	1511–39 (died 1539)*	Fath was Ald Nicholas Clere I; mr dau of Ald Robert Barker; dau mr gentry (William Bonham); sis mr Ald Robert Beste

Name	Origin	Occupation	Parish	Years as Alderman	Advantageous Alliances
Clere, Nicholas I	?	Clothier	St. James's	Inc 1491–92 (died 1500)*	Son mr dau of Ald Robert Barker; dau mr Ald Robert Beste
Clere, Nicholas II	Colchester	Clothier	St. Peter's	1562–70; then ref (still alive 1574)	Grandfath was Ald Nicholas Clere I; stepfath was Ald Beket
Clere, Nicholas III	Colchester	Clothier	St. James's	1573–79 (died 1579)*	Fath & grandfath were ald; bro Benjamin was ald
Cock, Thomas I	?	Shipowner	St. Leonard's	1531–44 (died 1544)*	Son prob mr dau of Ald Thomas Dybney; dau mr Ald Cock II
Cock, Thomas II	Fingringhoe, Essex adm 1568	Merchant	St. Leonard's	1575–93 (died 1595)*	Mr dau of Ald Cock I
Coksale, John	Hinden, Suffolk adm 1504	Innholder	St. Runwald's	1515–29 (died 1529)*	Sis prob mr Ald Brown I; nephew was Ald Brown II
Colle, John	Nayland, Suffolk adm 1498	Fuller; clothmaker	St. James's	1511–36 (died 1536)*	Prob mr dau of John Vertue

Name	Origin	Occupation	Parish	Dates	Notes
Cowbridge, Robert	?	Clothmaker	St. Mary's	Inc 1501–11 (died 1513)*	Dau mr son of Ald Bardfield
Debenham, William	Billericay, Essex adm 1510	(Gentleman)	St. Nicholas's	1517–20; then ref (died 1536)*	Stepson was Ald Buxston
Dybney, Thomas	Thetford, Norfolk adm 1521	Butcher	St. Martin's	1549–61 prob moved	Mr dau of John Mace, butcher; mr. stepdau of Ald Neve; dau prob mr son of Ald Cock I
Dybney, William	Colchester	?	?	1591–94	
Earnesbie, William	Olney, Buckinghamshire; London, adm 1581	?	St. James's	1586–88 (died 1588)*	Son mr dau of Ald Benjamin Clere
Flyngaunt, Robert	Colchester	"Paylemaker"	?	1542–52 (died 1552)	Fath was Ald Thomas Flyngaunt
Flyngaunt, Thomas	Prob Colchester	Clothier	St. James's	1520–41 (died 1541)*	Mr into Northern family

Name	Origin	Occupation	Parish	Years as Alderman	Advantageous Alliances
Fowle, John	Burnham, Essex adm 1547	Merchant; mariner	St. Leonard's	1568–72 (died 1572)*	Mr dau of Ald Robert Lambert; uncle was Ald Nicholas Clere III
Fynche, Ralph	?	Cordwainer; then brewer	St. Nicholas's	1547–49 (back to council; died 1552)*	Mr wid of Ald Reve
Gardener, Robert	Creeting, Suffolk adm 1502	Pewterer	All Saints'	1516–17	Mr wid of John Vertue
Halke, Richard	?	?	?	Inc 1488–89 (died 1489)	
Hamond, Christopher	Nayland, Suffolk adm 1509	(Gentleman)	St. Leonard's	1525–31	
Haselwood, Thomas	B Sudbury; of Ballington, Suffolk adm 1583	Clothier; then merchant	St. James's	1591–96, 1603–19 (died 1619)*	Stepfath was Ald Nicholas Clere III; stepbro was Ald Nicholas Clere IV; stepsis mr Ald Thomas Thurston

Name	Origin	Occupation	Parish	Dates	Notes
Heckforde, Thomas	?	Apothecary	St. Runwald's	1595–1622	
Hervy, Richard	?	Clothmaker	St. Mary's	Inc 1487–87 (died 1487)	
Heynes, Richard	Layer-de-la-Haye adm 1484	(Gentleman)	St. Peter's	Inc 1488–97	Mr wid of town clerk Roger Purpit
Hunwick, John I	Sudbury, Suffolk adm 1559	Merchant (Merch Adv)	St. Leonard's	1574–75, 1577–86	
Hunwick, John II	? adm 1594	Merchant (Gentleman) (prob Merch Adv)	St. Leonard's	1593–94 (died 1594)*	Prob heir of Ald Hunwick I
Ingram, Thomas	Ipswich, Suffolk adm 1572	Clothier	St. Peter's	1594–97 (moved; died 1611)*	
Johns, John	Prob Colchester	Mariner	St. Leonard's	Inc 1501–11	
Jopson, Thomas	Heslington, Northumberland, adm 1462	Merchant	St. Runwald's	1477–1515	

Name	Origin	Occupation	Parish	Years as Alderman	Advantageous Alliances
Jopson, William	Colchester	?	St. Runwald's	1519–25	Fath was Ald Thomas Jopson
Lambert, Richard	Colchester	Merchant	St. Leonard's	1578–91 (died 1599)*	Fath was Ald Robert Lambert; mr Beriff dau; sis mr Ald John Fowle
Lambert, Robert	Wolberswick, Suffolk adm 1541	Fishmonger; then merchant	St. Leonard's	1559–86; then ref (died 1592)*	Dau mr Ald Fowle; son mr dau of Ald William Turner I; dau mr son of Ald Benjamin Clere
Lawrence, Thomas	B Repton, Derby; of Bildeston, Suffolk adm 1549	Woolen draper; clothier	St. James's	1569–94 (died 1594)*	Mr dau of Ald Austin Beriff; mr wid of Ald Earnesbie; son mr Byrde dau
Leche, Robert	Stoke Nayland, Suffolk adm no date	Mercer	St. Peter's	1536–54 (died 1559)	Mr wid of mercer, John Turner
Lowthe, Ambrose	?	Merchant	St. Botolph's	1516–36 (died 1545)*	

Name	Origin	Occupation	Parish	Dates	Notes
Markes, Richard	?	(Gentleman)	?	Inc 1471–94	Mr wid of gentleman Robert Rokwoode,
Mayken, John	Layer Marney adm 1490	Grocer	St. Runwald's	Inc 1503–36	
Maynard, John	Colchester	Clothier	St. James's	1552–69 (died 1569)*	Fath was councillor; bro was Ald Robert Maynard; two daus mr gentlemen
Maynard, Robert	Colchester	Clothier	St. Peter's	1551–59	Fath was councillor; bro was Ald John Maynard
Middleton, Robert	?	Clothier & draper	St. Runwald's	1559–80 (still alive 1603)	Mr granddau of Ald John Reynold; son mr wid of Ald Richard Thurston; dau mr Ald Robert Mott
Mott, Robert	Colchester	Salter	St. Runwald's	1572–1604 (died 1604)*	Fath was Ald William Mott; mr dau of Ald Middleton
Mott, William	Prob Colchester	Wax chandler; then haberdasher	St. Runwald's	1549–61 (died 1562)*	Prob mr dau of Thomas Wesden
Neve, John	Stowmarket, Suffolk adm 1515	Clothmaker	St. James's	1525–40 (died 1541)*	

Name	Origin	Occupation	Parish	Years as Alderman	Advantageous Alliances
Northen, Robert I	Colchester	Clothmaker	St. Peter's	Inc 1524–25 (died 1525)*	Mr dau of Ald Smalpece I; BIL was Ald Smalpece II
Northen, Robert II	Colchester	Clothier	St. James's	1559–71	
Northey, Ralph	Colchester	Mercer; then linen draper	St. Nicholas's	1589–1608	Fath was Ald Richard Northey
Northey, Richard	Bradwell, Essex adm 1535	Linen draper	St. Nicholas's	Inc 1562–73 (died 1573)*	Relative of town preacher
Osborne, Henry	Tamworth, Staffs. adm 1570	Glover	St. Giles's; then St. Peter's	1595–1614 (died 1614)*	BIL was Vicar Robert Lewis
Pakke, Richard	?	?	St. Botolph's	Inc 1504–16	
Plomer, Richard	?	Clothmaker	?	Inc 1480–88	
Pye, John	Colchester	Clothier	St. Peter's	1572–95 (died 1597)	Stepfath was Ald George Sayer

Reade, William	?	Beer brewer	St. Leonard's	1576–78 (died 1592)*	
Reve, Thomas	Matching, Essex adm 1534	Ironmonger	St. Nicholas's	1544–49 (died 1550)*	
Reynold, John	?	Capper	St. Nicholas's	1509–23 (died 1524)*	
Reynold, Thomas	Colchester	Draper	St. Nicholas's	1589–1602 (died 1602)	Grandfath was Ald John Reynold; sis mr Ald Middleton; niece mr Ald Robert Mott
Sayer, George	Colchester	Clothier	St. Peter's	1539–72 (died 1577)*	Fath was Ald John Sayer; mr dau of Thomas Wesden; dau mr gentry William Cardinal
Sayer, John	Colchester	?	St. Peter's	Inc 1508–09 (died 1509)	
Smalpece, John I	?	?	All Saints'	1511–19	Prob mr sis of Ald Robert Beste; dau mr Ald Northen I; dau mr son of Ald Aleyn

Name	Origin	Occupation	Parish	Years as Alderman	Advantageous Alliances
Smalpece, John II	Colchester	Clothmaker	All Saints'	1526–40 (died 1542)*	Fath was Ald Smalpece I; sis mr Ald Northen I
Stone, John	Prob Colchester	Clothier	St. Peter's	1549–51 (died 1551)*	Grandfath was prob Ald Richard Hervy
Strachye, William	Sudbury, Suffolk adm 1546	Merchant	St. Leonard's	1554–59 (died 1569)*	
Swayne, John	?	?	All Saints'	Inc 1498–1515 (died 1515)*	BILs were prob Ald Robert Beste & Thomas Christmas II
Symnell, Richard	Colchester	(Gentleman)	All Saints'	1598–1608 (died 1608)*	
Sympson, William	Hadley, Suffolk adm 1546	Haberdasher	St. Runwald's	1573–74 (died 1575)*	
Thurske, John	?	Clothmaker	St. Peter's	Inc 1495–96 (died 1502)*	

Name	Place	Occupation	Parish	Dates	Notes
Thurston, Richard	Colchester	?	St. Nicholas's	ref in 1572, 1574–81 (died 1581)*	Fath was prob Ald William Thurston
Thurston, William	Colchester	Potter	St. Botolph's	1536–42	
Tompson, William	Colchester adm 1577	Clothier	St. James's	1594–97 (died 1601)*	Fath, Jacques Tompson, refused to be alderman, 1571
Turner, Thomas	Colchester	Clothier (Gentleman)	St. Peter's	1570–75 (died 1575)*	Stepfath was Ald Leche
Turner, William I	?	Merchant	St. Leonard's	1576, 1579–86 (died 1586)	Dau mr son of Ald Robert Lambert
Turner, William II	Colchester	Merchant	St. Leonard's; then St. James's	1595–1607; then ref in 1607, 1611–23	Fath was Ald William Turner I
Upchar, John	?	?	Holy Trinity	Inc 1484–93 (died 1502)*	

Name	Origin	Occupation	Parish	Years as Alderman	Advantageous Alliances
Wade, Robert	?	(Gentleman)	St. Mary's	1598–1611 (died 1611)*	
Wilson, Edmund	Heaton, Northumberland adm 1551	Merchant	St. Leonard's	1571–73 (died 1573)*	

Town Clerks, Recorders, and Members of Parliament in Tudor Colchester

Town Clerks	Recorders	Members of Parliament*	
John Harvy ca.1486		1485: Thomas Christmas[A]	John Vertue[A]
		1487: Thomas Christmas[A]	Richard Heynes[A]
		1489: Thomas Christmas[A]	Thomas Jobson[A]
		1491: Richard Heynes[A]	Thomas Jobson[A]
William Tey[GO] 1510–13	Sir James Hobard[LO] 1510–11	1512: John Clere[A**]	John Makyn[A**]
John Barnabe 1514–15	Thomas Bonham[I] 1511–32	1515: John Clere[APr**]	John Maykn[A**]
Thomas Audley[I] 1514–32		1523: Thomas Audley[I]	Ambrose Lowth[A]
Richard Duke[I] 1532–43	Richard Rich[MO] 1532–44	1529: Sir John Raynsford[O]	Richard Anthony[O]
			Richard Rich[MO]
John Lucas[IOPr] 1543–48	Anthony Stapleton[IO] 1544–52	1545: John Lucas[IOPr]	Benjamin Clere[A]
William Morice[Pr] 1549–50		1547: John Ryther[O]	John Lucas[IOPr]
John Lucas[IOPr] 1550–56	Jerome Gilbert[M] 1553–54	1553: Sir Francis Jobson[PrS]	John Lucas[IOPr**]
		1553: John Lucas[IOPr]	John Beste[A]
	Anthony Stapleton[IO] 1554–60	1554: Sir Francis Jobson[PrS]	William Cardinall I[GO]
		1554: George Sayer[A]	Robert Browne[A]
		1555: Sir Francis Jobson[PrS]	John Hering[L]
John Carowel 1557–64		1558: George Christmas[S]	Thomas Lucas[SI]
		1559: Sir Francis Jobson[PrS]	William Cardinall I[GO]
Robert Gynes[I] 1564–66	William Cardinall I[GO] 1560–68	1563: Sir Francis Jobson[PrS]	William Cardinall I[GO]
Thomas Lucas[SI] 1566–72	Thomas Meade[M] 1568–72	1571: Henry Golding[OPr]	Francis Harvey[P]
William Cardinall II[GPSJ] 1572–76	Sir Thomas Lucas[SI] 1572–76	1572: Robert Christmas[OS]	Henry Golding[OPr]
			Nicholas Clere[A]
			Robert Middleton[IS]
James Morice[MPS] 1576–97	William Cardinall II[GPSJ] 1576–78	1584: James Morice[SP]	Francis Harvey[P]
	Sir Francis Walsingham[GP] 1578–90		

Francis Harvey[P]
Arthur Throckmorton
Martin Basell[A]

Richard Symnell[IJ]
Richard Symnell[AJ]

1586: James Morice[SP]
1588: James Morice[SP]
1592: James Morice[SP]

1597: Robert Barker[IJ]
1601: Robert Barker[IJ]

Sir Thomas Heneage[G]
1590–96
Robert Cecil[GJ] 1596–1612

Richard Symnell[IJ] 1596–97
Robert Barker[IJ] 1597–1618

*Parliaments are listed only if the Colchester members are known.
**Probable MP, but not certain
A = alderman of Colchester
G = educated at Gray's Inn
I = educated at the Inner Temple
J = educated at St. John's, Cambridge
L = educated at Lincoln's Inn
M = educated at the Middle Temple
O = connections with the earl of Oxford
P = Puritan
Pr = committed Protestant, even before Mary's reign
S = son of an alderman or a former town official

Appendix 4

The de Veres, the Earls of Oxford in the Tudor Period

John, twelfth earl. 1408–62. Succeeded his father in 1417. Executed as a Lancastrian.

John, thirteenth earl. 1443–1513. Succeeded his father in 1462. Fled England in 1471. Returned with Henry Tudor in 1485 and gained numerous offices under Henry VII. His widow, Elizabeth, lived at Wivenhoe until her death in 1537.

John, fourteenth earl. 1499–1526. Succeeded his uncle in 1513, at the age of fourteen. Extravagant and irresponsible. Died without issue, so direct line ended with his death.

John, fifteenth earl. 1490–1540. Succeeded his second cousin in 1526, but with a diminished estate. Was a courtier, loyal to Henry VIII's policies.

John, sixteenth earl. 1512–62. Succeeded his father in 1540. Was Protestant.

Edward, seventeenth earl. 1550–1604. Succeeded his father in 1562, at the age of twelve. Had an unhappy marriage with Anne, daughter of Lord Burghley. Was a poet; some believe he was the author of Shakespeare's plays.

Henry, eighteenth earl. 1593–1625. Succeeded his father in 1604.

Information from William Addison, *Essex Worthies* (London: Phillimore, 1973), 189–91; S. T. Bindoff, *The House of Commons, 1509–1558* (London: Secker and Warburg, 1982), 3:241.

Appendix 5
Parish Churches

Parish Churches	Value of Benefice*	Patron before the Reformation	Patron after the Reformation
Within the Walls			
1. All Saints'	not listed	St. Botolph's Priory	Bishop of London
2. Holy Trinity	£6 13s. 4d.	St. John's Abbey	Crown
3. St. James's	£11 10s.	St. Botolph's Priory	Audley family (Crown,1585)
4. St. Martin's	£6 13s. 4d.	St. Botolph's Priory	Audley family
5. St. Mary-at-Wall	£10	Bishop of London	Bishop of London (Crown, 1596)
6. St. Nicholas's	£10	St. John's Abbey	Crown
7. St. Peter's	£10	St. Botolph's Priory	Audley family (Crown, 1589)
8. St. Runwald's	£7 13s. 4d.	Tey family	Bishop of London
Outside the Walls			
9. St. Botolph's	not listed	St. Botolph's Priory	Audley family (bishop of London, 1557)
10. St. Giles's	not listed— only a curacy	St. John's Abbey	Lucas family

11. St. Leonard's	£10	St. John's Abbey	Audley family, 1539; Crown, 1550–
12. St. Mary Magdalen's	£11, when part of hospital	St. John's Abbey	Uncertain; lapsed part of the time
Village Churches			
13. Berechurch (West Donyland)	not listed—only a curacy	St. John's Abbey	Audley family
14. Greenstead	100s.	St. John's Abbey	Crown
15. Lexden	£12	Radcliff family	Earl of Sussex
16. Mile End	£7	St. Botolph's Priory	Thomas Audley, Lucas family (bishop of London, 1555)

*Figures are from a return made in 1574 (PRO SP 12/101). They agree with the 1535 *Valor Ecclesiasticus*, except that the figure for St. James's was slightly lower in the earlier report. Also, the figure for St. Mary Magdalen's comes from the *Valor*.

Parish Priests, Ministers, and Curates

All Saints'	Holy Trinity	St. James's	St. Martin's	St. Mary-at-Wall	St. Nicholas's
William Bryan,† 1485–86r	Henry Corkar,† 1486–?	John Adam,† 1470–93d	William Twycross,† 1480–90r	Thomas Kerver, A.M.† 1483–1503r	Robert Alwether,† 1485–99r
William Belle, 1487–94d		John Lowth, 1493–1505d	Richard Friere,† 1490–1501d	Robert Lownde, L.B.,† 1503–?	
William Hintlesham,† 1494–97r	Richard Gildinwater,† 1502–1505r		John Ector,† 1502–18d	Thomas Chanon, A.B., 1504	Thomas Wilkinson,† 1499–1518?
Robert Butley, 1497–?	Edward Squire,† 1505–10depr	Thomas Knightby, B.D.,† 1505–10r			

† beneficed incumbent

d = died

depr = deprived

r = resigned

Information from Newcourt, vol. 2; Morant, vol. 2; registers, Bishop of London, Guildhall MSS 9537/1–13; visitation act book, Bishop of London, Guildhall MSS 9537/1–8; J. C. Challenor Smith, "Some Additions to Newcourt's *Repertorium*—Volume II," *TEAS*, n.s., 6 (1898): 238–41. Additional sources for each parish follow.

All Saints': on Havyn, *RPB*, 87; on Plumpton, W. Gurney Benham, *Historical Notes about the Churches of All Saints and St. Nicholas-cum-St. Runwald, Colchester* (n.d.), 11.

Holy Trinity: on Correnbeck, ERO D/ACA21/278 and Emmison, *Morals*, 209; on Copland, ERO D/ACV2/10.

St. James's: on Spencer, ERO D/ACR6/465; on Cock, ERO D/ACA10/157; on Miller, ERO D/ACA17/266; on Turner, ERO D/ACA17/259; on Agar, unpublished notes by the late Hilda Grieve.

St. Martin's: on Spencer, ERO D/ACA9/90, 228, and D/ACA14/50; on Correnbeck, Guildhall MS 9537/8, f. 53.

St.-Mary-at-Wall: on Chanon, PRO 8 Holgrave; on Wilkinson, CR89/25, 25d; on Rawlyns, ERO D/ABW16/9; on Oswester, CR103/26; on Walford, Morant, 2.5.

St. Nicholas's: on Remey, ERO D/ACR1/171; on Hartley, PRO 21 Bodfelde; on Borowe, *RPB*, 88; on Havyn, CR104/3; on Swadell, ERO D/ABW25/85; on Shelbury, ERO D/ACA14/9; on Farrar, ERO D/ACA14/217; on Banbrig, ERO D/ACV2/10; on Archer, ERO D/ACV3.

St. Peter's: on Harvie, Guildhall MS 9537/2, f. 63v.

St. Runwald's: on Lewis, ERO D/ACV1/6; on Copland, ERO D/ACV2/10; on Cole, ERO D/ACA24/113.

St. Giles's: on Aunger, unpublished notes by Hilda Grieve.

St. Leonard's: on Wilkinson, PRO 13 Dogett; on Forster, PRO 18 Adeane.

Greenstead: on Denman, ERO D/ACV2/78.

Lexden: on Kelsey, ERO D/ACR1/117; I believe Kelsey is the same as Newcourt's "Peter Kelsham."

All Saints'	Holy Trinity	St. James's	St. Martin's	St. Mary-at-Wall	St. Nicholas's
					William Remey, 1510
	John Dyson,† 1510–11d				
Hugo Fetherston,† ca.1510–25r	Ralph Tylney,† 1511–18r	John Wayne, D.L.,† 1510–36d			
	John Swan, A.B.,† 1518–25r		John Stow,† 1518–24d	Thomas Wilkinson,† ca. 1514–29r	
	Thomas Nicholas, 1526–30r		Henry Bromfeld,† 1524–37d		John Hartley, 1524
Thomas Hunden,† 1525–?	Robert Dent, A.M.,† 1530–31r			Nicolas Rawlyns,† 1529–30	Robert Lownde, L.B.† 1529–30d
	William Jay, A.M.,† 1531–54?			Edmund Campion, S.T.B.,† 1531–32depr	Richard Langryge, S.T.B.,† 1530–37r
William Havyn, 1534				John Clarke,† 1532–39r	Robert Borowe, 1534
		John PeKyns,† 1536–39r	Thomas Ydell,† 1537–?	Edward Oswester, curate, 1533–34	William Havyn, curate, 1535
		John Cornish,† 1539–41d		Thomas Kyrkham,† 1540–51d	William Bikerstaff,† 1537–?
Robert Plumpton,† ca. 1540–ca. 1544		John Blauncke, A.M.,† 1541–?		Marmaduke Smyth,† 1551–55depr	
John Pepper,† 1546–53				Thomas Gale, curate, 1554	William Swadell, curate, 1550
John Dixon,† 1542?–57depr	William Nevard, curate, 1554				

John Lukyn, A.M.,† 1557–59r
William Cowson,† 1559–69?

Oliver Pigge,† June 1569–?
John Walford,† October 1571–1609

Thomas Hilles, alias Theodorus Van den Berghe, preacher, 1588–92

Lawrence Agar, curate, 1559

William Lyon,† 1561–85d

Thomas Rosse, curate, 1583
Robert Good,† 1585–97?

Henry Corenbeck, 1592–94

John Copland, 1597–98
William Read,† 1597–?
William Bird,† 1597–?

John Thorpe,† 1555–56r
John Francis,† 1556d
Thomas Dyconson,† 1556–58d
Thomas Browne,† 1558–62
Hugo Allen,† 1562–65
John Walford, curate, 1577
John Walford,† ca. 1580–96

Richard Boniar, curate, 1577
Richard Spenser, 1580–83
Robert Goode, curate, 1584

John Spencer, 1576
Richard Glover, curate, 1577
William Cock, 1580–84
Robert Holmes,† 1585–ca. 1591
Miller, curate, 1589

Turner, curate, 1589–?96
George Northey, M.A., preacher, 1589–92
Thomas Farrar, 1591–1610d

William Cooke, sequestrator, 1577
Gerrard Shelbury, curate, ca. 1580–86
Thomas Farrar, B.A., 1587–90
Thomas Hilles, alias Theodorus Van den Berghe, preacher, 1588
William Banbrick, curate, 1592–97
George Archer, curate, 1597–1601

Henry Corenbeck, sequestrator, 1592

George Archer,† 1596–1603d
Thomas Taylcott,† 1603–?

St. Peter's	St. Runwald's	St. Botolph's	St. Giles's	St. Leonard's	St. Mary Magdalen's
William Browne,† 1485–94d	Thomas Nutak,† 1479–1513d			Thomas Skypwith,† 1482–87r	
				William Stokdale, S.T.B.† 1487	
					Thomas Skipwith, 1499
Richard Caumond, A.M.,† 1494–1535d		Richard White, curate, 1496		Thomas Wilkinson, curate, 1492–1501	Richard Pigall, 1504
			John Tawnton, 1504		
				James Forster, 1506	
		John Grewe, curate, 1509	William Fenning, curate, 1509–13	Thomas Chanon, A.B.,† 1509–13	
	Christopher Swallowe, A.M.,† 1513–16r			Robert Lownde, L.B.,† 1513–28r	
		Thomas Hale, 1514	John Colchester, curate, 1514		Thomas Chanon, 1514
			John Taunton, 1514		
			John Stoke, curate, 1515		John Wayne, 1516
	John Farfurth, L.B.,† 1516–19r	Walter Dowe, 1517			John Phelypps, 1516–17
					Thomas Smith, 1520
	Robert Knotsford,† 1519–25r		John Fraunces, curate, 1521		
	William Fawcett, A.M.,† 1525–44r	John Thixtill, 1525			
			Edward Oswestry, curate, 1528	John Smith,† 1528–29r	
			Harry Dyer, curate, 1529	Robert Harvey,† 1529–39r	John Swan, 1534
Robert Bachcroft,† 1535–37d					
Henry Beck,† 1537–45d					Ralph Lee, 1538–42
				William Wright, alias Smith,† 1539–50depr	

John Thorpe,† 1545–65d

William Townson,† 1544–?

Bevys Wright, 1545

John Fraunces, curate, 1545, 1554

Nicholas Davye,† 1550–53?depr

Thomas Gale, 1554

John Champinyes, curate, 1554

William Wright, alias Smith,† restored 155?–57d

Thomas Harvie, 1562

Nicholas Welles, curate, 1557

Thomas Gale, S.T.B.,† 1557r

Hugo Allen, 1563

Marcellinus Outred,† 1565–?

Thomas Aunger (Ager), curate, 1557–62

Peter Walker,† 1557–70d

Michael Goodeare,† curate, 1561–69; beneficed, 1570–71

Oliver Pigge,† 1569–71

Richard Glover, 1571

Thomas Upcher,† curate, 1561–?; beneficed, 1572–82r

John Elliot, 1569–72?

Richard Spencer, curate, 1575–83

Richard Spenser, curate, 1580

Richard Glover, curate, 1577

William Kirby, curate, 1577–84

Gerrard Shelbury, curate, 1580

Ralph Leaver 1582–84?

Thomas Lowe,† 1582–1615d

John Kinge, curate, 1583

Robert Lewis,† 1579–88

Thomas Holland, curate,1583–86

Robert Lewis, curate, 1583–88

Thomas Knevett, A.M.,† 1584–86

Edward Gutter, sequestrator, 1592

William Cock, 1588

William Cock,† curate, 1585–1619d

Thomas Lowe, curate, 1588–92

Thomas Taverner, A.M.,† 1588–90r

Thomas Farrar, curate, 1588–1607

Edward Gutter, A.M.,† 1590–93r

John Copland, sequestrator, 1597

Thomas Fryer, 1597–99

William Cole,† 1593–1600r

William Cole, A.B. 1597–1600

Stephen Newcomen,† 1600–29d

Berechurch	Greenstead	Lexden	Mile End
Henry Corkar,† 1486–?	William Hasan,† ?–1495d	John Mounford,† 1468–92d	Robert Alwether,† 1478–88r
	Richard Gildingwater,† 1495–?	John Ratcliff,† 1492–99r	John Lowth,† 1488–94r
		John Jackson,† 1499–?	Thomas Skipwith,† 1494r
Edward Squire, 1505–10depr		Simon Kelsey,† 1505?–6?	Simon Kelsey,† 1494–1503r
John Dyson, 1510–11d	William Boteler,† ?–1510r		William Ripon,† 1503–10r
Ralph Tylney, 1511–18r	Richard Powes,† 1511–38d	John Collings, D.B.† ?–1524d	Roger Cherch,† 1510–27d
John Swan, A.B., 1518–25r			
Thomas Nicholas, 1526–30r		William Grant,† 1524–37d	
Robert Dent, A.M., 1530–31r	William Jenkenson,† 1538r		
William Jay, A.M., 1531–?	William Kerchin,† 1538–40r	Roger Gorstelowe,† 1538–67d	Richard Sharples,† 1537–42d
	Patrick Collins, 1540		John Gyppes,† 1542–51r
	William Tayler,† 1540–41d		

William Fyske,† 1551–55depr
John Parkinson,† 1555–60r
William Lyon,† 1560–84d

Thomas Knevett, A.M.,† 1584–1608?

John Price,† 1567–76r

Robert Searle,† 1576–1610d

Robert Cooke, minister, 1587
Thomas Farrar, 1588

Thomas Talcoat, 1597–1636?

John Jenner, 1599

William Patch,† 1541–42d
William Bikerstaffe,† 1542–46d
Richard Alvey,† 1546–48r
Nicholas Davy,† 1548–?
Ralph Moer, curate, 1554
Michael Goodyeare,† 1563–69
Richard Spencer,† 1574–80
Gerard Shelbury,† 1580–85r
Robert Holmes,† 1585–89?
John Watson,† 1589
William Banbrick,† 1590–98r
John Worshipp,† 1598
William Denman, 1598–1601
William Weden, 1601
Sam Baldock,† ?

Thomas Aunger, curate, 1554

William Lyon, 1561–85d

Phillips, ca. 1584
Thomas Holland,† 1585–ca.90
Phillip Blunt,† 1588–92
William Cole, A.B.† 1592–ca. 98
Greene, 1593
William Hills, 1597
Richard Nuthall, 1597–99
William Read,† 1598–1612
Thomas Gallymor 1600–1601

Appendix 7

Perpetual Chantries in Colchester

Chantry	Founded	In the Gift of	Location	Later Developments	At Dissolution
John of Colchester	1321–22	Bailiffs and commonalty	St. Helen's Chapel		1539; to Corporation
Joseph Elianore	1348	Bailiffs and commonalty	Church of St. Mary-at-Wall	1535: listed in *Valor Ecclesiasticus*	1539; to Corporation
Richolda de Cosford	1395	Bailiffs and commonalty	St. Helen's Chapel	1535: still at St. Helen's	1539; to Corporation
Holy Cross	Early 15th century, by Guild of St. Helen	Guild of St. Helen	Chapel of Crossed Friars		1537 or 1539; to Audley
Thomas Fraunceys	1416	Guild of St. Helen	St. Nicholas's Church	1535: listed in *Valor Ecclesiasticus*	1539; to Audley
Edmund Haverland	1431	Guild of St. Helen	Chapel of Crossed Friars		1539; to Audley

Information from Morant, 2:45–51; *Valor Ecclesiasticus* (1810), 1:443; J. H. Round, *St. Helen's Chapel, Colchester* (London: Elliot Stock, n.d.), 18; BL, Stowe MS 834, pp. 72–73, 77; Guildhall MS 9531; PRO E301/20; ERO D/DRg 6/8.

Chantry	Founded	In the Gift of	Location	Later Developments	At Dissolution
Thomas Godston	Mid-15th century	Probably Guild of St. Helen	Chapel of Crossed Friars	1496: to stay at Crossed Friars 1510, 1518: to Crossed Friars	1537
Richard Heynes	ca. 1470	Executors	St. Peter's Church	1535: listed in *Valor Ecclesiasticus*	1547–48; to Crown
Peter Barwick	ca. 1480		St. Leonard's Church	1535: listed in *Valor Ecclesiasticus*	1547–48; to Crown
Edmund Harmanson	ca. 1485		St. Leonard's Church	1535: listed in *Valor Ecclesiasticus*	Property to Audley before his death in 1544

Appendix 8

Survey of Colchester Ministers, Mid-1580s

I. Ignorant and unpreaching ministers
   Master Shelbury, parson of St. Nicholas's
   Master Holland, curate of St. Botolph's
   Master Phillips, curate of Berechurch, a drunkard
   Master Golde, curate of Holy Trinity, also sometime a mender of saddles and panels
   Master Walford, parson of St. Mary-at-Wall
II. Double beneficed men [pluralists]
   Master Lowe, vicar of St. Leonard's
   Master Walford, vicar of All Saints'
   Master Holmes, of St. James's
   Master Golde, of St. Martin's
III. The sufficient painful and careful preachers and ministers . . . who have been sundry times molested and vexed, partly for refusing the late urged subscription, and partly for not wearing the surplice, and omitting the cross in baptism and the like
   Master Northey, preacher of Colchester; suspended by the bishop of London for the space of a whole year.
   Master Knevett, parson of Mile End, Colchester, was suspended since the bishop's visitation, for preaching in his own charge without a license.

Taken from the survey of Essex ministers printed in Thomas William Davids, *Annals of Evangelical Nonconformity in the County of Essex* (London: Jackson, Walford, and Hodder, 1863), 98, 104, 106, 111, 113–14, using the wording in Davids, though with some omissions, with spelling modernized, and with the names of some of the churches amended for clarity. This survey was first compiled in the summer of 1584, but it reflects two additions made in 1585, that is, Masters Holmes and Cock, who entered into their benefices in 1585. Patrick Collinson, *The Elizabethan Puritan Movement* (Berkeley: University of California Press, 1967), 489n, says that the Essex survey contains references to Bishop Aylmer's visitation in 1586. The survey is also printed in Peel's *The Seconde Parte of a Register*, which is a calendar of manuscripts compiled for publication by the Puritans, ca. 1593; see Harold Smith, *Ecclesiastical History of Essex under the Long Parliament and Commonwealth* (Colchester: Benham, n.d.), 9.

405

Master Searles, pastor of Lexden, hath, since the bishop's visitation, a day set for him for deprivation, for not yielding to wear the surplice.

Master Lewis, pastor of St. Peter's, Colchester, suspended at the time of the subscription, and being restored again, hath now, since the bishop's last visitation, a day set for deprivation for not wearing the surplice.

Master Cock, pastor of St. Giles's, Colchester, hath, since the bishop's last visitation, a day set for deprivation, for not yielding to wear the surplice.

Bibliography

Manuscript Sources

British Library

    Harley Manuscripts 416, 421, 595.
    Stowe Manuscripts 150, 829–31, 834–41.

Essex Record Office, Chelmsford

    Commissary Court of the Bishop of London. Registered and Original Wills.
        D/ABW.
    The Court of the Archdeacon of Colchester. Act Books. D/ACA1–24.
    The Court of the Archdeacon of Colchester. Original Wills. D/ACW.
    The Court of the Archdeacon of Colchester. Registered Probate Wills.
        D/ACR.
    The Court of the Archdeacon of Colchester. Visitation Act Books.
        D/ACV1–3.

Essex Record Office, Colchester

    Borough of Colchester. Assembly Book, 1576–98. D/B5 Gb1.
    Borough of Colchester. Assembly Book, 1600–1620. D/B5 Gb2.
    Borough of Colchester. Book of Examinations and Recognizances. D/B5
        Sb2/1–6.
    Borough of Colchester. Book of Examinations and Recognizances, 1562–72.
        Also known as *Liber ordinacionum*. D/B5 R5.
    Borough of Colchester. Contribution Book to the Poor (1581–82).
    Borough of Colchester. Court Rolls. CR82–161.
    Borough of Colchester. Monday Court Book, 1571–76. D/B5 R7.
    Colchester Parish Churches. Parish Registers. D/P178, 203, 245–46, 323–25,
        381; or a transcript, T/R108/2, 5.
    Morant Manuscripts. D/Y2/2–10.

Guildhall Library, London

Bishop of London. Registers. Guildhall Manuscripts 9531/7–13.
Bishop of London. Visitation Act Book. Guildhall Manuscripts 9537/1–8.

Public Record Office

Chantry Certificates. E301.
Poll Tax Returns. E179.
Prerogative Court of Canterbury. Registered Probate Wills.

Other

Corpus Christi College Manuscript 122.
Lambeth Cart. Misc. Vol. 13, pt. 2, no. 57.

Printed Primary Sources

Acts of the Privy Council of England. Ed. J. R. Dasent. 32 vols. London: HMSO, 1890–1907.

Benham, W. Gurney. *Translated Abstracts of the Court Rolls, 1310–1602, Borough of Colchester.* 33 vols. Colchester: handwritten by Benham, 1930s–1940s.

Benton, G. Montagu, ed. "Essex Wills at Canterbury." *TEAS,* n.s., 21 (1937): 234–69.

Boyd's Marriage Index, Essex. N.p., n.d.

"Calendar of Queen's Bench Indictments Ancient Relating to Essex, 1558–1603, in the Public Record Office." Typescript. Essex Record Office, Chelmsford, n.d.

Calendar of Patent Rolls: Edward VI. 6 vols. London: HMSO, 1924–29.

Calendar of Patent Rolls: Elizabeth I. 9 vols. London: HMSO, 1939–86.

Calendar of State Papers, Domestic: Edward VI, Mary, Elizabeth, and James I. 12 vols. London: HMSO, 1856–72.

Calendar of State Papers, Spanish. London: HMSO, 1862.

Cockburn, J. S., ed. *Calendar of Assize Records, Essex Indictments: Elizabeth I.* London: HMSO, 1978.

Cook, G. H., ed. *Letters to Cromwell and Others on the Suppression of the Monasteries.* London: John Baker, 1965.

Dickens, A. G., and Dorothy Carr, eds. *The Reformation in England to the Accession of Elizabeth I.* New York: St. Martin's Press, 1968.

Dickin, Edward P. "Embezzled Church Goods of Essex." *TEAS,* n.s., 13 (1915): 157–71.

Elton, G. R., ed. *Renaissance and Reformation, 1300–1648.* New York: Macmillan, 1963.

Emmison, F. G., ed. *Elizabethan Life: Wills of Essex Gentry and Merchants.* Chelmsford: Essex County Council, 1978.

———. *Elizabethan Life: Wills of Essex Gentry and Yeomen.* Chelmsford: Essex County Council, 1980.

Feet of Fines for Essex. Vol. 4, *1423–1547.* Ed. P. H. Reaney and Marc Fitch. Colchester: Essex Archaeological Society, 1964.

Feet of Fines for Essex. Vol. 5, *1547–1580.* Ed. Marc Fitch and Frederick Emmison. Oxford: Leopard's Head Press, 1991.

Foster, Joseph, ed. *London Marriage Licenses, 1521–1869.* London: Bernard Quaritch, 1887.

Foxe, John. *The Acts and Monuments of John Foxe.* Ed. Stephen Reed Cattley. 8 vols. London: R. B. Seeley and W. Burnside, 1841.

Fraser, S. "A Pynson Indulgence of 1523." *Sussex Archaeological Collections* 50 (1907): 109–16.

Harrison, William. *The Description of England.* Ed. Georges Edelen. Ithaca, N.Y.: Cornell University Press, 1968.

Latimer, Hugh. *Sermons.* Ed. George Elwes Corrie. Cambridge: Cambridge University Press, 1844.

Letters and Papers, Foreign and Domestic, of the Reign of Henry VIII. Ed. J. S. Brewer, James Gairdner, and R. H. Brodie. 21 vols. London: HMSO, 1864–1932.

Moens, William John Charles, ed. *Register of Baptisms in the Dutch Church at Colchester.* Lymington: Charles T. King, 1905.

Myrc, John. *Instructions to Parish Priests.* Ed. Edward Peacock. London: Kegan Paul, Trench, Trübner, and Company, 1898.

The Oath Book or Red Parchment Book of Colchester. Trans. W. Gurney Benham. Colchester: *Essex County Standard* Office, 1907.

Pronay, Nicholas, and John Taylor, eds. *Parliamentary Texts of the Later Middle Ages.* Oxford: Clarendon Press, 1980.

Prothero, G. W., ed. *Select Statutes and Other Constitutional Documents Illustrative of the Reigns of Elizabeth and James I.* 4th ed. Oxford: Clarendon Press, 1913.

The Red Paper Book of Colchester. Trans. W. Gurney Benham. Colchester: *Essex County Standard* Office, 1902.

A Relation, or Rather a True Account, of the Island of England. Trans. Charlotte Augusta Sneyd. London: Camden Society, 1897.

Seymour-Smith, Martin, ed. *The English Sermon, an Anthology.* 3 vols. Cheadle, Cheshire: Carcanet Press, 1976.

Smith, Sir Thomas. *De Republica Anglorum.* London, 1583.

Strype, John. *Annals of the Reformation.* 4 vols. Oxford: Clarendon Press, 1824.

————. *Ecclesiastical Memorials.* 3 vols. Oxford: Clarendon Press, 1822.

Tanner, J. R., ed. *Tudor Constitutional Documents,* A.D. *1485–1603, with an Historical Commentary.* Cambridge: Cambridge University Press, 1948.

Valor Ecclesiasticus. 6 vols. 1810.

Secondary Sources

Addison, William. *Essex Worthies.* London: Phillimore, 1973.

Addy, John. "The Archdeacon and Ecclesiastical Discipline in Yorkshire, 1598–1714: Clergy and Churchwardens." *Borthwick Papers* 24 (1963): 1–33.

Alexander, H. G. *Religion in England, 1558–1662.* London: University of London Press, 1968.

Alldridge, Nick. "Loyalty and Identity in Chester Parishes, 1540–1640." In *Parish, Church, and People: Local Studies in Lay Religion, 1350–1750,* ed. Susan J. Wright. London: Hutchinson, 1988.

Anderson, M. D. *History and Imagery in British Churches.* London: John Murray, 1971.

Anglin, Jay Pascal. "The Court of the Archdeacon of Essex, 1571–1609." Ph.D. diss., University of California, 1965.

————. "The Essex Puritan Movement and 'Bawdy' Courts." In *Tudor Men and Institutions: Studies in English Law and Government,* ed. Arthur J. Slavin. Baton Rouge: Louisiana State University Press, 1972.

————. *The Third University: A Survey of Schools and School Masters in the Elizabethan Diocese of London.* Norwood, Pa.: Norwood Editions, 1985.

Archer, Rowena E., and B. E. Ferme. "Testamentary Procedure with Special Reference to the Executrix." *Reading Medieval Studies* 15 (1989): 3–34.

Aries, Philippe. *The Hour of Our Death.* Trans. Helen Weaver. New York: Alfred A. Knopf, 1981.

Aston, Margaret. *Lollards and Reformers.* London: Hambledon Press, 1984.

Baker, Alan R. H. "Changes in the Later Middle Ages." In *A New Historical Geography of England,* ed. H. C. Darby. Cambridge: Cambridge University Press, 1973.

Beer, Barrett L. "London Parish Clergy and the Protestant Reformation, 1547–1559." *Albion* 18 (1986): 375–93.

Beier, A. L. *The Problem of the Poor in Tudor and Early Stuart England.* New York: Methuen, 1983.

Benham, W. Gurney. "The Chapel of the Holy Cross in Crouch Street, Colchester." *ER* 45 (1936): 33–35.

————. Introduction to *Court Rolls of the Borough of Colchester,* ed. and trans. Isaac Herbert Jeayes. 4 vols. Colchester: Colchester Town Council, 1921–41.

————. "A Parliamentary Election in Colchester in 1571." *ER* 49 (1940): 185–90.

Bennett, H. S. *English Books and Readers*. 2d ed. 3 vols. Cambridge: Cambridge University Press, 1965–70.

———. *The Pastons and Their England*. Cambridge: Cambridge University Press, 1968.

Bernard, G. W. "The Church of England, c. 1529–c. 1642." *History* 75 (1990): 183–206.

Bettey, J. H. *Church and Community: The Parish Church in English Life*. Bradford-on-Avon, Wiltshire: Moonraker Press, 1979.

Bindoff, S. T., ed. *The House of Commons, 1509–1558*. 3 vols. London: Secker and Warburg, 1982.

———. *Tudor England*. Baltimore: Penguin Books, 1950.

Bossy, John. *Christianity in the West, 1400–1700*. Oxford: Oxford University Press, 1985.

———. "The Mass as a Social Institution, 1200–1700." *PP* 100 (1983): 29–61.

Bowker, Margaret. *The Secular Clergy in the Diocese of Lincoln, 1495–1520*. Cambridge: Cambridge University Press, 1968.

Brigden, Susan. *London and the Reformation*. Oxford: Clarendon Press, 1989.

Britnell, R. H. "Bailiffs and Burgesses in Colchester, 1400–1525." *EAH* 21 (1990): 103–9.

———. "Colchester Courts and Court Records, 1310–1525." *EAH* 17 (1986): 133–40.

———. *Growth and Decline in Colchester, 1300–1525*. Cambridge: Cambridge University Press, 1986.

———. "The Oath Book of Colchester and the Borough Constitution, 1372–1404." *EAH* 14 (1982): 94–101.

Brooks, C. W. *Pettyfoggers and Vipers of the Commonwealth: The "Lower Branch" of the Legal Profession in Early Modern England*. Cambridge: Cambridge University Press, 1986.

Brown, Andrew. *Popular Piety in Late Medieval England: The Diocese of Salisbury, 1250–1550*. Oxford: Clarendon Press, 1995.

Burgess, Clive. "'By Quick and by Dead': Wills and Pious Provision in Late Medieval Bristol." *EHR* 102 (1987): 837–58.

———. "Late Medieval Wills and Pious Convention: Testamentary Evidence Reconsidered." In *Profit, Piety, and the Professions in Later Medieval England*, ed. Michael Hicks. Gloucester: Alan Sutton, 1990.

Byford, M. S. "The Price of Protestantism—Assessing the Impact of Religious Change in Elizabethan Essex: The Cases of Heydon and Colchester, 1558–1594." Ph.D. diss., Oxford University, 1988.

Camp, Anthony J. *Wills and Their Whereabouts*. 4th ed. London: n.p., 1974.

Carlson, Eric Josef. "Clerical Marriage and the English Reformation." *JBS* 31 (1992): 1–31.

Carpenter, Christine. "The Religion of the Gentry of Fifteenth-Century England." In *England in the Fifteenth Century: Proceedings of the 1986 Harlaxton Symposium,* ed. Daniel Williams. Woodbridge, Suffolk: Boydell and Brewer, 1987.

Christy, Miller, W. W. Porteous, and E. Bertram Smith. "The Monumental Brasses of Colchester." *TEAS,* n.s., 13 (1915): 39–52.

Clark, Peter. *English Provincial Society from the Reformation to the Revolution: Religion, Politics, and Society in Kent, 1500–1640.* Hassocks, Sussex: Harvester Press, 1977.

Clark, Peter, and Paul Slack. *English Towns in Transition, 1500–1700.* London: Oxford University Press, 1976.

Cliffe, J. T. *The Puritan Gentry: The Great Puritan Families of Early Stuart England.* London: Routledge and Kegan Paul, 1984.

Coldewey, John Christopher. "Early Essex Drama." Ph.D. diss., University of Colorado, 1972.

Collins, Stephen L. *From Divine Cosmos to Sovereign State: An Intellectual History of Consciousness and the Idea of Order in Renaissance England.* New York: Oxford University Press, 1989.

Collinson, Patrick. *The Birthpangs of Protestant England: Religious and Cultural Change in the Sixteenth and Seventeenth Centuries.* New York: St. Martin's Press, 1988.

———. "The Elizabethan Church and the New Religion." In *The Reign of Elizabeth I,* ed. Christopher Haigh. London: Macmillan, 1984.

———. *The Elizabethan Puritan Movement.* Berkeley: University of California Press, 1967.

———. *The Religion of Protestants: The Church in English Society, 1559–1625.* Oxford: Clarendon Press, 1982.

Cooper, Janet. "Civic Ceremonial in Tudor and Stuart Colchester." *Essex Journal* 23 (1988): 65–67.

Cressy, David. "A Drudgery of Schoolmasters: The Teaching Profession in Elizabethan and Stuart England." In *The Professions in Early Modern England,* ed. Wilfrid Prest. London: Croom Helm, 1987.

———. *Literacy and the Social Order: Reading and Writing in Tudor and Stuart England.* Cambridge: Cambridge University Press, 1980.

Cromwell, Thomas Kitson. *History and Description of the Ancient Town and Borough of Colchester.* 2 vols. London: Robert Jennings, 1825.

Cross, Claire. *Church and People, 1450–1660: The Triumph of the Laity in the English Church.* London: Fontana, 1976.

———. " 'Great Reasoners in Scripture': The Activities of Women Lollards, 1380–1530." In *Medieval Women,* ed. Derek Baker. Oxford: Basil Blackwell, 1978.

Crummy, Philip. *Aspects of Anglo-Saxon and Norman Colchester.* CBA Research Report 39. London: Council for British Archaeology, 1981.

Cutts, Edward L. *Colchester*. London: Longmans, Green, and Company, 1888.
———. *Parish Priests and Their People in the Middle Ages in England*. London: SPCK, 1914.
Davids, Thomas William. *Annals of Evangelical Nonconformity in the County of Essex*. London: Jackson, Walford, and Hodder, 1863.
Davis, James R. "Colchester, 1600–1662: Politics, Religion, and Officeholders in an English Provincial Town." Ph.D. diss., Brandeis University, 1980.
Davis, John. "Joan of Kent, Lollardy, and the English Reformation." *JEccH* 33 (1982): 225–33.
Davis, John F. "The Trials of Thomas Bylney and the English Reformation." *Historical Journal* 24 (1981): 775–90.
Dean, D. M. "Parliament and Locality." In *The Parliaments of Elizabethan England*, ed. D. M. Dean and N. L. Jones. Oxford: Basil Blackwell, 1990.
Dickens, A. G. *The English Reformation*. Rev. ed. London: Fontana/Collins, 1967.
———. *Lollards and Protestants in the Diocese of York, 1509–1558*. London: Oxford University Press, 1959.
Dickinson, John C. *The Later Middle Ages*. New York: Barnes and Noble, 1979.
Duffy, Eamon. *The Stripping of the Altars: Traditional Religion in England, c. 1400–c. 1580*. New Haven: Yale University Press, 1992.
Dugmore, C. W. *The Mass and the English Reformers*. London: Macmillan, 1958.
Dyer, Alan D. *The City of Worcester in the Sixteenth Century*. Leicester: Leicester University Press, 1973.
Dyer, Christopher. *Standards of Living in the Later Middle Ages: Social Change in England, c. 1200–1520*. Cambridge: Cambridge University Press, 1989.
Edwards, David L. *Christian England*. Vol. 2. London: Collins, 1983.
Elton, G. R. *Reform and Reformation, England, 1509–1558*. Cambridge: Harvard University Press, 1977.
Emmison, F. G. *Elizabethan Life: Disorder*. Chelmsford: Essex County Council, 1970.
———. *Elizabethan Life: Home, Work, and Land*. Chelmsford: Essex Record Office, with Friends of Historic Essex, 1991.
———. *Elizabethan Life: Morals and the Church Courts*. Chelmsford: Essex County Council, 1973.
———. *Guide to the Essex Record Office*. 2d ed. Chelmsford: Essex Record Office Publications, 1969.
———. "Tithes, Perambulations, and Sabbath-Breach in Elizabethan Essex." In *Tribute to an Antiquary: Essays Presented to Marc Fitch*, ed. F. G. Emmison and W. B. Stephens. London: Leopard's Head Press, 1976.
Emmison, F. G., ed. *Wills at Chelmsford*. Vol. 1, *1400–1619*. London: British Record Society, 1958.

Evans, N. R. "Testators, Literacy, Education, and Religious Belief." *Local Population Studies* 25 (1980): 42–50.

Fisher, J. L. "The Leger Book of St. John's Abbey, Colchester." *TEAS*, n.s., 24 (1944–49): 77–127.

Fowler, R. C. "The Friars Minor of Colchester." *TEAS*, n.s., 11 (1911): 367.

Garrett, Christina Hallowell. *The Marian Exiles: A Study in the Origins of Elizabethan Puritanism*. 1938. Reprint, Cambridge: Cambridge University Press, 1966.

Gasquet, F. A. *Parish Life in Mediaeval England*. 6th ed. London: Methuen, 1929.

Gillett, Edward, and Kenneth A. MacMahon. *A History of Hull*. 2d ed. Hull: Hull University Press, 1989.

Girouard, Mark. *The English Town: A History of Urban Life*. New Haven: Yale University Press, 1990.

Goldberg, P. J. P. "Women in Fifteenth-Century Town Life." In *Towns and Townspeople in the Fifteenth Century,* ed. J. A. F. Thomson. Gloucester: Alan Sutton Publishing, 1988.

Goose, Nigel. "The 'Dutch' in Colchester: The Economic Influence of an Immigrant Community in the Sixteenth and Seventeenth Centuries." *Immigrants and Minorities* 1 (1982): 261–80.

Gottfried, Robert S. "Bury St. Edmunds and the Populations of Late Medieval English Towns, 1270–1530." *JBS* 20 (1980): 1–31.

———. *Bury St. Edmunds and the Urban Crisis, 1290–1539*. Princeton: Princeton University Press, 1982.

Greaves, Richard L. *Society and Religion in Elizabethan England*. Minneapolis: University of Minnesota Press, 1981.

Green, Mrs. J. R. *Town Life in the Fifteenth Century*. 2 vols. London: Macmillan, 1894.

Guy, John. *Tudor England*. Oxford: Oxford University Press, 1990.

Haigh, Christopher. "The Church of England, the Catholics, and the People." In *The Reign of Elizabeth I,* ed. Christopher Haigh. London: Macmillan, 1984.

———. "The Recent Historiography of the English Reformation." *Historical Journal* 25 (1982): 995–1007.

Haller, William. *The Rise of Puritanism*. New York: Harper, 1957.

Harding, Alan. *The Law Courts of Medieval England*. London: George Allen and Unwin, 1973.

Harrod, Henry. *Report on the Records of the Borough of Colchester, 1865*. Colchester, 1865.

Hart, A. Tindal. *The Man in the Pew, 1558–1660*. New York: Humanities Press, 1966.

Hasler, P. W., ed. *The House of Commons, 1558–1603*. 3 vols. London: HMSO, for the History of Parliament Trust, 1981.

Heath, Peter. "Urban Piety in the Later Middle Ages: The Evidence of Hull Wills." In *The Church, Politics, and Patronage in the Fifteenth Century,* ed. R. Barrie Dobson. New York: St. Martin's Press, 1984.

Herrup, Cynthia. "Law and Morality in Seventeenth-Century England." *PP* 106 (1985): 102–23.

Hewitt, Gordon. *To Frame the Heart.* Chelmsford: Chelmsford Diocesan Print Unit, for the Trustees of Henry Batchelor's Gift, n.d.

Higgs, Laquita M. "Wills and Religious Mentality in Tudor Colchester." *EAH* 22 (1991): 87–100.

Hill, Christopher. *Society and Puritanism.* 2d ed. New York: Schocken Books, 1967.

Horrox, Rosemary. "Urban Patronage and Patrons in the Fifteenth Century." In *Patronage, the Crown, and the Provinces in Later Medieval England,* ed. Ralph A. Griffiths. Atlantic Highlands, N.J.: Humanities Press, 1981.

Hoskins, W. G. *The Age of Plunder: The England of Henry VIII, 1500–1547.* London: Longman, 1976.

———. *Provincial England: Essays on Social and Economic History.* New York: St. Martin's Press, 1963.

Houlbrooke, Ralph A. *Church Courts and the People during the English Reformation, 1520–1570.* Oxford: Oxford University Press, 1979.

Hughes, Philip. *The Reformation in England.* Rev. ed. 3 vols. London: Burns and Oates, 1963.

Hull, M. R. *Roman Colchester.* Reports of the Research Committee of the Society of Antiquaries of London, no. 20. Oxford: Oxford University Press, for the Society of Antiquaries and the Corporation of the Borough of Colchester, 1958.

Hunt, William. *The Puritan Moment: The Coming of Revolution in an English County.* Cambridge: Harvard University Press, 1983.

Ingram, Martin. *Church Courts, Sex, and Marriage in England, 1570–1640.* Cambridge: Cambridge University Press, 1987.

———. "Religion, Communities, and Moral Discipline in Late Sixteenth- and Early Seventeenth-Century England: Case Studies." In *Religion and Society in Early Modern Europe, 1500–1800,* ed. Kaspar von Greyerz. London: George Allen and Unwin, 1984.

Ives, E. W. *The Common Lawyers of Pre-Reformation England: Thomas Kebell, A Case Study.* Cambridge: Cambridge University Press, 1983.

James, Mervyn. "Ritual, Drama, and Social Body in the Late Medieval English Town." *PP* 98 (1983): 3–29.

Jedin, Hubert, and John Dolan, eds. *Handbook of Church History.* Vol. 4, *From the High Middle Ages to the Eve of the Reformation.* Trans. Anselm Biggs. Montreal: Palm Publications, n.d.

Jewell, Helen M. *English Local Administration in the Middle Ages.* New York: Barnes and Noble, 1972.

Jones, Norman L. "Elizabeth's First Year: The Conception and Birth of the Elizabethan Political World." In *The Reign of Elizabeth I,* ed. Christopher Haigh. London: Macmillan, 1984.

Jordan, Wilbur K. *Philanthropy in England, 1480–1660.* New York: Russell Sage, 1959.

Jungmann, Joseph A. *The Mass of the Roman Rite: Its Origins and Development.* Trans. Francis A. Brunner. 2 vols. New York: Benziger, 1951.

Kent, Joan. "Attitudes of Members of the House of Commons to the Regulation of 'Personal Conduct' in Late Elizabethan and Early Stuart England." *Bulletin of the Institute of Historical Research* 46 (1973): 41–71.

Kerridge, Eric. *Textile Manufactures in Early Modern England.* Manchester: Manchester University Press, 1985.

Kitching, Christopher. "The Disposal of Monastic and Chantry Lands." In *Church and Society in England: Henry VIII to James I,* ed. Felicity Heal and Rosemary O'Day. London: Macmillan, 1977.

Knowles, David. *The Religious Orders in England.* 3 vols. Cambridge: Cambridge University Press, 1956.

Kowaleski, Maryanne. "The History of Urban Families in Medieval England." *Journal of Medieval History* 14 (1988): 47–63.

Kreider, Alan. *English Chantries: The Road to Dissolution.* Cambridge: Harvard University Press, 1979.

Lake, P. G. "Calvinism and the English Church, 1570–1635." *PP* 114 (1987): 32–76.

LeGoff, Jacques. *The Birth of Purgatory.* Chicago: University of Chicago Press, 1984.

Lehmberg, Stanford E. "Sir Thomas Audley: A Soul as Black as Marble?" In *Tudor Men and Institutions: Studies in English Law and Government,* ed. A. J. Slavin. Baton Rouge: Louisiana State University Press, 1972.

Lenman, Bruce. "The Limits of Godly Discipline in the Early Modern Period with Particular Reference to England and Scotland." In *Religion and Society in Early Modern Europe, 1500–1800,* ed. Kaspar von Greyerz. London: George Allen and Unwin, 1984.

Leonard, E. M. *The Early History of English Poor Relief.* 1900. Reprint, London: Frank Cass, 1965.

Loades, David. *Politics, Censorship, and the English Reformation.* London: Pinter, 1991.

———. *Revolution in Religion: The English Reformation, 1530–1570.* Cardiff: University of Wales Press, 1992.

MacCaffrey, Wallace T. *Exeter, 1540–1640: The Growth of an English County Town.* Cambridge: Harvard University Press, 1958.

Mackie, J. D. *The Earlier Tudors, 1485–1558*. Oxford: Clarendon Press, 1952.

Manning, Bernard Lord. *The People's Faith in the Time of Wyclif*. 2d ed. Hassocks, Sussex: Harvester Press, 1975.

Martin, G. H. *Colchester: Official Guide*. 4th ed. Colchester: Benham and Company, 1973.

———. *The Story of Colchester from Roman Times to the Present Day*. Colchester: Benham Newspapers, 1959.

Martin, J. W. *Religious Radicals in Tudor England*. London: Hambledon Press, 1989.

Mason, Emma. "The Role of the English Parishioner, 1100–1500." *JEccH* 27 (1976): 17–29.

Matlock Population Studies Group. "Wills and Their Scribes." *Local Population Studies* 8 (1972): 55–57.

Mayhew, Graham. *Tudor Rye*. Brighton: University of Sussex Centre for Continuing Education, 1987.

McIntosh, Marjorie Keniston. *A Community Transformed: The Manor and Liberty of Havering, 1500–1620*. New York: Cambridge University Press, 1991.

———. "Local Responses to the Poor in Late Medieval and Tudor England." *Continuity and Change* 3 (1988): 209–45.

McRee, Ben R. "Religious Gilds and Civic Order: The Case of Norwich in the Late Middle Ages." *Speculum* 67 (1992): 69–97.

Moorman, John R. H. *Church Life in England in the Thirteenth Century*. Cambridge: Cambridge University Press, 1955.

Moran, Jo Ann Hoeppner. *The Growth of English Schooling, 1340–1548*. Princeton: Princeton University Press, 1985.

Morant, Philip. *The History and Antiquities of the Most Ancient Town and Borough of Colchester*. 1748. Reprint, Wakefield: S. R. Publishers, 1970.

Morgan, John. *Godly Learning: Puritan Attitudes towards Reason, Learning, and Education, 1560–1640*. Cambridge: Cambridge University Press, 1986.

Neale, J. E. *The Elizabethan House of Commons*. New Haven: Yale University Press, 1950.

———. *Queen Elizabeth I*. Garden City, N.Y.: Doubleday, Anchor Books, 1957.

Newcourt, Richard. *Repertorium Ecclesiasticum Parochiale Londinense*. 2 vols. London, 1710.

O'Day, Rosemary. "The Anatomy of a Profession: The Clergy of the Church of England." In *The Professions in Early Modern England*, ed. Wilfrid Prest. London: Croom Helm, 1987.

———. "Ecclesiastical Patronage: Who Controlled the Church?" In *Church and Society in England: Henry VIII to James I*, ed. Felicity Heal and Rosemary O'Day. London: Macmillan, 1977.

———. *Education and Society, 1500–1800*. London: Longman, 1982.

O'Dwyer, M. "Catholic Recusants in Essex, c. 1580–c. 1600." Master's thesis, University of London, 1960.

Orme, Nicholas. *Education and Society in Medieval and Renaissance England.* London: Hambledon Press, 1982.

Owst, G. R. *Preaching in Medieval England.* New York: Russell and Russell, 1965.

Oxley, J. E. *The Reformation in Essex to the Death of Mary.* Manchester: Manchester University Press, 1965.

Palliser, David M. *The Age of Elizabeth: England under the Later Tudors, 1547–1603.* London: Longman, 1983.

———. "Introduction: The Parish in Perspective." In *Parish, Church, and People: Local Studies in Lay Religion, 1350–1750,* ed. Susan J. Wright. London: Hutchinson, 1988.

———. "Popular Reactions to Reformation, 1530–70." In *Church and Society in England: Henry VIII to James I,* ed. Felicity Heal and Rosemary O'Day. London: Macmillan, 1977.

———. "The Reformation in York, 1534–1553." *Borthwick Papers* 40 (1971): 1–32.

———. *Tudor York.* Oxford: Oxford University Press, 1979.

Peers, C. R. *St. Botolph's Priory, Colchester.* London: HMSO, 1917.

Petchey, W. J. *A Prospect of Maldon, 1500–1689.* Chelmsford: Essex Record Office, 1991.

Peter, Sister Mary Justine. "A Study of the Administration of the Henrician Act of Supremacy in Canterbury Diocese." Ph.D. diss., Loyola University, 1959.

Phythian-Adams, Charles. "Ceremony and the Citizen: The Communal Year at Coventry, 1450–1550." In *Crisis and Order in English Towns, 1500–1700: Essays in Urban History,* ed. Peter Clark and Paul Slack. Toronto: University of Toronto Press, 1972.

———. *Desolation of a City: Coventry and the Urban Crisis of the Late Middle Ages.* Cambridge: Cambridge University Press, 1979.

Pilgrim, J. E. "The Rise of the 'New Draperies' in Essex." *University of Birmingham Historical Journal* 7 (1959–60): 36–59.

Platt, Colin. *The English Medieval Town.* London: Book Club Associates, 1976.

———. *The Parish Churches of Medieval England.* London: Secker and Warburg, 1981.

Plumb, Derek. "The Social and Economic Spread of Rural Lollardy: A Reappraisal." *Studies in Church History* 23 (1986): 111–29.

Poos, L. R. *A Rural Society after the Black Death: Essex, 1350–1525.* Cambridge: Cambridge University Press, 1991.

Powell, Ken, and Chris Cook. *English Historical Facts, 1485–1603.* Totowa, N.J.: Rowman and Littlefield, 1977.

Pressey, William J. "The Essex Churchwarden." *ER* 51 (1942): 145–50.

Reed, Michael. "Economic Structure and Change in Seventeenth-Century Ipswich." In *Country Towns in Pre-Industrial England,* ed. Peter Clark. Leicester: Leicester University Press, 1981.

Reynolds, Susan. *An Introduction to the History of English Medieval Towns.* Oxford: Clarendon Press, 1977.

———. "Medieval Urban History and the History of Political Thought." *Urban History Yearbook,* 1982, 14–23.

Rickword, George. "Members of Parliament for Colchester, 1547–1558." *ER* 4 (1895): 110–22.

———. "Members of Parliament for Colchester, 1559–1603." *ER* 4 (1895): 235–45.

Ritchie, J. Ewing. "James Morice, M.P. for Colchester, 1586–1593." *ER* 2 (1893): 165–68.

Rodes, Robert E. *Ecclesiastical Administration in Medieval England.* Notre Dame: University of Notre Dame Press, 1977.

Rogers, Alan. "Late Medieval Stamford." In *Perspectives in English Urban History,* ed. Alan Everitt. New York: Harper and Row, 1973.

Roker, L. "The Flemish and Dutch Community in Colchester in the Sixteenth and Seventeenth Centuries." Master's thesis, University of London, 1963.

Rosser, Gervase. "Communities of Parish and Guild in the Late Middle Ages." In *Parish, Church, and People: Local Studies in Lay Religion, 1350–1750,* ed. Susan J. Wright. London: Hutchinson, 1988.

———. *Medieval Westminster, 1200–1540.* Oxford: Clarendon Press, 1989.

Rothkrug, Lionel. "Popular Religion and Holy Shrines." In *Religion and the People, 800–1700,* ed. James Obelkevich. Chapel Hill: University of North Carolina Press, 1979.

Round, J. H. *St. Helen's Chapel, Colchester.* London: Elliot Stock, n.d.

———. "St. Peter's Church, Colchester." *TEAS,* n.s., 15 (1921): 94–95.

Royal Commission on Historical Monuments. *An Inventory of the Historical Monuments in Essex.* 4 vols. London: HMSO, 1916–23.

Russell, J. C. *British Medieval Population.* Albuquerque: University of New Mexico Press, 1948.

Sacks, David Harris. *The Widening Gate: Bristol and the Atlantic Economy, 1450–1700.* Berkeley: University of California Press, 1991.

Samaha, Joel. "Hanging for Felony: The Rule of Law in Elizabethan Colchester." *Historical Journal* 21 (1978): 763–82.

Scarisbrick, J. J. *Henry VIII.* Berkeley: University of California Press, 1968.

———. *The Reformation and the English People.* Oxford: Basil Blackwell, 1984.

Scott, John. "Tudor Adventurer." *British History Illustrated* 1 (1975): 56–63.

Scribner, Bob. "Religion, Society, and Culture: Reorientating the Reformation." *History Workshop Journal* 14 (1982): 2–22.

Seaver, Paul S. *The Puritan Lectureships: The Politics of Religious Dissent, 1560–1662.* Stanford: Stanford University Press, 1970.

Sharpe, J. A. *Early Modern England: A Social History, 1550–1760.* London: Edward Arnold, 1987.

———. *Crime in Early Modern England, 1550–1750.* New York: Longman, 1984.

Sheehan, Michael M. *The Will in Medieval England.* Toronto: Pontifical Institute of Mediaeval Studies, 1963.

Sheils, W. J. "Religion in Provincial Towns: Innovation and Tradition." In *Church and Society in England: Henry VIII to James I,* ed. Felicity Heal and Rosemary O'Day. London: Macmillan, 1977.

Skeeters, Martha C. *Community and Clergy: Bristol and the Reformation, c. 1530–c. 1570.* Oxford: Clarendon Press, 1993.

Slack, Paul. "Poverty in Elizabethan England." *History Today* 34 (1984): 5–13.

Smith, H. Maynard. *Pre-Reformation England.* 1938. Reprint, New York: Russell and Russell, 1963.

Smith, Harold. *Ecclesiastical History of Essex under the Long Parliament and Commonwealth.* Colchester: Benham, n.d.

Smith, J. C. Challenor. "Some Additions to Newcourt's *Repertorium*—Volume II." *TEAS,* n. s., 6 (1898): 228–57.

Smith, J. R. *Pilgrims and Adventurers.* Chelmsford: Essex Record Office, 1992.

Smith, Richard Dean. "Social Reform in an Urban Context: Colchester, Essex, 1570–1640." Ph.D. diss., University of Colorado, 1996.

Sommerville, C. John. *The Secularization of Early Modern England.* New York: Oxford University Press, 1992.

Spufford, Margaret. *Contrasting Communities: English Villagers in the Sixteenth and Seventeenth Centuries.* Cambridge: Cambridge University Press, 1974.

———. "Peasant Inheritance Customs and Land Distribution in Cambridgeshire from the Sixteenth to the Eighteenth Centuries." In *Family and Inheritance,* ed. Jack Goody, Joan Thirsk, and E. P. Thompson. Cambridge: Cambridge University Press, 1976.

———. "Puritanism and Social Control?" In *Order and Disorder in Early Modern England,* ed. Anthony Fletcher and John Stevenson. Cambridge: Cambridge University Press, 1985.

Stevenson, David. *The Book of Colchester.* Chesham, Buckinghamshire: Barracuda Books, 1978.

Strauss, Gerald. "Lutheranism and Literacy: A Reassessment." In *Religion and Society in Early Modern Europe, 1500–1800,* ed. Kaspar von Greyerz. London: George Allen and Unwin, 1984.

Swanson, R. N. *Church and Society in Late Medieval England.* Oxford: Basil Blackwell, 1989.

————. "The Problems of the Priesthood in Pre-Reformation England." *EHR* 105 (1990): 845–69.

Swete, Henry Barclay. *Church Services and Service-Books before the Reformation.* Rev. ed. New York: Macmillan, 1930.

Tanner, Norman P. *The Church in Late Medieval Norwich, 1370–1532.* Toronto: Pontifical Institute of Mediaeval Studies, 1984.

————. "The Reformation and Regionalism: Further Reflections on the Church in Late Medieval Norwich." In *Towns and Townspeople in the Fifteenth Century,* ed. J. A. F. Thomson. Gloucester: Alan Sutton, 1988.

Tate, W. E. *The Parish Chest.* 2d ed. Cambridge: Cambridge University Press, 1951.

Tentler, Thomas N. *Sin and Confession on the Eve of the Reformation.* Princeton: Princeton University Press, 1977.

Thomas, James H. *Town Government in the Sixteenth Century.* London: George Allen and Unwin, 1933.

Thomas, Keith. *Religion and the Decline of Magic.* New York: Charles Scribner's Sons, 1971.

Thompson, Alexander Hamilton. *The English Clergy and Their Organization in the Later Middle Ages.* Oxford: Clarendon Press, 1947.

Thomson, John A. F. *The Later Lollards, 1414–1520.* London: Oxford University Press, 1965.

————. "Piety and Charity in Late Medieval London." *JEccH* 16 (1965): 178–95.

Thrupp, Sylvia L. *The Merchant Class of Medieval London.* Ann Arbor: University of Michigan Press, 1962.

Tittler, Robert. *Architecture and Power: The Town Hall and the English Urban Community, c. 1500–1640.* Oxford: Clarendon Press, 1991.

————. "Elizabethan Towns and the 'Points of Contact': Parliament." *Parliamentary History* 8 (1989): 275–88.

————. "The Emergence of Urban Policy, 1536–58." In *The Mid-Tudor Polity, c. 1540–1560,* ed. Jennifer Loach and Robert Tittler. London: Macmillan, 1980.

————. "Seats of Honor, Seats of Power: The Symbolism of Public Seating in the English Urban Community, c. 1560–1620." *Albion* 24 (1992): 205–23.

Tromly, Frederic B. "'According to Sounde Religion': The Elizabethan Controversy over the Funeral Sermon." *Journal of Medieval and Renaissance Studies* 13 (1983): 293–312.

Underdown, David. *Fire from Heaven: Life in an English Town in the Seventeenth Century.* New Haven: Yale University Press, 1992.

————. *Revel, Riot, and Rebellion: Popular Politics and Culture in England, 1603–1660.* New York: Oxford University Press, 1985.

Venn, John, and J. A. Venn, eds. *Alumni Cantabrigienses: A Biographical List of*

All Known Students, Graduates, and Holders of Office at the University of Cambridge from the Earliest Times to 1900. Cambridge: Cambridge University Press, 1922.

Victoria History of the Counties of England: Essex. 9 vols. London, 1903–94.

Ward, Jennifer C. "The Reformation in Colchester, 1528–1558." *EAH* 15 (1983): 84–95.

———. "Wealth and Family in Early Sixteenth-Century Colchester." *EAH* 21 (1990): 100–17.

Webb, Sidney, and Beatrice Webb. *English Local Government.* Vol. 2, *The Manor and the Borough.* New York: Longmans, Green, and Company, 1908.

Wedgwood, Josiah C. *History of Parliament: Biographies of the Members of the Commons House, 1439–1509.* 2 vols. London: HMSO, 1936.

Westlake, Herbert Francis. *The Parish Gilds of Mediaeval England.* New York: Macmillan, 1919.

Whiting, Robert. "Abominable Idols: Images and Image-Breaking under Henry VIII." *JEccH* 33 (1982): 30–47.

———. *The Blind Devotion of the People: Popular Religion and the English Reformation.* Cambridge: Cambridge University Press, 1989.

Whitley, W. T. "Thomas Matthew of Colchester and Matthew's Bible of 1537." *ER* 43 (1934): 1–6, 82–87, 155–62, 227–34; 44 (1935): 40–44.

Williams, Penry. "The Crown and the Counties." In *The Reign of Elizabeth I,* ed. Christopher Haigh. London: Macmillan, 1984.

Wood-Legh, Kathleen L. *Perpetual Chantries in Britain.* Cambridge: Cambridge University Press, 1965.

Wright, Thomas. *St. Patrick's Purgatory.* 1844.

Wrightson, Keith. *English Society, 1580–1680.* London: Hutchinson, 1982.

Youings, Joyce. *The Dissolution of the Monasteries.* New York: Barnes and Noble, 1971.

Zell, Michael L. "The Use of Religious Preambles as a Measure of Religious Belief in the Sixteenth Century." *Bulletin of the Institute of Historical Research* 50 (1977): 246–49.

Index